Here we go
Stelers!

Tom OLeme
12/2?/22

Immaculate

PRAISE FOR *IMMACULATE*

In their defining tome on the subject of 1972's Immaculate Reception—arguably the greatest play in NFL history—Tom O'Lenic and Ray Hartjen not only chronicle the chain of events and circumstances that led to the iconic moment, they explore how the play became a catalyst for four Super Bowl victories in the ensuing decade, an enduring Steelers football dynasty and the very rebirth of the city of Pittsburgh. If you're a Steelers fan . . . heck, if you're a football fan . . . you're going to love *Immaculate*.

> —**Jim Fabio,** Emmy Award-winning producer/director of
> *The NFL Season: Immaculate Remembrance*

A half-century after Franco Harris's miraculous catch that may be the defining moment in Pittsburgh Steelers history, comes an immaculately researched book that does its best to define Pittsburgh, on and off the playing field. Essentially a love letter to the city, the co-authors appropriately co-mingle critical developments about life reliant on steel to life energized by Steelers. A history book as much as a sports book, readers will nod and smile at the introduction of an all-star cast, from players Terry Bradshaw, Frenchy Fuqua, and Jack Lambert, to all-star moments in Super Bowls, and even from a movie *The Fish That Saved Pittsburgh.* Just as the Steelers did, the co-authors show how Pittsburgh adapted from the twentieth to the twenty-first centuries.

> —**Lew Freedman,** prize-winning journalist and author of
> more than one hundred books

The Steelers, both as an organization and an identity, are Pittsburgh—full stop. There are precious few communities like it, and *Immaculate: How the Steelers Saved Pittsburgh*, is a collection of all the stories, past and present, that makes Pittsburgh a Steelers' town, and the Steelers a treasured source of Pittsburgh pride.

> —**Nick Mehta,** CEO of Gainsight (and self-proclaimed "wannabe Pittsburgh
> Steelers football player who plays day-job as a leader of technology companies")

The Immaculate Reception football is not just another football, as it's also an Immaculate Remembrance. Having 50 years of history, sparking a Pittsburgh Steeler dynasty, changing a city and my family forever. *Immaculate: How the Steelers Saved Pittsburgh* recounts this story and so much more to show readers how important the Steelers are to the city of Pittsburgh.

— **Jim Baker,** owner and custodian of the Immaculate Reception football

In their book, Tom O'Lenic and Ray Hartjen capture the history that shaped Pittsburgh, its citizens and, eventually, its football team. Then, they explore the pivot that ultimately allowed the Steelers and the city of Pittsburgh to come together to shape their collective future. *Immaculate: How the Steelers Saved Pittsburgh* provides a fascinating look at the community and why it is unique.

— **Robert O. Stakeley,** affiliates program manager, Senator John Heinz History Center

As a child of immigrants who grew up watching the Steelers in the '70s and '80s, I understand firsthand how the Steelers of that era brought our entire community together—both long-time residents and newcomers like my family, bonded through our common love of the Black and Gold. *Immaculate: How the Steelers Saved Pittsburgh* tells the story of how a city and community experienced a resurgence that mirrored the rise of one of the great football dynasties in the history of sports.

— **Ajay Agarwal,** Partner at Bain Capital Ventures

Come for the football, stay for the history lesson!

— **Cam Inman,** San Francisco 49ers' beat writer, Bay Area News Group

Immaculate: How the Steelers Saved Pittsburgh not only shares the stories of how Pittsburgh and its football club were built, but it also tells the story of how they both overcame adversity and rose to new heights. From U.S. Steel and other manufacturers advancing education throughout the valley to the Steelers ascending to become a bedrock of civic pride for us all, *Immaculate* tells the tales of what makes Pittsburgh someplace special.

— **Joe Sikora**, career-long foreman at the Homestead Works and Irwin Works mills

IMMACULATE

How the
Steelers
Saved
Pittsburgh

TOM O'LENIC & RAY HARTJEN

NEW YORK

LONDON • NASHVILLE • MELBOURNE • VANCOUVER

Immaculate

How the Steelers Saved Pittsburgh

Published in New York, New York, by Morgan James Publishing. Morgan James is a trademark of Morgan James, LLC. www.MorganJamesPublishing.com

Proudly distributed by Ingram Publisher Services.

Morgan James BOGO™

A **FREE** ebook edition is available for you or a friend with the purchase of this print book.

_____

CLEARLY SIGN YOUR NAME ABOVE

Instructions to claim your free ebook edition:
1. Visit MorganJamesBOGO.com
2. Sign your name CLEARLY in the space above
3. Complete the form and submit a photo of this entire page
4. You or your friend can download the ebook to your preferred device

ISBN 9781636980546 paperback
ISBN 9781636980553 ebook
Library of Congress Control Number: 2022945493

Cover & Interior Design by:
Christopher Kirk
www.GFSstudio.com

Morgan James PUBLISHING **Builds** with... **Habitat for Humanity** Peninsula and Greater Williamsburg

Morgan James is a proud partner of Habitat for Humanity Peninsula and Greater Williamsburg. Partners in building since 2006.

Get involved today! Visit MorganJamesPublishing.com/giving-back

From Tom,
To my grandparents, Baba and Dida, and my parents, Dorothy and Bill O'Lenic,
who sacrificed so much to allow me to live the American Dream.

From Ray,
To Lori, Olivia, and Raymond, as well as the cancer patient, cancer care provider,
and cancer patient caregiver communities. #punchtodayintheface

TABLE OF CONTENTS

PREFACE

Today, the city of Pittsburgh is known globally as a center of commerce, academia, and the cultural arts. Over the past several decades, it has distinguished itself in the fields of health care, education, environmental design, and technology, among others.

Modern-day Pittsburgh has captured the world's attention for all the right reasons. In 2015, Pittsburgh was listed among the eleven most livable cities *in the world*, according to The Metropolis Guide to the Best Cities to Live, Work, and Play.

However, it wasn't always like that.

Pittsburgh has a long, colorful history, and for many decades—more than a century—it was a commercial center of great prosperity.

Pittsburgh blossomed as a link between the Atlantic coast and the American Midwest, and with its rich natural resources, it became a manufacturing center without peer. Known as "the Steel City," Pittsburgh dominated the iron and steel industries, and led the way in glass, aluminum, and petroleum too. And, of course, those industries provided fertile ground to sprout and support tangential industries like banking and finance.

Consider that in 1950, Pittsburgh had a population of 675,000 people, and for most of the twentieth century, the city trailed only New York City and Chicago, cities with much bigger populations, in corporate headquarters employment.

Pittsburgh was an American success story.

Then, rather suddenly, it wasn't.

Global competition, complete with new, modern manufacturing methods and processes, quickly made Pittsburgh's legacy heavy industries obsolete. Seemingly overnight in the mid-1970s, Pittsburgh's foundational industries became uncompetitive. Tens of thousands lost their jobs, and the city shrank dramatically as a great number of families relocated in search of new opportunities.

The very viability of the city and the surrounding area was under threat. Pittsburgh, like a lot of American cities in the "Rust Belt," was on the brink of becoming just a shadow of its former self. It was a formidable time, and some cities have never really come back from it, like, arguably, Detroit.

Pittsburghers, however, changed the narrative, and I'm of the firm opinion that a big part of that can be tied to . . . the Pittsburgh Steelers professional football team.

Until the 1972 season, the city's beloved Steelers had been horrible. Coined the "lovable losers" by none other than late-night talk show host Johnny Carson, locals chronicled each dismal season with talk of the "same old Steelers."

The team's fortunes changed in that 1972 season, highlighted by the most memorable play in National Football League history, the "Immaculate Reception." And the Steelers' upward arc helped offset the city's bleak economic period.

The Steelers galvanized Pittsburgh through its darkest days. The team provided the city's citizens with a source of pride they could embrace, a thread that kept the community fabric intact, and, coupled with the success of baseball's Pirates in the late 1970s and early 1980s, Pittsburgh claimed the title of "the City of Champions."

All the while, the city struggled to reinvent itself. The Steelers' success—four Super Bowl Championships between 1975 and 1980—gave Pittsburghers something to hold on to and generated a civic pride that, to borrow from writer Dylan Thomas, would not go gentle into that good night.

It took time, but Pittsburgh survived its transition and now thrives in its transformation. And I'm convinced the Steelers provided the foundation for it to rebuild upon.

I'm a proud Pittsburgher. I'm not a Pennsylvanian, and not really even a western Pennsylvanian unless you're talking about places within an hour's drive of Pittsburgh. I'm a Pittsburgher.

My grandmother, Anna "Baba" Mikula, arrived in America through Ellis Island on the USS Lincoln on December 7, 1912. Being only fourteen, she lied about her age, stating she was sixteen, the minimum age at which one could travel alone. She entered the country with just $3, or about the equivalent of $91 in 2022. Her final destination was Donora, Pennsylvania, where she had extended family.

Like a lot of Eastern European immigrants who populated the area, my grandparents arrived in the area without speaking English. Luckily, labor jobs in the steel and coal industries were plentiful, and they didn't require extensive communication skills. There were long hours in often poor working conditions, but it was the start of the American Dream.

With the steel industry a fundamental part of life in the region, many, if not most, jobs in the area were connected to it. My father, an industrial engineer who earned a college degree through the G.I. Bill after returning stateside from World War II, worked for U.S. Steel for over thirty years. However, even as an engineer, he wasn't immune to the industry's downturn; he was forced to retire while I was a senior in high school.

I still remember the day vividly. Although it was a punch to the gut, it ultimately proved to be an eye-opening and motivating experience for me, personally.

In addition to the steel industry, sports have also been an integral part of life for Pittsburghers post-World War II, and it was especially true for my family. My father played baseball in the minor leagues, and my uncle is baseball Hall of Famer "Stan the Man" Musial.

For me, like most other Pittsburghers, local sports were not just a passion, but part of my identity. Before elementary school every morning, my friends and I would arrive early so we could play football or kickball, all the while pretending we were local sports heroes like Terry Bradshaw, Lynn Swann, Joe Greene, or Roberto Clemente. Monday mornings were always about the latest Steelers game, and if the Steelers had lost, the mood was somber and our games a bit more physical and aggressive.

I have discussed the idea of this book for many years, procrastinating far too many times for far too many reasons, including devoting time to raising my family and furthering my career. I knew I had to write this book after I attended a wedding in, of all places, Tampa, Florida. I had moved to California, and at that wedding, I was introduced to another ex-Pittsburgher. Learning where I was from, the first question she asked was, "Are you still a Steelers fan?"—Steelers, pronounced "Stillers" in the local yinzer lexicon, naturally.

No other topic was important enough to supplant that question. She wanted to start where so many of us Pittsburghers want to start: the Steelers.

The Steelers, the team of lovable losers, who, on an overcast December afternoon in 1972, had one play indelibly etched in the memories of so many, elevate the franchise and, in time, rescue an entire city.

Being from Pittsburgh is a peculiar thing. In college, when asked where they were from, people typically responded by naming their states: Florida, Virginia, New Jersey, etc. Not us Pittsburghers. We were from Pittsburgh.

I'm a Pittsburgher. I'm not from Pennsylvania. I'm from Pittsburgh. There's a difference, and that difference is important.

I'm proud of my city, and a big part of that pride rests in the Steelers, the first team to win four Super Bowls and the first franchise dynasty in the NFL's Super Bowl era.

~Tom O'Lenic

Chapter 1
GAME DAY

When dawn broke in Pittsburgh on December 23, 1972, it revealed a rather overcast morning, like so many other typically overcast December mornings Pittsburghers wake up to. This day was a little different, though, and more so than because of the relatively mild temperatures.

With Christmas just two days away, people had been finishing their last-minute holiday shopping and, of course, stopping by Giant Eagle and Foodland to pick up the traditional local delicacies like chipped ham and kielbasa. Throughout, there was a buzz permeating the air, and it was that buzz that made this December morning distinctly different. It wasn't just a holiday buzz; it was also very much a Pittsburgh Steelers buzz.

An eager, optimistic Steelers buzz was a rather novel affair; yet, here it was, and the team was the talk of the town and, for once, for good reason. Just four years before, the team had completed a dismal one-win, thirteen-loss season. They were called the "loveable losers" by no less a national cultural icon than Johnny Carson, host of NBC's popular *Tonight Show*. In their less than illustrious thirty-nine-year history, the franchise and its devout fan base had experienced just eight winning seasons and a single, solitary playoff game, a 21–0 blanking suffered at the hands of the cross-state rival Philadelphia Eagles in 1947.

But this Steelers team, it was hoped, was different. The Steelers were finally back in the NFL playoffs!

Six days before, the Steelers had faced off with the San Diego Chargers in the final game of the regular season, a must-win if the Steelers were to wrap up the American Football Conference's Central Division over the archrival Cleveland Browns. The game had started inauspiciously as quarterback Terry Bradshaw had been sacked in his own end zone, resulting in a safety and a quick 2–0 deficit. However, the Steelers, sparked by a stifling defense and touchdowns from running backs

Franco Harris and John "Frenchy" Fuqua, stormed back to score twenty-four unanswered points en route to a title-clinching 24–2 victory.

Spirits in Pittsburgh were sky high, even if there was some anxiety about a short turnaround time after a long cross-country trip back home for the young ball club.

The anxiety was compounded by the playoff opponent, the notorious Oakland Raiders, a team quickly earning a reputation as the NFL's "bad boy" franchise. The playoff game would be a rematch of the season opener, a tense, sloppy, turnover-plagued game that eventually ended in a 34–28 Steeler victory.

In that first game, the Steelers had stormed out to a 17–0 lead, and the Raiders played a sort of musical chairs game at the quarterback position, first replacing starter Kenny Stabler with veteran George Blanda after Stabler threw three interceptions, then replacing an ineffective Blanda with third-stringer Daryle Lamonica. The Raiders hung tough, though, and kept themselves in the game with two interceptions of their own, one each by safeties Jack Tatum and George Atkinson, players who were to become Public Enemies No. 1 and No. 2 to Steeler fans who felt the two had a propensity to level illegal cheap shots to Steeler receivers.

The Raiders fought back in the fourth quarter behind two touchdown passes from Lamonica, but the Steelers hung on behind a strong running game led by Preston Pearson and the quiet rookie, Harris. The victory had set the tone for a very solid 11–3 season.

The 10–3–1 Raiders were coming into town led by their demonstrative head coach, John Madden, whereas the Steelers were led by the meticulously reserved Chuck Noll. Both men were completing their fourth seasons as head coaches, and both had been building their deep rosters through successful drafts.

Madden had burst on the scene as an almost instant success, boasting a regular season record of 38–12–6 coming into the game. While the Steelers' record under Noll was just 23–33, Noll's teams had improved every year since he took over the reins in 1969. Both teams had finished the season strongly, with the Raiders chalking up six consecutive wins and the Steelers four, including a 30–0 drubbing of the Browns in Week Twelve.

The game was shaping up to be as big as it got. Only here's the thing: It wasn't going to be televised in the Pittsburgh area because of the NFL's policy restricting televising home games. That policy would change the following year to allow for the live televising of games if tickets were sold-out at least seventy-two hours before kickoff. So, if you weren't already one of the more than 50,000 lucky Steeler fans with tickets to the biggest professional football game in Pittsburgh's history, you were going to have to follow the game by tuning into the WTAE radio broadcast.

WTAE had become the radio home of the Steelers in 1970, after Dan Rooney, the son of team owner Art Rooney, moved the broadcast rights over from KDKA because he felt the Pittsburgh Pirates baseball team was being given preferential treatment. It had been a somewhat surprising move, considering the pedigree of KDKA, the first-ever radio station in the United States, and its large, loyal following. But football fans made the move alongside the team and were glued to their radios and the voices of play-by-play host Jack Fleming and "the voice of the Pittsburgh Steelers," color commentator Myron Cope, a local treasure with his distinctive high-pitched, nasal voice and heavy yinzer, or Pittsburgher, accent.

The game was set to kick off at 1:00 p.m. EST, the first of the playoff games on the NFL's busy weekend schedule. The boisterous and hopeful crowd filed into Three Rivers Stadium, nested beside the Allegheny River near the confluence of the Monongahela River that forms the Ohio River. All around town, televisions were turned off and radios were turned up as fans huddled around to listen to the game. After the Pepsi commercial—"You've got a lot to live, and Pepsi's got a lot to give"—the kickoff was just minutes away.

As the game began, so did the story about how the Steelers saved Pittsburgh.

Chapter 2

EARLY PENNSYLVANIANS

The stories of both the Pittsburgh Steelers and the city of Pittsburgh begin with the story of Pennsylvania. However, the story of Pennsylvania starts long before it became known as Pennsylvania.

For many years, what some might call *ages*, the oldest evidence of human existence in all of North America dated back some 12,000 years. But that was before Albert Miller took a strange liking to a freshly dug groundhog hole one day as he was walking along his property he called Meadowcroft, near Avella in Jefferson Township, Washington County, about twenty-seven miles west-southwest of Pittsburgh.

Miller had long held a theory that Native Americans had once lived on his land, and he took advantage of what the groundhog had begun with his own excavation to find archeological evidence. He dug out the hole and soon found artifacts that supported his claim.

Those initial finds by Miller occurred in 1955, but he played his discovery close to the vest to not attract the attention of vandals and looters. Miller delayed reporting his findings for eighteen years, when he then contacted James M. Adovasio, who led the first excavations of the site from 1973 to 1979 under the oversight of the Cultural Resource Management Program of the University of Pittsburgh.

Over the years, Meadowcroft produced a literal treasure trove of artifacts, including tools, pottery, projectile points, stones worked to have flakes removed from both sides—what scientists refer to as *bifaces*—and a variety of stone fragments and chipping debris. Then, research in the laboratory redefined the timeframe for the earliest humans in North America. Or, rather, it may have.

Radiocarbon dating of Meadowcroft, now known as the Meadowcroft Rockshelter, and its artifacts suggested occupancy by humans beginning 16,000 years ago—and maybe as far back as 19,000 years ago—blowing the lid off the previous evidence from 12,000 years ago. However, the Meadowcroft findings are still somewhat controversial, as some scientists claim possible contamination from ancient carbon from coal-bearing strata, or sedimentary rock layers, in the watershed.

Back to the age controversy, the Meadowcroft samples were retested, and those results showed no evidence of contamination from groundwater activity. Accelerator mass spectrometry tests also supported the initial findings. Because this is a book about Pittsburgh by a Pittsburgher, we're going to go with the original findings as being authentic, scientifically proven, and confirmed.

With that, Meadowcroft Rockshelter became the oldest known site of human habitation in North America, providing a look into the lives of prehistoric hunters and gatherers. The site has produced remains that pre-date the Clovis culture, the Paleoamerican culture named for the archeological finds near Clovis, New Mexico, in the 1920s, as well as the remains from the Paleoindian, Archaic, and Woodland periods.

Artifacts from the site also paint a picture of the lives of those prehistoric peoples. There are fragments of flint from Ohio, jasper from eastern Pennsylvania, and seashells from the Atlantic coast, all suggesting inhabitants were both mobile and involved in long-distance trade. The dig also produced the remains of 149 separate species of animals and remnants of corn, squash, fruits, nuts, and seeds, providing insights into the hunting and gathering nature of existence.

It's a remarkable story, particularly when remembering all that discovery began with the inauspicious burrowing of a boot into a freshly dug groundhog hole.

After the prehistoric peoples, but well before European settlement, Pennsylvania was inhabited by many Native American tribes, including the Erie, Honniasont, Huron, Seneca and Oneida Iroquois, Leni Lenape, Munsee, Shawnee, Susquehannock, and others. However, today there are no federally recognized tribes or nations in Pennsylvania. It's not that those cultures are extinct; rather, the cultures were displaced by colonial expansion coming from the east.

Until recently, there's been a tendency to white-wash history, not just in America, but throughout the world. What many of us learned in school was often a story told from a single perspective, and most of the time, that was from the perspective of a white male.

A fantastic resource on the subject is *Lies My Teacher Told Me: Everything Your American History Textbook Got Wrong*, a 1995 book by sociologist James W. Loewen. In its pages, Loewen critically examines a dozen popular American high school history textbooks and concludes their authors propagated false, Eurocentric, and mythologized views of American history.

Don't fall prey to the thought that Native American culture and life were static, frozen in time, up to the arrival of European settlers and the advent of written, recorded history. Over time, Native cultures developed, diversified, and prospered as they adapted to the pristine, natural geographies they inhabited, spurring an evolving collection of distinctive cultural groups with different languages and customs.

Native tribes communicated and traded with one another, in the process sharing knowledge and experience, improving their collective methodologies for hunting, fishing, farming, pottery, tool-making, and more. And they didn't learn war from Europeans, as they had plenty of experience in that arena before white settlers encroached on the land.

A thousand years before US Route 30 bisected the state, Native peoples turned the Susquehanna Valley into their own migratory superhighway, connecting communities from the Great Lakes all the way east to the shores of Chesapeake Bay. Even Pennsylvania's mining heritage can be drawn back to Native peoples, as rock quarries in the Lehigh and Delaware Valleys were mined for commodities traded with other Native cultures as far away as coastal New England.

Change in the lives of Native peoples accelerated when they crossed paths with the strange white settlers from across the ocean. European settlers brought with them new technologies and goods that quickly worked themselves into daily Native life. Woven cloth soon complemented Indigenous clothing, and sharp-edged iron tools started replacing worked stones.

It was a two-way street as the Native peoples traded for those goods with goods of their own—in particular, animal pelts. Eventually, however, demand for goods from settlers outpaced an ability to trade in furs, leading to the precedent of trading land as payment.

Now, there are all sorts of cultural implications to consider when looking at land from a historical perspective, from ideologies as polar opposite as living in harmony with the land—"we are the land"—to one of land ownership and control, manipulating and shaping the land to fit man's needs. Regardless, when land was traded for goods, the wheels were put into motion for what was to come.

Indebtedness caused by trade not only resulted in the selling of land to settle up with trade partners but also wars between Native peoples for new lands and their wealth of fur-bearing animals, as well as migration to create space and a buffer from encroaching white settlers. In hindsight, more space was needed as diseases carried by European settlers devastated Native communities, and trade in alcohol damaged entire Native peoples' social constructs.

Despite the dynamics of the fur trade, European Christianity missionary activities, and other cultural conflicts, Native-European relations were generally one of peaceful coexistence. The tipping point that changed that paradigm rather abruptly was the outbreak of the French and Indian War in 1754.

However, to do justice to any explanation of the French and Indian War, it's necessary to provide some context around that story, and to do that, we need to go back in time a bit and tell a parallel narrative of the Native American story. It's here where we'll introduce William Penn.

William Penn was born on October 14, 1644, at Tower Hill, London, to Margaret Jasper and English Captain William Penn. Penn's mother was from the Netherlands, the daughter of a wealthy Rotterdam merchant, and the recent widow of a Dutch captain. At the time of his son William's birth, Captain Penn was an ambitious twenty-three-year-old officer serving in the Commonwealth Navy during the English Civil War, responsible for quelling ongoing Irish Catholic unrest through tactics like blockading Irish ports.

After the war, Oliver Cromwell, who had led armies of the Parliament of England against King Charles, rewarded Captain Penn with estates in Ireland and a promotion to the rank of admiral, affording a certain degree of privilege to his young family.

Penn the younger grew up during the Puritan rule of Cromwell, but despite his father's rank and status, Penn's young childhood was far from picture-perfect and idyllic. First, his father was often away from home, at sea. More importantly, though, Penn the younger contracted smallpox, which left him hairless. He wore wigs up through young adulthood. In response to his condition, the family moved to an estate in Essex, in the southeast of England. It was there, in the English countryside, that Penn the younger began his lifelong affinity for horticulture.

In his teens, Penn's family was exiled to their lands in Ireland, a punishment for a failed mission at sea. It was there the younger Penn met Thomas Loe, a Quaker missionary who was much maligned by wary Protestants and Catholics alike. It was with Loe that young Penn wrote later, ". . . the Lord visited me and gave me divine Impressions of Himself."[1]

Things soon returned full circle for the Penn family. Cromwell died, and royalists strengthened their resurgence. The Penn family returned to England, where, in

1660, Admiral Penn was sent on a secret mission to retrieve Prince Charles and return him to the throne that had been vacated after his father, Charles I, was beheaded in 1647. It was for his daring bravado in restoring the monarchy that Admiral Penn was knighted and awarded the powerful position of Lord Commissioner of the Admiralty.

From captain to admiral, from William Penn to Sir William Penn, there's no doubting Penn the elder had a distinguished career marked by upward mobility.

Meanwhile, in 1660, Penn the younger began his collegiate studies at Oxford. Oxford's student body was a boiling mix of Cavaliers—those aristocratic Anglicans whose families supported Charles I and the monarchy in the English Civil War—ultra-conservative Puritans, and nonconforming Quakers. With the newly restored royal government discouraging religious dissent, the Cavaliers were essentially empowered to persecute the other two minority groups.

At the time, Penn would have been considered a Cavalier, primarily because of his father's high-ranking position and elevated social status. But the influence of Loe on his formative teen years led him to sympathize with the Quakers. Avoiding the conflict, Penn withdrew from the religious-based political infighting and concentrated on being a reclusive scholar.

At Oxford, Penn was a follower of theologian John Owen, and he stood faithfully beside him as he was first fired from his position as dean and then further censured. For his continued support, the university fined and reprimanded young Penn.

The university then adopted stronger, more strict religious requirements, including daily chapel attendance. Penn rebelled against the enforced worship and was subsequently expelled. If the admiral was disappointed by the earlier fine and reprimand, just imagine his thoughts on his son's expulsion.

The admiral kicked young Penn out of the family home, attacking him with a cane. With that as the catalyst, young Penn, just eighteen years old, was dispatched to Paris, in large part to get him out of sight, out of mind.

Young William Penn spent two years in France, one of which he spent under the spiritual direction of a mentor, French Protestant theologian Moise Amyraut, at the Saumur commune in western France. Influenced by Amyraut's belief in free will, Penn migrated further away from rigid Puritanical beliefs and was inspired to search out his own religious path, a key determinant of his actions later in life.

Young Penn returned to England a more polished, more mature young gentleman, and his parents had designs on him easing into the aristocracy. The admiral had his son enroll in law school, but with war looming with the Dutch, the younger Penn left school to, believe it or not, follow his father onto the seas, soon serving as an emissary between the admiral and the king.

When the Penns returned to England, they found London was firmly in the grips of the plague. Even amid the direst societal needs, Penn the younger saw how Quakers were continually harassed by followers of other religions and even blamed for causing the plague. Again, this experience would shape Penn's beliefs and fuel his future ambitions and actions.

In 1666, Penn the younger went to Ireland to tend to the family's estates, and it was there he became a soldier and served in duty to suppress an Irish rebellion. During this same period, King Charles leveled further restrictions against all religious sects other than the Anglican Church, with the penalty for unauthorized worship being imprisonment or deportation. Quakers were especially targeted.

So what was the Crown's issue with Quakers? The Quakers were strict Christians; it wasn't that. It was the firm Quaker belief that all men were equal under God (sorry, women, but it was, after all, the seventeenth century and a very unenlightened time in many respects). That single, fundamental Quaker belief was a polar opposite and a direct, irreconcilable conflict with the idea of a monarchy, built and supported by an unwavering belief that the monarch was divinely appointed by God. Quakers would never swear oaths of loyalty to the monarchy—they refused to bow or take off their hats to higher classes of society. In return, the Crown labeled Quakers as heretics.

It's easy to see why the Crown felt threatened, but what about the Anglican Church? Quakers held no rituals and had no professional clergy. The belief was that God communicated directly with individuals, and if individuals felt so inspired, they could share revelations and thoughts with others.

With the Crown and the Church both threatened, they found strength together, in numbers. With their majority, coupled with their wealth and control of both the legal system and the army, they continued to tighten the noose around the Quakers.

Penn, however, was not dissuaded by the tougher restrictions and persecutions, and he attended Quaker meetings. An unplanned chance reunion with Loe further spurred Penn toward the sect. Eventually, Penn publicly declared himself a member and formally joined the Quakers, despite an earlier arrest. In his defense, Penn argued the Quakers, unlike the Puritans a couple of decades before, had no political agenda, and therefore should not be subjected to the laws that restricted the activities of non-Anglican religions.

Penn's argument didn't carry any weight with the court, but his father's rank and social standing did. Penn was released from jail and called home by the admiral, only to be cut out of the family.

With no home to turn to, Penn sought refuge with his extended Quaker family, and he traveled extensively for the next ten years, writing a number of essays and pamphlets. He became a close friend and confidant of George Fox, the founder of the Quakers, and Penn's writings included a detailed explanation of Quakerism in his introduction to Fox's autobiography, the *Journal of George Fox*. That written introduction essentially served as the religion's written doctrine, helping it establish its public standing. It also made Penn its de facto theologian.

Penn's writings were highly controversial, to say the least, and he continually drew the ire of both the Anglican Church and the king. As a result, Penn was no stranger to running afoul of the law. He even spent an eight-month stint in solitary confinement while imprisoned in the Tower of London.

Before the admiral's death, he and his son reconciled, the father having begrudgingly gained respect for his son's integrity and courage. However, the admiral also knew that upon his death, his son would lose the protection afforded by his rank and social standing. The admiral wrote a letter to the heir to the throne, the Duke of York, and soon thereafter, the duke and the king, in a tip of the hat to the admiral's service to the Crown, promised Penn the younger would be made a royal counselor and receive a shield of protection.

Over the next few years, the situation didn't get better for the Quakers as their persecution only intensified. In response, Penn proposed to the Crown a somewhat novel solution: a mass migration of Quakers to the New World.

Some Quakers had already emigrated to the New World, settling in the New England region. But they found the Puritans there to be every bit as hostile toward them as the Anglicans they had left in England, and some had even been banished to the Caribbean.

One can only assume the banished Quakers felt some small justice was served when winters rolled around.

Penn, a wealthy man, as he had not been disinherited, participated in a coalition of prominent Quakers and purchased the entire colonial province of West Jersey, which is now half the state of New Jersey. With a presence already secured in the New World, Penn pressed his case further with the Crown, and, let's just say, his persistence paid off.

Somewhere along the line, the Crown had been indebted to the admiral to the tune of £16,000. Whether in sympathy for the plight of young Penn and the

Quakers or just a political move to peacefully remove dissidents from the country, the king decided to settle the debt by bestowing upon Penn the charter to over 45,000 square miles of land in America. With a stroke of a pen, Penn became the world's largest non-royal landowner and the sole proprietor of a tract west of New Jersey and north of Lord Baltimore's Maryland, and he was granted sovereign rule of the territory with all rights and privileges associated, except the power to declare war.

Penn initially named the territory New Wales, before changing it to Sylvania, Latin for forests or "woods." King Charles II, ever the king, decreed the name should be Pennsylvania, in honor of the admiral. And so, on March 4, 1681, the king's signature made it official.

With land deed in hand, Penn, perhaps feeling penned in—pun only partially intended—decided to expand the territory's land holdings, negotiating a purchase from the Lenape tribe. In the deal, Penn, a man of idealistic principles shaped by his past experiences and Quaker faith, included a provision that allowed the Lenape to retain the rights to traverse the lands for fishing, hunting, and gathering.

Penn had multiple goals for his New World land. He drafted a charter of liberties for the settlement, with designs on creating a province marked by freedom of religion, freedom from unjust imprisonment, fair trial by jury, and free elections. Certainly motivated by religious freedom, Penn was also motivated by profit. To that end, he was committed to exploiting neither the Native peoples nor new immigrants, writing, "I would not abuse His love, nor act unworthy of His providence, and so defile what came to me clean."[2]

Penn's first New World commercial challenge was attracting settlers, especially fellow Quakers looking for a safe haven. However, the cross-Atlantic voyage was no easy trip to consider, leading Penn to write a prospectus to lure travelers. Within six months, Penn had convinced over 250 adventurers, mostly well-to-do Quakers from London, to make the journey, doling out over 300,000 acres of land as incentives. His writings continued to attract settlers, particularly persecuted religious minorities from western Europe and the Nordics.

Penn returned to England in 1684, tending to his European affairs while governing his colony from afar. A shoddy businessman, he unknowingly signed over the property rights to Pennsylvania to his embezzling business manager, fellow Quaker Philip Ford, an act that complicated his life—and his estate—in later years.

In 1699, Penn returned to Pennsylvania intending to stay, and he found a colony much different from the frontier land he left fifteen years before. The population of Pennsylvania had grown rapidly, with nearly 20,000 residents in the state and over 3,000 in Philadelphia. The society was firmly anchored in religious diversity, and schools were producing a literate workforce, putting Philadelphia, in particular, on the path to being a leader in science and medicine.

It's fairly clear that William Penn had good intentions with his future ambitions for Pennsylvania, including interactions with the Native peoples. Peaceful coexistence was ideal, and in the early history of the colony, it was generally realized. However, it's important to note that peaceful coexistence was not a multidirectional give-and-take, built upon a level playing field. Rather, it was cultural imperialism, with, for the most part, European settlers taking and Native peoples giving.

As the European settler communities grew in population, those Native peoples who remained within close proximity of their ancestral homelands found it necessary—almost mandatory—to accommodate themselves to the colonists and assimilate into their imported cultures. A great many of those who stayed adopted farming or other European craftwork and converted to Christianity, all along facing pressure to abandon their cultural heritage.

Other Native peoples moved west, migrating into the Allegheny, Susquehanna, and Ohio Valleys. There, they established new communities, many of which featured mixed tribal affiliations, including members of the Iroquois, Shawnee, Delaware, Nanticoke, Tutelo, and others. As the colonial frontier, and the fur trade that accompanied it, moved further west, some of these new mixed Native communities gained newfound status and power.

Despite the eastern Native people adopting a colonial way of life, including its culture and religion, they still experienced prejudice that not only stifled their ultimate success but also threatened their very safety and security. Those who had fled to the west eventually saw the European colonists follow, and they grew weary of the constant colonial expansion, an increasingly one-sided fur trade, and European settlers' relentless Christian missionary activities.

While there might have been an idyllic initial vision of harmony, as is too often the case with humans, reality teetered toward something else entirely. The peaceful coexistence of the early eighteenth century gradually eroded until it hit its flash point with the outbreak of the French and Indian War.

The French and Indian War began in 1754, and it was the North American theater of a larger conflict between Great Britain and France, the Seven Years' War.

Until the war, England controlled the thirteen North American colonies up to the Appalachian Mountains. However, the land that lay beyond was known as New France, a large, sparsely settled colony that stretched from Louisiana up through the Mississippi River valley and the Great Lakes, and into Canada.

The border between British and French rule was neither clearly defined nor completely agreed upon. A particularly disputed territory was the upper Ohio River valley.

To strengthen its claim, the French constructed several forts in the region. In 1754, British forces led by then Lt. Colonel George Washington—yes, that George Washington—brazenly warned the French to leave in an attempt to seize control of the disputed lands.

In North America, the war pitted France, its French colonists, and allied Native peoples against Great Britain, its Anglo-American colonists, and one Native nation, the Iroquois Confederacy, who controlled upstate New York and portions of northern Pennsylvania. The French gained an early upper hand in the war, and present-day Pittsburgh played a starring role. It was at Fort Duquesne where the French killed General Edward Braddock, the commander in chief of British North American forces, in an ambush of his troops' failed sortie to capture the post.

By 1763, the French and Spanish appetite for war had abated, and the Treaty of Paris was signed, with Great Britain securing a giant territorial gain in North America, including all the French territories east of the Mississippi River and all of previously Spanish-held Florida.

So the English and Great Britain had secured a hard-fought victory, right? Not so fast.

The Seven Years' War, in large part because of its incredible global scope, had been costly, and the British government sought to partially recoup its investment by imposing taxes on the North American colonists. The colonists viewed these taxes as yet another attempt by England to flex and expand its imperial authority in the New World, and it garnered sweeping resentment. That growing resentment, stoked repeatedly year after year, led to a series of colonial uprisings and, eventually, the American Revolution.

The French and Indian War had seen armed conflict between Native peoples and colonial settlers, and that conflict didn't end when the war ended with the treaty signing in 1763. On the heels of the Treaty of Paris, a new conflict erupted in the New World, initiated by a confederation of Native tribes challenging British rule in the Great Lakes region. Known as Pontiac's Rebellion or Pontiac's War, the conflict burned white hot for a short period, with eight British forts destroyed and hundreds killed on both sides.

Ruthless, war-time atrocities were widespread over the span of both wars, on both sides of the ledger. Prisoners were executed, and civilians were repeatedly attacked. Pittsburgh, with its highly strategic position at the confluence of the Monongahela and Allegheny rivers, again played a role.

During the height of the French and Indian War, between 1759 and 1761, Fort Pitt had been built near the site of the aforementioned Fort Duquesne, which had been destroyed by the British in 1758. It was at Fort Pitt where one of the most infamous, most fiercely debated wartime atrocities took place—when British officers attempted to infect Native Peoples with smallpox-contaminated blankets.

It's not clear if this early biological warfare tactic worked, but it was symbolic of the growing, irreconcilable divide between European settlers and Native peoples. Tensions escalated with almost every encounter between the groups throughout a multi-generational period of war and violence, from the French and Indian War, through Pontiac's Rebellion, and onto, and throughout, the American Revolution.

With murderous atrocities committed by both sides, the ethnic gulf widened to where white settlers almost unanimously favored Native peoples' dispossession and exile to lands further west, while Native peoples became devoted to movements that rejected all of colonial society. By the turn of the nineteenth century, most Native tribal nations had abandoned ancestral homelands within Pennsylvania and fled to Ohio, parts further north in Canada, or further west.

Today, Native American culture in Pennsylvania is a distant memory, despite its indelible imprint on language and the names we're so familiar with—Ohio, Aliquippa, Youghiogheny, Monongahela, and so many more are derived, of course, from Native languages, not European languages. There is a small settlement of descendants of the Seneca on the Allegheny River near Warren, a grant from the commonwealth to Chief Complanter, who is buried at the site and to whom a monument was erected in 1866 by a special act of the Commonwealth's Assembly.

Descendants of other tribal nations are spread throughout the state, having been assimilated over time into Americana. Other descendants of the Native peoples of the Pennsylvania area were displaced and relocated en masse to the central plains. Descendants of the Delaware are with the Cherokee and Wichita in Oklahoma, the Stockbridge in Wisconsin, and the Chippewa in Kansas. Others migrated further north and are integrated with the Iroquois in Ontario, Canada.

Chapter 3

A FIRST HALF DOMINATED BY DEFENSE

Back to December 1972, as the pre-game festivities subsided and the band marched off the Tartan Turf field of Three Rivers Stadium, nervous anticipation floated through the crowd of over 50,000 fans. It had been a long wait for the first-ever home playoff game in franchise history, and, adding to the tension, the Steelers were just two-point favorites, a far tighter point spread than typical for a home team in a playoff game. Even bettors were every bit as uncertain about the outcome as were the fans in attendance. A cool, winter breeze gently furled the flags and banners hung by fans throughout the stadium, showing support for their beloved Steelers—"Franco's Italian Army" and "Count Fuqua's Foreign Legion" flying among them.

The Steelers' running back tandem of rookie Franco Harris and fourth-year veteran John "Frenchy" Fuqua was a formidable pair on the field and complete opposites off the field.

In 1969, Fuqua had been an eleventh-round draft pick of the New York Giants out of Morgan State University, a small, historically Black research university in Baltimore, Maryland. Fuqua had given himself the nickname, "The French Count," and over time, most everyone had shortened it to "Frenchy."

Frenchy Fuqua is still fondly recalled as one of the flashiest dressers in NFL history, and he really stood out in the pre-disco days of the early seventies. How flashy a dresser was Fuqua? Fuqua sometimes ventured out wearing platform shoes with transparent heels that contained water and a live tropical fish he plucked from his home aquarium to match the color of his outfit that day.

Yeah, that flashy.

His running mate in the Steeler backfield was Harris, a shy introvert who had been selected by the Steelers in the first round of the 1972 draft out of the major college football powerhouse, Penn State University. Harris had been the thirteenth overall pick in the draft, twenty-nine spots earlier than the running back he mainly *blocked for* in college, first-team All-American Lydell Mitchell.

Harris's African-American father served in World War II and met Harris's Italian mother while stationed overseas. With his Italian-American heritage, locals like Al Vento, proprietor of Vento's Pizza, and Tony Stagno, another Pittsburgher business-man, started what became one of the most iconic fan clubs in the city's history, Fran-co's Italian Army. Group members wore classic Army-issue World War II helmets while drinking Italian wine out of large goblets and devouring Italian cuisine before, during, and after Steelers games. The boisterous group hoisted signs and chanted, "Run Paisano, Run." Members attended charity events with Harris, and they once flew to Southern California to induct Frank Sinatra into Franco's Italian Army as a one-star general.

Together, Fuqua and Harris were a productive pair for the Steelers during the 1972 season, accounting for over 1,700 rushing yards, at an average of over five yards an attempt, and tacking on an additional thirty-nine combined receptions for over 300 yards. They were the centerpiece of the offensive side of the team, and the Steelers used them in their run-heavy offense, amassing 2,520 rushing yards throughout the fourteen-game regular season, far more than their 1,958 total passing yards gained.

Note, and as the statistics above indicate, professional football in the 1970s was a much different game than today. In today's NFL, rules have been created to provide a decided advantage for the offensive side. One case in point is the automatic first down given with every penalty against the defensive side, save one—offsides.

The biggest rule change that provided a boost to the offense in the modern era of football was the illegal contact rule brought into the game ahead of the 1978 season. That rule prohibited defensive players from contacting an opponent's receiv-ers beyond five yards from the line of scrimmage. After five yards, receivers today are left protected, allowed to run their routes with precision, opening up big passing lanes for modern quarterbacks. In today's NFL, when quarterbacks are under pres-sure from the pass rush, they often throw the ball to a spot on the field, confident their intended receiver will run his route and meet the ball at the spot.

In 1972, not so much. Back then, receivers were mugged wherever they dared to tread. Defensive backs grabbed, tugged, pushed, hit, and generally harassed receivers whenever they had an opportunity. Quarterbacks wouldn't dare throw the ball to a spot and had tiny windows in which to throw the ball at all. The rules allowed defen-sive coaches to call a lot of man-to-man-coverage, and, in doing so, freed teams to crowd the line of scrimmage with linebackers and safeties to defend against the rush.

In the 2021 season, Tampa Bay Buccaneers quarterback Tom Brady led the league with 5,316 yards passing in a seventeen-game season, completing 67.5 percent of his passes. In 1972, Archie Manning of the New Orleans Saints led the league with 2,781 yards passing over a fourteen-game season, completing just 51 percent of his passes. Pittsburgh's Terry Bradshaw, a future Hall of Fame quarterback, finished his season completing less than 48 percent of his passes for a total of just 1,887 yards.

Statistics like Bradshaw's 1972 stat line no longer get you in the Hall of Fame. In fact, they don't even get a quarterback into a team's starting lineup in today's NFL.

Terry Bradshaw is a professional football icon. Not only did the Blonde Bomber suit up for fourteen seasons with the Steelers, but after he retired, he became a staple on the *Fox NFL Sunday* pre-game, halftime, and post-game studio shows. When Fox telecasts the Super Bowl, as it does every three years, Bradshaw is the personality that hosts the on-field presentation of the Lombardi Trophy.

Bradshaw has developed into a popular culture celebrity, too, taking supporting roles in several television shows and movies, and he's even released music albums.

Yes, Bradshaw is a legend and is considered royalty in Pittsburgh. But it didn't start that way, not by any stretch of the imagination.

A native of Shreveport, Louisiana, Bradshaw stayed close to home and played college football at nearby Louisiana Tech University in Ruston. In Bradshaw's first two collegiate seasons, he was the backup quarterback and understudy to Phil Robertson, who much later grew to fame as the patriarch of the *Duck Dynasty* family, popularized in the long-running A&E television series.

It's true. You can't make that up.

During his junior and senior collegiate seasons, Bradshaw shined. In his first year as a starter, he led the NCAA in passing yardage and guided his team to a 9–2 record and a bowl game victory. His final year at Tech was a good one, with an 8–2 record and a healthy stat line considering he played little in the second half of most games. Most professional scouts thought he was the best quarterback available in the 1970 NFL draft.

The Steelers, limping off a dismal 1–13 season in 1969, held the rights to the first overall draft pick, having won a coin flip tiebreaker with the Chicago Bears, who had finished the season with an identical record. The Steelers won the flip and, with it, the right to draft first.

Take a moment and feel sorry for the Bears fans of 1969–1970. The team won one game all season and then lost a coin flip for the first overall pick. The Bears didn't get much better for several seasons, but ahead of the 1975 NFL draft, their luck in coin tosses changed. That year, they won a coin toss tiebreaker with the Cleveland Browns. Their prize in the 1975 draft? None other than the legendary Hall of Fame running back Walter Payton.

The Steelers selected Bradshaw with the first overall pick, and then, nothing much happened. In his rookie season, Bradshaw shared time with second-year pro Terry Hanratty. Bradshaw appeared in thirteen games, starting eight, and was . . . dismal. The team was 3–5 in his eight starts, with a 5–9 campaign overall, and in Bradshaw's 218 passing attempts, he threw an astounding twenty-four interceptions against just six touchdowns. A full 11 percent of his passes ended up as interceptions!

Bradshaw won the starting job ahead of the 1971 season, and both the team and he were marginally better. The Steelers finished the season 6–8, and Bradshaw threw *only* twenty-two interceptions. Twenty-two inceptions was an improvement, though, considering Bradshaw heaved 373 pass attempts. Still, Bradshaw was prone to turning the ball over, and fans and media alike took notice.

Many perceived Bradshaw, with his Southern accent and down-home country-boy charm, as being too dumb to play quarterback in the NFL.

In the 1972 season, Bradshaw turned it around. The team blossomed under his leadership and improved their play, finishing with that startling 11–3 record. For his part, Bradshaw threw only twelve interceptions, a marked improvement, matching his twelve touchdown passes.

In 1974, Bradshaw briefly lost his starting position to Joe Gilliam. He won the job back during the season, and from then on, Bradshaw never looked back. Over his career, he led the Steelers to eight divisional titles and four Super Bowl championships.

Bradshaw's tough, gritty play endeared himself into the hearts of the fans in Pittsburgh. Again, his era was before current rules were put into place to protect quarterbacks. In Bradshaw's day, quarterbacks were just another player, albeit one who touched the ball with every offensive play. A hit to the head was treated just like a hit to the head of any other player. No penalty. A hit below the knees, the same thing—no penalty. The result was a sort of open season on quarterbacks for defensemen across the league.

Bradshaw was tough, and he showed up for work every day, just like all those Pittsburghers in the mills. Viewing that week after week, season after season, Steelers fans embraced Bradshaw as one of their own.

Bradshaw was inducted into the Pro Football Hall of Fame in his first year of eligibility, 1989. He was also inducted into the College Football Hall of Fame in 1996.

In 1972, the Steelers, like most teams, relied on running the football, controlling field position and ball possession, and tenaciously defending every blade of grass—or Tartan Turf as the case may be—with a tough, stout defense.

The Steelers were stellar on defense, allowing the second least number of points scored during the season and forcing a league-leading forty-eight turnovers. The centerpiece of the defense was its dominant defensive line, led by All-Pro "Mean Joe" Greene and composed of a fearsome rotation that included Dwight White, Ernie "Fats" Holmes, LC Greenwood, Ben McGee, and Steve Furness.

By its performance alone, the defensive line had a great deal of notoriety in the public eye across the country. The line's mystique was even more amplified by its nickname, "The Steel Curtain," a play on both the region's steel industry and Winston Churchill's "Iron Curtain" description of the political boundary separating the Soviet bloc from the west. The Steel Curtain name originated from a 1971 contest conducted by local radio station WTAE and won by Gregory Kronz, a ninth-grade student at Montour High School. In a cruel twist of fate, Kronz was too young to fully enjoy the grand prize, a four-day trip to Miami to watch the Steelers play the Dolphins. Instead, he gave the prize package to his parents. One can only hope that he was duly compensated by his parents on birthdays and Christmases from then on out.

The Pittsburgh Steelers' defense of the 1970s was a fearsome lot, and no one was more feared by opponents than defensive tackle "Mean Joe" Greene.

Greene joined the Steelers as their first-round draft pick, and fourth selection overall, in the 1969 NFL Draft. A native Texan, Greene had starred at North Texas State University, now known as the University of North Texas, where he earned consensus All-America honors as a senior. His impact with the Steelers was immediate.

Mean Joe was named the NFL Defensive Rookie of the Year after the 1969 season, rather remarkably as the team miserably crawled to a 1–13 record. That was an indication of how good Greene was, and his reputation grew quickly around the league, because of both his play and his catchy nickname—a name that Greene, himself, didn't particularly care for.

When Greene first entered North Texas State, the team's mascot was the Eagles. Quickly though, the university adopted the moniker, "the Mean Green." How that name came about is disputed.

Two accounts have emerged, both with origins from fans at a North Texas game in 1966. What's not in dispute is that the name developed from cheering on the green-clad team, not one particular player in green named, appropriately, Greene.

However, it wasn't long before the two became one and the same. Joe Greene became Mean Joe Greene, and it was a name that bristled him over time. He wanted to be known as an exceptional player for championship teams and not be thought of, and remembered, as simply being mean.

There's more to the nickname that many devout Steelers fans don't know about. You see, Joe isn't Mean Joe Greene's first name. For real.

Greene was born on September 24, 1946, in Temple, Texas, as Charles Edward Greene. Joe was a nickname given to him by one of his aunts, who thought young Charles's build looked rather like boxing champion Joe Louis. The name stuck and combined with "Mean," it's a name cemented forever in football folklore.

While it's arguable, as with practically everything else in organized sports, Greene was probably the best, most dominant player in the NFL during the early 1970s, and that includes players from both sides of the ball, offensive and defensive. Greene's presence on the field simply affected every single play run by the opposition.

Greene won two NFL Defensive Player of the Year awards in his first five seasons in the league. Additionally, he was selected first-team All-Pro five times, and he had ten Pro Bowl appearances.

In Super Bowl IX, in January 1975, Greene had what many think is the greatest individual defensive Super Bowl performance ever, when he recorded an interception, a forced fumble, and a fumble recovery. For the game, a 16–6 victory and first Super Bowl championship for the Steelers, Greene and the Steel Curtain held the Vikings to just 119 total yards on offense and a paltry seventeen total yards rushing.

A known quantity among professional football fans everywhere, Greene became a definitive popular culture icon with his starring role in a Coca-Cola commercial that debuted in the autumn of 1979. In the commercial, a tired, weary Greene is seen limping down the tunnel toward the locker room as the game continues in the background. A kid asks him if he's okay, tells him he thinks he's the best ever, and offers him his bottle of Coke. After first refusing, Greene takes the Coke, and while he tips it back and chugs the entire bottle, the kid turns and walks away while the "Have a Coke and a Smile" song plays. Greene, finished with the Coke, says, "Hey, kid," and when the kid turns around, he says, "Catch," and tosses him his jersey. The kid's giant smile at the end of the commercial says it all.

Mean Joe Greene was inducted into the Pro Football Hall of Fame in 1987, in a class that included Oakland Raiders offensive guard Gene Upshaw, who on December 23, 1972, was suiting up in the visitors' locker room opposite the Steelers in Three Rivers Stadium.

Heading into the game, Steelers coaches knew their defensive unit would face a considerable challenge from the potent Raiders' offense. The Raiders' offense was led by 1,100-yard rusher, Marv Hubbard, a tough, bruising back who ran behind Gene Upshaw, between the tackles, and was a difficult runner to stop. Strong-armed Daryle Lamonica was the quarterback, and his receivers included the All-Pro tandem of split end Fred Biletnikoff and tight end Raymond Chester.

In the cast of characters that made up the Raiders roster in the 1970s, Biletnikoff was one of the notables. Never the most fleet afoot, Biletnikoff was blessed with great hands, and if the ball was remotely close to him, he came down with the catch much more often than not. Biletnikoff was such a great collegiate and professional wide receiver, the award given annually to the most outstanding receiver in NCAA Division I FBS football is named in his honor, the Biletnikoff Award.

The legend of Biletnikoff grew to Bunyanesque proportions, not because of his hands, though, but what he put *on* his hands. And his socks. And his forearms. His helmet, and nearly every place on his uniform and body. Biletnikoff used a liberal amount of a sticky, glue-like substance called Stickum, abundantly slathering it on various parts of his uniform where he could quickly replenish the coats on his hands should he need to.

Stickum was banned by the NFL in 1981, but by that time, Biletnikoff had retired, and what a career he had—589 receptions, seventy-six touchdowns, six Pro Bowl selections, and two appearances on the All-Pro team. In 1972, he was coming off a fifty-eight-catch season and poised to make big catches in the playoffs.

In fact, all the Raiders were ready to make big plays in the big games that were the NFL playoffs. Over the previous decade, no team had won more games than the Raiders, and they were very accustomed to playing in important games and performing well.

The Raiders began the game running behind their dominant left side of the offensive line, tackle Art Shell and Upshaw, which just so happened to be on the side away from Greene—a strategic win-win for the Raiders. Oakland found a modicum of success early, until Lamonica threw a pass that fell into the arms of Steelers linebacker Andy Russell.

With the ball in good field position, the Steelers began their first offensive series very conservatively, and when Bradshaw was stopped on a run just shy of the first down marker, Coach Noll brought in placekicker Roy Gerela to attempt a fifty-two-yard field goal to get the first points on the board. Unfortunately, Gerela's kick fell considerably short of the goalpost, nipping that scoring threat in the bud.

Gerela was in his fourth year in the NFL, completing his second season with the Steelers after having broken into the league with their division rival, the Houston Oilers. He would enjoy another six seasons in Pittsburgh and become a rather unlikely fan favorite—unlikely, in that he was a placekicker. Just as Harris had his Franco's Italian Army fan club, Gerela was the centerpiece of Gerela's Gorillas, and the sight of fans in head-to-toe gorilla costumes would become a game day staple at Three Rivers for the better part of a decade.

Off the heels of a missed scoring opportunity, the Steelers' defense continued to stymie the Raiders' offense, and running back Charlie Smith seemed to take the brunt of the punishment, weathering vicious, bone-jarring hits. Lamonica continued to struggle, with his longest completion being an eleven-yard pass to Biletnikoff. When the whistle blew to end the first quarter, the score remained deadlocked at 0–0.

Switching things up a bit, the Steelers began the second quarter moving the ball with quick, short passes—two caught by the Steelers' top pass receiver, Ron Shanklin. On a fourth-and-two at Oakland's thirty-one-yard line, Pittsburgh decided to go for it instead of attempting another field goal. Frenchy Fuqua ran up the middle and was halted in his tracks with a big hit by Raiders' safety Tatum.

Tatum, of course, was another of the more interesting characters who dressed for the game. In only his second year, Tatum had established a well-earned reputation as a tough, physical, intimidating presence in the middle of the field. For some, that description was the kinder, more gentle description of his on-field demeanor. Detractors bemoaned a repeated history of violent hits that unnecessarily crossed over the line of fair play. Years later, known then as "The Assassin" for his hard-hitting play, Tatum was forever linked to a hit on New England Patriots wide receiver Darryl Stingley in a preseason game, one that left Stingley paralyzed.

The second quarter continued, with both teams feeling one another out, probing for competitive weaknesses that could be exploited. On the Raiders defensive line, rookie tackle Otis Sistrunk, one of the very few NFL players in the modern era to have never played collegiate football, was having a huge impact, mauling the Steelers running backs whenever they dared try the middle. On passing plays, Bradshaw faced immense pressure from the likes of Tony Cline, often ending up on his backside and suffering large chunks of lost yardage. While the "sack" didn't become an official statistic of the NFL until 1982, its impact had always been felt in games, and this game was proving to be no exception.

As the hard-fought, rather conservatively played first half ended, it was still a scoreless tie. Both teams retreated to their respective locker rooms, knowing points would be coming at a premium, and one play could very well determine the outcome of the game.

Chapter 4

THE FOUNDING OF PITTSBURGH

A s European settlers descended on the New World, Pittsburgh, or at least
some settlement on the site of present-day Pittsburgh, was destined to
happen by geography and natural resources alone. Native peoples saw the
benefit of the confluence where the Allegheny and the Monongahela join to form
the Ohio River, and when the first European settlers arrived and saw the confluence,
they wrote home about it.

Literally.

In 1717, Michael Bezallion described the forks of the Ohio in a manuscript, and
later that same year, traders established posts and settlements in the vicinity.

Settlements began in earnest in the late 1740s, when an English land speculation
consortium, the Ohio Company of Virginia, won a 200,000-acre land grant from
England to organize the settlement of the Ohio Country by Virginians.

The French, who had also claimed the area, didn't exactly see eye-to-eye with
either the British or the Ohio Company, and that conflict reached its zenith with the
French and Indian War introduced earlier in Chapter 2.

French aspirations for the region began in 1749 when an expedition led by Céleron
de Bienville, a military officer, traveled down the Allegheny and the Ohio Rivers to
reinforce France's claim to the land. Along the journey, de Bienville and his troops
posted markers claiming ownership of the territory and drove off any English traders
they encountered on the way.

Four years later, in 1753, a larger expedition was sent into the region, and Fort
Presque Isle was established on the shores of Lake Erie at what is now present-day
Erie, Pennsylvania. From Fort Presque Isle, the expedition pressed farther inland,

cutting a road through the forest until reaching what they named French Creek, where they promptly constructed Fort Le Boeuf.

At high water, it was possible for the French and their Native compatriots to ride the current of French Creek all the way to the Allegheny. Doing just that, they wintered at the confluence and then established Fort Machault at the site the next year.

All this French movement into the region naturally caused concern for the Virginians, and Governor Robert Dinwiddie sent an army major, young George Washington, to warn the French they needed to withdraw their forces.

In the French style, Washington and his men were met with courtesy. Alas, also in the French style, they very independently refused to heed the governor's written warning. Despite the setback, Washington seemed to recover well, rising in the military ranks, becoming one of the Founding Fathers of the United States of America, later serving as the country's first president, and having his image memorialized on currency—Washington's profile is perhaps the most recognizable of anyone in American history. Quite remarkable, considering he lived over two hundred years before Instagram.

Mildly discouraged, but committed not to be outdone by the French, Governor Dinwiddie sent army Captain William Trent westward, and in early 1754, Trent and his men started to build Fort Prince George at a site that is now Pittsburgh.

Fort Prince George was never finished. Catching wind of this new intrusion into what they considered their land, the French marched over 500 troops to the site. The sheer size of their force, over ten times the number of troops and colonists at Trent's disposal, sent the British scurrying back to Virginia. Freed from the intrusion of the Brits, the French razed Fort Prince George and built their own fortification, Fort Duquesne.

Perhaps believing the third time to be charmed, Governor Dinwiddie ordered yet another expedition west, this time under the command of Colonel Joshua Fry and seconded by Washington. In May 1754, the French and British first clashed, and the resulting bloodshed contributed mightily to the start of the French and Indian War, a conflict that grew to span much of the world.

Several years of armed skirmishes ensued, with the French enjoying the upper hand early on, including the killing of General Braddock on the outskirts of Fort Duquesne. The pendulum, though, swung the other direction in 1758; although it probably didn't seem that way at the time.

In the summer of 1758, British General John Forbes led a combined force of 7,000 British Army and colonial troops on a campaign to capture Fort Duquesne. Along their march, they constructed both Fort Ligonier and Fort Bedford, and they cut a wagon road over the Allegheny Mountains, later named, quite appropriately, Forbes' Road.

Then, disaster struck. On the night of September 13, 1758, a scouting party under the direction of Major James Grant was massacred at the Battle of Fort Duquesne. After this defeat, Forbes set his mind to wait until spring to commence a retaliatory attack.

But that changed. Hearing through the grapevine that the French had lost Fort Frontenac and had, for the most part, evacuated Fort Duquesne, Forbes reversed his course and pressed on. The French, seeing they were completely outnumbered, beat a hasty retreat, razing their own Fort Duquesne in the process.

Seizing control of the burned-out fort on November 25, 1758, Forbes ordered the construction of Fort Pitt, named in honor of British Secretary of State William Pitt the Elder. Additionally, he named the settlement between the rivers Pittsbrough. Yes, Pittsbrough—that's not a typo.

What's in a name?

When it comes to the city of Pittsburgh, it was a good question for many years. In the last one hundred years or so, not so much.

With the defeat of the French at Fort Duquesne and the subsequent building of both Fort Pitt and the settlement, General Forbes referenced both in letters sent out in November 1758. Later, various sources published quotes from those letters, and the name of the settlement was referred to as Pittsburg, Pittsburgh, and even Pittsbourgh.

A Scot, General Forbes most likely pronounced the settlement's name similar to how he and his countrymen pronounced Edinburgh, "*pitsbərə*." The suffix "-burgh" is the Scottish-English cognate of the English "borough," and historically was used in names for locations that were generally thought of as being defensible, like a fort. In December 1758, the *Pennsylvania Gazette* published a letter from a member of Forbes's troops from "Pittsburgh."

Early municipal documents typically spelled the name with a final *h*, Pitts-burgh, but a notable exception is in the city charter enacted by the Commonwealth's legislature in 1816. From then on, throughout the 1800s, the variable spellings persisted. Even the city's local newspapers couldn't agree. The *Pittsburgh Gazette* celebrated the *h*; however, the city's largest newspaper, *The Pittsburg Press*, went *h*-less until 1921, as did both *The Pittsburg Dispatch* and *The Pittsburg Leader*—all the way into 1923.

The federal government even got into the act.

In 1890, the United States Board on Geographic Names was created to develop a standardization of location names used across the various departments and agencies of the rapidly growing US government. As part of its processes, the Board unilaterally adopted thirteen general principles, one of which determined the final *h* would be dropped from location names ending in "-burgh." In 1891, the Board published a report of location names in which the city's name, for purposes of the federal government, was declared to be Pittsburg. A supporting argument, of course, was the city charter from 1816.

The Board's decision on Pittsburg took effect at all federal government agencies, including the United States Postal Service. However, outside of the federal government, the Board's decision, while certainly influential and attached with a degree of political clout, was not officially binding. As such, the Pittsburgh city government continued with its spelling, *h* inclusive, as did big civic institutions, such as the University of Pittsburgh, the Pittsburgh Chamber of Commerce, and the Pittsburgh Stock Exchange.

In 1908, the Chamber chartered a committee to review historical documents, and based on the findings, endorsed Pittsburgh as the correct and most proper way to spell the city's name. From there, a lobbying effort started.

On July 19, tired of fighting a fight that needn't be fought, and bowing a bit to increasing political pressure from Republican Senator George T. Oliver, a longtime Pittsburgh resident and newspaper tycoon, the Board reversed its decision and officially added an *h* to its spelling of the city's name.

And that, for the most part, ended the controversy. Sort of.

California, Florida, Kansas, New Hampshire, Oklahoma, and Texas all have cities or towns named Pittsburg. Tennessee has a town named South Pittsburg, and a bunch of unincorporated municipalities in the United States are spelled Pittsburg. In fact, Pittsburgh, Pennsylvania is the only Pittsburgh, with an *h*, and one of the exceptionally few city or town names ending in a "-burg" that includes an *h*.

Pittsburgh slowly took shape as traders and settlers built out two sections of the settlement, the "lower town," nestled in nicely by the walls of the fort, and the "upper town," a collection of buildings along the Monongahela. In a census conducted in April 1761, a whopping 104 houses and 332 people were counted.

You'll recall the French and Indian War was not the only war that affected the early start of Pittsburgh. Rule over the land had transferred from the French to the British, and the Native peoples were no better off for it, and their dissatisfaction only grew. It eventually led to the outbreak of Pontiac's War.

Also known as Obwandiyag, Pontiac was an Odawa war chief, and he is forever linked to the war that took his name. However, his role—and his overall importance—in the conflict has been greatly debated over the centuries. Early on and through the 1800s, he was portrayed as the leader of the Native peoples' uprising. Subsequent studies by historians now suggest his role was greatly exaggerated. Generally, Pontiac is today remembered as an important Native leader at the local level who influenced a more encompassing initiative but who did not command it.

In May 1763, the Native revolt took aim at British forts, and Fort Pitt, in particular, was viewed as a big prize. However, Fort Pitt, then under the command of Swiss officer Captain Simeon Ecuyer, prepared accordingly. He ordered the clearing of the "lower town," razing the buildings to afford his troops a clear line of sight, and gathered supplies to weather a prolonged attack. Then he ordered every settler into the fort—330 men, 104 women, and 196 children joined his soldiers in the encampment.

The Native peoples attacked Fort Pitt on June 22, 1763, and the resulting siege lasted over six weeks. A force of approximately 500 soldiers, led by Colonel Henry Bouquet, made haste to reinforce Fort Pitt, and when the Natives peeled away from the fort to confront them, the Battle of Bushy Run took place. Over August 5 and 6, the British soldiers defeated the Native warriors, and further strengthened their hold over the Ohio River valley.

The next year, in 1764, Colonel Bouquet had his troops add a supplementary fortification to Fort Pitt, named the Fort Pitt Blockhouse. That structure still stands, and it is the sole remaining structure from Fort Pitt. Additionally, it's the oldest authenticated building west of the Allegheny Mountains.

A big threat repelled, Fort Pitt was hardly freed from conflict, as violent skirmishes marked the next 20 years. When the Iroquois signed the Fort Stanwix Treaty of 1768, they formally ceded all lands south of the Ohio to the British Crown. Naturally, this resulted in an increase of white European settlers in the region which, of course, continued to stoke tensions with the Native peoples.

Acts of violence were common, and they grew in intensity and frequency until the eruption of Lord Dunmore's War in 1774, named for the governor of Virginia, John Murray, Fourth Earl of Dunmore. Those formal hostilities ended that same year, with the Ohio River recognized as the boundary between the Native nations and the British colonies, and with the Natives ceding their right to hunt on colony lands.

Then, in 1776, the American Revolution started, with the colonies seeking independence from the British Crown. Native warriors viewed the Revolution opportunistically, launching attacks on the colonies' western front, hoping to win back lands as settlers' attention was focused elsewhere.

During the Revolution, Fort Pitt transitioned to become a United States fort when Brigadier General Edward Hand took command in 1777. It was also during the war, in 1780, when Pennsylvania and Virginia agreed on their border, creating the state lines that have carried forth to today and, once and for all, determining Pittsburgh as being Pennsylvanian.

When the Revolution ended in 1783, the might of the colonists' firepower brought closure to the Native conflict, this time with a 1784 Treaty of Fort Stanwix.

Early life in the Pittsburgh area was not easy. The frequent skirmishes with Native peoples highlighted the difficulties, but everyday life was tough and certainly not for the weak of either body or spirit.

White settlers in the area included English, Scottish, Irish, Welsh, German, and others, and they tended to settle together in smaller, farming-centered communities. Mostly, European settler life meant clearing forests and removing stumps to create farmland. Then the hard work started: building homes and barns; planting, caring for, and harvesting crops, and building nearly everything by hand, including farming and manufacturing tools, as well as furniture and other household goods.

On the farm, one of the most bountiful crops was corn, and farmers took to distilling their corn into whiskey, for a lot of different reasons. First, well, it was whiskey, and who doesn't like a taste every now and then? But, most importantly, distilling corn into whiskey increased the value of farmers' harvests tremendously—whiskey grew to become a form of currency.

When word of the value of whiskey got back to the federal government, it did what governments of the era—of all eras—did and imposed excise taxes. Fresh off a revolution driven, in large part, by objections to taxes, farmers in western Pennsylvania took umbrage, gathering at a rally on Braddock's Field and marching on the city of Pittsburgh. The Whiskey Rebellion of 1794 was short-lived, though, as then-President George Washington sent in troops to restore order.

With post-war peace, Pittsburgh continued to grow as European settlers moved west to seek a better life. With life on the river ripe with so much opportunity, it's no wonder that one of the region's first industries was boatbuilding. Boatyards sprung up along the rivers, first building flatboats and keelboats, and then, over time, building ocean-going vessels for commercial shipping as far away as Europe.

In 1800, a census put the population of Pittsburgh at 1,565, supporting over sixty different kinds of commercial shops—general stores, bakeries, and the like. But with the river fueling commercial trade and boatbuilding, and with its location on top of coal, petroleum, and natural gas, and alongside lush forests and productive farm country, Pittsburgh was becoming a manufacturing town.

Iron City was on the horizon.

Chapter 5

THE BIRTH OF IRON CITY

From its early days of settlement, Pittsburgh was practically destined to become a commercial center. The rivers, of course, supplied easy transportation, both in materials shipped to town and materials and finished products shipped out. The mountains to the east made heavy transport rather difficult and demanded the region be somewhat self-sufficient. And the region was blessed with an abundance of natural resources, with lush forests sprouting from fertile soil and an almost embarrassment of riches below ground, including coal, oil, natural gas, and limestone.

As mentioned in Chapter 4, one of the first businesses to boom in Pittsburgh was boatbuilding. The bounty of the rich forests to the north and northeast could be floated downriver to Pittsburgh, and from there, trees became lumber and lumber became boats.

The earliest boats were flatboats, and they were used exclusively for going down-river—basically, they were large rafts. Dimensions varied from twenty to one hundred feet long and twelve to twenty feet wide, and the average boat could be loaded down with fifty tons of tradable goods. Every town downriver from Pittsburgh was a potential destination, and the farthest port, New Orleans, was just a four-week trip. Once docked and unloaded of her goods, the flatboats were then scavenged and sold off as salvaged lumber.

Keelboats were used for upriver runs, but the journeys were slow. That four-week flatboat trip downriver to New Orleans became a four-month return trip upriver on a keelboat.

All that changed in 1811 with the first steamboat built in Pittsburgh, the *New Orleans*. Owned by Robert Fulton and Robert R. Livingston, and built by Nicholas Roosevelt, its maiden voyage from Pittsburgh, through Cincinnati and Louisville, to New Orleans, marked the start of commercial steamboat navigation on western and mid-western continental rivers.

Roosevelt brought shipbuilders and mechanics from New York to build the steamboat at a shipyard on the banks of the Monongahela River, a short distance from its junction with the Allegheny River at "The Point." The majority of the machinery for the boat was made in New York and transported overland to the shipyard because Pittsburgh didn't have a local manufacturer with sufficient capacity or capability.

Of course, that would quickly change. Steamboats brought more change. With steamboats now on the river, commerce became a two-way endeavor, downstream and upstream. All that was left was to take advantage of the opportunities presented.

Another catalyst for the growth of Pittsburgh was the fortuitous—for Pittsburgh, that is—outbreak of the War of 1812. At the time, Britain was the world center of manufacturing, and the war cut off the supply of finished goods to the relatively young America, forcing it to grow its own manufacturing capabilities. As Britain ruled the seas, it effectively enforced a blockade on America, forcing the country's hand to level up its manufacturing game and become self-reliant. More importantly, coal imports from Liverpool, England evaporated completely. More on that later.

With overseas trade stalled, America was forced to build its inland trade, and that opened up the flow of both raw materials and finished goods from all directions into, and through, a young Pittsburgh. The settlement took advantage of the boom town catalyst, and in 1815, estimated annual production included $764,000 in iron, $249,000 in brass and tin, and $235,000 in finished glass products.

By the time Pittsburgh was officially incorporated as a city in March 1816, its identity was already firmly rooted in its extensive manufacturing and commercial capabilities. However, to continue to grow and flourish, it needed to build and benefit from an even more conducive transportation infrastructure.

The National Road, also referred to as the Cumberland Road, was the original highway project built and paid for by the United States federal government. Construction started in 1811 in Cumberland, Maryland, outside of Baltimore, and started moving west, with the intention of connecting the Potomac and Ohio Rivers. The 620-mile route was destined to be the main thoroughfare for tens of thousands of European settlers, along with the commerce that was to follow alongside them.

Unfortunately for the commercial prospects of a young Pittsburgh, the National Road bypassed the city altogether, instead routing itself through Wheeling when the first segment was completed in 1818. Luckily, that wasn't the defining closing chapter in the story of Pittsburgh.

After its incorporation, and with the foresight of its civic leaders, Pittsburgh made tremendous improvements in its transportation infrastructure. In 1818, the region's first river bridge, made entirely of wood, opened at Smithfield Street. Being wooden, of course, it's not the bridge that stands today—that Smithfield Street Bridge was assembled in 1883 and eventually was designated a National Historic Landmark in 1976.

The original bridge, however, laid the foundation for Pittsburgh to become known as "the City of Bridges." The city had started building bridges, and it may not have ever stopped. One hundred years later, in the first half of the twentieth century, the city really kicked up its bridge-building spree, and most of Pittsburgh's oldest bridges today have origins from that period. When the country began expanding its interstate highway system in the latter half of the twentieth century, even more bridges were built to accommodate increased traffic, higher speeds, and heavier commercial transport loads.

The result of over 150 years of bridge building is an impressive collection of 446 bridges, including a bridge inside the USX Tower and a bridge, the Bellefield Bridge, that was buried and now lies underneath a fountain in Oakland, in a park between the Carnegie and Hillman libraries. In 2006, because of the research of Bob Regan, a visiting professor at the University of Pittsburgh, the city of Pittsburgh claimed its title as the city with the most bridges, surpassing the incumbent, Venice, Italy, by three.

Many of the bridges in downtown Pittsburgh are painted in the color of Aztec Gold. Naturally, it's not a coincidence.

Some might think the reason is that those bridges are in close proximity to the city's "Golden Triangle." But the colors go back much further than that, long before commercial titans laid claim to large patches of downtown.

When Pittsburgh was officially chartered as a city in 1816, efforts formalized its official colors, the colors that had been unofficial since the mid-1700s. The city's Great Seal and official standard were adopted based on Sir William Pitt's family coat of arms. More formally, in 1899, the city council set up an ordinance establishing the "flags and colors for the city of Pittsburgh," and decreed them to be black and gold.

So in painting bridges, it was rather natural to consider either black or gold. Perhaps wanting to add a little zing to a city that seemed to be perpetually buried under a cloud of coal dust in its early days, gold became the favored choice.

Black and gold, of course, are the colors adopted by the Pittsburgh Steelers. In fact, *all* of Pittsburgh's professional sports teams use the colors, making it the only city in the country where its teams have done so.

The city's original hockey team, the Pittsburgh Pirates, was the first sports team to embrace the colors, doing so in 1925. The Steelers adopted the colors upon their founding in 1933, and their first uniforms included the city's Great Seal. In 1948, the Pittsburgh Pirates baseball team changed its colors to black and gold from its original red, white, and blue. Then, finally, the current hockey team, the Penguins, latched onto the black and gold colors to start their 1980 season.

With its transportation infrastructure serving as a critical foundation to empower the city's growing manufacturing and commercial interests, Pittsburgh continued to make access to and from its borders more readily available. In 1834, the Pennsylvania Main Line Canal was completed, part of the Main Line of Public Works legislation package developed in the mid-1820s. The vision was to create a commercial transportation network connecting Philadelphia in the east and Pittsburgh in the west. It started with canals and later grew to include railroads.

Railroads were no doubt the future, and in 1835, McClurg, Wade and Co. built the first locomotive west of the Allegheny Mountains, further putting Pittsburgh on the map regarding its ability to manufacture the most important products and machines of the era. Pittsburgh was a frontier town no more; it had grown into a full-fledged city, one of the biggest in the west.

Between 1820 and 1840, the city's population tripled to over 21,000 people. However, like cities both before and after, the size of the city and its denizens grew at a faster pace than the city's infrastructure of essential services and, in particular, its ability to deliver water across the city, complete with dependable water pressure.

That annoyance developed into a significant problem on April 10, 1845, as a great fire almost destroyed the entire city. It was a "perfect storm" of a variety of factors, and its aftermath was devastating.

Pittsburgh's rapid growth and expansion had resulted in many wooden structures, residences primarily, built closely together in a high density across the city's footprint. Iron and glass industries were becoming dominant in the area, and their furnaces filled the city's air with a seemingly permanent haze of coal dust and soot. Other industrial concerns released flour dust and cotton fibers into the air, further completing a cloud of threatening incendiary dust that settled over the entirety of Pittsburgh.

Then there was the water supply. In 1844, the city completed the construction of a new reservoir, retiring the previous one. However, its pumps and water lines were inadequate for the size of the city. Just two water mains served the entire city of almost 30,000 people.

Last, the city had ten fire companies, all of them staffed by volunteers. However, common to the day, those fire stations were far more gentlemen's social clubs than civil service, and they were woefully ill-equipped. The companies simply did not have the lengths of hose necessary to reach from the rivers to center city.

You can imagine where this is going.

By April 10, 1845, Pittsburgh was in the middle of a drought that had deprived it of rain for six weeks, lowering the level of its water reservoir and making the city one big tinder box. To make matters worse, the day was windy.

The great fire can be traced to a single identifiable person, believe it or not. A woman named Ann Brooks worked for businessman Colonel William Diehl, and she had built a fire to heat water for washing. Leaving it briefly unattended, a spark from the fire was pushed by the wind to a nearby wooden building, where it quickly ignited into a proper blaze.

The first fire department responders found only a trickle of water emerging from their hoses, and the wind took care of the rest. The fire quickly spread and consumed several buildings owned by Diehl, including his home, and then engulfed the Globe Cotton Factory. The wooden cornice of the Third Presbyterian Church caught fire but was dropped into the street to save the church. Its stone walls served as a barrier to the fire spreading further to the north and west.

Blocked on one side, the winds took the fire toward the southeast. At the height of the firestorm, the large congregation of citizens fighting the fire left in an attempt to save their personal possessions. The fire moved unabated across the city, block by methodical block. Even the Bank of Pittsburgh, considered fireproof, fell victim, a total loss, save the contents of its vault. Other notable buildings destroyed included the elegant Monongahela House hotel, the cupola of the Western University of Pennsylvania (the precursor of the University of Pittsburgh), and the homes of both the university president and the city's mayor.

By daybreak on April 11, a third of Pittsburgh had burned to the ground. The fire destroyed 1,200 buildings and displaced approximately 12,000 people. Despite the chaos of the fire and its devastating impact on the city, only two people perished in the blaze.

Financially, losses were estimated as high as a quarter of a billion dollars in today's valuation. Very little of it was recoverable, and the fire forced all but one of the city's insurers into bankruptcy.

Spurred by grants and tax waivers given by the state, as well as charitable donations from across the country and as far away as Europe, rebuilding began almost as soon as the smoke had settled. Within just two months, over 400 newly constructed buildings sprouted up in the burned-out area of town.

Contrary to what many Pittsburghers might believe, the iron and steel industries weren't invented in Pittsburgh.

I know, right?

Iron has been known to human civilizations since ancient times and was initially sourced from meteorites. It's difficult to date ancient iron artifacts because, well, they're made of iron and not gold or silver. Iron corrodes easily, while those other two elements do not. So many iron artifacts from ancient times have simply been lost to time, having literally corroded away.

However, artifacts like iron beads dating from 5000 BCE have been discovered in Egyptian tombs. Artifacts made of smelted iron have been found dating from about 3000 BCE in Egypt and Mesopotamia. Back in those days, iron was truly rare and special—writings indicate iron was worth eight times as much as gold.

The world's iron age began about 1300 BCE when iron became cheap enough to replace bronze. Then, around 1000 BCE, someone somewhere probably made a mistake, letting his molten iron fall into the charcoal of his smelting fire. That introduction of carbon to iron gave humans the first steel.

That likely accident was a game-changer. Improving upon iron by adding carbon to make steel and the ability to cold work, or shaping metal when it is below its recrystallization temperature, made it much more preferable to work with than bronze.

Of course, another great advantage is the availability of iron. One-third of Earth's mass is believed to be iron, most of which is thought to lie at its core. With our natural supply, iron has turned into the cheapest, and most used, metal, accounting for about 95 percent of the world's total metal production.

In the 1600s, Britain had an insatiable appetite for iron as it served as a foundational catalyst for its growth in construction and manufacturing. But the iron manufacturing process required charcoal, and that required trees. Lots and lots of trees.

As Britain leveled its once-abundant forests, it became increasingly dependent on supplementing its domestic iron production with imports, including imports from its very European neighbors who were frequent wartime adversaries. However, turning an eye toward the west and the emerging colonies, Britain saw vast, relatively untouched forests.

With forests as fuel, British investors looked to build iron furnaces in the New World, and as transportation to England was paramount, settled their interests around the Chesapeake Bay, where bog iron ore was widely abundant. By 1751, Virginia and Maryland exported nearly 3,000 tons of pig iron to Britain annually, about 15 percent of annual British production.

The Chesapeake Bay furnaces were built for export. But the growing colonies needed iron for their consumption, too, so additional furnaces sprouted across the land. Simple business economics dictated that plants be built near critical resources—rivers to supply water power, forests to supply charcoal, iron ore deposits for basic raw materials, and limestone for flux in the smelting process. And, of course, close proximity to a major market or easy transportation for the distribution of finished products.

You know, places like Pittsburgh.

Coal had been part of Pittsburgh's history from the beginning. One of the first mentions of coal was by Gabriel Thomas in a letter to William Penn, where he speculated coal might be underground as the water had the same coloring as the water in Wales.

The marking of coal on a map was first recorded in 1753 by a Native peoples trader named John Pattin, although it's lost in history whether it was he or another who made the actual discovery.

The first actual coal mine recorded was a bituminous mine in Fort Pitt near the top of "Coal Hill," or what we now call "downtown Pittsburgh," denoted for posterity's sake in 1761 on the Plan of Fort Pitts and Parts Adjacent Map. Anthracite coal was discovered soon after, in 1762, by Obadiah and Daniel Gore, two brothers who were the first to use anthracite coal for their blacksmithing purposes at their shop in Wilkes Barre.

The coal industry figuratively exploded in the region and quite literally later on during its role in the great fire. Three hundred and fifty tons of coal were mined in Pennsylvania in 1810, and that number increased dramatically during the War of 1812 when the wartime shortage of British bituminous fuel caused Americans to look elsewhere for their fuel.

With the war rather forcing the hands of iron makers, they began experimenting with anthracite coal as fuel in their production. In 1840, David Thomas introduced Welsh hot blast technology to the Lehigh Crane Iron Company in eastern Pennsylvania, and it marked the debut of successfully using anthracite to smelt iron.

Iron producers discovered that using anthracite saved up to 25 percent of the cost of production, with the added benefit that the iron produced was of better quality. Using anthracite became a "no-brainer," and by the 1850s, half of all crude iron produced in the United States used anthracite. Pittsburgh, of course, was poised to take advantage.

Infrastructure improvements in transportation aided in putting Pittsburgh on the map, so to speak. First, it was the canals; then came the railroads. The Ohio and Pennsylvania Railroad began service in 1851, connecting Allegheny City, annexed by Pittsburgh in 1907 and now known as the North Side, and Cleveland. It was followed in 1854 by the Pennsylvania Railroad, connecting Pittsburgh with Philadelphia.

At that point, Pittsburgh's commercial leaders took off and never looked back, at least not for over a century. In 1857, Pittsburgh was still a city with less than 50,000 people, or roughly 10 percent the size of Philadelphia. That makes the following output, as recorded in an 1857 article in *Ballou's Pictorial Drawing-Room Companion*, even more remarkable. Consider the following Pittsburgh statistics from that year:

- 939 factories in Pittsburgh and Allegheny City
- Over 10,000 workers employed by those factories (well over 20 percent of the city's entire population)
- 400 steam engines in production
- 22 million bushels of coal used in manufacturing
- 127 tons of iron used in manufacturing
- $12 million of total goods produced[3]

In terms of steam tonnage, Pittsburgh was the third busiest port in the nation in 1857, trailing only New York City, population of about a million, and New Orleans, population of well over 100,000.

Pittsburgh, first with coal, then as "Iron City," was getting it done!

Chapter 6

THE STAGE IS SET

Coming out of the dressing rooms for the second half of the game, both teams were looking for something—anything—on which to build an offensive attack.

In the first half, the Raiders had tried to lean on the running game, running most often to their left side and away from Mean Joe Greene. While they had some modicum of success on a handful of plays, it was evident they would not be able to mount any long, sustained drives based entirely on the run game.

The loud crowd knew it too. Spurred on by the scoreboard flashing DEE and FENSE, each Raider possession had been greeted with a deafening din. It was only going to get louder in the second half, and the Raiders were going to need to find a solution.

It wasn't going to be an easy feat either, as the Raiders also knew they needed to find some answer to the Steelers' stifling pass defense, one of the strongest in the NFL. Not only were the Steelers stingy in giving up yards, but their twenty-eight interceptions in the fourteen-game regular season led the league.

In the first half, the Raiders' longest pass play was an eleven-yard gain, made possible only by the exceptional catch of glue-fingered Biletnikoff, who snatched the ball off his shoe tops while blanketed in coverage.

However, on the other sideline, the Steelers' offense had not fared much better. Raiders defensive lineman Sistrunk was having his way on the line of scrimmage, stopping Steelers running backs before they could garner any headway. Whenever he dropped back to pass and looked to push the ball deep downfield, Bradshaw had been constantly harassed, and, as a result, suffered a couple of sacks for big losses of yardage.

Starting the third quarter, Noll directed the Steelers to mix it up, with Bradshaw taking shorter drops, looking to get the ball out quickly before the Raiders could collapse his protective pocket. Short drops meant short, quick routes by his receivers, under the Raiders' deep coverage, and Bradshaw worked the ball out to Harris, who was sweeping out of the backfield and into the short flats on either side.

Those short passes allowed Harris to get some running room away from the shackles of Sistrunk and his linemates, and the Steelers moved the ball a bit. Yet, they had done that on occasions in the first half but had come up short.

Catching the Raiders focusing on Harris a bit too much, Bradshaw struck deeper downfield, hitting receiver Ron Shanklin for a nice gain down the right sideline and a first down deep in Raiders' territory. The Steelers tried to force their way in for a touchdown but were held back by the Raiders.

Perhaps weary of losing another good scoring opportunity with a failure on fourth down like they suffered in the first half, the Steelers trotted out Gerela for a little chip shot, an eighteen-yard field goal.

Gerela split the uprights, and the Steelers had broken the scoreless battle. The Black and Gold were now up, 3–0.

The Raiders persisted with Lamonica at quarterback, but any newfound success against the Steelers' tough-as-steel defense continued to be elusive. The Raiders, growing more and more frustrated on offense, simply couldn't get anything going. Lamonica did connect with Raymond Chester on a nineteen-yard reception, but that promising start to a drive quickly fizzled.

Despite their struggles on offense, the Raiders' defense continued to play inspired football. They made their counter adjustments to the Steelers' revised short-passing game plan, and they tightened down their own clamps on Bradshaw and company.

When the referee's whistle signaled the end of the third quarter, Gerela's score remained the only marker, and the Steelers clung to a narrow 3–0 lead heading into the fourth.

After the Steelers began the fourth quarter without getting much going and having their possession stopped by an Art Thoms's sack of Bradshaw, they punted the ball away to the Raiders. Perhaps desperately, Lamonica let loose an ill-advised long pass down the right sideline in the general direction of Biletnikoff, who was double-covered. Outside linebacker Jack Ham picked off the pass, Lamonica's second interception of the game.

Maybe Lamonica couldn't believe a linebacker like Ham could make his way so far downfield in coverage on a wide receiver. Regardless, the Steelers took over possession, and fans began thinking maybe they'd witness the Steelers win a 3–0 grind fest of a game.

Doing their part, the Raiders' defense continued to pick up the slack for their struggling offense. Repeatedly winning on the line of scrimmage, they once again clamped down on the Steelers' offense and forced a punt.

By this time, Oakland head coach Madden had seen enough of Lamonica on this particular day. Needing a spark, he turned to backup quarterback Ken Stabler, a third-year player out of the University of Alabama.

Eventually inducted into the Hall of Fame, Stabler was much less experienced than Lamonica, having started just two games in his career. For the entire 1972 season, Stabler had attempted just seventy-four passes, with four touchdowns and three interceptions.

Steelers fans grew more excited as their beloved Steel Curtain eyed fresh prey.

Greene and company made sure Stabler's introduction to the game was a rude one. Harassing him with pressure on every drop back, the Steelers continued to shut down the Raiders before the slightest hint of an offensive threat could be generated.

Not that it mattered to the Raiders' defense. Determined to show that what the Steelers could do, they could do better, the Raiders generated a turnover of their own when cornerback Nemiah Wilson snagged an errant Bradshaw pass. The defensive pendulum, having swung back and forth the entire game, did so yet one more time.

On the Raiders' possession, the Steel Curtain reintroduced itself to Stabler once more, pressuring him as he rolled out to his left. When Stabler prolonged the play by dancing around, looking for an open receiver, the ball was punched out of his grasp—in part, by his own lineman, guard Upshaw. The ball shot forward about ten yards where it was gathered in by safety Mike Wagner, who just beat a diving Jim Otto, the Raiders center, for the fumble recovery.

First down, Steelers, on the Raiders' own thirty-five-yard line!

In possession of the ball, with a slim three-point lead and the clock clicking steadily down, the Steelers were content to play it relatively close to the vest. Their conservative play-calling rendered a first down and advanced the ball slightly before they had to settle for a twenty-nine-yard Gerela field goal.

The crowd celebrated the 6–0 score. With the dominance displayed by the Steelers' defense the entire game, a wave of optimism swelled over the hometown crowd.

This was happening!

Forced by the dwindling time remaining and the Steelers' defense, Madden tossed out his painstakingly prepared offensive game plan. From the Raiders' perspective, the game was now in the hands of Stabler.

Finding time in the pocket for the first time, the "Snake" started the Raiders' drive by hitting Chester with a short pass to gain a first down and move the chains.

Then Stabler dropped back and came under pressure from the entire Steelers defensive line. But it was a ruse, as the Oakland offensive line let the Steelers rush while they set up a screen pass for fullback Pete Banaszak. Banaszak, on his only touch of the ball the entire game, rumbled twelve yards for another Raiders first down.

Stabler then connected on a down-and-out pattern with Biletnikoff for yet another first down. In quick succession, the Raiders were enjoying their most sustained offensive success of the entire game.

Inside the two-minute warning, Stabler, rolling to his left under pressure, first from Steeler defensive tackle Ernie Holmes and then by end Dwight White, delivered a strike to receiver Mike Siani, his first reception of the game. The completion advanced the ball, and Siani stopped the clock when he went out of bounds.

For the first time in the game, the Raiders were finding success on offense, and they were doing so with the short passing game. Thus, it was no surprise to anyone, fans and players alike, when Stabler took the snap on the Steelers' thirty-yard line and dropped back once again to pass.

A left-handed passer, Stabler naturally looked to elude pass rushers by rolling to his left—it made for an easier, more accurate throw than rolling to his right. Faced with the mighty Steelers pass rush, he had been doing it on nearly all of his drop backs.

On this play, Stabler anticipated pressure coming from his right side when he saw linebacker Ham creep up to the line of scrimmage pre-snap, prepared to blitz with all his might. By getting an early start to roll left, Stabler just eluded defensive end Craig Hanneman, who had beaten Banaszak's block on the play.

Evading the pass rushers, Stabler was flushed all the way back to the forty-yard line, and when he looked downfield he saw . . . a lot of open space down the left sideline. Still gripping the ball in his left hand like he was going to pass, Stabler took off toward the end zone.

Never the most fleet afoot, Stabler nevertheless easily ran by end Greenwood. Then he benefited from a great block by Siani on Mel Blount at the goal line. Stabler only had to get past Wagner, and he did so by diving into the end zone.

Stabler was mobbed by his teammates as he made his way back to the sidelines, and the crowd was left standing in shocked silence.

When George Blanda added the extra point, the Raiders, rather remarkably, held a 7–6 lead, with less than a minute and a half remaining.

Chapter 7

THE RISE OF STEEL CITY

Much like the War of 1812, the American Civil War provided a boost to the welfare of Pittsburgh's iron and steel businesses and, in turn, its citizens. Local manufacturers were inundated with orders for iron and steel, and even finished armaments, like ironclad warships and cannons.

By the end of the Civil War, Pittsburgh was responsible for over half of all steel manufactured in the United States, and post-war reconstruction only spurred growth further. The steel business grew year over year and became one of the most dominant industries in the latter half of the nineteenth century.

Pittsburgh mills brought forward new technologies in the manufacturing process, further cementing its place as the industry's epicenter. Before the Civil War, coke-fire smelting was brought to the region. Soon after the war, local factories were producing steel rail using the Bessemer process, which allowed the high carbon content of pig iron to be burnt away in a controlled and rapid manner during steel production.

Steelwork has never been easy, but in the mid- to late-1800s, it was downright difficult. Materials and finished products were extraordinarily dense and heavy, and the manufacturing process was hot, dusty, smokey, and more than a little dangerous. When workplace accidents happened, they were serious, often with catastrophic consequences to both limb and, too often, life.

However, it was the life of Pittsburghers.

As the steel industry grew, it far out-paced other professions in the greater Pittsburgh economy. Almost every family had ties to a mill, and many families had economic ties only to mills. Pittsburgh was steel, and Pittsburghers were strong as steel.

While steelwork was good work and allowed workers to provide for their families, the steel business brought even better rewards to those industrialists who owned the enterprises and the tangential businesses spawned by the steel industry. Steel and its related businesses delivered vast fortunes to a handful of the world's richest men in the late nineteenth and early twentieth centuries.

Industrialists Andrew Carnegie, Henry Clay Frick, Andrew W. Mellon, and Charles M. Schwab all amassed fortunes that were almost unimaginable at the time, with steel holdings being the heart of their expansive portfolios. Pittsburgh banks grew to be regional giants, financing the steel barons with massive loans for new manufacturing technologies and innovations, upgraded plants and infrastructure, and merger and acquisition plays to vertically integrate their industries.

Not all the Pittsburgh elite were players in the steel game, however. Pittsburgh was also home to George Westinghouse, who, after serving first in the New York National Guard, then the Union Army, and finally, in the Union Navy during the Civil War; founded over sixty companies over his lifetime, including Westinghouse Air and Brake Company, Union Switch & Signal, and, most notably, the Westinghouse Electric Company.

Then, of course, there was Henry J. Heinz, who co-founded a small horseradish production company. Unfortunately, that business never really took off and eventually shuttered its doors. But, as the old saying states, when one door closes, another opens. Heinz created a second business and focused it on tomato ketchup and other condiments. That business grew to be the H. J. Heinz Company, a pillar of Pittsburgh for well over 130 years. To this day, many Pittsburghers refuse to use any ketchup other than Heinz. Period.

The "Mount Rushmore" of Pittsburgh steel barons probably begins with Andrew Carnegie. Carnegie was born in Dunfermline, Scotland, in 1835 and emigrated to the United States with his parents in 1848 at age twelve. Looking for a better life and having borrowed money to make the move, the family settled in Allegheny.

Carnegie's father was a weaver, but he had trouble establishing a business in Allegheny. It wasn't long before he started working at a Scottish-owned cotton mill, Anchor Cotton, alongside his son. Andrew started his first job in 1848, working as a bobbin boy, changing spools of thread in the cotton mill during twelve-hour shifts, six days a week, all for the tidy sum of $1.20 per week (or the equivalent of $43 in 2022).

In 1849, Carnegie shifted to work as a telegraph messenger boy in the Pittsburgh office of the Ohio Telegraph Company. He worked hard, made several connections, and impressed people so much that he was promoted to an operator position within a year.

Carnegie loved to read, and his thirst for knowledge, and the self-education it provided, led him to take advantage of the sweeping generosity of Colonel James Anderson, a local educator, railroad contractor, and Army officer, who availed his

400-volume personal library to working boys like Carnegie every Saturday night. That simple act of kindness and mentoring would shape Carnegie's future philanthropic pursuits.

In 1853, at the age of eighteen, Carnegie pivoted from the telegraph business to railroads and the Pennsylvania Railroad Company, as he believed it would afford better career growth. Railroads were huge—the first really big business on the continent—and the Pennsylvania was the biggest of them all.

Under the tutelage of Thomas Alexander Scott, a future US Assistant Secretary of War, and John Edgar Thomson, the president of the Pennsylvania Railroad, Carnegie made his first investments. In hindsight, they were can't-miss bets, as they were investments made on insider knowledge of companies that were involved in business deals with the railroad.

Carnegie advanced rapidly with the Pennsylvania Railroad Company and served under Scott during the Civil War as the superintendent of the Military Railways and the Union Government's telegraph lines in the East.

In 1864, Carnegie was one of the early investors in the Columbia Oil Company in Venango County. With the war machine demanding fuel for iron and steel concerns, he and his co-investors made money hand-over-fist. After the war, Carnegie made another pivot, leaving the railroad and concentrating on ironworks, eventually forming the Keystone Bridge Works and the Union Ironworks in Pittsburgh. Of course, his close ties to Scott and Thomson—Carnegie named his first steel plant after Thomson—ensured the Pennsylvania was his biggest customer.

Carnegie made the vast majority of his fortune in steel. His leadership in the industry came from two primary innovations. Adopting the Bessemer process, he could mass produce steel efficiently and inexpensively. Additionally, he vertically integrated nearly all suppliers of raw materials to be under one organizational roof.

He further grew his businesses by using his cozy relationships with railroads to negotiate favorable transport prices. It was a quid pro quo arrangement, as Carnegie's ironworks supplied steel rail for the railroads, and the mutually beneficial relationship usurped any free market competition. As Carnegie's fortune amassed, he acquired rival companies, further building his enormous portfolio.

A big win for Carnegie and his business concerns occurred when the Eads Bridge, spanning the Mississippi River in St. Louis, was completed in 1874. That massive, and highly visible, project essentially served as a proof of concept for engineering and building with steel. The bridge's successful completion further stoked the embers of a white-hot industry by opening up new, previously untapped applications and markets.

As Carnegie's wealth grew, he gobbled up other related steelmaking concerns. By the late 1880s, early 1890s, the United States' output of steel, the majority of it centered in Pittsburgh, exceeded that of the United Kingdom. And Carnegie owned the lion's share of that American trade.

By the turn of the century, Carnegie, in his early sixties, eyed retirement. Preparing to divest, he converted his holdings into a joint stock corporation. From there, he worked with John Pierpont Morgan, the country's preeminent banker and financial deal maker, and, later, the namesake of the prestigious J. P. Morgan and Co banking firm.

Morgan set his sights on an integrated steel industry for the next era of industrialization, but to realize that vision, he needed to buy out Carnegie and other titans to consolidate into a single company. Morgan got the deal done on March 2, 1901, forming the United States Steel Corporation.

At its formation, U.S. Steel was the world's first corporation with a market capitalization of over $1 billion, and it busted through that ceiling quite handily. Tipping the scales at a hefty $1.4 billion in valuation, it represented about four percent of the US gross domestic product (GDP). One company!

Individually, Carnegie walked away from the deal with over $225 million, the equivalent of over $7 billion in 2022.

Entering a new phase of life, Carnegie transitioned from a shrewd, market-manipulating industrialist to a generous philanthropist.

A lasting legacy of his charitable contributions was the establishment of public libraries throughout the United States, Canada, Britain, and other English-speaking countries. His model centered on donating funds to build and equip a library, on the condition the local authority complemented those contributions by providing the land and budgets for administration and maintenance.

The first Carnegie library opened in 1883 in his birthplace, Dunfermline, Scotland. Over time, Carnegie funded over 3,000 libraries in forty-seven US states and multiple English-speaking countries.

In Pittsburgh, Carnegie donated $2 million in 1900 to fund the Carnegie Institute of Technology (CIT) for the advancement of scientific research and discovery. That institution lives today as Carnegie Mellon University after it merged with the Mellon Institute of Industrial Research.

A decade later, Carnegie boosted his contributions to CIT with an additional $10 million, rather forcefully suggesting the money be invested in a manner to help expedite the construction of George Ellery Hale's ambitious endeavor to build the 100-inch Hooker Telescope at Mount Wilson, outside Los Angeles. Carnegie desperately wanted to see the telescope come to fruition before he died. The telescope became operational in 1917, and Carnegie was alive to revel in its success.

Another academic-related pursuit was the 1905 establishment of a pension fund for American college professors. Over time, this fund grew to become TIAA-CREF, a Fortune 100 financial services organization that is the leading provider of financial services in the academic, research, medical, cultural, and governmental fields.

Among his other philanthropic pursuits, Carnegie funded the construction of over 7,000 church organs. Additionally, his love of music led him to build the famed Carnegie Hall in New York.

Carnegie was also a large benefactor to Booker T. Washington and the Tuskegee Institute for African-American education. Within that relationship, he helped Washington create the National Negro Business League.

Carnegie died on August 11, 1919, at his Shadow Brook estate in Lenox, Massachusetts. With his market manipulation and aggressive lobbying for self-protective steel tariffs that tremendously contributed to his wealth, Carnegie shouldn't be remembered as a saint-like businessman. However, compared to other industrialists of his time, history views him much more favorably, as a more humane protagonist in the great American story.

The latter part of his life certainly balanced any transgressions of his earlier professional life, as Carnegie donated well north of $300 million over his lifetime. He left an indelible mark on a number of places, Pittsburgh among them, and his legacy stands strongly today.

The mega steel barons owned the enormous companies, but Pittsburgh was also home to several small, independent iron and steel manufacturers, and they created wealth for both their owners and the community as a whole.

These smaller firms focused their businesses on specialized products, like structural steel, where the economies of scale of the enormous steel companies couldn't carve out a competitive advantage. The specialty products required the smaller companies to employ more highly skilled labor, and the businesses were successful.

This produced a rapid expansion of the steel industry and a subsequent search for more space and resources. What began as a fairly centralized industry in Pittsburgh ballooned out to become a sprawling regional industrial complex throughout Allegheny County. The city of Pittsburgh, however, centered the region and remained its crown jewel.

Iron and steel were making many rich—wealthy almost beyond compare in the United States. And the industries were pumping money into the Pittsburgh area's economy, too, providing a multiplier effect where almost everyone could trace some part of their good fortune to the industries.

But there was still an enormous wealth gap between the steel barons and their workers. Coupled with the fact that iron and steelwork was difficult, dirty, and dangerous, that wealth gap quickly stoked the fires of labor unrest. The solution, for workers, came in the form of unions and collective bargaining.

The relationships between organized labor and steel companies were contentious from nearly the very start. And don't think for a second that those contentious relationships weren't a driving force for companies moving out into the countryside.

Vandergrift is a good example. Vandergrift, a borough of a little over 5,000 people today, sits in Westmoreland County, about thirty miles northeast of Pittsburgh. In the early 1900s, it was home to the largest sheet steel mill in the world.

In the 1890s, George McMurtry's Apollo Iron and Steel Company was entrenched in a bitter dispute with labor. Seeing no end in sight, he oversaw a lockout and brought in replacement workers from Pittsburgh's surrounding communities. In doing so, a bigger idea came to fruition in his head.

To avoid future labor problems, McMurtry sought a solution to develop a community and ecosystem so intertwined that dependable, and relatively inexpensive, labor was always available. He based his plan on the philosophies driving reform movements in western Europe and the United States—what we would call welfare capitalism today. Ideally, an industrial concern would go above and beyond basic paychecks as compensation to employees, incorporating provisions for the social well-being of its workers into its value proposition. If he could successfully do so, McMurtry believed he would nurture a happier, more productive workforce.

In 1895, it all came together. Apollo Iron and Steel built a new, integrated, and non-unionized steelworks plant. At the same time, McMurtry hired the country's preeminent landscape architectural firm, Olmsted, Olmsted and Eliot, whose partner Frederick Law Olmsted was the principal designer of the 1893 Chicago World's Fair, to design his new model industrial town, Vandergrift, named for Capt. JJ Vandergrift, a director at his company.

Based on direction from McMurtry, the architects designed an urban area with foundations in comprehensive infrastructure planning, environmentalism, social reform, and home ownership. In 1904, when a model of the town was displayed at the St. Louis World's Fair, the town's design won two gold medals.

Workers loved Vandergrift, and they became very loyal to McMurtry and the company. So loyal that McMurtry used Vandergrift in 1901 to break the first major organized labor strike against the U.S. Steel Corporation.

By 1940, the population of Vandergrift had swelled to almost 11,000 people. In 1988, the steel mill was purchased by the Allegheny Ludlum Corporation, a specialty steel maker. Investments in the plant upgraded it to a modern, state-of-the-art mill.

As Pittsburgh's industrial complex swelled, its wealthiest denizens lived in East Liberty, a neighborhood in the east end of Pittsburgh. One hundred years before the richest of the rich built their impressive mansions, it was a free grazing area for the animals of local farmers. Its name, East Liberty, is literally derived from that. East, for the location, and Liberty, as the old English designation for common land on the outskirts of a town.

In the early days, two farming patriarchs, John Conrad Winebiddle and Alexander Negley, owned much of the land in the area. When Winebiddle's daughter Barbara married Negley's son Jacob, the families' holdings merged into a single collective.

The land holdings alone were enough to generate great wealth. Then, as if land management wasn't lucrative enough, when the Pittsburgh-Greensburg turnpike was routed through East Liberty, the area became a robust trading center, and its destiny for bigger and better was firmly rooted.

With their wealth, Barbara and Jacob built a stately mansion, one that caught the attention of a great many eyes. Among those dutifully impressed was Thomas Mellon, who first sighted the mansion as a ten-year-old visiting the area.

Reaching adulthood, Mellon became an attorney and married none other than Sarah Jane Negley, daughter of Barbara and Jacob. As a successful attorney from a well-off banking family, Mellon was already wealthy. However, by renting and selling much of his wife's property holdings, he financed much of Pittsburgh's burgeoning industrial complex, laying the foundation for a vast, multi-generational family fortune.

The most famous of the Mellons, though, was perhaps his son, Andrew Mellon.

Andrew Mellon was born in Pittsburgh on March 24, 1855, the sixth child—and fourth son—of his parents. His father didn't trust either public or private schools, so he built a schoolhouse and hired teachers to teach his children. That homeschooling formed the educational foundation for young Andrew and his siblings.

Andrew eventually attended Western University but did not graduate. After briefly paying his dues in the lumber and coal industries, and while still in his teens, he joined his father at the family bank in 1873.

Andrew's financial career didn't start with smooth sailing. Rather, in his first few months, the seas proved tumultuous. The Panic of 1873 ravaged the national economy, and the local Pittsburgh economy proved no exception. The result was a precipitous decline in the family fortune.

It was a temporary setback, however. By the end of 1874, the bank had fully recovered, and much of the credit seemed to be linked to Andrew's leadership.

Andrew's influence at the bank continued to grow, and in 1876, he was given power of attorney to direct the operations of the bank. In 1882, his father granted Andrew full ownership of the bank.

Early in his career, Andrew befriended a customer of the bank, Henry Clay Frick, a co-founder of the Frick Coke Company, a business that transformed coal into coke for the local steel manufacturing industry. Together, Mellon and Frick, who would later become the chairman of Carnegie Steel, invested in, and integrated, a great number of local businesses.

During the 1880s, Andrew leveraged the family's wealth to broaden its financial holdings, as well as diversify its portfolio with companies in adjacent industries. Mellon acquired or co-founded several financial institutions, served as director of the Pittsburgh Petroleum Exchange, and co-founded two natural gas companies that collectively controlled 35,000 acres of gas lands.

In 1889, Andrew struck gold in the form of aluminum. Mellon granted a modest loan to the Pittsburgh Reduction Company, a relatively small outfit that sought to become the first sustainable industrial producer of aluminum. In 1891, as a director of the company, Andrew was influential in establishing aluminum factories in New Kensington, eighteen miles northeast of Pittsburgh along the Allegheny River, and Niagara Falls, New York. The company's explosive growth made it the jewel of the Mellon portfolio, and it was one of the most profitable ventures of the family's many profitable investments. In 1907, that company changed its name to one that we're much more familiar with—Alcoa.

The Mellon family's oil and gas investments also did well, and by 1894, their vertically integrated companies produced approximately 10 percent of the total amount of oil exported by the United States. Just one year later, the family profitably divested its petroleum interests by selling to Standard Oil.

Business was good during Andrew Mellon's early career, but everything didn't come up roses. Mellon and Frick enjoyed a social relationship, too, and that included poker games with local bigwigs like Westinghouse and attorney Philander Knox. Frick eventually chartered the South Fork Fishing and Hunting Club for his cronies, and Mellon was one of its first members.

The club built the South Fork Dam, which created an artificial lake club members used for boating and fishing. Those particular fun and games for the region's rich and powerful abruptly ended in 1889 when the dam broke, resulting in the Johnstown Flood. The tragic flood claimed the lives of over 2,000 people and destroyed more than 1,600 homes. As proof that it pays to have friends in high places, Knox personally led a legal defense that successfully argued the club bore no legal responsibility for the flood.

On Mellon's business side, banking and investments in coal, gas, steel, streetcars, shipbuilding, his pal Westinghouse's company, and others all paid off handsomely. In 1902, Andrew reorganized T. Mellon & Sons into the Mellon National Bank, a federally chartered National Bank, and the Mellon banks grew steadily early in the new century.

During that same period, Andrew Mellon also helped establish the Guffey Company with J.M Guffey to take advantage of the Texas oil boom. In 1907, the Mellon family ousted Guffey and renamed the business Gulf Oil, inserting Andrew's older brother, James Ross Mellon, as its head.

Andrew's power and influence continued to grow in the early twentieth century, and the Panic of 1907 resulted in only a modest hiccup to his business portfolio. The family's original business, banking, continued to click along, performing quite well. By the end of 1913, Mellon National Bank held more money in deposits than any other Pittsburgh bank. Moreover, the second-largest bank in terms of deposits, Farmers Deposit National Bank, was controlled by Mellon's Union Trust Company.

Like the War of 1812 and the Civil War, World War I brought prosperity to some while doling out tragedy to others. The Mellons prospered by financing a great part of the war, using Union Trust Company and other Mellon institutions to grant millions of dollars in loans to both Britain and France.

Always a supporter of the Republican party, and chafed by the antitrust actions of the (Theodore) Roosevelt, Taft, and Wilson presidential administrations, Andrew Mellon became more politically inclined after the war. Mellon attended the 1920 Republican National Convention with the hope his associate, Knox, would win the nomination. However, when Senator Warren G. Harding of Ohio emerged from the convention as the party's presidential nominee, Mellon, fully aligned with the party's conservative platform, served as an influential fundraiser for Harding's campaign.

Following Harding's victory in the 1920 presidential election, Mellon accepted his appointment as Secretary of the Treasury in February 1921. Before joining Harding's cabinet, Mellon sold his bank holdings to his brother, Richard, but kept his non-banking holdings. Regardless, Andrew got by just fine. By several accounts, at one point in the 1920s, only John D. Rockefeller and Henry Ford paid more federal income taxes than did Mellon.

President Harding died from the effects of a stroke in August 1923, and he was succeeded by Vice President Calvin Coolidge. With Coolidge, Mellon enjoyed an even closer relationship than with Harding, and he exerted tremendous influence on the administration.

Originally slated to serve just one term as secretary, Mellon, desiring to usher in extensive tax cuts—for what some might view cynically as obvious, very personal reasons—extended his commitment when Coolidge won reelection in 1924. In 1928, with his hand forced by Coolidge's surprise decision to not seek reelection, Secretary Mellon provided his last-minute support to Herbert Hoover. However, his general distrust and dislike of Hoover led him to continue on yet again for another term as Secretary of the Treasury.

On October 29, 1929, the New York Stock Exchange suffered the worst crash in its history, and "Black Tuesday" opened the door for the Great Depression. Most Americans didn't have stock holdings, so the impact had little immediate effect on most in the country. Mellon, for his part, felt little sympathy for the losses suffered by stock speculators.

Mellon, like Hoover, thought the worst of the aftereffects had already occurred by mid-1930. They were, of course, wrong. With the national economy in the throes of a deep, deep slump, Democrats won control of Congress in the country's 1930 midterm elections. Mellon, himself, became a highly loathed figure, viewed by the masses as a villain. He certainly wasn't helped when the Bank of Pittsburgh, the sole remaining major Pittsburgh bank not controlled by the Mellon family, went under in late 1931.

In early 1932, Congressman Wright Patman of Texas began impeachment proceedings against Mellon, contending Mellon violated numerous federal laws designed to prevent conflicts of interest. Although Mellon had overcome similar investigations in the past, his slumping reputation left little in the way of providing any real opposition. Moving quickly to save the situation, Hoover removed Mellon from Washington by offering him the position of ambassador to the United Kingdom.

Hoover was defeated by Franklin D. Roosevelt in the 1932 presidential election, but before Mellon left office at the conclusion of Hoover's term in 1933, he managed to convince the British to allow Gulf Oil to operate in Kuwait, Britain's protectorate in the Persian Gulf. Going down swinging, Mellon used his waning influence to hit one last home run.

Back in private life, Mellon continued to draw the ire of the public. In 1933, he was the subject of Harvey O'Connor's best-selling and highly unfavorable biography, *Mellon's Millions*. When the board game Monopoly was released, the cartoon figure in the black top hat and tails and sporting a white mustache was modeled after Mellon.

Mellon was unpopular most everywhere, and increasingly so in his hometown. As a result, he lived most of his final years elsewhere, including in Washington, DC.

Mellon was diagnosed with cancer in late 1936. An art collector for most of his adult life, he donated a collection valued at $25 million to the US government in 1937 before he passed. Among the distinguished works were Raphael's Alba Madonna and twenty-three Rembrandts. In addition to the works, Mellon donated $15 million to build the National Gallery of Art, which opened its doors in 1941, to house the collection.

Andrew Mellon died on August 26, 1937. He is buried at Trinity Episcopal Church Cemetery in Upperville, Virginia.

Pittsburgh further reinforced its rather colorful reputation during the Prohibition era. Prohibition was a nationwide constitutional ban on the production, importation, transportation, and sale of alcoholic beverages in the United States, and it lasted from 1920 to 1933.

Apparently, Pittsburgh and its citizens were late in getting the memo.

By most accounts, Pittsburgh was a hotbed of bootlegging and illicit alcohol consumption. The term speakeasy—an illegal drinking establishment—is said to have originated in the Pittsburgh enclave of McKeesport, at the Blind Pig tavern. Even now, speakeasies are also known as blind pigs (as well as blind tigers) in some locales.

Looking back, history showed that fighting back against Prohibition should not have come as a surprise. Pittsburgh was a city of immigrants, chock full of Europeans. In the late 1800s, immigrants continued to flow into the city from Britain and Germany, but the real influx came from poor rural areas in southern and eastern Europe, like Italy, the Balkans, the Austro-Hungarian Empire, and the Russian Empire. Jobs in construction, mining, factories, and, of course, steel mills were magnets attracting unskilled immigrants looking for opportunities and a better life.

Pittsburghers' experience with government, both local, from the new country, and from former home countries, had led to high levels of anti-establishment sentiment and distrust of government. It was a long-held tradition in the region, with the Whiskey Rebellion tax protests of 1791–1794 just one memorable proof point.

The illegal party continued until Prohibition was repealed when the 21st Amendment was ratified on December 5, 1933. However, while the illegal parties prospered, legal businesses suffered. Pittsburgh's last distillery, Joseph S. Finch's, ceased operations at the onset of Prohibition. In December 2011, Wigle Whiskey, a family-owned craft distillery, opened, becoming the first since Finch's closure.

Politically, Pittsburgh and the surrounding region were Republican strongholds from the late 1800s, until 1930. Pittsburgh offered highly skilled, high-paying jobs to European immigrants and the African-Americans migrating from the segregated South. Essentially, Republican governments traded job opportunities for votes, and they stayed in control for over fifty years.

That all changed, like so much throughout the country, during the Great Depression. Nationally, the Democratic victory in the 1932 election swept in many changes, and as the depression grew worse before it got better, Pittsburgh's ethnic and racial groups, in a bit of desperation for change, threw their support to the Democratic Party. Local midterm 1934 elections presented strong victories for the Democrats, and Pittsburgh became a central figure in the New Deal Coalition that provided the foundation for the party up through the 1960s.

Democrats pushed forward with platforms built on jobs and economic relief, and Pittsburghers took notice. The Works Progress Administration (WPA), renamed later as the Work Projects Administration, was a New Deal agency that employed millions of job seekers across the country to carry out public works projects, and it was just the promise hard-hit American workers were looking for, Pittsburghers being no exception.

With the old Republicans, like Mellon and his network, out of the local and national scene, the Democrats took credit for the country's—and the Pittsburgh region's—economic recovery. Democrats were strongly in power as the United States got drawn into World War II in Europe.

Chapter 8

ART ROONEY & THE FOUNDING OF THE PITTSBURGH STEELERS

The story of the Pittsburgh Steelers begins by first telling the story of the larger-than-life man synonymous with the team for over fifty years, the "Chief," Art Rooney. Arthur Joseph Rooney was born on January 27, 1901, in Coulter, Pennsylvania, the first son of Dan and Margaret, or Maggie, Rooney. He was the oldest of eight children in a succession of large families, with a long Irish Catholic lineage tracing back multiple generations to the Emerald Isle.

Rooney's great-grandparents escaped Ireland's Great Famine in the 1840s by immigrating to Canada. Later on, they sailed back across the Atlantic yet again to settle in the United Kingdom, this time in Wales, taking their son, also named Arthur, Art's grandfather, with them.

In Wales, that particular Arthur Rooney met and wed another Irish Catholic, Catherine Regan. Their second-born child was a son they named Dan, who would become Art's father.

When Dan was two years old, his father packed up the family and re-traced his father's footsteps to Canada, eventually making their way to Pittsburgh in 1884. There, the Rooney family settled and grew its western Pennsylvanian roots, and the immediate family swelled to include Dan and an additional eight brothers and sisters.

Dan Rooney stayed in the Pittsburgh area, and he opened a saloon in the coal town of Coulter, in Allegheny County. Coulter is where Dan met Maggie, a coal miner's daughter, and, once married, started a family.

Shortly thereafter, in 1913, Dan and Maggie settled in Pittsburgh's North Side, where they occupied a three-story building at the corner of Corry Street and General Robinson Street. Dan ran the Dan Rooney Cafe & Bar on the first floor, and the family lived in the space above.

It was a pretty colorful start to the story of Art Rooney, founder and owner of the Pittsburgh Steelers, and a start that Art would add more than his own fair share of pigment to over the years.

Art Rooney was an athlete. With plenty of kids in the neighborhood—including his own four brothers and three sisters—Rooney spent his youth outside playing sports, including football, basketball, baseball, and a favorite pastime of youth in the era (and area), boxing.

Growing up, Rooney attended St. Peter's Catholic School and Duquesne University Prep School. Then, he enrolled at the Indiana Normal School, now the Indiana University of Pennsylvania, where he competed in football and basketball. But he really left his mark on the baseball diamond, where he was considered a major league prospect center fielder.

He was also no slouch in the boxing ring, either, where he won an Amateur Athletic Union (AAU) welterweight title and an automatic invitation to participate in the 1920 Olympic Games, which he ultimately declined.

Rooney's athletic career continued well after college. He played minor league professional baseball for both the Flint (Michigan) Vehicles and the Wheeling (West Virginia) Stogies. In 1925, he served as the Stogies player-manager, alongside his brother Dan, who was a catcher on the team. That year, Art led the Middle Athletic League in games played, hits, runs, and stolen bases. He also finished second in the league in batting average, with his brother coming in right behind him in third.

And then there was, of course, football. As a teenager, he started a semi-professional team, the Hope-Harveys, and he later played for the Majestic Radio, a team he eventually took over and renamed the J. P. Rooneys.

As good as Rooney was at participating and playing in organized sports, he was perhaps best of all at handicapping horse racing. His success at the track was legendary, and it has spawned a number of "folklorish" tales.

Many Pittsburgh Steelers fans understand the franchise fee was paid for by Rooney's winnings at the racetrack. The story goes that on a weekend trip to New York's Empire City and Saratoga Springs race tracks, Art parlayed his bets to net a nice haul of winnings. The precise numbers of Rooney's windfall vary by who's telling the story, but the consensus falls between $250,000 to $350,000, a pretty penny indeed when considering the country was in the midst of the Great Depression.

It's a great story. And it's true. But it's not how Rooney founded the Steelers. That weekend trip to the track occurred in 1937, four years after Rooney founded the football club in 1933. The track winnings most certainly did help the Steelers, but that story comes a little later.

Professional football was created in western Pennsylvania.

No joke.

In 1892, two players, Pudge Heffelfinger and Ben "Sport" Donnelly, were paid to play for the Allegheny Athletic Association of the Western Pennsylvania Senior Independent Football Conference. And thus, with a couple of hefty cash handouts, pro football was born.

In its infancy, football was a regional sport, and many times, primarily just an intrastate activity for its teams. There were no national leagues or championships, although there were plenty of attempts to get one started, including a league backed by Major League Baseball.

Western Pennsylvania was a hotbed of football, but the most prominent football of the early twentieth century came from its neighbors in Ohio and the Ohio League, whose players included the most famous athlete of the time, the legendary Jim Thorpe.

New York, with both its population and media, boasted a few well-publicized teams, as well, including the Rochester Jeffersons, owned by Leo Lyons. Lyons had visions of a nationwide league, but his dreams kept getting derailed, first by the country's involvement in World War I, and then by the flu pandemic that swept across the United States in 1918.

Regional football had its drawbacks, particularly on the cost containment side. The barnstorming clubs bid liberally to poach the best players from competing clubs, and climbing salaries caused many teams to experience financial difficulties that eventually caused them to cease operations completely. Professional football had grown to be a disheveled mess, with no clear vision or direction, and was much more vaudeville entertainment than organized sport.

By 1919, two primary interstate barnstorming circuits had formed. One centered around New York and New Jersey and included Philadelphia, and they played mostly on Saturdays. The other primary circuit covered the northern Midwest, including Wisconsin, Minnesota, Illinois, Indiana, Ohio, and upstate New York, and those teams typically played their games on Sundays.

Finally, in 1920, the dreams of Lyons and so many others were realized, and the National Football League was founded. The founding fathers ironed out the charter details in a Hupmobile auto dealership in Canton, Ohio, and originally named the venture the American Professional Football Conference. That name, however, was rather short-lived. Just one month later, the league swapped out

Conference for Association and became the APFA, or American Professional Football Association.

The league had fourteen charter clubs in thirteen different cities: the Akron Pros, Buffalo All-Americans, Canton Bulldogs, Racine (Illinois) Cardinals, Chicago Tigers, Cleveland Tigers, Columbus Panhandles, Dayton Triangles, Decatur (Illinois) Staleys, Detroit Heralds, Hammond (Indiana) Pros, Muncie (Indiana) Flyers, Rock Island (Illinois) Independents, and Rochester (New York) Jeffersons. Thorpe, still playing for the Canton Bulldogs, was chosen as the league's first president.

On an interesting side note, two charter members, the Cardinals (now the Arizona Cardinals) and the Staleys (now the Chicago Bears), are still in existence. Founded in 1919, the Green Bay Packers are the oldest professional football team to have not changed locations, but they did not join the league until 1921.

The first league title went to the undefeated Akron Pros, and despite a season full of challenges, the first campaign was considered a success, and other clubs clamored to gain admission into what was generally viewed as the future of football. Ahead of its second season, the league swelled to twenty-two teams.

In 1922, the Association became the League, officially changing its name to the National Football League. However grand its name might have been, the league struggled to gain national acceptance and rise to the level of being recognized as a major national sport. Teams had difficulty gaining traction in their local markets, and clubs came and went throughout the 1920s.

Pittsburgh was a big football market, buoyed by the success of the collegiate Pitt Panthers, who were legitimate national championship contenders more years than not. The NFL definitely wanted to tap into the western Pennsylvania market. So why the wait?

While the NFL was founded in 1920 and the working-class city of Pittsburgh seemed an ideal fit for the rough and tumble sport, there was no team in either Pittsburgh or across the state in Philadelphia. There were a lot of contributing factors, but certainly, a big factor was Pennsylvania's "blue laws."

Blue laws were laws passed at the state level across the country, and they were designed to preserve Sunday as "the Lord's Day," setting it aside as the one day of the week devoted for prayer, church attendance, and, being the seventh day and all, rest.

No state adopted blue laws as vigorously and as widely as Pennsylvania, which passed its first blue law in 1779. In 1794, one was passed that very specifically denoted the illegality of any "unlawful game, hunting, shooting, sport, or diversion whatsoever."

As blue laws aged, they became more and more controversial, with the argument against centering on the laws being out of touch with more modern attitudes about . . . well, nearly everything. While waiting for the laws to be repealed, businesses and sports teams took creative measures to get around them.

The Baltimore, Maryland baseball team, for instance, allowed spectators to attend for free on Sundays, technically sidestepping the state law prohibiting professional baseball games. Fans got into the stadium without charge, but once in the stadium, they reportedly had to buy a program, and the program was priced differently depending on where a spectator sat. You know, sort of *exactly* like a ticket.

Most blue laws, both in Pennsylvania and other states, were simply ignored. Others, for reasons that are difficult to determine, were firmly enforced. That paradox exists today; it's why you still can't buy a car from an automobile dealership on Sunday in the state of Pennsylvania.

In 1933, with political change in the air, Rooney, then just thirty-two years old, took a gamble, another sure thing in his eyes, and paid his $2,500 franchise fee to become an NFL owner. Later that year, compromise legislation was introduced that allowed professional football and baseball to be played on Sundays between the hours of 2:00 and 6:00 p.m., as long as it was approved by voters in local referendums.

Rooney had won another bet.

Art Rooney was as big a baseball fan as he was an exceptional baseball player, and growing up in such close proximity to the ballpark of Major League Baseball's Pittsburgh Pirates, he was a devoted fan. Thus, when it came time to name his newly minted NFL franchise, Rooney chose the name *Pirates*.

The early Steelers, er Pirates, struggled to find success. More truthfully, they struggled to find mediocrity.

The club's initial roster consisted mainly of the players on the J. P. Rooneys semi-professional team. Forrest Douds, a tackle, was named the first-ever coach, or player-coach, of the Pirates. The club's first game took place on September 20, 1933, a 23–2 loss at home to the New York Giants in front of a large crowd of around 20,000. John Oehler scored the franchise's first-ever points when he blocked a punt through the end zone, resulting in a safety.

It took just one more game for the Pirates to secure their maiden victory, a 14–13 win over the visiting Cardinals. That game featured the club's first-ever touchdown, an interception returned ninety-nine yards by Martin Kottler.

Defense certainly has a legacy in Pittsburgh. The club's first points were a safety off special teams, and the first touchdown was an interception return by the defense.

The winning point of that victory was the point after touchdown kicked by Mose Kelsch, a holdover from the semi-professional Majestics. At thirty-six, he was the oldest player in the NFL that season, four years older than the Chief himself, Rooney.

One of the charter members of the team was tackle Ray Kemp, a coal miner by trade immediately upon graduation from high school and later a decorated player at Duquesne University. Besides being a well-respected football player, Kemp was also notable for being Black. Being the team's first season, Kemp was the Steelers' first Black player, and just one of two Black players in the entire NFL in 1933, the other being the Cardinals' Joe Lillard.

Kemp played in the Steelers' first three games and then was cut by Douds, who, as player-coach, also played the tackle position. After the Steelers went 2–5 over their next seven games, Kemp rejoined the team and, after just two days of practice, started in the season finale against the New York Giants at the famed Polo Grounds. That 27–3 Steeler loss signaled not only the end of the Steelers' inaugural season, but also Kemp's career as a professional player.

Kemp and Lilliard were both out of the league by the start of the 1934 season, and the NFL, led by Washington Redskins owner George Preston Marshall's "gentlemen's agreement" among club owners to not sign Black players, remained segregated until 1946. It took the breakthroughs of Kenny Washington and Woody Strode, with the Los Angeles Rams, and Bill Willis and Marion Motley, with the Cleveland Browns, to close that most shameful chapter of NFL history, one year before Jackie Robinson did the same to Major League Baseball.

In that inaugural season, Douds's lone season at the helm, the team compiled a record of three wins, six losses, and two ties.

The football Pirates didn't achieve any better success in their second season. While Douds played for the team for two additional years, he was replaced as head coach by Luby DiMelio, a former captain for the Pitt Panthers, for the 1934 season. However, despite the change of leadership, the club regressed slightly to finish with a record of 2–10.

For the club's third season, Joe Bach was named the head coach, and the team improved to 4–8, finishing third in the East division. Returning for another year, Bach led the Pirates to their first non-losing season, posting a record of 6–6 in 1936 to finish second in the division. It would take until 1942 before the franchise finished a season with a winning record.

The club spent its first five seasons mostly off of the national radar. Frankly, they weren't that big of a deal, even in the city of Pittsburgh. For example, in their first season, attendance for the Pirates' five home games totaled less than the attendance at the University of Pittsburgh versus Duquesne game. However, in 1938, the team made big news, signing Byron "Whizzer" White to what was, at the time, the biggest contract in league history.

A native of Colorado, Whizzer White starred in football, basketball, and baseball for the University of Colorado, where he finished runner-up in voting for the Heisman Trophy in 1937. The Pirates made the gifted tailback their first-round selection in the 1938 NFL draft and signed him to a record contract of nearly $16,000 to suit up for the team. To put the sum into perspective, consider player-coach Johnny "Blood" McNally earned just $3,500.

White made an instant impression, leading the league in rushing with 567 yards on 152 attempts, scoring four touchdowns, and being named first-team All-Pro. However, it wasn't enough to lift the Pirates' fortunes, as the club finished the year fifth in the division, losing its final six games and closing with a 2–9 record.

Off the field, White made an impression too. On road trips, the team took trains, and almost every player took part in card games. Not the scholarly White, for he was a reader and could always be found with his nose in a good book.

White played just a single season for the Pirates. Having graduated Phi Beta Kappa and valedictorian from the University of Colorado with a Bachelor's Degree in Economics, White had deferred his Rhodes Scholarship to attend the University of Oxford to play for the Pirates. In 1939, he continued his studies at Hertford College, a constituent college of the University of Oxford in England.

White finished his professional football career with two seasons in Detroit, where, in addition to being recognized once again as a first-team All-Pro, he also attended Yale Law School. White is best known not for his record-setting contract and his All-Pro seasons, but for his distinguished law career and his service as a United States Supreme Court Justice from 1962 to 1993.

White was picked in the 1938 NFL Draft. The first draft took place just two years earlier, in 1936. Rooney and the Pirates were instrumental in developing the draft as a way of attempting to level the playing field, with the teams with the worst records from the preceding season choosing players ahead of the teams with the best records.

The first-ever draft choice of the Pittsburgh Pirates, you might ask? Well, none other than . . . William Shakespeare.

No, seriously. But not *that* William Shakespeare—although both Shakespeares had something in common in that neither ever played a game in the NFL.

Shakespeare, the football player, was a star halfback and punter for collegiate powerhouse Notre Dame. He was a first-team All-American in 1935 and had a distinguished collegiate career that earned him induction into the College Football Hall of Fame in 1983.

With such an on-field pedigree, why didn't the talented Shakespeare, the first pick of the Pirates and the third-ever NFL Draft pick, never play professional football? Well, pro football didn't pay a lot of money, so Shakespeare decided to pursue a more lucrative career in business with the Cincinnati Rubber Company.

Shakespeare's time at the company was interrupted only by his service in the Army during World War II. A captain who commanded a machine-gun platoon of the 424th Infantry Regiment, Shakespeare was awarded four battle stars, the Combat Infantryman Badge, and the Bronze Star for gallantry during the infamous Battle of the Bulge in the Ardennes forest of Belgium.

The Pirates franchise started right in the middle of the Great Depression, the worldwide economic depression that began in late October 1929, with a devastating collapse of the US stock market. Whether the market crash caused the depression or was a symptom is still argued by economists today, but the financial hardships that swept the world were very real.

International trade was almost immediately halved, and personal income fell sharply. Unemployment in the United States rose to 23 percent, and some countries suffered from unemployment rates as high as 33 percent. Heavy industry was significantly impacted and so was farming, too, with crop prices falling by almost 60 percent.

Times were tough, and purse strings were pulled tightly. One extravagance that was often put off was paying to attend a professional football game, a sport that paled in comparison to the draw of college football. The Pirates suffered from poor attendance, and Rooney oversaw a team that was in financial turmoil, with expenses well above gate receipts.

Losing on the field, the Pirates were also losing at the box office. In an era in football when teams came and went with alarming regularity, the Pittsburgh club wasn't a sustainable enterprise. It needed an owner with deep pockets to fund the team through its money-losing formative years.

Now, Rooney didn't come from money. He was the son of a hard-working saloon owner. But you don't live over a saloon your entire upbringing without learning a thing or two about bookmakers and placing a wager. Placing wagers, or most appropriately, winning wagers, provided Rooney with more than enough money to adequately bankroll his NFL franchise.

Rooney was an all-time great horse handicapper. The proof, as they say, is in the pudding. And while Rooney had experienced ample success at the horse track earlier, he became a truly legendary horseplayer on the national scene after an August weekend in 1936, when he went on a winning streak few bettors have surpassed, before or after.

Rooney's weekend began with the Saturday card at New York's Empire City track, later called Yonkers Raceway, and even later yet, purchased by Rooney's adult sons. The Chief's first winning bet was an $8,000 wager on Quel Jeu, a six-year-old, 8–1 longshot who had previously won the Remsen Handicap Grade II stakes race in 1932.

Keep in mind, Rooney's $8,000 wager was right smack in the middle of the Great Depression, and it was more than double the salary of any of his players. It was reflective of Rooney's confidence in his analyses—he later espoused that horse racing wasn't really gambling if you did your homework properly.

The race was a photo finish. In short order, Quel Jeu was declared the winner, and Rooney was, well, off and running to borrow a phrase. That first race was the first of five long-shots he hit among his seven winners on the day. That was seven winners on an eight-race card, by the way.

A day for the ages, no doubt. But the Chief was just getting started.

On Monday, Rooney took his action to opening day at Saratoga Race Course, in nearby Saratoga Springs, New York. That day was even more successful—maybe $250,000 or more. Like all good stories, it's difficult to nail down the exact facts, and you can bet, no pun intended, Rooney, ever the wise and charming storyteller, wasn't about to report out his specifics. Be that as it may, it was rumored that Saratoga officials offered Rooney a Brink's armored truck to transport his winnings to New York City.

After two days at the track, Rooney walked away with something well north of $250,000, in a year where the average hourly wage of an American worker was fifty-eight cents per hour.

It also wasn't the only time Rooney made the news for his horse-wagering prowess. In 1937, *Time* magazine actually ran a photo of the Chief talking to a fellow race track patron alongside a story of him having won over $300,000 at Aqueduct Racetrack in Queens, New York.

The Pirates needed money to keep operating. Thanks to his shrewd horse handicapping and a bit of good fortune, Rooney had the money.

Rooney's success at the track funded his beloved Pirates. His winnings enabled him to sign the players he wanted and successfully recruit the services of player-coach Blood McNally, an eleven-year veteran who had suited up for the Pirates in 1934. "Johnny Blood" was a colorful character, and Rooney had high hopes that his charisma, along with a winning record, would spur box office ticket sales.

The 1937 season started out wonderfully, with the Pirates winning the first two games. Then, the wheels fell off, with the club losing five consecutive games on its way to a 4–7 record and third place in the East division.

The year 1938, of course, brought Whizzer White and high expectations for the football team. Quoted in *The Gettysburg Times* ahead of the season, McNally said of White, "We had calculated on a championship without him, and since we have him it looks like we can't miss."[4]

White, as mentioned, earned his high salary by leading the league in rushing and being named All-Pro. The Pirates as a whole, on the other hand, underperformed dramatically to preseason aspirations, regressing to 2–9 and falling to fifth place in the division.

At this point, Rooney had seen six seasons of less than inspiring football from the Pirates. He hadn't had much success doling out big money for a star player the year before, so for the 1939 season, he tried to spark the team to success by spending big to bring in a star head coach. His target? None other than the legendary Jock Sutherland of the University of Pittsburgh.

Jock Sutherland had recently resigned his head coach position of the Pitt Panthers, where he had served since taking over from his former coach and mentor, Pop Warner. Over his fifteen seasons at the helm of the Panthers, his teams produced a record of 111–20–12, earned five Rose Bowl invitations (they played in four, and turned down the offer in 1938), and won five national championships.

Sutherland had left Pitt after the school's Chancellor, John Gabbert Bowman, pushed through new policies that targeted the school's nationally renowned football program, eliminating athletic scholarships, student-athlete stipends, and recruiting funds. The timing was perfect, and for Pirates fans, it appeared as though the stars had aligned.

However, Sutherland spurned Rooney's big offer, which had been rumored to have been a significant raise over his salary at Pitt. Thus, the Pirates went into 1939 with Johnny Blood, since retired as an active player, as the head coach.

The Pirates started the 1939 season with losses in their first three games. On the heels of the six consecutive losses to end the 1939 campaign, Johnny Blood had had enough and resigned as the coach, putting a lid on his career as a head coach with a lifetime 6–19 record. Blood had much more success as a player than a coach, and surely, that was the merit on which his 1963 induction into the Pro Football Hall of Fame was based.

Walt Kiesling took over as head coach, but the change at the top didn't produce a much different result. The Pirates finished 1–6–1 and in a tie for fourth—or written differently, tied for last, in the division. The only real bright spot of the campaign had been the lone win, in the season's final game, against the cross-state Eagles. It wasn't much to lay one's hat on, as the Eagles had defeated the Pirates earlier in the season, and they, too, were equally inept, as they were the team that shared the divisional cellar with the Pirates.

At the end of the 1930s and the Pirates' seven seasons, Rooney's Pirates had just twenty-two victories in eighty games, five head coaches, no winning seasons, and a best finish of second in the division. Rooney needed a change.

In early 1940, the Chief collaborated with the *Pittsburgh Post-Gazette* to sponsor a contest to find a new name to replace the Pirate moniker. Former coach Joe Bach, who had led the team to its 6–6 record and second-place finish in 1936, headed the panel that would make the suggestion.

Spoiler alert: "Steelers" won out. Never mind that at least one high school in the area played as the Steelers. The name won out as it represented the working class of Pittsburgh citizens and its dominant industry.

In the contest, twenty-one entries suggested Steelers, and each won a pair of season tickets for the coming season to watch one of the league's worst teams try to break out of its futility.

Alas, they, as well as the rest of the club's supporters, were not rewarded in 1940. With Kiesling continuing as coach, the Steelers bumbled their way to a 2–7–2 record. In an era of football with low scores compared to today, the Steelers took low scoring to an art form, tallying just sixty points for the entire season. The Chicago Bears scored seventy-three points in their shutout of the Washington Redskins in the championship game of that same year.

Rooney was done. Sort of.

Over eight seasons, the Steelers had lost money hand over fist, all for a paltry 24–62–5 total record. The country was getting more and more involved in the war in Europe, and a military selective service draft was going to greatly affect the availability of young men to suit up as professional players. At the same time, Alexis Thompson, a twenty-six-year-old multi-millionaire heir of the Republic Iron and Steel fortune, had repeatedly inquired to Rooney as to the purchase of his team.

Rooney took the bait. Or, rather, Rooney set the bait. Here's what happened.

The Detroit Lions had recently been sold for $225,000. But they were a successful franchise that had a 1935 NFL Championship to their credit. With that in mind, Rooney and Thompson agreed on a reported price of $160,000 for the Steelers. The transaction was confirmed on the same day of the Bears crushing defeat of the Redskins for the title.

The Chief took $80,000 of his proceeds and went across the state to purchase at least a 50 percent stake in the Philadelphia Eagles (some reports go as high as an 80 percent stake), owned by his pal, Bert Bell. Yes, Steelers fans, Art Rooney both sold the Steelers and bought into the Eagles. And if that wasn't weird enough, things got even weirder from there.

Rooney, Bell, and Thompson pooled together the rosters of both the Steelers and the Eagles and conducted a draft between themselves to divvy up the talent, resulting in the fifty-one players under contract to the two clubs being reallocated across the teams. The Eagles ended up being joined by eleven players of the 1940 Steelers team. The Steelers were joined by seven players who were part of the 1940 Eagles team.

Simple, right?

The weirdness continued.

Thompson had originally entered negotiations for the Steelers intending to relocate the team to Boston, a rather convenient train ride from his home in New York. If Thompson was going to go through with that plan, Rooney, the faithful Pittsburgh native, and Bell were going to split the Eagles' home games between both Philadelphia and Pittsburgh.

By March 1941, Thompson hadn't opened a local Pittsburgh office, and Rooney was fearful that "his" beloved Steelers would be moving. So Rooney and Bell convinced Thompson that Philadelphia, the City of Brotherly Love, was an even more convenient train ride from his home, and together, they engineered a swap of the franchises.

So to keep track of this, Rooney sold the Steelers outright, bought into the Eagles, participated in pooling the two teams' players, and then allocating them out; then, after choosing rosters for each team, he traded the Eagles for the Steelers. At the end of the day, in a manner of speaking, Rooney still owned the Steelers—this time in partnership with Bell—and had the titles co-owner and vice president. For his part, Thompson owned the Eagles, who were still based in Philadelphia.

Thompson renamed his team the Iron Men. And while Pittsburgh played as the Steelers, the business organization operated under the name the "Philadelphia Eagles Football Club, Inc." for the next several years.

It's a confusing bit of Steelers and NFL history, for certain. In some circles, the entire escapade became known as the "Pennsylvania Polka."

So what did all the shenanigans do to improve the Steelers' fortune on the playing field?

Not a thing. The team finished last in the division, with a 1–9–1 record. Of course, being the Steelers, there was much, much more of a story than just an under-performing team on the field.

The country was plainly veering into World War II, and Rooney and Bell were hesitant to enter into a long-term agreement with a coach with so much uncertainty in the air. So Bell, who had coached the Eagles to five consecutive losing seasons, was named the head coach, with Kiesling as his assistant.

The Steelers started the year 0–2, and Rooney and Bell accepted the fact that Bell wasn't going to be the coach that lifted the team's performance. Their target was Aldo "Buff" Donelli, the head football coach at nearby Duquesne University. There was just one problem: Donelli was under contract with the university for another full season.

Never one not to be imaginative, with the Pennsylvania Polka as a solid proof point, Rooney and Bell, along with Donelli, got creative. Donelli would keep his position as head coach at Duquesne and moonlight by coaching the Steelers in his spare time. For practice, he'd coach the Steelers in the morning and the Dukes in the afternoon. As for games, on Saturdays, he'd patrol the sidelines for the Dukes; on Sunday, the Steelers.

That would work, right?

NFL commissioner Elmer Layden didn't think so. Layden, who had coached Donelli previously at Duquesne, believed it to be impossible to coach two different football teams at the same time. To get out of the predicament with the league office, Donelli resigned as the football coach at Duquesne but kept his role as athletic director. That allowed him to accept the role of head coach of the Steelers. In all practicality, of course, nothing really changed. Donelli attended all of the Dukes' practices and games and was very much considered the head coach, despite not having the official title.

Donelli switched things up for the Steelers, installing a new offense, the Wing T, all the rage in the college game. The Steelers did not show any improvement whatsoever, going on a 0–5 skid. The Dukes, on the other hand, were having a monster year.

Come early November, the coaching carousel fantasy crashed and burned. It seemed no one had taken a close look at the schedule. On a single autumn weekend, Duquesne was scheduled to play Saint Mary's College in California the day before a Steelers game in Philadelphia. Commissioner Layden, concerned about the integrity of the fledgling professional league, ordered Donelli to be on the sidelines in Philadelphia on Sunday. Faced with an impossible dilemma, Donelli made the choice of sticking with his undefeated Duquesne Dukes and abandoning the hapless Steelers.

Thus, the Donelli era ended with an 0–5 record. Kiesling took the reins once again and led the club to its only victory of the season. The 1–9–1 record matched the 1939 record for the worst since the team's founding.

Two weeks before the 1941 NFL Championship Game, the Japanese bombed Pearl Harbor, and the country tumbled perilously into the ravages of war on both sides of the globe.

Chapter 9

WORLD WAR II & THE "PITTSBURGH RENAISSANCE"

When the world became engulfed in World War II, American president Franklin D. Roosevelt tried to keep US troops out of combat. As Nazi Germany occupied much of Europe by the middle of 1940, Roosevelt delivered a radio broadcast on December 29, 1940, pledging America's "Arsenal of Democracy" in assisting Winston Churchill and Great Britain in fighting off Adolf Hitler's advances.

The Arsenal of Democracy was America's industrial might, with Pittsburgh right alongside other major industrial cities like Detroit, Chicago, and Philadelphia. Pittsburgh's mills pumped out iron and steel just like always, but other industrial concerns pivoted into the manufacturing of weapons and other military products. For example, Detroit's famed automobile manufacturing lines started producing aircraft for the war effort, and Singer, of sewing machine fame, started producing pistols. The United States became the primary supplier of material in the Allied war effort.

The Japanese surprise attack on Pearl Harbor almost a year later, on December 7, 1941, changed the war for all Americans. No longer just a supplier of raw materials and finished wartime goods, American troops were now thrust into combat around the globe.

If Pittsburgh's mills weren't already busy enough, they became even busier. Estimates place Pittsburgh's production of steel for the wartime effort at ninety-five million tons. To put that number in perspective, consider it represented 20 percent of the entire worldwide production. Forty-one percent of the nation's steel was produced within a thirty-minute train ride from Pittsburgh.

That ambitious production schedule created labor shortages, particularly with so many young men conscripted into the armed forces. As a result, Pittsburgh was once again a destination for yet another migration of Black Americans from the deep south, adding yet another ribbon of cultural diversity to the woven fabric of Pittsburgh's population.

Despite the upheavals related to a world war and the remarkable throughput of steel and other manufactured materials, Pittsburgh's population rather plateaued. Businesses were making a lot of profits, and working families in the region were benefiting little—not nearly as much as the corporations but still better off, slightly, year after year. However, the population remained relatively stagnant.

In 1930, Pittsburgh was the nation's tenth largest city, with a population of nearly 670,000. Ten years later, in 1940, the city was still the country's tenth largest, but its population over that ten years increased by less than 2,000 people. In 1950, after the war, the population was just under 677,000, and the city had slipped to the twelfth largest.

In twenty years, from 1930 to 1950, the city had grown by just 7,000 people.

While the population floundered somewhat, Pittsburgh's local businesses were doing well, and their public works helped modernize the development of the local area. Yes, they paid workers, but the millworker was never independently wealthy. They worked hard, and there was enough money to go around to raise a family with relative stability. It wasn't a life of luxury, but it was a good living.

The prosperous corporations and their wealthy owners and executives contributed mostly with funding for the civil works projects and countless cultural amenities around the arts. They took pride in their hometown, and they wanted it to prosper.

But to get Pittsburgh from where it was to where they wanted it to be, they had to clean it up.

With its heavy industry, Pittsburgh had always been dirty. Output from steel mill furnaces produced soot and smog in almost unimaginable quantities. For generations, the sooty smog was so prevalent in Pittsburgh that it wasn't uncommon for street lights to be illuminated during the day! Along with poor air quality, local rivers presented their own pollution challenge, as they were fed enormous amounts of industrial waste daily.

In 1948, Donora, Pennsylvania, just twenty-eight miles south of Pittsburgh, was the site of the country's worst air pollution disaster, not only up to that time, but up to our current time. Carnegie Steel had set up shop in the area in 1902, and in 1915, Donora Zinc Works began operating. It wasn't long before Donora and its neighboring community of Webster noticed the environmental impact.

During the 1920s, landowners, tenants, and farmers began suing for damages attributed to smelter effluent—the zinc plant alone pumped large volumes of heavy metal dust and carbon monoxide into the air. At the height of the depression, a group of families in Webster brought legal action against Zinc Works, claiming air pollution damaged their health. However, the might of U.S. Steel fought them off with interminable legal proceedings. Moreover, plans to update the Zinc Works furnaces were shelved by the company in September 1948 because they'd be too costly for business.

The infamous, noxious "Donora Smog" appeared throughout the town on Tuesday, October 26. By the weekend, scared residents were calling doctors and hospitals to report difficulty breathing. A local doctor, Dr. William Rongaus, had to resort to carrying a lantern and leading an ambulance by foot through streets made unnavigable by the smog.

The fatalities started early in the weekend, and the number of victims grew steadily, eventually reaching twenty. In addition, hundreds of patients were seen at area hospitals, and hundreds more with respiratory and cardiac conditions were told to evacuate the area.

Finally, Sunday midday, the rain came and beat down the smog, bringing relief to the besieged communities. An untold number of lives were saved by that rain. Dr. Rongaus is quoted as estimating the death toll could have been 1,000 rather than twenty. Even accounting for a great exaggeration, it was clear that the community's disaster could have been much, much worse.

The first investigators to the scene were reportedly run off by gun-toting locals. On the surface, that might be counterintuitive. But, keep in mind, over half of Donora's population of 14,000 were employed by the mill, and the other half were surely dependent upon it.

All stakeholders—government, businesses, and citizens—knew they had to get to the bottom of the root causes of the event. As state investigators were thought to be too friendly to industries, the hands that literally kept their mouths fed, they called upon the federal government to launch an investigation, led by the newly formed United States Public Health Service.

The agency sent a large contingent of investigators to the area and conducted an extensive environmental study. At the end of the study, they reported more than 5,000 of the 14,000 residents had experienced smog-related symptoms ranging from moderate to severe and that the American Steel & Wire Plant and the Donora Zinc Works emitted a combination of poisonous gasses, heavy metals, and fine particulate matter into the air. All that, of course, was rather obvious at the outset.

But the report went further, careful not to point too many fingers at the steel industry as the primary culprit. Rather, the report also blamed a temperature inversion that trapped the Donora Smog in the valley, as well as pollution from other sources, including river traffic and residents' coal-burning heaters.

For its part, in response to repeated lawsuits from locals, American Steel & Wire asserted the entire event was an Act of God. Claims were eventually settled without the company accepting blame for the incident.

The Donora Smog spurned an interest in expanding public health research, moving beyond studying epidemics and including long-term exposures to environmental pollutants. It also influenced President Harry S. Truman to convene the first national air pollution conference in 1950.

In the region, local civic leaders, led by Pittsburgh Mayor David L. Lawrence, began smoke abatement control and urban renewal revitalization projects.

The Pittsburgh air might have become cleaner, but the city still suffered in many other ways.

Looking back at history, it probably started with the American Housing Act of 1949, part of President Harry Truman's "Fair Deal" domestic initiative. It produced a sweeping expansion of the federal government's role in mortgage insurance and issuance and the construction of public housing.

One of the first urban renewal projects in the United States was the Gateway Center, a complex of office, residential, and hotel buildings, constructed in Pittsburgh between Commonwealth Place and Stanwix Street at the western edge of the city's central business district, immediately to the east of Point State Park. However, for Pittsburgh to get the Gateway Center, it first had to clear a wide swath of land—over twenty-five acres—of its previous buildings and their inhabitants.

Be that as it may, for the Gateway Center's better or worse, urban renewal was decidedly worse for the city's lower Hill District.

From the late 1950s and into the early 1960s, the lower Hill District was destroyed, adversely impacting the neighborhood's primarily African-American population. With the city using eminent domain, the power of a local municipality to take private property for public use, it forcibly displaced more than 8,000 residents, the vast majority of them Black, along with hundreds of small businesses. Ninety-five acres were cleared for a planned cultural center with the Civic Arena, opened in 1961, as its crown jewel. Other than a single apartment building, none of the other buildings of the planned cultural center were ever built.

East Liberty wasn't spared either. Once home to the Pittsburgh elite, in the early 1960s, over 125 acres of the neighborhood were demolished and replaced by, among other things, three twenty-story public housing apartments—known, even now, as "the projects." It was not a boon to the local area—local businesses went from about 600 in 1959 to less than 300 ten years later.

A lot, but not everything, fell prey to the urban renewal efforts. Revitalization plans were resisted by neighborhood groups, and in 1964, the Pittsburgh History and Landmarks Foundation was formed to support the preservation of historic buildings and neighborhoods.

Thankfully, a great many of those efforts paid off. Some of Pittsburgh's coolest architectural heritage was saved in neighborhoods like Manchester, Allegheny West, and the Mexican War Streets, originally the Buena Vista Tract.

During all the neighborhood upheaval, Pittsburgh's industrial machine marched on, unabated. Companies like U.S. Steel, Alcoa, Westinghouse, Pittsburgh Plate Glass, and H.J. Heinz were stalwarts of the American economy. In 1970, U.S. Steel, Alcoa, and Westinghouse were three of the thirty companies that made up the famed Dow Jones Industrial Average that was broadly reported daily through the news.

By 1970, most of the building projects that signaled the city's first Renaissance period were completed, with two of the final touches being the U.S. Steel Tower downtown and, of course, Three Rivers Stadium, the Steelers' home nestled at the confluence.

Chapter 10

THE IMMACULATE RECEPTION

L ike the late afternoon shadows, a weird sort of raucous bedlam encompassed the crowd in Three Rivers Stadium. The boisterous pre-game optimism and the nervous anxiety of the ebb and flow of the game were distant memories. In their place, a foreboding acceptance of defeat was beginning to creep.

Now, Pittsburghers, as a group, are tough, persistent, and resilient—characteristics proudly worn by citizens as badges of honor in their hardscrabble, hard-working town. But with Stabler's thirty-yard scramble putting the Raiders up 7–6, the outcome looked bleak for the Black and Gold.

The Steelers hadn't mounted much offense throughout the game. To this point in the game, they had managed a paltry 172 yards in total offense. Granted, the Raiders hadn't been much better with their 216 yards, but they had the lead.

The good news was that the Steelers only needed a field goal to win. The bad news is that Gerela had already come up very short in a fifty-two-yard attempt in the first quarter. To have any real probability of success, the Steelers needed to penetrate at least as far as the Raiders' forty-yard line. The thirty-yard line would be better. Remember, Steelers' coach Noll passed on a field goal attempt in the first half from the thirty-one-yard line, believing the odds of a successful kick were too long.

Compounding the bad news, the Steelers didn't get an opportunity to return the kickoff. The ball hit the goalpost, resulting in the kick being ruled a touchback. Steelers ball, first and ten on their twenty-yard line. Forty to fifty yards away from scoring position. Only seventy-three seconds left to tick off the clock.

How improbable would a Steelers comeback be? How's this for an indication: owner Rooney left his box before the final drive began, wanting to work his way to the locker room to both console his players when they arrived after the game, as well as congratulate them for one of the greatest seasons in Steelers history.

On first down, Bradshaw took the snap and dropped back to pass, fading to his right, where he dumped off a short screen pass to Harris, who followed a blocker to reach the twenty-nine-yard line. Second down, one yard to go for a new set of downs.

The Steelers elected to keep the game clock running, saving their timeouts for later in the drive. The Raiders, wily old veterans they were, used a little gamesmanship of their own to burn the clock. Defensive tackle Art Thoms took nearly ten seconds to get to the Raiders' side of the line of scrimmage so the teams could line up for the next play.

At the snap on second down, Bradshaw again dropped back to pass, finding Fuqua in the flat for the first down and then some, as Fuqua moved the ball up to the Steelers' own forty-yard line. At the whistle, Pittsburgh called time out.

Twenty to thirty yards to field goal range. First down. The clock stopped with just thirty-seven seconds.

Nearly the entire crowd was on their feet. Bradshaw dropped back again, freeing a pass into Raiders' territory toward rookie tight end John McMakin, a third-round pick who had all of twenty-one receptions over the regular season. Raider safety Tatum dove at the last moment, breaking up the play and forcing an incompletion.

Thirty-one seconds. Second down.

Bradshaw dropped back yet again, throwing deep down the center of the field to his intended receiver, Shanklin, where the play was broken up by the Raiders' other star safety, George Atkinson.

Only five seconds had elapsed, leaving twenty-six ticks left. But, besides time, the Steelers were also running out of downs.

Third down and ten, the line of scrimmage still at the Steelers' forty-yard line. Sixty yards from the Raiders' goal line and pay dirt, twenty to thirty yards from a long field goal attempt.

Bradshaw took the snap, dropped straight back into a well-protected pocket, and fired the ball down the center of the field, past the fifty-yard line, once again toward McMakin. Just like before, Tatum broke up the play.

Fourth down, ten yards to go for a new set of downs. Ball placed on the Steelers' own forty-yard line. Twenty-two seconds left in the game, and the Steelers without a timeout to burn.

Even if the Steelers could convert the first down, if they did it in the field of play, without a timeout, they'd likely be able to run just one more desperation play. Even if they did convert a first down and stopped the clock by running out of bounds, at most, just two plays would remain in the game.

This was it. One play for the ballgame.

Charles Henry "Chuck" Noll was born on January 5, 1932, in Cleveland, Ohio, the youngest, by eight years, of three children to William and Katherine. They lived in the very same house Katherine had grown up in.

William Noll was a butcher but, suffering from Parkinson's disease, was frequently left unable to work. Chuck, doing his part, started working as a seventh grader. By the time high school came around, he had saved enough money to pay tuition to the private Roman Catholic college preparatory boys' school, Benedictine High School.

In high school, Noll excelled academically and athletically. On the football field, he starred as both a running back and a tackle and was named to the Ohio All-State team.

Noll wanted to play football at national powerhouse Notre Dame, but in practice ahead of his freshman year, he suffered a seizure on the field. When coach Frank Leahy refused to take on the risk of Noll suiting up for the Fighting Irish, Noll accepted a scholarship to play at the University of Dayton.

His hometown Cleveland Browns selected Noll in the twentieth round of the 1953 NFL Draft with the 239th overall pick, and Noll played on great Browns teams from the very start of his career.

In his rookie season, the Browns advanced to the NFL Championship Game, where they lost to the Detroit Lions. However, in the next two seasons, the Browns and Noll finished as league champions.

The Browns were coached by the legendary football pioneer, Paul Brown, and Brown utilized Noll, originally drafted as a linebacker, as a guard. Brown would use Noll as a messenger of sorts, telling Noll the play he wanted to run and having Noll, in turn, relay it to the quarterback to call out the play in the huddle for the rest of the offensive unit.

It's said that Noll hated that messenger role so much that, as a head coach, he allowed his quarterback to call plays in the huddle.

Noll retired as a player at the end of the 1959 season, and as a twenty-seven-year-old, expected to start his coaching career at the University of Dayton. However, when Dayton refused to name him to an open position on its coaching staff, Noll accepted a job as an assistant coach to Sid Gillman of the Los Angeles Chargers, ahead of the team's inaugural season.

Noll, always an academic at heart, studied under the tutelage of Gillman—to this day considered one of the greatest offensive masterminds the game of football has seen. During his tenure with the Chargers, who relocated to San Diego after their first season, Noll was on the same coaching staff as Al Davis, who would later become the coach, general manager, and, eventually, owner of the Oakland Raiders.

From Gillman, Noll then moved to an understudy position with head coach Don Shula at the Baltimore Colts. Shula, perhaps best known as the multiple Super Bowl-winning coach of the Miami Dolphins, holds the record of the most coaching wins in NFL history at a staggering 328. He was also at the helm of the Dolphins during the only undefeated season in NFL history—we'll get to that later.

Noll's last game as an assistant coach was on the Colts' sidelines during Super Bowl III when the heavily favored Colts lost to Beaver Falls native Joe Namath and his New York Jets team, 16–7. The very next day, Noll interviewed to become the next head coach of the Pittsburgh Steelers, and the rest, as is said, is history.

But there's a bit to the history that isn't that well known, and it's pretty interesting. In speaking to John Madden's oldest son, Mike, in preparing this book, he shared an interesting bit of family folklore. In early 1969, Al Davis, owner of the Raiders, seemed to be dragging his feet a bit in naming the Raiders' next head coach. During that time, Madden was considering an offer to join Noll's staff in Pittsburgh as the defensive coordinator. In fact, according to Mike, his mother, Virginia, told her husband, "John, if it makes sense for your career to go to Pittsburgh, then we should go."

Alas, that move never happened, and NFL history is probably better off for it. But just imagine what a Madden-coached Steelers' defense would have been!

Noll was just thirty-seven years old, the youngest head coach in the NFL, when he was named the fourteenth head coach of the Pittsburgh Steelers. Until that time, there had been a revolving door of coaches spearheading the team. Noll changed all that.

Noll coached the Steelers for twenty-three seasons, compiling a regular season record of 193–148–1, and leading the team to four Super Bowl championships. Only three head coaches had ever had as long a tenure with one club in the NFL. He was elected to the Pro Football Hall of Fame in 1993.

Noll built the foundation for the stability of the Steelers' head coaching position. When he retired at the end of the 1991 season, he was succeeded by Bill Cowher, who manned the position for fifteen seasons, delivering a 149–90–1 record and a Super Bowl Championship.

Upon Cowher's retirement, the helm was taken over by current head coach Mike Tomlin, who as of this writing, just completed his fifteenth season in the position.

Prior to Noll, the Steelers had thirteen head coaches. In the fifty-three seasons and counting since, just three, Noll included.

With one play to decide the game, Noll ordered a pass play called 66 Circle Option, with the intended receiver being Barry Pearson, a rookie who, like a lot of Steelers, was playing in his first professional football playoff game. Unlike the rest of the Steelers, however, Pearson was also playing in his first professional football game.

Ever!

What? With one play to run, Noll called on Pearson?

Yes, he did.

At the snap, Bradshaw dropped back deep, planting his right foot at his own thirty-yard line. On this play, the Raiders mustered up a strong pass rush, and Bradshaw didn't have a real chance to look Pearson's way. Pressure stormed in from both sides; defensive end Horace Jones pushed in from Bradshaw's left, while defensive end Tony Cline joined the party from Bradshaw's right.

Feeling the pressure, Bradshaw brought the ball down, ducked, and scrambled out to his right, followed in hot pursuit by both Jones and Cline. He dodged Jones with a quick sidestep to his own left, planted his right foot at the twenty-nine-yard line, and fired a pass deep down the middle, all the way down to the Raiders' thirty-four-yard line.

The intended receiver was Fuqua, and again, Tatum was on the scene, delivering a big hit that separated the two of them and the ball. In fact, the ball shot backward, toward Bradshaw and the line of scrimmage, about ten yards.

Raider defensive back Jimmy Warren, a thirty-three-year-old veteran of nine professional football seasons, threw his arms up in the air in triumph.

In 1972, many NFL rules were different from those today. One such rule was related to the legality of receptions. The rule in 1972 stated that once an offensive player touched a forward pass, he was the only offensive player eligible to catch that pass. On the other hand, ". . . if a [defensive] player touches [the] pass first, or simultaneously with or subsequent to its having been touched by only one [offensive] player, then all [offensive] players become and remain eligible" receivers who can catch the pass.

After Tatum collided into the scene, the ball tumbled backward, end over end, in a downward line drive of sorts toward the artificial turf. There, right above the turf, the ball met the outstretched hands of Franco Harris.

Harris had been a blocker on the play, and as the play wore on, he had released and started working his way downfield, perhaps to be a target for a scrambling Bradshaw or a blocker for a teammate who caught the pass.

But now, Harris had caught the pass, right off his shoe tops.

All the Raiders players had been moving toward the play, and most had relaxed for just a split second, thinking the play was over. Suddenly, in that split second, they found themselves with a charging Harris running right at them.

Raiders defenders stopped their forward momentum and quickly changed direction, pursuing Harris at an angle toward the sideline. Raiders linebacker Villapiano was blocked by McMakin, and fellow linebacker Gerald Irons was too late changing direction and quickly eluded by Harris.

That left Harris, now at full speed, streaking down the sideline on his left, with just one Raider to beat—the aforementioned Warren.

With the play happening too quickly for the crowd to know better to be stunned by its sheer improbability, they erupted in a thunderous, cascading wave of noise.

Harris, ball cradled in his left arm, continued full tilt downfield, too fast for Warren to get a proper angle on him and force him out of bounds. At the twelve-yard line, in desperation, Warren dove for Harris, arms outstretched, only to be pushed off with a glancing stiff arm from Harris.

That little stiff arm, however, redirected Harris's forward momentum just a bit to his left, toward the sideline. Harris barely kept his right foot in bounds at the three, tight-roped the boundary with his left foot inside the one, and slipped into the end zone just inside the orange pylon at the goal line.

Touchdown, Steelers!

To those fans listening on the radio, Harris's run must have seemed like it took forever. But was it worth it or what? The Steelers had finally won a playoff game—and in the most unimaginable way possible.

Unbelievable!

In the most improbable manner, the Steelers had won. Or had they?

While the whistle had blown and the action on the field had stopped, the play, in the minds of many, and in particular those playing for the Silver and Black and their fans in Raider Nation, the play continued on. In fact, the controversy still lives on to this day, fifty years later.

Had the catch been legal under the rules?

The crux of the matter is simply, who did the football touch in the Fuqua/Tatum collision? If the ball bounced off Fuqua without subsequently also bouncing off Tatum, then no other Steeler would have become an eligible receiver, and Harris's reception would have been invalid. The result of the play would then be an incompletion, and the Raiders would take possession on a Steelers loss of downs; Raiders' ball, first and ten, on the Steelers' forty-yard line.

However, if the ball bounced only off of Tatum, or both players for that matter, then the reception was legal. Touchdown, Steelers, and a 12–6 lead.

At the conclusion of the play, one game official, back judge Adrian Burk, signaled the play was a touchdown. The other officials, however, made no signal at all—neither a touchdown nor an incomplete pass.

The referee crew huddled, and after a brief discussion . . . nothing. No confirmation signal of a touchdown, no conflicting signal of an incompletion.

Then, to add to the already bizarre, something even more improbable happened. Referee Fred Swearingen went to the Steelers sideline and asked to be taken to a telephone. Now, this was highly irregular. Today, it's a familiar sight for the referee to go to the sidelines and look at slow-motion video replays to confirm or reverse a call on the field. In 1972, the league was still far away from instant replay reviews.

Steeler staffer Jim Boston took Swearingen to one of the Three Rivers Stadium baseball dugouts. Once there, Swearingen dialed up the press box at the top of the stadium to speak with Art McNally, the NFL's supervisor of officials.

Different accounts vary on who answered the call into the press box. Some reported Dan Rooney, son of Steelers team owner Art, answered the call. Others reported Steelers public relations director Joe Gordon picked up first. Regardless, McNally was quickly put on the line.

Oh, if only there was an audio recording of that call!

It wasn't a long conversation. But the fact that it took place at all only further stokes the flames of controversy. According to published reports, McNally stated that Swearingen never once inquired about the rule and that he stated his crew saw Tatum touch the ball.

If that was the case, then why did Swearingen make the call in the first place? Keep in mind, throughout his entire career as an official, he had never called up to a press box to preview a call before notifying the players on the field and the crowd. For that matter, he never did it again afterward, either.

Regardless, after a brief conversation, Swearingen hung up the phone, returned to the field, and signaled touchdown. The Steelers were officially in the lead.

There was a video monitor in the dugout where Swearingen made his phone call, but he never once accessed it. The NFL immediately denied that neither television replays were used nor the decision was made by McNally in the press box.

Two days after the game, the Oakland Tribune published an article that stated Steelers publicist Gordon told the pool of reporters in the press box that the final decision had been made using video replay for confirmation. Gordon has denied those claims.

Of course, even if video replay had been used, it would have confirmed the call on the field. The outcome of the game shouldn't be in doubt. Besides, you've undoubtedly seen replays of the play—can you determine what really happened? Only Frenchy Fuqua might—and that's a big might—know for certain, and he's still, after all these years, playing it coy, relishing the attention that is focused on him whenever the topic comes up.

While the controversy started immediately at the play's end, it has never really stopped, not for want of people wanting to prove one outcome or another. A physicist, John Fetkovich, an emeritus professor of physics at Carnegie Mellon University, even conducted a study in 2004 based on archival film and videotape. He came to the conclusion that the ball had to have hit Tatum, as his forward momentum toward the line of scrimmage was the only force that could have knocked the ball as far backward as it flew. Fuqua was running across the field, and if the ball had deflected off of him, it would most likely have gone toward one side or another.

Bradshaw, as you might expect, agreed with that conclusion, stating he didn't feel he threw the ball hard enough, at the distance it traveled downfield, for it to bounce as far back upfield as it did.

Then again, there was one more controversial element: did the ball touch the ground before Harris caught it? Because of the nature of the play, cameras were moving downfield with the flight of Bradshaw's pass. With the Tatum/Fuqua collision and the speed of the football flying now in the opposite direction, by the time cameras reversed direction and captured Harris, he already had the ball. Various low-level shots of the play, both from the sidelines and from an NBC camera in the back of the end zone, recorded such tight shots that the actual catch is out of the frame.

Regardless of where the arguments go, at the end of the conversation, the Raiders' faithful will forever declare the play the "Immaculate Deception." In NFL history and Pittsburgh Steelers lore, however, the play has become known as the "Immaculate Reception," and it's the single most identifiable play in Steelers—and professional football—history.

Football fans around the world celebrated the 100th season of NFL football in 2019. To denote the centennial, the NFL Network, the league's privately owned television network, produced programming around "the best" of its colorful history, as determined by a panel of national media.

One list produced was the NFL's 100 Greatest Plays. Any guess on what one, single play topped the list?

That's right, the Immaculate Reception was agreed upon by the media as the greatest play in league history, coming in ahead of other notable plays, such as "The Catch," a game-winning touchdown pass from San Francisco quarterback Joe Montana, a Donora native, to receiver Dwight Clark, and "the helmet catch" New York Giants receiver David Tyree made off an Eli Manning pass in Super Bowl XLII.

The Immaculate Reception survived an additional forty-six years of football history to stake a claim as the NFL's greatest play. Will it ever be supplanted at the top?

Never in the hearts and minds of Steel City.

With the election of the Class of 2020 into the Pro Football Hall of Fame in Canton, Ohio, there are now 346 members enshrined in the Hall. Of those 346, seventeen were associated with the Immaculate Reception game.

Eight Oakland Raiders who were involved with the game were later enshrined in the Hall. They are owner and founder Al Davis, head coach John Madden, center Jim Otto, guard Gene Upshaw, tackle Art Shell, tackle Bob Brown, quarterback and kicker George Blanda, and quarterback Ken Stabler.

Nine Pittsburgh Steelers who were involved with the game were later inducted into Canton. They are owner and founder Art Rooney Sr., head coach Chuck Noll, executive Dan Rooney, scout and executive Bill Nunn, running back Franco Harris, quarterback Terry Bradshaw, defensive tackle Joe Greene, linebacker Jack Ham, and cornerback Mel Blount.

A lot of football has been played since that fateful game on December 23, 1972. Still, even today, fifty years after the fact, a full 5 percent of the inductees into the Hall of Fame played a role in that game.

You might be wondering, "Whatever happened to the football Franco Harris scored with on the 'Immaculate Reception' play?" Perhaps it rests in the Pro Football Hall of Fame in Canton? Or, maybe it sits in the center of a trophy case in Franco Harris's house?

Those would be two great guesses. However, they're both incorrect.

Rather unbelievably, the historic ball has spent almost all of the past fifty years secured in a safe in the offices of a Pittsburgh insurance agency.

In 1972, Jim Baker was a twenty-six-year-old from West Mifflin, breaking into the insurance business, and to get the necessary capital to get his business off the ground, he had sold off his Steelers season tickets. The only reason he was at the game in the first place was through his cousin's last-minute gift of two tickets in Box 57 near the thirty-yard line.

Just four days before the game, Baker's wife Mary had given birth to the couple's second son, Sam. But, hey, that wasn't going to stop a dyed-in-the-wool Steelers fan. Baker's cousin was a photographer who was going to be working the game for *Pitt Press*, so he gave Baker two tickets on the condition his son, thirteen-year-old Bobby Pavuchak, would accompany Baker to the game. That condition was all good with Baker, as not only was he going to the biggest game in the franchise's history, but he would be able to work on little Bobby for some future babysitting assistance.

Like the rest of the 50,000-plus in attendance, Jim and Bobby sat through the tense defensive struggle until all heck broke loose in the game's final two minutes. First up, of course, was when Raiders quarterback Stabler dove into the end zone with 1:13 remaining, tying the score at 6–6. Veteran Blanda kicked the PAT, and Oakland had its first lead of the game.

Baker and Pavuchak stood through the tumultuous final drive, hoping and praying the Steelers' offense could pull a proverbial rabbit out of its hat after having been stymied by the Raiders' defense all game long.

Then, of course, came the Immaculate Reception, and Harris's touchdown scamper down the sideline to win the game. During the play, the crowd erupted, and within seconds after Harris scored, bedlam ensued, with hundreds of spectators jumping out of the stands and onto the field.

In a 2012 interview with Kim Gamble for an article on Grantland.com, Harris remembered the ensuing madness, recalling, "People jumped on me. I had the football in my hand. Someone hit my arm, and the football rolled into oblivion."[5]

Harris remembers it all wrong, of course. As he went to hug receiver Ron Shanklin, Harris gave a little underhanded toss of the football, probably intending to get it to a referee for the extra point. The football bounced around in the end zone for a second while the television broadcast cut to a shot of Steelers fans going berserk in the stands.

Amid the chaos, Baker kept his eye on the ball.

In that same Grantland article, Pavuchak recalled the moment. "It all happened so fast," he said. "Uncle Jim yanked my arm and yelled, 'Let's go!'"

The two ran down the aisle, jumped on the roof of the Pittsburgh Pirates dugout, and then spilled onto the field.

Then Swearingen made his infamous call to the press box while the celebrations in Three Rivers Stadium raged on.

During the delay, stadium security pushed everyone on the field, including Baker and Pavuchak, to the back of the end zone. All along, Baker kept his eye on the ball—Baker told the authors of this book he watched it from the moment it left Harris's right hand to when it was placed in play for the Steelers PAT attempt.

When play resumed, Steelers kicker Roy Gerela split the uprights with his kick, the ball hitting a cement wall before bouncing into the corner of the end zone where it was swarmed upon by a pile of people, Baker included.

Baker, a former high school wrestler, emerged with the ball. Worried there might be some altercations with others if the ball was visible during their exit from the stadium, he and Bobby tucked it under Pavuchak's coat, and together, they made a beeline out of Three Rivers.

As they left the stadium, Baker recalled in an interview with the authors, they came across a couple of fans in a 1958 Pontiac. Baker tapped on the window and said, "Can I give you some money to take us off the bridge to the Pitt Press office?" The driver asked why. Baker told him, "Because I have the game ball!" The driver told them to get in, and he refused any money.

Of course, it's impossible to prove Baker's ball is *the* ball, but a strong indication that it is authentic comes from the fact that not a single conflicting story has emerged after all these years.

In today's NFL, each team provides twelve primary game balls and twelve alternative game balls. Remember Dallas Cowboys running back Emmitt Smith coming back to the sideline with every single football he ever scored with—175 in total for his career? He could do that in his era, as there were a lot of footballs to go around. However, back in 1972, there was usually just a single ball available for the game.

During the play, Adrian Burk was the line judge who followed Harris up the field, and he would have been the logical referee to retrieve the football and put it in position for the extra point. Burk, who passed away in 2003, is the only person who could have confirmed he placed the same football in play for the extra point. McNally's take is the following: "In those years, the number of balls was so limited. The official's not gonna turn around, go to the bench, and ask for another ball. I'm very confident it's the same one."[6]

Celebrating a victory snatched from the clutches of defeat, Baker stopped on the way home to show the ball to friends at his neighborhood bar, The Seven Knights. Word spread quickly, and by nightfall, much of Pittsburgh had heard the story.

Long before the era of eBay and online auctions, Baker didn't envision selling the football. Feeling that the ball did rightfully belong to Harris and the Steelers, Baker offered to give the team the ball in exchange for two lifetime season tickets and some autographs. When the Steelers declined, he put the ball in his safe, bringing it out from time to time to show it off, and sometimes, believe it or not, play catch with it.

Over the years, Baker has turned down offers for the ball, including a reported $150,000 offer in 1979 from Ray Anthony International, a Pittsburgh-based provider of cranes and other heavy equipment. The ball has, in so many ways, become intertwined in the lives of Baker and his family, and his attachment to the ball carries a great deal of sentimentality, particularly in light of the death of his son, Sam, born four days before the game, in May 2005 at the tender age of just thirty-three.

Sam was survived by his wife, Joanna, and two young sons, Sam Jr. and Alex. Baker has talked in interviews about leveraging the ball for a degree of financial security for his grandsons, perhaps as a means for a college education.

In the meantime, the ball rests secure, an indelible piece of history—of Pittsburgh, the Steelers, Harris, and the NFL. Baker refers to the ball as an Immaculate Remembrance. It's arguably the most prized bit of NFL memorabilia, and no matter where it ends up after Baker, it will be the centerpiece of a truly *Immaculate* collection.

Chapter 11

THE SAME OLD STEELERS

W orld War II had a sweeping effect over the globe, and professional football was certainly no exception. The federal government had started the military draft with the Selective Training and Service Act of 1940, passed in September of that year. At first, the draft didn't have a significant impact on the NFL.

That changed, of course, after the attack on Pearl Harbor on December 7, 1941. With that single act, the United States was now thrust into war in two different theaters. The United States needed soldiers, much more so than the NFL needed football players.

The Steelers, fresh off their last-place finish, owned the first pick of the 1942 NFL Draft. Rooney and Bell lobbied for the draft to be delayed, what with the uncertainty of the war effort and all. After their effort was rebuked by the rest of the league's owners, they selected "Bullet" Bill Dudley, a halfback out of the University of Virginia, with the first pick. After that, the Steelers, believe it or not, concentrated on drafting and signing married players, with the long view that those players would have a lower draft status and be less likely to be conscripted into service, at least ahead of the 1942 season.

Several players from the team joined the military before the start of the season, including both quarterbacks and their leading rusher. Dudley, too, intended to enlist, but the backlog of young men entering the military delayed his service and allowed him to play his rookie season.

In his first season, Dudley, who would later be inducted into the Hall of Fame, led the league in rushing with 696 yards on 162 attempts. A versatile threat, he also recorded thirty-five receptions for 438 yards receiving. His impact on the team, and the league, was immediate, and he was runner-up to Green Bay's Don Hutson in voting for the league's Most Valuable Player award.

The Steelers had started the season as the same old Steelers, losing their first two games. But then, behind Dudley, they won seven out of eight, before falling to

Hutson's Packers in the final game of the season. That 7–4 record represented the first winning season in the club's history.

The Steelers were on a roll but so was the Allied war effort.

The league's owners contemplated canceling the 1943 season entirely. But, in the spring of 1943, they collectively decided to continue playing, except for the Cleveland Rams, who elected to suspend operations for the year. Knowing that finding players would be a struggle, the league voted to trim rosters from thirty-three players to twenty-five.

League owners didn't know the half of it when it came to finding players. By summer, the Steelers had only five players under contract. It was clear to Rooney that it would be almost impossible for him to field a team in the coming season.

Almost out of desperation, Rooney and Bell reached out to Thompson to propose merging their two clubs, the Steelers and the Eagles, to form one unit for the upcoming season. Thompson was keen, but the other league owners, fearing a super-team juggernaut might result, initially balked. After much debate and some arm-wringing, they acquiesced, though, and the combined team prepared to suit up for the 1943 season.

Officially, the team was known as the Eagles, and they had no city affiliation. However, they were familiarly known as the Philadelphia/Pittsburgh "Steagles," slated to split their home games between the two cities; four in Philly, two in Pittsburgh, with coaching duties shared between Eagles coach Greasy Neale and Kiesling.

Neale and Kiesling were far from friends, and they apparently didn't get along well at all. As a remedy, each took responsibility for one side of the ball, one coaching offense, the other defense. It served as a precursor to how coaching staffs are formed today, with both an offensive and defensive coordinator reporting to a single head coach.

The Steagles got through the season with a 5–4 record, the Eagles' first-ever winning season, and the second consecutive winning season for the Steelers.

Still in the throes of a world war, Rooney and Bell decided another merger made sense for the 1944 season, although this time around the partner of convenience was chosen to be the Chicago Cardinals.

The team was known as Card-Pitt, but it soon devolved into the "Carpets," and for good reason as the team sank to the floor of the standings, completing the season with a winless record.

In 1945, the Steelers went back to operating on their own, but they finished yet another dismal season at just 2–8. Prospects got brighter though during the 1946 season, as Dudley, back from his service, led the team to a 5–5–1 record on his way to winning the league's MVP award.

Born in Virginia, Dudley tried out and made his high school football team as a junior. He was a punter and a placekicker, and he was good enough to be awarded a scholarship to the University of Virginia as just a sixteen-year-old incoming freshman.

Seeing his athleticism, coaches moved Dudley to the halfback position, and by his sophomore year, he was appearing in games. In his junior year, he started every game, and by his senior year, he became the first Virginia player to earn All-America honors on his way to being awarded the Maxwell Award for best college football player of the year.

The backlog of men entering the military and the subsequent postponement of Dudley's enlistment allowed him to play his rookie season for the Steelers in 1942, and he scored a touchdown in his very first professional game. After a sterling rookie season, Dudley then entered the service with the US Army Air Corps.

Dudley returned from the service in time for the final four games of the 1945 season, ending the season as the club's leading scorer and setting the stage for a magnificent season the very next year.

In 1946, throughout that 5–5–1 season, Dudley was seemingly everywhere. He led the league in rushing, and coupled with his fantastic results as a punt returner, he led the league in all-purpose yards as well. Defensively, he led the league with ten interceptions and seven recovered fumbles. At the end of the season, he was named All-Pro and selected as the NFL's Most Valuable Player.

Alas, before the 1947 season, Dudley was traded to the Detroit Lions, where he captained the club for all three seasons he was there. From Detroit, he finished his professional career with Washington, retiring after the completion of the 1953 season,

Over his career, Dudley was named first- or second-team All-NFL six times and named to three Pro Bowls. He is still the only NFL player to record touchdowns by rushing, receiving, punt return, kickoff return, interception return, fumble return, and throwing a pass. Oh, and he also kicked PATs and field goals.

Deservingly so, Dudley was inducted into the Pro Football Hall of Fame in 1966, the same year as his Steelers coach, Walt Kiesling.

The 1947 season proved to be the Steelers' most successful season to date. Behind quarterback Johnny Clement, the first and only player to wear the number zero on

the Steelers, the club finished the season with an 8–4 record, tying the Eagles for the division crown.

The season tie led Clement, second in the league in rushing yards that year, and the Steelers to Philadelphia for the team's first-ever playoff game. Over 35,000 fans showed up for the intrastate clash.

Unfortunately, the Steelers' offense didn't show up, at least not in their best form. They struggled all day to move the football and sustain drives, netting just fifty-two yards passing all day on the way to 154 yards of total offense.

The Eagles scored touchdowns in both the first and second quarters to take a 14–0 lead by halftime. Then, the killing blow came in the form of a seventy-nine-yard punt return for a touchdown by Bosh Pritchard in the third quarter. The Steelers ended up closing their season with a 21–0 defeat.

It would be the Steelers' last playoff game for twenty-five years.

In the offseason, in April 1948, head coach Jock Sutherland was found in a confused state of mind in his car in Kentucky while on a scouting trip. Diagnosed with exhaustion, Sutherland flew back to Pittsburgh for more thorough medical examinations. He died a few days later following surgery to remove a malignant brain tumor.

Shaken, the Steelers struggled that season, finishing with a 4–8 record.

In 1949, the Steelers started the season with a look to turn things around again but stumbled down the stretch to finish 6–5–1. That winning season would be the last for quite a while.

The 1950s started with the following season records:

- 1950: 6–6
- 1951: 4–7–1
- 1952: 5–7
- 1953: 6–6
- 1954: 5–7

But that stretch of mediocrity was set to change heading into the 1955 season. You see, in the 1955 NFL Draft, the Steelers selected quarterback Johnny Unitas in the ninth round.

Johnny Unitas joined the Steelers for training camp as one of four quarterbacks competing for three positions on the team's roster. Head coach Kiesling, however, believed Unitas lacked the intelligence to play quarterback in the NFL. In training camp practices, Unitas was given very few plays to prove his worth. Not surprisingly, he was cut from the roster before the season began.

Married, Unitas took construction work in Pittsburgh to support his family, filling his weekends by playing quarterback, safety, and punter on the local semi-professional team, the Bloomfield Rams. For his football efforts, Unitas was rewarded with a tidy $6 per game.

How did football work out for Unitas going forward? Well, not too poorly.

In the months leading up to the 1956 season, Unitas signed with the Baltimore Colts, led by legendary coach Weeb Ewbank. Beginning with his rookie season, Unitas threw at least one touchdown pass in forty-seven consecutive games, a league record that stood for fifty-two years. It was just one of many records Unitas established over the course of his seventeen-year career.

On his way to receiving ten Pro Bowl and five first-team All-Pro honors, Unitas was named Most Valuable Player three times, in 1959, 1964, and 1967. He led the Colts to four championships, including a victory in Super Bowl V.

Unitas's first championship game, at the conclusion of the 1958 season, was played in Yankee Stadium, where the Colts defeated the New York Giants 23–17 in overtime. The game is regarded as "The Greatest Game Ever Played," and an estimated forty-five million Americans watched it unfold on the nationwide telecast. The game, and Unitas's big role in the outcome, spurred the beginning of the NFL's huge popularity surge and eventual rise to the top of the United States' televised sports market.

Johnny Unitas, he of the "Golden Arm," was inducted into the Pro Football Hall of Fame in 1979. He never played a single down for the Pittsburgh Steelers.

Without Unitas, the Steelers suffered through two more losing seasons, posting records of 4–8 and 5–7 in 1955 and 1956, respectively. Buddy Parker then replaced Kiesling as head coach prior to the 1957 season. While the Steelers showed modest improvement in finishing with a 6–6 record, the season is most noteworthy for the Steelers hiring Lowell Perry as their receivers coach, the NFL's first African-American coach.

Perry, whose father was a respected dentist and civic leader, was born in Ypsilanti, Michigan, in 1931. He played collegiately at the University of Michigan, where he starred as an end, a safety, and a punt returner.

The Steelers drafted Perry in the eighth round of the 1953 NFL Draft. Professional football, however, came second to Perry's Reserve Officers' Training Corps (ROTC) obligations, and Perry joined the United States Air Force, where he eventually rose to the rank of second lieutenant.

Perry joined the Steelers in 1956, and he made an immediate impact. On his first-ever professional play, in a pre-season game against the Detroit Lions, he ran ninety-three yards for a touchdown.

In his first six regular season games, Perry caught fourteen passes for 334 receiving yards and two touchdowns, including a seventy-five-yard touchdown catch. Perry was a star in the making. Alas, in that sixth game, Perry sustained a fractured pelvis and dislocated hip, injuries that forced him into a premature retirement.

Perry spent thirteen weeks in Pittsburgh's Mercy Hospital following the injury and joined the Steelers' coaching staff for the next season. For the 1958 season, Perry transitioned to the role of Steelers scout. He also attended law school.

Pivoting away from professional football, Perry moved to Detroit, completed his law degree at the Detroit College of Law in 1960, and clerked for US District Court Judge Frank A. Picard, a former Michigan Wolverines quarterback.

In 1963, Perry began what would be a seventeen-year career at Chrysler, where, in 1973, he was appointed the plant manager of Chrysler's Eldon Avenue Axle Plant in Detroit, the first African-American to be appointed the plant manager position at a US automobile company.

At Chrysler, Perry also moonlighted, hired in 1966 as a color analyst for CBS Television, where he broadcasted Steelers games alongside play-by-play commentator Joe Tucker. In doing so, Perry became the first African-American to broadcast an NFL game to a national audience.

But that's not all. In 1975, Perry was appointed by President Gerald Ford to be commissioner of the US Equal Employment Opportunity Commission, a post he held for a year until he returned to Chrysler.

A budding superstar on the field whose career was cut short, Perry was a remarkable success in his other professional endeavors, achieving a number of notable firsts along the way.

The 1958 season held plenty of promise for the Steelers, at least after the first two weeks of the season. They started the year with two losses out of the gate, but then Rooney swung a trade for veteran quarterback Bobby Layne, who had led the

Detroit Lions to three championships over his decorated ten-year career up to the 1958 season.

Layne immediately turned the fortunes around for the Steelers, and they closed the season on a 7–2–1 tear. While still two games out of first place in the division and a playoff spot, their 7–4–1 record was the club's first winning season in nine years.

Layne, as great as he was, was on the tail end of his brilliant career, and he, alone, couldn't quite get the Steelers over the hump. With Layne starting at quarterback, the Steelers finished the next two seasons, 1959 and 1960, with decidedly mediocre records of 6–5–1 and 5–6–1.

During the 1961 season, journeyman quarterback Rudy Bukich supplanted Layne as the starter, but the club's fortunes fared no better, and they closed the campaign with a 6–8 record.

The 1962 season came with a new look for the Steelers. Literally.

Ahead of the season, the team adopted its current logo, based on that of the "Steelmark" used by the American Iron and Steel Institute (AISI). Previously, the Steelers' helmets had been golden, with players' numbers on each side, but as the new logo had gold in it, on a white background, they changed their helmet color to black for the logo to stand out visually.

So what's the deal with the Steelers' logo being only on the right side of their helmets, the only team in the NFL to do so? Well, it's a pretty simple story.

Dan Rooney, Art's son, asked long-time equipment manager, Jack Hart, to place the logo decals on the helmet. Apparently, as Dan wasn't specific in his request, Hart arbitrarily decided to put the stickers on the right side of the helmets, and the right side only. It's been that way ever since.

The Steelers had worked with the AISI to use their logo and changed the word "Steel" in the circular image to "Steelers." As for the three diamonds in the logo, their colors represent the three materials used to make steel: yellow for coal, red for iron, and blue for steel scrap.

The new-look Steelers had a banner year in 1962, with Layne again at the helm. They finished the season with their best record yet, 9–5, good for second in the division.

The star of the 1962 Steelers was running back John Henry Johnson. Johnson was actually the Steelers' second-round draft pick, and the eighteenth overall selection, in the 1953 NFL Draft. However, Johnson didn't suit up for the Steelers until the 1960 season.

After being drafted, Johnson first played in Canada for the Calgary Stampeders of the Western Interprovincial Football Union (WIFU). Legend has it that Johnson received more money from Calgary, but Rooney was on record that he believed

Johnson, who had played collegiately in both California and Arizona, thought Pittsburgh would be too cold in fall and winter.

After one season in Canada, Johnson, known simply as John Henry as a nod to the African-American freedman legend of the same name, spent three seasons apiece with the San Francisco 49ers and the Detroit Lions. He joined the Steelers ahead of the 1960 campaign, seemingly at the end of his career.

It turned out, Johnson was just getting started.

In 1960, Johnson rushed for 621 yards, the second-best total of his career, on just 118 carries. He followed that up with a career-best 787 yards in 1961.

Then, Johnson really got going in the 1962 season, at age thirty-three, rushing for 1,141 yards, second in the league to the Green Bay Packers' Jim Taylor.

Two seasons later, John Henry again broke the 1,000-yard rushing mark, tallying 1,048 yards on the ground, third-best in the league behind Taylor and the legendary Jim Brown of the Cleveland Browns. To this day, John Henry remains the oldest player, along with the Washington Redskins' John Riggins, to rush for over 1,000 yards in a season.

Despite John Henry's late-career resurgence, the Steelers started trending down, completing the 1963 season in fourth place in the division with a 7–4–3 record. If those three ties on the season had been victories, what a difference it may have made.

In 1964, the downward trend continued, with the team recording a 5–9 record and slipping to a sixth place finish in the division. In an otherwise unremarkable season, 1964 was the Steelers' first year away from their original home, Forbes Field. In 1958, they started playing some of their home games at Pitt Stadium, on the campus of the University of Pittsburgh. By the 1964 season, the Steelers had bid farewell completely to Forbes Field and made Pitt Stadium their new home.

After head coach Buddy Parker retired, Mike Nixon took the helm ahead of the 1965 campaign. The result was a dismal disaster, as the Steelers finished with a league-worst 2–12 record.

Bill Olson took over the head coaching duties but never turned things around over his three seasons, 1966–1968. His best season was his debut season, 1966, when the club improved slightly to 5–8–1. From there, seasons of 4–9–1 and 2–11–1 led the Chief to replace him with Chuck Noll.

The savior of the Pittsburgh Steelers had arrived. Only, the fans in Pittsburgh didn't know it quite yet.

Pittsburgh Steelers fans look back on Chuck Noll's twenty-three seasons with the club as the turning point in the franchise's fortune. Until his arrival, the team had been, for the most part, the "same old Steelers," a squad that seemed to consistently fall short of the big expectations the community held for them.

But for the decision of Penn State's Joe Paterno to turn down Rooney's offer to coach the Steelers, Noll's tenure with the team would have never happened.

After serving a one-year stint in the Army, Paterno attended Brown University, where he quarterbacked the football team. Upon graduating, he planned on attending the Boston University School of Law. Then, he received an assistant coaching position offer from Penn State head coach Rip Engle. Thoughts of being an attorney were quickly replaced with that of coaching on the gridiron.

Paterno stayed on Engle's staff, advancing steadily until Engle retired ahead of the 1966 season, whereupon Paterno took over the head position. By his third season, 1968, the Nittany Lions were an undefeated 11–0, with an Orange Bowl victory and a number two ranking behind only the national champion Ohio State Buckeyes. Paterno had definitely caught the Chief's eye.

Paterno didn't bite at the Steelers' offer though. He stayed at Penn State, where the club produced another undefeated season in 1969, further launching Paterno to a historic career that produced a record 409 coaching victories.

When Paterno spurned the Steelers' advances, Rooney turned to Noll. But, before all of the club's success with Noll at the reins, there remained a few years of struggle. So much so, Noll almost wasn't around for the team's turnaround.

Noll's tenure started well, as the team won its first game of the 1969 campaign, defeating the Lions. Then the wheels came off. And off. And off again. And they continued to fall off until the very end of the season. After a promising start, the Steelers reeled off thirteen consecutive losses to finish the season at 1–13, tied for the worst record in the NFL.

That tie for the worst record in the league led to a coin toss with the Chicago Bears to determine who would select first in the 1970 NFL Draft. The Steelers won the toss, setting themselves up to take Bradshaw with the first overall selection.

The year 1970 was a monumental year in the history of the Pittsburgh Steelers. Sure, Bradshaw joined the club, but that was just the beginning of it.

In 1970, the NFL merged with the rival American Football League. As part of that merger, the Steelers, along with the Cleveland Browns and Baltimore Colts, joined the former AFL teams to create the new American Football Conference, whose champion would play the National Football Conference's champion annually in the Super Bowl. Part of that move included the Steelers procuring a $3 million relocation fee, a much-needed financial boost for a club seeking to attract higher caliber players.

To top it off, the Steelers had a sparkling new home, Three Rivers Stadium. There might be a tendency to look back at the stadium now with a bit of ridicule, as it proved to be a pretty nondescript, cookie-cutter type of venue that resembled so many other stadiums of the era, like Cincinnati's Riverfront Stadium. But, at the time, Three Rivers was some kind of special.

The new stadium began as an initiative of the baseball Pirates, who sought a bigger stadium that could produce bigger revenues. To get the ball rolling, they sold Forbes Field, the second-oldest stadium to Philadelphia's Connie Mack Stadium in the major leagues, to the University of Pittsburgh in 1958 and leased the property back from the school until a replacement stadium was built.

That took over ten years. Various stadium designs were produced, but the real sticking points proved to be location and good, old-fashioned politicking about funding, particularly the contributions of both the Pirates and the Steelers.

Finally, stadium construction broke ground in April 1968 and took a rather pedestrian twenty-nine months to complete, at a total cost of $55 million. The hope was the stadium would play host to the Pirates' Opening Day in April 1970, but those dreams faded down the schedule's stretch run. After an emergency infusion of $3 million from the city to push the construction's completion, a new target date was set for the end of May.

Alas, more delays ensued, and the stadium's lights weren't yet installed, leading to yet another postponement of its grand opening. Finally, in their first game after the All-Star Break, the Pirates christened the stadium against the Cincinnati Reds on Thursday, July 16. The outcome: a 3–2 Pirates' defeat.

The field and spectator stands had been ready, but the parking lot, the Pirates' and Steelers' team offices, the Allegheny Club, and the press boxes were still not open due to extended labor union work stoppages. For the stadium's opening day, the Pirates had the parking lot closed and asked fans to either park downtown and walk to the stadium or take shuttle buses. All in all, a rather inauspicious opening.

But, in time, both the Pirates and the Steelers had a new home. And just as Yankee Stadium was known as "The House that (Babe) Ruth Built," many Pittsburghers took to referring to Three Rivers Stadium as "The House that Clemente Built."

Fifty years after his death, Roberto Clemente Walker remains a revered figure in Pittsburgh civic and sports history.

Clemente played 18 seasons for the Pittsburgh Pirates and contributed mightily to two World Series titles. Over his career, he recorded 3,000 hits to produce a batting average of .317, was a twelve-time All-Star, and won the Most Valuable Player award at the end of the 1966 season. In his last regular season game, October 3, 1972, he tied Honus Wagner's record for games played as a Pittsburgh Pirate—his 2,433rd game played.

Throughout his career, Clemente gave back to communities with his charitable work. Early in December 1972, he visited the capital city of Nicaragua, Managua, and the city and its citizens made an impact on him.

On December 23, 1972, the day of the Immaculate Reception game in The House that Clemente Built, Managua was hit by a catastrophic earthquake. In response, Clemente arranged a number of emergency relief flights to provide support and aid.

Clemente chartered a Douglas DC-7 cargo plane for a New Year's Eve flight from his native Puerto Rico to Managua. The plane, missing both a flight engineer and a copilot, and overloaded by over two tons, crashed into the Atlantic Ocean immediately after takeoff.

Clemente's body was never found.

Both Pittsburgh and Puerto Rico lost one of their most treasured citizens on December 31, 1972.

On March 20, 1973, the Baseball Writers' Association of America held a special election for the Baseball Hall of Fame, where they voted to waive the waiting period for Clemente and posthumously elected him for immediate induction.

Besides a new stadium and a new divisional and conference alignment, 1970 also brought another change to the Pittsburgh Steelers. It was that year that Myron Cope began his thirty-five-year run in the Steelers' broadcast booth.

Myron Cope was born Myron Sidney Kopelman on January 23, 1929, in Pittsburgh. After graduating from Taylor Allderdice High School, he stayed local and attended the University of Pittsburgh, where he studied journalism.

It was in journalism, as a writer, where Cope left his first marks on both Pittsburgh and the world of sports. His first job was with the *Daily Times* in Erie, Pennsylvania, but in short order, he was back in Pittsburgh with the *Pittsburgh Post-Gazette*.

It wasn't long before Cope became a freelance journalist, adding contributions to notable publications like *Sports Illustrated* and the *Saturday Evening Post* to his work with the *Post-Gazette*.

Cope was a distinguished sportswriter. In 1963, he was awarded the E. P. Dutton Prize for Best Magazine Sportswriting in the Nation for his portrayal of young heavyweight boxing contender Cassius Clay (who changed his name shortly thereafter to Muhammad Ali). Celebrating its fiftieth anniversary in 2004, *Sports Illustrated* selected Cope's 1967 profile of Howard Cosell as one of the fifty best-written articles ever published in its magazine.

As accomplished as Cope was behind the typewriter, Steelers fans best remember him from his time in the broadcasting booth behind the microphone.

In 1968, Cope ventured into radio, voicing daily commentaries for WTAE radio. His distinctive, high-pitched, nasally voice and Pittsburgher accent caught the attention of listeners. Among those listeners were Rooney and other Steelers officials, who, in turn, brought Cope into the Steelers' game-day radio broadcast booth.

Cope immediately endeared himself to Pittsburgh fans as a unique character. He often peppered his commentary with Yiddish expressions, and "Yoi!" became one of his trademark catchphrases, along with "Double Yoi!" and, on those truly extraordinary occasions, "Triple Yoi!"

Cope was also the creator of many a nickname for players, both Steelers and opposing players alike. Additionally, opposing teams weren't immune from his sharp wit and tongue, with the Cincinnati "Bungles" being repeated by sportscasters to this day whenever the Cincinnati Bengals underperform.

While Cope's thirty-five-year broadcasting career would have made him a Pittsburgh-area legend in its own right, what really cemented his status was a bit of common household linen.

In the days leading up to a 1975 playoff game with the Baltimore Colts, Cope wanted to create a simple way to energize the Steelers' fan base, particularly those who would be in attendance at Three Rivers. His idea was to use something everyone already had so as to not require any unnecessary spending. He settled on towels.

Specifically, yellow, gold, or black dish towels. His thought was if fans didn't have a dish towel in one of those colors, they could either go out and buy one or just dye one of the dish towels they likely had lying around the house.

Hence, the Terrible Towel was born. It proved to be popular right away—an immediate hit! It has persevered over the years, and today, it might be the most iconic symbol of professional sports fandom around the globe. If you know a Steelers fan who doesn't have at least one Terrible Towel, you now have an instant holiday gift idea.

In 1996, Cope, whose son was severely autistic, granted his commercial rights to the Terrible Towel to the Allegheny Valley School in Coraopolis, Pennsylvania, an institution that provides service and care to those with intellectual and physical disabilities.

In the summer of 2005, Cope retired from broadcasting, citing ongoing health concerns. The Steelers have never replaced him, deciding instead to continue broadcasting with just a two-person broadcast team.

Myron Cope died of respiratory failure on February 27, 2008, at seventy-nine years of age. He is remembered as a one-of-a-kind Pittsburgher personality and a local treasure.

So the 1970 season promised a new beginning for long-suffering Steelers fans. The team had a sparkling new stadium, a wonderfully wacky radio announcer, and a new quarterback who had been the first overall pick of the NFL Draft.

The Steelers proved to be better than their 1–13 team the season prior, but not tremendously better. Bradshaw, like many rookie quarterbacks throughout the history of professional football, struggled for much of the campaign.

Rather remarkably, Bradshaw was tackled for a safety in each of the Steelers' first three games. How is that even possible?

On the season, Bradshaw completed just 38 percent of his passes and threw twenty-four interceptions, or an interception every nine pass attempts. Given that offensive inefficiency, the Steelers stumbled to a 5–9 record.

In the 1971 NFL Draft, the Steelers selected Frank Lewis, a wide receiver out of Grambling, with their first-round pick. Lewis proved to be a solid, if unspectacular, professional, playing seven years for the Steelers before finishing his career with six seasons with the Buffalo Bills.

However, the 1971 Draft is best remembered by Pittsburgh faithful as the year the club drafted linebacker Jack Ham (round two), defensive end Dwight White (fourth round), defensive tackle Ernie Holmes (eighth round), and defensive back Mike Wagner (eleventh round). Those four players laid the foundation for a fierce Steelers' defense for several years.

The team was getting better, but the building process remained slow. Bradshaw, while improved, continued to struggle in his second season, and he threw twenty-two interceptions against just thirteen touchdowns. The team finished the 1971 season slightly better than the year before, posting a 6–8 record, good enough for second place in the AFC Central Division.

History shows that the pieces of the puzzle were coming together. But Steelers fans were left unaware and resigned themselves to lamenting the "same old Steelers."

Chapter 12

A TEAM ON THE ASCENT, A CITY AT THE PRECIPICE

oll continued to build his Steelers roster with the 1972 NFL Draft, selecting running back Harris in the first round. Additionally, five other selections from the '72 draft class made the team's roster after training camp, including fifth-round choice Steve Furness, a defensive tackle out of Rhode Island who went on to be a solid contributor to the Steelers over ten NFL seasons.

The 1972 season started with an opening game victory against the Raiders at Three Rivers Stadium, a wild 34–28 tilt. The Raiders rolled into the game coming off an 8–4–2 record the season before, aiming to be a playoff-contending team once again. The Steelers jumped on them early, opening up a 17–0 lead early in the second quarter.

After Bradshaw scored on a two-yard run to make the score 24–7 entering the fourth quarter, it looked like the Steelers would open the season with a comfortable win.

Not so fast!

The Raiders stormed back in the fourth quarter to make it interesting, although the Steelers prevailed in the end. Despite allowing twenty-eight points, the defense really saved the day with five forced turnovers on the afternoon.

Opening day enthusiasm evaporated just a week later with a 15–10 loss to the division-rival Bengals in Cincinnati. The offense struggled the entire game, but the defense looked sharp—the only points allowed to the Bengals were five Horst Muhlmann field goals.

With a record level at 1–1, the Steelers played their next two games on the road, defeating the St. Louis Cardinals 25–19 and losing to the Dallas Cowboys 17–13.

From there, Noll and the Steelers went on a tear, rolling off five consecutive victories. The offense, behind both Bradshaw and Harris, began to jell, and the Steelers posted thirty or more points on three consecutive weekends, culminating in a 40–17 thrashing of the Bengals on November 5.

The very next week, the Steelers defeated the Kansas City Chiefs at Three Rivers to run their record to 7–2. Long-suffering Steelers fans were beginning to think this team was for real.

Not even a heart-breaking 26–24 loss to the Browns at Cleveland Memorial Stadium in Week Ten could ebb the tide of optimism for long. The Steelers ran off four consecutive wins at the end of the season, including road victories over the Houston Oilers and San Diego Chargers in the final two weeks.

Then, of course, came the divisional playoff game hosting the Raiders, a rematch of the season-opening game won by the Steelers. The Immaculate Reception and the resultant victory upped the Steelers' record to 12–3, and advanced the club to the AFC Championship Game, just one game away from a berth in Super Bowl VII.

Home field advantage is a big factor in all sports, and the bigger the game, the more important a home field—and a team's crazed, hometown fans—can be in creating a seemingly less-than-level playing field.

In all of today's major sports leagues, the home team designation for playoff games is awarded to teams who have won their division or secured the best regular season record. In 1972, however, the NFL still determined the location of its playoff games based on a divisional rotation, with the exception being the wild card team—the best team outside of the divisional winners in each conference—being required to play on the road. Thus, the Steelers, division champions in their own right and coming off the extraordinary drama of the Immaculate Reception game, were set to host the undefeated Miami Dolphins for the right to represent the AFC in Super Bowl VII.

The 1972 Miami Dolphins might arguably be the best team in NFL history. They rolled through the regular season with a perfect 14–0 record. Their No-Name Defense, named as such for their lack of high-profile players, secured three shutouts over the season, including a 52–0 thumping of the New England Patriots in Week Nine and a regular season-closing 16–0 win over the Baltimore Colts.

The Dolphins had been battle-tested too. They lost starting quarterback Bob Griese to a broken ankle in a Week Five game against the Chargers and played the rest of the season with thirty-eight-year-old veteran journeyman Earl Morrall under center. They were also familiar with playing close, competitive games, too, winning games by one, two, and four points along the way.

Remarkably, the 1972 season was only the seventh season of Dolphins football, and just their third season in the NFL after the league's merger with the AFL. At the helm was head coach Don Shula, who was in his third season leading the team after a successful seven-season run coaching the Baltimore Colts.

The Dolphins had ended the previous season with a stinging 24–3 loss in Super Bowl VI at the hands of the Dallas Cowboys. Having lost to the New York Jets in Super Bowl III while in Baltimore, it was Shula's second Super Bowl defeat, and he and his rock-solid team looked to get over the proverbial hump.

Morrall was steady, if unspectacular, controlling the offense. The real headliners on the Dolphins' offensive side of the ball were its running back trio of Larry Csonka, Mercury Morris, and Jim Kiick. Both Csonka and Morris rushed for over 1,000 yards during the season, the first time NFL teammates had accomplished the feat in the same season. For his part, Kiick posted over 500 rushing yards for good measure.

The Dolphins' No-Name Defense was led by middle linebacker Nick Buoniconti, a future Hall of Famer, and safeties Dick Anderson and Jake Scott. They were a stingy defensive unit, leading the league in allowing just 171 points on the season, just four fewer points allowed than the Steelers themselves. Their forty-six takeaways, or turnovers forced, were second only to the Steelers' forty-eight.

The 1972 AFC Championship Game was set up to be another bruising, defensive-minded affair.

Pittsburgh fans came out in droves, packing Three Rivers for the second consecutive week, eager to cheer their hometown heroes to another victory. A pleasant Pittsburgh winter day greeted the visiting Dolphins, but the fans and the Steelers themselves conspired to make the stadium as ungracious as possible for their fair-weather foes.

The Dolphins began the game in possession of the ball and, being a visiting team in a hostile environment in a critical playoff game, played relatively conservatively on their first handful of plays. Looking to get Csonka and Morris involved in the game early, the Dolphins pushed the ball out to midfield.

However, after a couple of first downs, Morrall tried to catch the Steelers napping, faking a handoff to Csonka and tossing a pass deep downfield. His pass went over the head of his intended receiver and right into the hands of waiting Steelers safety Glen Edwards. Edwards returned the interception past the fifty-yard line, setting up the Steelers' offense with a short field for their first possession.

Like the Dolphins, the Steelers wanted to make a strong first impression with its running attack early in the game, and they set off for the end zone with an impressive eleven-play march, all on the ground. They had their fair share of good fortune along the way.

First, Harris fumbled on a sweep, with the football luckily bouncing out of bounds, allowing the Steelers to keep possession. Then, two plays later, on third down and goal from the two-yard line, Bradshaw took matters into his own hands and tried to sweep around the left side into the end zone. Dolphins safety Scott, however, tackled Bradshaw with a dive at the quarterback's knees. On his way down, Bradshaw fumbled, and the ball rolled into the end zone where . . . it was recovered by offensive tackle Gerry Mullins.

Touchdown Steelers, and with Gerela's extra point, a 7–0 lead! First the Immaculate Reception, and now a fumble recovery in the end zone for a touchdown—maybe, just maybe, the Steelers were destined to be champions.

Initially lost in the celebration though was the fact that Bradshaw laid still on the Tartan Turf of Three Rivers, in visible pain from a shoulder injury suffered on the play. The buzz quickly faded from the stadium; maybe the Steelers weren't so charmed after all.

Still leading 7–0, Bradshaw came out for the Steelers' second possession of the game in a gutsy effort to lead his team. But it was readily apparent that he was injured too badly to be productive for the offense. He ended up sitting out the entire second quarter, turning the reins of the offense over to backup quarterback Terry Hanratty.

The Steelers' defense was still carrying its share and then some. They were allowing the Dolphins to find some moderate success in the running and short passing game, but they were locking them down once the ball got to midfield.

Then, on a fourth down late in the first quarter, the course of the game changed completely.

Receiving the snap, Dolphins punter Larry Seiple took a couple of steps in an apparent kicking motion, but also alertly looked at the Steelers rush. When the Steelers turned to run back and block for a punt return, Seiple took off running, first up the middle and then slanting to the right.

Seiple's fake punt surprised the entire stadium—Shula included. His thirty-seven-yard run advanced the ball to the twelve-yard line, and led to a Morrall touchdown pass to Csonka in short time, tying the game at 7–7.

The first half ended in that tie, with each team's defense rising to the occasion and putting the clamps on the opponent's offense. It was apparent that this game featured two evenly matched teams.

The Steelers started the third quarter with Hanratty blasting out of the gates immediately. After shaking off the cobwebs from his inactivity as Bradshaw's season-long backup, Hanratty completed two long passes. Then, changing the pace, he handed the ball off to Fuqua on a delayed draw run, and Fuqua's twenty-four-yard scamper to the Dolphins' fourteen-yard line was the Steelers' third straight gain of twenty or more yards.

The opening drive of the half stalled near the goal line, and the Steelers had to settle for a short field goal by Gerela and a 10–7 lead. It proved to be the last Steeler lead of the game.

Shula brought the still-recovering Griese into the game at quarterback, and his decision paid immediate rewards. Griese completed a short pass to receiver Paul Warfield that turned into a fifty-two-yard catch and run, and the Dolphins had created some offensive momentum.

Steeler linebacker Ham seemed to abruptly halt that momentum with an interception of Griese. However, an offsides penalty called on defensive end White negated the play. Instead of Steelers ball, the Dolphins retained possession deep in Steelers territory.

A few plays later, Kiick scored on a two-yard run, and the Dolphins had their first lead of the game. After that, the No-Name Defense got back to making it tough on Hanratty and the Steelers. They began to exert their dominance, and when Miami's special teams blocked a long field goal attempt by Gerela, everything seemed to be falling the way of the Dolphins.

Kiick tacked on another short touchdown run, this one from three yards out, and the Dolphins were up eleven points after Garo Yepremian's extra point, 21–10.

Bradshaw courageously returned to the game, and in less than two minutes, led the Steelers to a touchdown, a drive capped by a nifty one-handed catch by second-year receiver Al Young.

The Steelers' defense quickly forced the Dolphins to punt, and with three minutes left, Bradshaw and the offense took over, looking for another miraculous, last-minute playoff victory. The Dolphins had other designs in mind. Linebacker Buoniconti intercepted a third-down Bradshaw pass at midfield.

The relentless Dolphin rushing game looked to put the game on ice, running out the clock. They marched down toward the Steelers' goal line, precious seconds ticking off the game clock along the way. But on fourth down and one from the Steeler nine-yard line, Steelers safety Edwards stopped Csonka in his tracks.

With less than a minute left, the Steelers had possession, ninety yards away from a go-ahead score. After the Immaculate Reception the week before, anything was possible, right? Would there be another miracle at Three Rivers?

Pittsburgh's dreams ended when Dolphin linebacker Mike Kolen intercepted an underthrown Bradshaw pass intended for Young.

The Steelers' best-ever, storybook-like season had come to a sudden end, concluding without a fairytale ending. But they had grittily played through a hard-luck injury to their starting quarterback and went toe-to-toe, blow-to-blow with a Dolphins team that concluded its season two weeks later with a 14–7 victory over the Washington Redskins, completing what is still the only undefeated season in NFL history.

Surprisingly, Rooney's football team had risen from the "same old Steelers" to become the pride of Pittsburgh. The 1972 season proved the team was set to take its place among the NFL's best.

For the city of Pittsburgh and the entire region, at the same time, storm clouds were brewing on the distant horizon. As they closed in, they would prove to rattle the city and its citizens to their very core.

Like the late 1960s before it, the early 1970s were a tumultuous time in United States history. Nearly all national news was viewed through the context of dual filters, one being the continuation of a highly unpopular war in Vietnam; the other being a menacing threat of the Cold War with the Soviet Union escalating beyond the stockpiling of enormous quantities of atomic weapons.

The Vietnam War started in the 1950s, and its origins came from the French colonization of the country in the late 1800s, what France called French Indochina. From there, the entire region morphed into a powder keg beginning early in the 1920s.

Future president Hồ Chí Minh, who probably spent time as a baker at Boston's famed Parker House Hotel in 1912, was trained in the Soviet Union in the early 1920s as an agent of the Communist International, an international organization that advocated world communism. In 1930, Hồ was instrumental in the formation of the Indochinese Communist Party at a meeting in Hong Kong.

Later in the decade, of course, World War II erupted throughout Europe. In 1940, Nazi Germany occupied France. With its attention firmly rooted in dire matters within its own country's borders, the French had nothing left to protect its interests in French Indochina, which included Laos and Cambodia. Seeing an open opportunity, the Japanese pounced and invaded.

In response, Hồ Chi Minh and his colleagues established the League for the Independence of Vietnam, also known as Viet Minh, and proactively began a resistance against both Japanese and French control of his ancestral homeland.

In early 1945, the Japanese announced the end of the French colonial era and declared Vietnam, Laos, and Cambodia independent. However, just a few months later, on August 14, 1945, US President Harry S. Truman accepted Japan's unconditional surrender that ceased the military actions of World War II. The conclusion of the war and the elimination of Japan's military might created a power vacuum in the French Indochina region, and it caught the fervent attention of governments around the globe.

France wanted its colony back. Hồ declared the independence of North Vietnam and modeled his declaration on the United States' own Declaration of Independence, in what proved to be a futile effort to win the support of the US. On polar opposites, Hồ and the French could not, or would not, come to terms, and Hồ began a guerilla war against the French occupiers.

Communism grew, and the United States' fear of the spread of communism grew proportionately. Truman introduced foreign policy doctrine that made it the United States' duty to assist any country in peril of falling into communism. Shortly thereafter, communist leader Mao Zedong declared the creation of the People's Republic of China after twenty-plus years of intermittent civil war. In the meantime, the Soviet Union developed and tested its first atomic weapons.

Together, in January 1950, both the People's Republic of China and the Soviet Union formally recognized Hồ's communist Democratic Republic of Vietnam and began to supply economic and military aid to communist fighters within Vietnam. In return, the United States felt it had no other recourse than to identify the Viet Minh as a clear communist threat, and as a result, foreign policy dictated a significant increase in American military aid provided to France for their own operations.

Over the next few years, the Viet Minh made progress, and rather surprisingly, they fought to an improbable victory in the nearly two-month battle of Dien Bien Phu in 1954. That victory essentially marked the end of French colonial rule in Vietnam.

It was during that battle that US President Dwight D. Eisenhower stated the fall of Vietnam into the hands of communist rule would result in a domino effect of other countries subsequently falling into communism, thereby contributing a direct threat to the American way of life. That "domino theory" would guide the United States' involvement in the Vietnam conflict to its very end.

US soldiers began to get killed in Vietnam in 1959, the first of over 58,000 US military fatalities of the Vietnam War.

Almost from the very start, the Vietnam War was a political lightning rod in the United States, spanning the administrations of five American presidents. It was the first conflict with American troops where, nightly, the news divisions of national television networks broadcasted graphic video images of frontline combat directly into households across the country.

As the horror of warfare became daily news, opposition to the war effort grew, and American servicemen and servicewomen often drew the blunt end. It was a very different era than that of World War II or the more recent armed conflicts in the Persian Gulf and other countries where the war on terror has been fought. Returning military personnel weren't being welcomed home with applause and gratitude—conversely, there were numerous reports in the media of returning service personnel being spat upon at airports.

There were high-profile dissents from celebrity ranks, as well. Heavyweight champion Muhammad Ali engaged in a lengthy battle against the legality of the military draft based on his conscientious objector status, an act that caused him to be stripped of his title and put his boxing career on hold for three years.

Even more controversially, activist actress Jane Fonda visited troops in 1972—North Vietnamese troops. Her trip to Hanoi, which led to the creation of the derisive nickname "Hanoi Jane," included multiple radio appearances where she spoke out against American military policy in Vietnam and also featured a well-publicized photograph of her sitting on an anti-aircraft gun, giving the impression to some she was prepared to shoot down American planes.

The Vietnam War certainly had its impact on the country's economy too. Immediately after World War II, the country's economy flourished. However, by the 1960s, it had begun to slow down.

By nature, Eisenhower was a conservative leader, and his administration's policies had ushered in a cautious period of growth; the economy was growing but in steps rather than the leaps of the 1950s.

President John F. Kennedy and his modern-day Camelot brought a country-wide swell of pride and enthusiasm, and the administration inspired big, bold, and audacious challenges—like winning the space race with the Soviets and sending astronauts to the moon. The Kennedy administration was steadfast in its goals to stimulate rapid growth of the economy, reduce unemployment, and, of course, position the United States as the worldwide leader in the advocacy of democracy over communism.

After Kennedy's life was cut short on the afternoon of November 22, 1963, Lyndon Johnson ascended to the role of president and looked to continue Kennedy's political agenda, including eradicating poverty, obtaining equal rights for racial minorities and women, and winning the Vietnam War.

History affords the luxury of hindsight, and looking back at the decade of the 1960s, it's quite apparent there was a lot going on. A *lot*. Something had to give, and it turned out the economy bore the brunt of blowback. As a result, ultimately, the country's citizens were the ones that would be left holding the short straw.

There was massive government spending on infrastructure, social initiatives, and the war. At the same time, there was a determined effort to create jobs, designed to generate full employment for the country's workforce. Stoking it all was an "easy money" monetary policy, where the US Federal Reserve freed up the money supply, allowing cash to flood the nation's banking system.

The US dollar, for the first time ever, lost its stability. Coupled with the constraints of the international monetary system as a whole, the result was a significant increase in domestic inflation in the United States. The year 1965 marked the beginning of a period in US economic history that is now called The Great Inflation.

For context, consider the following. In 1964, inflation was 1 percent, and unemployment was 5 percent. Ten years later, in 1974, inflation would be over 12 percent and unemployment above 7 percent.

The entire country would feel the pain, and Pittsburghers would not be immune. Furthermore, domestic economic conditions would get worse before they got better. By mid-1980, inflation would soar to nearly 14.5 percent, and unemployment would approach 8 percent.

The war was a divisive issue across the country, but all Americans were concerned about the rising cost of living. For their part, industries, including Pittsburgh's steel titans, feared the ongoing rise in the cost of production, from expensive labor to more and more expensive raw materials, especially petroleum.

The Vietnam war and the domestic economy would prove to be pivotal in both the 1968 and 1972 US presidential elections. Emotionally and physically fatigued by the crisis in Vietnam, Johnson chose not to seek the Democratic Party's nomination in the 1968 race after only narrowly winning the party's first primary in New Hampshire. With Johnson out of the race, his vice president, Hubert Humphrey, would get the nod.

On the Republican side, former Vice President Richard Nixon earned his party's nomination over liberal New York Governor Nelson Rockefeller and conservative California Governor, and future president, Ronald Reagan.

The election year of 1968 was extraordinarily volatile. In April, civil rights leader Martin Luther King Jr. was assassinated, and widespread riots subsequently embroiled communities across the country. Two months later, former US Attorney General and sitting New York Senator Robert F. Kennedy, brother to former President Kennedy, was assassinated.

As if that wasn't enough, American casualties were stacking up in Vietnam, beginning with the defense against North Vietnam's deadly Tet Offensive in January. Throughout the election year, there were almost constant protests on college campuses nationwide in opposition to the escalating conflict in Vietnam.

In the first presidential election after the passage of the Voting Rights Act of 1965, the federal legislation that prohibited racial discrimination in voting, Nixon easily won the electoral college after narrowly winning the popular vote.

Over Nixon's first term, the Vietnam War continued to rage on, and the economy continued to worsen. In November 1968, the Dow Jones Industrial Average, the price-weighted market index of stock exchanges in the United States, was at 8,000 points. After falling as low as 5,000 points in June 1970, it was still below 7,000 points by election day in 1972.

Despite troubles at home and abroad, incumbent Nixon handily defeated Democratic challenger George McGovern in the 1972 election, in what is still the largest margin of victory in any presidential election. Nixon sidestepped inflationary concerns by touting the strength of employment and his vast experience in foreign affairs. McGovern ran his campaign on the promise of an immediate end to American involvement in Vietnam and a guaranteed minimum income for US citizens.

American voters responded to Nixon, and he won nearly 61 percent of the popular vote and forty-nine of the fifty states in his landslide victory. Left completely unsettled at the time of the election was the arrest of five men on charges of attempted burglary and attempted interception of telephone and other communications at the offices of the Democratic National Committee's headquarters in the Watergate Complex in Washington, DC.

So, as the Steelers' season came to a disappointing end on the last day of 1972, there remained a still unbridled enthusiasm for the team and its promising future. However, Pittsburghers, while seemingly safe and secure with jobs aplenty in the steel industry-dependent region, were faced with an increasingly high cost of living and a murky national political scene.

Any story of the Pittsburgh Steelers without mention of running back Rocky Bleier would be incomplete, for his legacy epitomizes both the team and the city: tough, resourceful, and often underrated. Within the context of the Vietnam War, any omission of Bleier would be grossly inadequate and just downright inexcusable.

Robert Bleier was born March 5, 1946, in Appleton, Wisconsin, the oldest of four children. As an infant, young Robert was stocky, well-built, and muscular. His father's friends would inquire how his "little rock" was doing, and the nickname "Rocky" was born.

In high school, Bleier was a standout basketball player. However, he really shined on the gridiron, starring as a three-time All-State selection as a running back, in addition to receiving All-Conference honors at both linebacker and defensive back. His football prowess earned him a spot at Notre Dame, where, after helping the Fighting Irish win the national championship as a junior, he served as a team captain his senior year.

The Steelers drafted Bleier in the sixteenth round of the 1968 NFL Draft, the 417th overall pick. Local legend has it Rooney drafted Bleier not necessarily for his football skills, but also on the assumption that having gone to Notre Dame, Bleier was Catholic.

Bleier wasn't; he was Presbyterian. So much for the religious connection.

By all accounts, Bleier was a longshot to make the Steelers roster; after all, he was a sixteenth-round selection. Keep in mind, today's NFL Draft consists of just seven rounds.

Compared to his NFL brethren, Bleier was relatively small in physical stature, and he wasn't particularly fast. But he was intelligent and a hard worker, and he seemed to always be in the correct position, making the correct decision on the field.

Remarkably, Bleier overcame the long adds and made the 1968 Steelers roster. In his rookie season, he appeared in ten games, carrying the ball six times for thirty-nine yards and tacking on three receptions for another sixty-eight yards in the Steelers' dismal 2–11–1 campaign.

Just before the conclusion of his rookie season, on December 4, 1968, Bleier was drafted into the US Army. In May 1969, as his Steelers teammates were preparing to go to training camp, Bleier was shipped out to Vietnam, assigned as a squad grenadier to Company C, 4th Battalion (Light), 31st Infantry, 196th Light Infantry Brigade.

While on patrol on August 20, 1969, Bleier's platoon was ambushed, and he was shot in his left thigh. While he was down and tending to his wound, an enemy grenade landed nearby, and when it exploded, shrapnel blasted throughout his lower right leg, leading him to lose part of his right foot. For his military service, Bleier was awarded both the Bronze Star and a Purple Heart.

During his recovery, doctors advised Bleier that playing football was likely no longer in his future. Coping with his injuries and an uncertain future, Bleier received a postcard from Rooney while he was in a hospital in Tokyo. The Chief simply wrote, "Rock—the team's not doing well. We need you."

It was the spark that reignited Bleier's competitive fire.

Bleier started the rehabilitation of his injuries and joined his Steelers teammates at training camp in 1970. However, his ordeal had caused him to lose a substantial amount of weight, all of it muscle mass, and he weighed just 180 pounds. Additionally, he still could not walk without pain, much less run.

The Steelers placed Bleier on the injured reserve list, and he sat out the entire 1970 season as he continued his rehabilitation.

With unwavering commitment, Bleier continued to work hard on his physical recovery and conditioning, and he returned for the 1971 season in much better shape. He made the roster as a reserve running back and special teams player, and he suited up for six games.

A victory of sorts, for sure, but Bleier was not done yet. Not by a long shot.

On the 1972 Steelers team, Bleier was again a special teams contributor, suiting up for every game of the season. On the 1973 team, Bleier was released on a couple of occasions but brought back to again contribute on special teams.

Throughout this long period of repeated trials and tribulations, almost five years since his injuries, Bleier continued to pursue his dreams with his trademark fiery determination. His endless days of hard work and worrisome nights began to pay off in 1974.

At training camp in 1974, Bleier was a stout, rock-like 212 pounds, and his impressive showings in practice and preseason games earned him a slot in the Steelers' starting lineup. Ostensibly a blocking back for Harris, who was, in fact, three inches taller and twenty pounds heavier, Bleier also became a potent offensive threat with the ball. By the end of the 1976 season, at thirty years of age, Bleier was a 1,000-yard rusher in his own right, pairing with Harris in the second-ever backfield to feature two backs to hit that milestone in the same season.

Bleier played a key role in the Steelers' first four Super Bowl-winning seasons. In Super Bowl XII, he caught a touchdown pass from Bradshaw that gave the Steelers a lead they would never relinquish, and his recovery of Dallas' onside kick in the waning moments of that same game sealed the team's third Super Bowl victory.

In the NFL, thirty years of age is getting up there for those in the running back position. Bleier's playing time shrunk over the 1979 and 1980 seasons, but he was still a key contributor both on the playing field come game day and as a leader in the locker room and practice field. After the 1980 season and the Steelers' fourth Super Bowl championship, Bleier retired from football.

Rocky Bleier overcame almost impossible odds to become a revered Pittsburgh legend. Throughout his illustrious eleven-season career, including those three limited seasons when he was in the throes of recovering from his wartime injuries, Bleier amassed 3,865 yards rushing and 1,294 receiving yards, with twenty-five total touchdowns scored. He played in eighteen playoff games, gaining 682 total yards and crossing the goal line six times, and he contributed mightily to those four Super Bowl-winning teams.

Rocky Bleier was inducted into the Steelers Hall of Honor in 2018.

Chapter 13

KNOCKING ON THE DOOR

The Steelers entered the 1973 offseason with a strong sense of optimism. Sure, their improbable championship dreams the season before had been dashed by the Dolphins. But, then again, the Dolphins had been the only undefeated championship team in NFL history, and it had taken a tough, spirited game to get by the young, gritty Steelers.

The 1972 team had definitely not been the "same old Steelers," and Rooney, Noll, and company were determined to keep the momentum going.

In the 1973 NFL Draft, the team added to its already strong defense with its selections of defensive back JT Thomas in the first round and linebacker Loren Toews in the eighth round. With the taste of the previous season's success in their mouths, the Steelers, led by its Steel Curtain defense, were hungry for more.

In their opener at home against the Detroit Lions, the Steelers, perhaps still wiping the sleep out of their eyes, stumbled out to a 3–0 halftime lead. The Lions made it a ballgame tying the score at 10–10 in the third quarter, but the Steelers' quality and depth showed in the fourth quarter, and the Black and Gold pulled away to win 24–10. In a foreshadowing of what was to come, the defense shined that day, limiting the Lions to 301 total yards of offense, sacking Lion quarterback Greg Landry four times, and intercepting three of Landry's passes.

Having worked out the rust against the Lions, the Steelers dominated their next three games, thrashing the Cleveland Browns (33–6), the Houston Oilers (36–7), and the San Diego Chargers (38–21) in short order. The offense was efficiently scoring points, but it was the defense that was the real story, squeezing the life out of opponents' offenses with an anaconda-like ruthlessness.

During those three games, the Steel Curtain gave up 208, 178, and 348 yards respectively, and forced a collective fourteen turnovers. And the only reason the Chargers put up some points and collected some yards was that the Steelers somewhat coasted through the fourth quarter after dashing out to a 38–0 lead.

The fast start set up a Week Five showdown with the division-rival Bengals at Cincinnati's Riverfront Stadium. There, the Steelers ran into a methodical buzz saw.

Cincinnati attacked the Steelers' defense with a disciplined running game, but the Steel Curtain kept the Bengals out of the end zone in the first half, limiting them to three short field goals. Meanwhile, the Bengals' defense was giving Bradshaw and company all they could handle, and then some.

Harris sat out the game because of an injury suffered the week before, and the Steelers proved to be rather inept without him. For the day, they put up only 138 yards of total offense, and that included a sixty-seven-yard pass completion to Ron Shanklin. On the ground, the Steelers were limited to only seventy-one yards on twenty-two carries.

Spotting the Bengals a 19–0 lead, the Steelers finally got on the scoreboard on a one-yard touchdown run by running back Preston Pearson. Too little, too late, however, and the Steelers returned home nursing the wounds of a 19–7 defeat.

The Steelers quickly rebounded though, reeling off victories in their next four games, including a rematch against the Bengals in Three Rivers just two weeks after their first matchup.

In the return tilt with the Bengals on the last Sunday of October, the battle for divisional supremacy was a similarly hard-hitting contest, only this time with a different outcome. Harris had returned the week before and had delivered a standout game against the Jets, rushing for over one hundred yards and a touchdown. Against the Bengals, he was somewhat stymied though, rushing for just forty-three yards on twenty-one carries.

Despite being hemmed in, Harris still contributed to an opportunistic offense. Backup quarterback Hanratty excelled in relief of an injured Bradshaw, and his fifty-one-yard touchdown pass to Shanklin in the second quarter put the Steelers ahead for good. The Steel Curtain again reigned supreme, forcing five turnovers and limiting the Bengals to 318 yards of total offense and one touchdown, the final score in a well-earned 20–13 Steelers victory.

Against the Washington Redskins the very next week, a nationally televised *Monday Night Football* game at Three Rivers, the Steelers prevailed 21–16 despite the four interceptions thrown by Hanratty and Joe Gilliam, both pressed into duty in the continued absence of Bradshaw. Once again, the story of the game was the Steelers' defense, with the unit forcing four turnovers and limiting the Redskins to less than 200 yards of offense.

With a dominating defense and a record of 7–1, all eyes were on the Steelers as they headed west to play the Oakland Raiders in a Week Nine rematch of the

Immaculate Reception game. The game between the two protagonists would be the third time squaring off in only fourteen months; the clubs knew each other very well.

The Raiders were still smarting from the Immaculate Reception call, believing that it should have been ruled an incomplete pass and they should have been awarded the ball to run out the clock and take the victory. They hadn't forgotten, not by a long shot, and neither had their fans. Heck, fifty years later, Raider Nation *still* hasn't gotten over the Immaculate Reception.

Fans of the Silver and Black flooded into Oakland-Alameda County Coliseum for the afternoon game, and they were treated to another hard-hitting affair on a sloppy grass field.

Hanratty started the game in place of the injured Bradshaw once again, and he struggled through most of the afternoon, completing just six of nineteen passes for a paltry eighty-six yards through the air. On the other sideline, the Raiders had quarterback issues of their own. Their starter, Ken Stabler, could only play the first quarter before an injured knee sent him to the sideline, turning the duties of leading the league's top-rated offense to the quarterback who started the Immaculate Reception game, Daryle Lamonica.

Lamonica had a few moments, including a twenty-seven-yard touchdown strike to Biletnikoff in the fourth quarter to close the scoring. But the Steel Curtain had a great many more moments, harassing Lamonica nearly non-stop, racking up five sacks in total and intercepting four of his passes—two of them by defensive end Dwight White. While the Steelers recovered only one Raiders fumble, they caused another four, further disrupting the Raiders' offense in another dominant display. That impenetrable defense allowed the Steelers to squelch any thought of a Raiders' revenge, and the Steelers were rewarded with a 17–9 victory.

Nine games into the 1973 season, the Steelers were 8–1 and sitting comfortably atop the AFC's Central Division with a two-and-a-half game lead over the Cleveland Browns.

As part of ongoing peace negotiations, President Nixon suspended US military offensive actions in Vietnam just a couple of weeks into 1973. Three days after he was sworn into his second term as president, Nixon announced a peace treaty had been agreed upon. Four days later, the Paris Peace Accords were signed, signaling the end of US involvement in Vietnam.

A dark cloud in American history was beginning to dissipate. Others were brewing in its wake.

Politically, G. Gordon Liddy was found guilty on counts of conspiracy, burglary, and illegal wiretapping for his role in the Watergate scandal, just three days after the administration celebrated the success of the Peace Accords. The chief operative in the covert White House Special Investigations Unit, also referred to as the White House Plumbers, Liddy's conviction only intensified the already explosive scandal.

Over the spring and summer, Nixon, looking for scapegoats and trying to quell the growing scandal, fired White House Counsel John Dean and accepted the resignation of Attorney General Richard Kleindienst and his staffers, HR Haldeman and John Ehrlichman. Televised hearings began, and it wouldn't be long before Dean testified. Even more condemning for the president was the testimony of former White House aide, Alexander Butterfield, who informed the investigative committee that Nixon had secretly recorded incriminating conversations.

Excruciatingly for the American public, the White House drama dragged along. Beleaguered by an investigation of criminal conspiracy, bribery, extortion, and tax fraud during his time as Baltimore County Executive and Governor of Maryland, Vice President Spiro Agnew resigned his office on October 10, replaced by Gerald Ford. Although never implicated in the Watergate scandal, his no-contest plea to a charge of tax evasion was another black eye on the Nixon Administration.

Just a week and a half later came the so-called "Saturday Night Massacre," when Nixon ordered Attorney General Elliot Richardson to dismiss Watergate Special Prosecutor Archibald Cox. Richardson, for his part, refused and, along with Deputy Attorney General William Ruckelshaus, submitted his resignation. Those actions left Solicitor General Robert Bork, third in line at the Department of Justice, to fire Cox, which he dutifully did.

Chaos erupted on the US political scene, and immediate calls for Nixon's impeachment rang out. A few weeks later, Nixon uttered his famous words, "I am not a crook."

Economically, the US dollar was devalued as part of the continuation of Nixon's policies initiated in his first term. The aftereffects of those policies are referred to by historians as the "Nixon Shock," and very notably, it led to the dissolution of the Bretton Woods system of fixed exchange rates that went into effect after World War II.

Needing to win elections, Nixon's policies were centered on creating more and better jobs to protect against a skyrocketing cost of living, as well as protecting the dollar from speculators in the international money markets. Economists continue to debate the merits and aftereffects of those policies. At the time, though, the actions of Nixon and his administration were viewed as a political success, an America-versus-the-world type of story.

Still, Pittsburghers, like all Americans, felt the pain of stagflation, the wicked combination of high inflation rates, slowing economic growth rates, and a steadily high unemployment rate. Overall, the American economy was writing checks it couldn't cash. Sooner or later, the bill was going to come due, and it wasn't going to be pretty.

Even more worrisome was the direction of the steel industry, and the chinks in the industry's armor were becoming not only more visible but more troublesome as well. Like the confluence of Pittsburgh's rivers, multiple factors combined to put increasing pressure on the industry.

Partially in response to Nixon's policies as related to the gold standard, the twelve member countries who made up the Organization of the Petroleum Exporting Countries, better known as OPEC, instituted an embargo on October 19, 1973, where they stopped the exportation of oil to the United States. Domestic US oil producers were already at full capacity, and they were unable to take up the slack.

Over the next six months, oil prices quadrupled. In turn, gas prices skyrocketed, and long lines of cars queuing to have their tanks filled before prices went even higher—or stations ran out of fuel completely—became a common sight across the country.

Rising fuel prices only aggravated the inflationary environment. With more money spent on fuel, Americans had less money to spend on other goods and services, and that lower demand, coupled with plummeting consumer confidence, ushered in a recession that didn't ease until 1975.

Desperate to uncover a monetary policy solution, the Federal Reserve Board began a series of interest rate adjustments, both up and down, in a futile attempt to find a silver bullet-like solution. However, with interest rates bouncing up and down, it became almost impossible for companies, including those in the capital-intensive steel industry, to effectively plan their operations.

The post-World War II boom in construction projects around the country had been the catalyst for an enormous expansion of the domestic steel industry, particularly those plants in the Pittsburgh area (as well as those in Youngstown, Ohio; Gary, Indiana, and other steel-making cities). Those massive facilities were incorporated around machinery and methods that were rapidly becoming outdated. Global competitors in Japan and Germany, assisted in part by American post-war reconstruction aid, were gaining an advantage with more efficient (i.e., less costly) manufacturing capabilities.

On the raw materials side, no relief was to be found for Pittsburgh steelmakers either. In fact, depleted coke and iron ore deposits in the region only exacerbated the situation.

Finally, there was labor and its historically hostile relationship with management across the steel industry. There have been several books that have explored in depth the contentious relationship between management and organized labor in the steel industry, and neither side comes off looking very good. The action of both parties resulted in a race to the bottom.

In a recessionary period, with rising materials and transportation costs, increasing competition from both global concerns and domestic, union-free "mini-mills," and outdated, inefficient machinery and processes, labor costs were threatening to be the proverbial straw that broke the camel's back. However, union labor was not going to be the first to acquiesce, and they steadfastly resisted any talk of wage cuts.

The year 1973 would prove to be the year that steel production peaked in the United States, when 111.4 million tons were produced.

The Steelers returned from their triumphant victory over the Raiders in Oakland to host the Denver Broncos the very next Sunday. With Bradshaw still unable to play, the Steelers' struggles on the offensive side of the ball finally came back to haunt them.

The teams traded field goals in each of the first two quarters, heading into the locker rooms at halftime deadlocked, 6–6. The Steelers' field goals were both short attempts by Gerela, from fifteen and thirteen yards out, respectively. The Broncos' defense bucked up and held when it mattered most, keeping Harris and company away from pay dirt.

The Broncos scored the game's first touchdown in the third quarter, but Hanratty leveled the game again with a forty-seven-yard touchdown strike to Shanklin.

Having feasted on turnovers all year long, the Steelers' defense could not force the Broncos into a costly mistake. To compound matters, Steelers ball carriers were uncharacteristically butterfingered, fumbling three times and losing possession on each occasion. The Broncos pulled away with ten points scored in the fourth quarter to earn a 23–13 victory, dropping the Steelers to 8–2.

With four games left in the season, the Steelers were still in first place in the division and in control of their own destiny. They couldn't, however, capitalize on the opportunity.

They lost the next week in Cleveland, against the Browns, 21–16. Despite getting only ten first downs, gaining just 250 yards in total offense, and turning the ball over four times to the Steelers, the Browns won by maximizing their few opportunities, scoring touchdowns instead of settling for field goals.

Being opportunistic against a stingy Steelers' defense paid off for the Browns. The Steelers, conversely, led by quarterback Joe Gilliam in relief of Hanratty, moved the ball up and down the field, gaining 380 yards. But when close to the end zone, their momentum was stifled by the Browns, and they had to settle for Gerela field goals of fourteen, twenty, and twenty-four yards. It was the difference in the ballgame, and now, with a record of 8–3, the Steelers were falling back into the grasp of the resurgent Bengals, winners of three straight and holders of a 7–4 record.

Week Twelve wouldn't bring a reprieve to the Steelers, though, for they had to visit Miami and face off against the defending Super Bowl champion Dolphins.

Fresh off their undefeated campaign the season before, the Dolphins had lost their second game of the season, on the road, against the Oakland Raiders. They hadn't lost since, reeling off nine consecutive victories ahead of hosting the Steelers in a nationally televised *Monday Night Football* game.

The game was the first-ever career start of Joe Gilliam, and he had a horrible game. He didn't complete any of his seven passes. Worse, he threw three interceptions in those seven passes, all of them picked off by safety Anderson, one of which he returned thirty-eight yards for a touchdown.

After Anderson's "Pick Six" score, the Dolphins had a 27–0 lead in the second quarter. Noll plucked Gilliam from the fire and replaced him with the not fully mended Bradshaw. With Bradshaw under center, the Steelers mounted a furious comeback.

Down 30–3 at halftime, the Steelers roared back. The defense did its part, dominating the Dolphins' offense, allowing only eight first downs and just 189 yards of total offense the entire night. Bradshaw, guiding a pass-heavy offense required to play catch-up, threw two touchdown passes, and Harris, who rushed for 105 yards, added a scoring run. When White sacked Griese in the end zone for a safety and two points, the Steelers had clawed their way back to just a 30–26 deficit.

Alas, the Dolphins held on, and the Steelers dropped their third straight game, falling into a tie with the Bengals atop the division with an 8–4 record.

The Bengals' last two games were against their cross-state rivals, the Cleveland Browns, and the hapless Houston Oilers, who had won only one game all season. Luckily, the Steelers got a shot at the Oilers also, in Week Thirteen, and the divisional rival from Texas proved to be just the team with which to get the Steelers back to their winning ways.

Pittsburgh outclassed the over-matched Oilers after a back-and-forth first quarter, reeling off thirty unanswered points to close out the game easily, 33–7.

The Steelers rushed for nearly 200 yards, and the defense was up to its task, exceeding even its high standards, causing nine Oilers turnovers—five fumbles and four interceptions—on the way to relinquishing only eighty-three yards of total offense.

The final game of the regular season saw the Steelers travel back to the northern California Bay area, this time as visitors to Candlestick Park, the home of the San Francisco 49ers. The defense had its way with the 49ers' offense, forcing six turnovers and allowing just one offensive touchdown, the last score of the game.

It took a little over a quarter to work off the jet lag, but once the Steelers' offense got rolling, they stretched a 7–7 tie in the second quarter to a 37–7 fourth-quarter lead and left the west coast with a very convincing 37–14 victory.

The win in San Francisco lifted the Steelers' record to 10–4. Unfortunately, the Bengals also won their final game of the season, holding off a furious fourth-quarter comeback from the Oilers, to also finish the season with a 10–4 record. By virtue of a better record against AFC opponents, the Bengals earned the Central Division title. The reward: a first-round matchup with the defending Super Bowl champion Miami Dolphins, winners of the AFC East Division with a 12–2 record.

Securing second in the Central Division earned the Steelers a wild card berth in the playoffs. Their opponent was to be the winners of the AFC West Division, the Oakland Raiders, in a rematch of not only Week Nine but also of the previous year's Immaculate Reception game.

Any professional football historian debating the best-ever defensive unit would have to consider the 1973 Pittsburgh Steelers. No matter how small the list of candidates might be on that best-ever list, the Steel Curtain deserves its place.

The Steelers' defense presented a nightmare matchup for quarterbacks. Opponent signal callers completed only 45.7 percent of their passes, for just 1,923 yards throughout the fourteen-game regular season, a measly 5.36 yards per pass attempt. Opposing quarterbacks managed to throw just eleven touchdown passes against— get a load of this statistic—thirty-seven Steelers inceptions!

In the complicated formula used to determine quarterback passer ratings, the Steel Curtain rated a 33.1, still an NFL record for the Super Bowl era of the NFL.

Eleven members of the defense recorded interceptions, and safety Wagner led the team with eight, tied for the league lead with Miami's Anderson. Including recovered fumbles, the Steelers led the league with an astonishing fifty-five takeaways. Additionally, eight players recorded one or more sacks, and defensive end L.C. Greenwood led the way with 8.5 of the team's total of thirty-three.

The old adage states that "defense wins championships." The Steelers headed off on a return trip to Oakland looking to prove just that.

Finishing second place in the division and qualifying for the playoffs as the wild card team meant the Steelers would have to travel over 2,500 miles to their second game in seven days—and their third game in six weeks—in the Bay area in northern California. Having beaten the Raiders three times previously in the past seventeen months, Rooney's club was confident.

On the Raiders side, they entered the game believing they had to play great defense and special teams, for they knew the strength of the Steel Curtain first-hand from their Week Nine drubbing on the same field.

The Raiders received the early afternoon kickoff and, trying to avoid the potent Steeler pass rush and dangerous secondary, set off to establish an effective running game. And did they ever.

The Raiders offensive line dominated the line of scrimmage, opening holes for Raiders runners. The result was a sixteen-play, eighty-two-yard drive for the game's first score, a grinding one-yard plunge by Marv Hubbard. The possession milked almost ten minutes off the game clock and staked the Raiders to a 7–0 lead.

The Steelers, on the other hand, had difficulty getting their running game started, a theme that would continue throughout most of the afternoon. Forced by the Raiders' defense to turn to a short passing game to earn first downs and move the sticks, Bradshaw found moderate success. But just when the Steelers looked to generate some momentum on offense late in the first quarter, a deflected Bradshaw pass found its way into the arms of Raiders linebacker Phil Villapiano. The interception ended a promising drive, and the quarter subsequently ended with the Raiders leading 7–0.

Early in the second quarter, Stabler had the Raiders on the move and threatening to score another touchdown when Greene's strong bull rush up the middle forced him to scramble to his right, where end Greenwood and linebacker Russell met him and planted him for a big loss. Having to settle for a short Blanda field goal, the Raiders extended their lead to 10–0.

In the closing minutes of the first half, Bradshaw got the Steelers' offense moving. Big chunks of yardage came courtesy of a twenty-four-yard completion to Preston Pearson and a roughing-the-passer call on the Raiders' defense. With the ball on the four-yard line, Bradshaw connected on a pass in the short right flat to receiver Barry Pearson, who narrowly got over the goal line before being tackled out of bounds. Despite being thoroughly outplayed over the first thirty minutes, the Steelers entered halftime trailing only 10–7.

The Raiders' offensive game plan was keyed around preventing the turnovers that had plagued Steelers' opponents all season long. Protecting the ball behind a steady running game and an effective short-passing game that served as a change of pace, Stabler engineered two drives in the third quarter, both ending in short Blanda field goals to extend Oakland's lead to 16–7.

While damaging to the Steelers' chances, the two field goals were not lethal blows to them. They were still very much in the ballgame, until, that is, a turnover of their own turned the tide and placed their entire season in peril.

At midfield, Bradshaw faked a handoff on a play-action pass and tossed a pass in the left flat to his intended receiver, Preston Pearson. The fake didn't fool Raiders cornerback Willie Brown, who stepped inside Pearson for an easy interception and an unobstructed jog into the end zone for a touchdown.

The fans of Raider Nation erupted in Oakland-Alameda County Coliseum. Brown's dagger had given the Raiders a 23–7 lead, and it appeared the Raiders were on their way to erasing the sting of losing the Immaculate Reception game the year before.

Facing a big deficit and unable to get anything going with Harris and the running game, Bradshaw was forced into a pass-heavy scheme to try to overcome the deficit. Two plays into their next possession, he overthrew a pass deep down the middle that was intercepted by safety Atkinson.

Raiders running back Charlie Smith then took a handoff from Stabler and scampered forty yards down the left sideline, deep into Steelers territory. The game very much felt like it was slipping away from the Black and Gold and that it was all over but the kicking and screaming.

The Steel Curtain closed tightly, however, and forced another short Blanda field goal at the start of the fourth quarter. With less than fifteen minutes to play, the Steelers trailed 26–7.

Bradshaw and the offense predictably were forced to play catch-up by passing the ball, and that invited a heavy Raiders' pass rush. Despite a continually collapsing pocket and a number of hits, Bradshaw began to move the Steelers downfield, using short passes to Fuqua out of the backfield as a catalyst.

A sneaky run by Fuqua on a draw got the Steelers close, and on a third down from the twenty-six-yard line, Bradshaw laced a scoring pass to receiver Frank Lewis to close the gap to twelve points, 26–14.

However, it was far too little, far too late. The Raiders, just as they had at the beginning of the game, pounded the Steel Curtain with running play after running play, eating up large chunks of both yardage and game clock alike. Their methodical drive ended with another one-yard touchdown run by Hubbard with just thirty-five seconds remaining in the game.

The Raiders had exacted their long-awaited revenge, winning the 1973 AFC Divisional playoff game decisively, 33–14. The Steelers, for all the hope their once sparkling 8–1 record had provided just six weeks before, had their season unceremoniously ended.

A must-read for any Pittsburgh Steelers fan is Roy Blount Jr.'s 1974 book, *About Three Bricks Shy of a Load: A Highly Irregular Lowdown on the Year the Pittsburgh Steelers Were Super but Missed the Bowl*. The book chronicles the Steelers' 1974 season in detail, from preseason training to the bitter end. It's a wonderful read and full of anecdotes that provide glimpses into the complex characters of a season-long drama.

To go along with The Terrible Towel, there's another holiday gift idea for the Steelers fans in your life.

Chapter 14

A FANTASY DRAFT & A SEASON OF QUARTERBACK ROULETTE

Late summer of every year, football fans of all ages begin their participation in a season of fantasy football with a fantasy draft. In that fantasy draft, they take turns among other players in their leagues of friends and co-workers in drafting the absolute best of the NFL to their teams. They might not draft every player they want, but round after round, they draft talented, star players.

In the off-season leading up to the 1974 season, the Steelers conducted a fantasy draft of their own, only this was in real life. Their draft class in the 1974 NFL Draft was the best ever selected.

Ever.

Four of the Steelers' first five draft picks went on to have Hall of Fame careers—receiver Lynn Swann, linebacker Jack Lambert, receiver John Stallworth, and center Mike Webster.

Their fourth selection, defensive back Jimmy Allen, goes almost forgotten, despite the fact he played eight years in the NFL—his first four seasons with the Steelers—and tallied thirty-one career interceptions.

Noll and the Steelers drafted receiver Swann in the first round with the twenty-first overall selection. A high-gifted receiver with soft hands that caught nearly everything within an arm's distance, Swann starred on the University of Southern California's 1974 national championship winning team, earning consensus All-America honors along the way. His selection by the Steelers was pretty much a "no-brainer" when their turn finally arrived during the first round.

In the second round, the Steelers may have stretched just a wee bit in selecting middle linebacker Lambert, who had earned two All-Mid-American Conference honors while starring at Kent State University in Kent, Ohio. At Kent State, Lambert was a teammate of Nick Saban, who later embarked on a legendary collegiate coaching career.

Saban has shared an anecdote of just how Lambert ascended into his starting role at Kent State. According to Saban, who was a defensive back at Kent State, he and a few of his other teammates were asked to act as security at a Rolling Stones concert. Among those teammates was Bob Bender, the starting middle linebacker on the team.

As Mick Jagger, the iconic singer of the Rolling Stones, was walking off the stage that night, Bender spied a fan winding up to throw something at the singer. Acting swiftly, Bender, right in front of Jagger, knocked the object out of the fan's hand. Jagger, on the spot, hired Bender onto the Stones' permanent security team.

When fall football camp came around, Bender was nowhere to be found. Lambert stepped up to fill his spot.

The Steelers didn't have a third-round pick in the 1974 NFL Draft, but they made up for it with two selections in the fourth round. With their first of those two selections, the eighty-second pick overall, the team drafted John Stallworth, an athletic receiver from the small football program Alabama A&M in Huntsville, Alabama. Stallworth, who went unrecruited by coach Bear Bryant at the University of Alabama, was fast and blessed with great leaping ability. Drafting Stallworth was a testament to the Steelers' scouting department, and as a fourth-round selection, he was a virtual steal as his talent warranted him being selected much higher.

In the fifth round, Noll and the Steelers drafted center Webster from the University of Wisconsin. Initially a back-up to longstanding starter and mentor Ray Mansfield, Webster would take over at the center of the Steelers offensive line in 1976 and start 150 consecutive games at one of the most physically demanding positions in the game, serving as the Steelers' offensive captain for nine seasons.

While every team is always hopeful their draft class will go down as being, if not the best in NFL history, at least a superb class, Noll and the Steelers were optimistic about their selections. They had carefully targeted opportunities to improve the roster, and they had added a number of players who could immediately contribute to a team that already had a strong foundation from the previous two seasons.

While the Steelers felt good about the upcoming 1974 season, league-wide, there was a growing chasm between the players and the league. At the heart of the matter was the desire for the freedom of free agency once contracts had expired, something that would take a couple of more decades to come into full effect.

Players wanted to eliminate the option clause, in which a club held the exclusive rights to a player—their option—for one full year after an expiring contract. In effect, when a player played out his contract with a team, he would still be beholden to that team for an additional year, preventing him from signing with another football team. In a sport with notoriously short careers, almost every player just couldn't afford to take an entire season off.

Just as restrictive was the so-called "Rozelle Rule," named after NFL Commissioner Pete Rozelle, which required any team signing a free agent to compensate the player's former team. Both points were untenable to the players, but they had additional concerns too. In total, the players' union, the National Football League Players' Association (NFLPA), had sixty-three total demands it wanted to be addressed by the league.

With the league and its owners turning a deaf ear, the NFLPA resorted to its only meaningful bargaining chip, and that was a work stoppage in the form of a players' strike. Locked in a bitter dispute, players went on strike on July 1 and stayed away from training camps that opened later in the month.

The highlight, or rather a lowlight, of the forty-two-day strike was the circus-like environment created by the players' boycott of the Hall of Fame game, one of the centerpieces of the annual Hall of Fame celebration weekend in Canton, Ohio, when new classes of players are inducted into the shrine and a general celebration of professional football goes on for days.

The game between the Buffalo Bills and the St. Louis Cardinals was played almost entirely with replacement players, and it was accompanied by picket lines featuring NFL stalwarts, like Alan Page, defensive lineman for the Minnesota Vikings, and Dan Pastorini, quarterback for the Oilers, carrying signs with the NFLPA's rallying cry, "No Freedom, No Football."

Times were a bit troubled, and there looked to be a possible void in professional football in 1974, as the Canadian Football League was also enduring player unrest. Looking to take advantage of that void was the opportunistic World Football League, a new league founded by Gary Davidson, who had previously helped launch the American Basketball Association and the World Hockey League as competitors to more entrenched professional sports leagues.

When Davidson announced the formation of the WFL in October 1973, his original intention was to begin games in 1975. The labor uncertainty experienced by the NFL led him to move forward more quickly with his plan.

Teams in the WFL began signing current NFL players to "futures contracts," where players would play out their existing NFL contracts and then plan to jump to the new league. But, while there was a publicity boost with each signing, the product on the field was still very much inferior to the established NFL.

The WFL kicked off its inaugural season in early July, and they played a full slate of twenty games, six more than the NFL's regular season schedule, over just nineteen weeks. At first, it looked to be a resounding success, as fans flocked to stadiums. However, it wasn't long before it became apparent that a great many fans had been given free tickets.

Teams began relocating in the middle of the season, and two teams were shut down completely in-season. Additionally, Davidson was forced out of the top office in October. Finally, the season came to an end with the Birmingham Americans winning the World Bowl, 22–21 over the Florida Blazers.

After barely making it through its first year, the WFL folded in the middle of its second season in 1975. And while it didn't succeed as a viable enterprise, it very much succeeded in lifting the stagnant player salaries that were commonplace in the NFL. Salaries for professional football players were among the lowest of the major professional sports leagues.

During the start of the inaugural WFL season in July 1974, players began to break from the solidarity of the NFLPA, with many players crossing the picket lines and entering camp. Some, of course, did it to play out their contracts and possibly be rewarded the next season in a new league. Others just needed to make a living.

After hundreds of veteran players reported to camp, the NFLPA conceded, although, as history would prove later, only temporarily. Still, the work stoppage affected teams' preseason preparations, and even more uncertainty than usual presented itself before the Week One kickoff.

Economically, the United States continued to struggle in 1974, from the beginning of the year until the end. The stock market crash that had begun in January of the previous year continued, and ultimately the New York Stock Exchange's Dow Jones Industrial Average would suffer the seventh-worst bear market in its history, losing over 45 percent of its value through December 1974.

The collapse of the Bretton Woods system, the subsequent devaluation of the dollar, the resultant OPEC oil embargo, and the rest of the "Nixon Shock" sent much of the world into a deep economic depression. Inflation in the United States was over 11 percent. Communities in every corner of the country were feeling pain, and Pittsburgh's dependence on the steel industry was setting the local region up to feel more than its fair share.

In the post-World War II economic boom, the steel industry in the United States flourished. Yet imported steel was also thriving, growing at a substantially higher rate at that. In 1946, the US imported less than 150 million tons of steel into the country. By 1959, the US had become a net *importer* of steel, bringing more foreign-made steel into the country than what was being produced domestically.

Wanting to protect the domestic industry and keep employment steadily high—and courting votes along the way—the government instituted steel import quotas starting in 1969. But all those measures did was increase the cost of steel and contribute more to the inflationary economic environment.

Corresponding with the increased importation of steel, jobs were being lost in the industry. Employment peaked in 1953 at 650,000 employees. By 1974, the number of workers had declined over 20 percent, to 512.000. The worst was yet to come.

In 1974, the economic pain being felt in the steel industry wasn't exactly everywhere in the industry. While those in the mills were faced with possible job loss, those in the executive offices and boardrooms were enjoying a period of prosperity.

Oddly, despite the glut of bad industry and economic news globally, steel companies were generally performing well financially throughout 1974. Sure, challenges were in the marketplace and new ones were sprouting on the near-term horizon, but at the same time, companies posted big profits. The nation's largest steel producer, US Steel, reported record profits of $634.9 million, up 94.9 percent from 1973 and four times its profits from 1972.

Additionally, most forecasters were bullish on future steel demand, predicting significant growth globally over the next ten-year period. Those forecasts sparked major production expansion projects outside of the United States. Those new plants, with modernized machinery and more efficient production methods, were sure to present a serious threat to domestic US steel producers.

On the US domestic political front, no relief was to be found over the course of the year. In fact, 1974 proved to be one of the most tumultuous years in US politics in memory for most voters.

Set in motion years prior, the Watergate scandal unraveled at a furious pace for the Nixon administration.

On March 1, 1974, a Washington, DC, grand jury indicted seven former aides of Nixon, who collectively became known as the "Watergate Seven," for conspiring to hinder the Watergate investigation. The grand jury secretly named Nixon as an unindicted co-conspirator, dissuaded from formally indicting him by the special prosecutor, who argued a president can only be indicted after he has left office.

Indictments and convictions on previous indictments continued to follow. In time, sixty-nine people were indicted in the scandal, and forty-eight were eventually convicted, many of them top officials in the Nixon Administration.

At the end of April, after weeks of internal debate within the administration, audio tapes of White House meetings were released, edited to omit profanity and vulgarity. Worrisome gaps in the tapes were said to be important national security conversations that were redacted. Even edited, the transcripts of the tapes painted Nixon in an unflattering light. Within days, calls for Nixon's resignation or impeachment rang out.

The process played out in the media and the public eye with a dizzying speed. On July 27, the House Judiciary Committee voted to recommend the first article of impeachment against the president, obstruction of justice. Then, on the 29th, the Committee recommended the second article, abuse of power, and on the 30th, the third article, contempt of Congress.

Also on July 30, responding to a Supreme Court decision a week earlier, the Nixon White House released additional tapes from the Oval Office. Then, on August 5, the White House released a previously unknown audio tape recorded in the immediate aftermath of the Watergate break-in, and its content was incriminatory, documenting the initial stages of a cover-up from the highest public office in the land.

That final tape destroyed Nixon's last political stand. The congressmen who had supported the president and voted against all three articles of impeachment in the House Judiciary Committee announced they would change course and support the impeachment articles when they came up before the full House of Representatives.

With impeachment inevitable, Nixon announced his intention to resign in a nationally televised address from the Oval Office on August 8. The next morning, Vice President Gerald R. Ford was sworn in as the 38th President of the United States.

A funny thing happened along the way to the start of the Pittsburgh Steelers' 1974 season. They found a new starting quarterback.

Breaking camp, Joe Gilliam was named the starter, usurping incumbent Terry Bradshaw. Bradshaw hadn't exactly set the league on fire early in his career, and his first two seasons, 1970 and 1971, were noticeable primarily for interceptions. He threw forty-six combined interceptions during those first two seasons, or one about every fourteen pass attempts. Against those forty-six interceptions, Bradshaw had thrown only nineteen touchdowns.

Bradshaw had shown improvement from his rookie year to his second year, though, and he did the same from his second year to his third. In 1972, Bradshaw threw an interception on average every twenty-five pass attempts, and he totaled as many touchdowns passes, twelve, as interceptions.

Bradshaw had regressed, however, during his injury-riddled 1973 campaign. His interceptions had climbed to fifteen against just ten touchdowns, or about one interception every twelve pass attempts.

With a strong defense returning, Noll wanted more efficiency from his offense. More touchdowns would be nice, of course. But he didn't mind punting the ball away too often, for that required teams to mount long, sustained drives against the Steel Curtain—a rather unlikely occurrence that he was comfortable playing with the odds in his favor. What Noll couldn't entertain was turning the ball over and giving opponents a relatively short field in which to get points.

Gilliam had been selected by the Steelers in the eleventh round of the 1972 NFL Draft, the 273rd overall pick, out of Tennessee State, where his father was a longtime defensive coordinator on the football coaching staff. After playing sparingly his first season and a half, Gilliam saw expanding playing time in 1973 due to Bradshaw's injuries and the spotty play of backup Terry Hanratty. As you might recall, Gilliam even started one game in 1973, a late-season *Monday Night Football* game against the Dolphins in Miami.

It had been a dismal performance. Gilliam threw seven passes, without a completion. Three passes were caught, but all three were interceptions by Dolphins safety Dick Anderson, one of which he returned for a touchdown. Gilliam was ingloriously pulled from the nationally televised contest.

However, Gilliam won the open competition in training camp to become the Steelers' starter. It was notable around the country for Gilliam was an African-American, and when Noll named him to the starting position, Gilliam became the first Black quarterback to start a season opener since the NFL-AFL merger.

Younger readers might not understand. In that era of the NFL, and very much reflective of the racial dynamics of the country at the time, every other quarterback was, simply, a quarterback. Gilliam was a Black quarterback, and the media attention was very high.

On September 15, the Steelers opened their 1974 campaign by trouncing the Baltimore Colts, 30–0. Picking up from where they had left off the year prior, the Steel Curtain was dominant, limiting the Colts to just 166 total yards of offense while tallying two recovered fumbles, two interceptions, and six sacks.

Gilliam was good, completing seventeen of thirty-one passes for 257 yards and two touchdowns, including a fifty-four-yarder to rookie Swann, and throwing only one interception. For his efforts, Gilliam was featured on the cover of that week's *Sports Illustrated*.

In Week Two, the Steelers traveled to Denver to square off against the Broncos, and the game proved to be a wild, back-and-forth affair. The Steelers had success running the ball—for the game, they gained 160 yards on forty rushes. But, despite that success on the ground, Gilliam repeatedly called his own number in the huddle, resulting in a team-record fifty passing attempts in the game, of which he completed thirty-one for 348 yards with one score and two interceptions. In the end, the two teams settled for a 35–35 tie.

The Steelers returned home to Three Rivers to face off against the rival Raiders, but chinks were appearing in the Steelers' armor, and Noll was growing increasingly concerned with Gilliam's apparent fixation on the passing game. Behind a strong running game and an opportunistic passing game, the Raiders plowed out to a 17–0 lead by the second quarter. From there, it was a game of the Raiders being on cruise control, forcing a total of four Steelers turnovers and playing keep away with the ball until time finally expired on a 17–0 shutout win.

Gilliam was not good in the game and produced a horrible stat line of just eight completed passes in thirty-one attempts, good for only 106 yards. He also threw two interceptions and suffered another two quarterback sacks. The Steelers' record dropped to 1–1–1, and local fans were beginning to voice their displeasure with Gilliam, pounding a steady drumbeat for the return of Bradshaw to the starting lineup.

Week Four was an opportunity for the Steelers to break out of their funk against the hapless Oilers in Houston. Buy, once again, the Steelers' offense faltered, and the culprit, yet again, was Gilliam's inability to come up big on key plays. The running game carried its weight, with Preston Pearson rushing for 117 yards in place of the injured Harris, and the team totaling 184 yards on the ground on just thirty-eight carries. Too often, though, the offense was stalled through the air.

Gilliam continued not to be shy about calling pass plays, and he tallied thirty-two attempts on the day. However, he completed just half, sixteen, for only 202 yards, all the while throwing an additional two interceptions. Despite the less-than-stellar performance, the Steelers escaped with a 13–7 victory courtesy of a Pearson nine-yard scoring run in the fourth quarter.

The next week, in Kansas City against the Chiefs, the Steelers won another wild one, 34–24, thanks to a difficult-to-imagine nine turnovers forced by the Steel Curtain, including one interception returned forty-nine yards by Glen Edwards for a touchdown. Once again, Gilliam was less than impressive, completing fourteen of thirty-six passes for 214 yards, with one touchdown and one interception.

Week Six, the Steelers hosted the division cellar-dwelling Browns at Three Rivers, and they were fortunate to escape with a 20–16 victory, lifting their record to 4–1–1. In what proved to be the final straw for Noll, Gilliam was downright ineffective against the Browns, completing just five of eighteen passes for seventy-eight yards.

Despite being in first place in the division, Noll believed the team was capable of playing much better, producing a much bigger margin against rather undistinguished foes like the Oilers, Chiefs, and Browns. Gilliam's on-field performances had been sub-par. Additionally, Gilliam was also apparently guilty of breaking established team rules and ignoring carefully crafted game plans with his signal calls.

Knowing the potential he had with his roster, Noll made a switch at the quarterback position, elevating Bradshaw back to the starting spot. Bradshaw would start in Week Seven, a nationally televised *Monday Night Football* game against the Atlanta Falcons.

Not surprisingly, Bradshaw was a bit rusty from a lack of game action, and it showed in his performance. His stat line of nine completions in twenty-one attempts for 130 yards and two interceptions were as poor as most any Gilliam performance. Fortunately, Harris had a big game on the ground, rushing for 141 yards and a touchdown, and the Steelers pulled away in the second half for a 24–17 victory.

At the halfway point of the season, the Steelers were in first place in the AFC Central Division with a 5–1–1 record. They had a stout defense and could control the pace and flow of a game from the defensive side. However, on the offensive side, the Steelers lacked a cohesive identity, and they were suffering from a lack of effective leadership at the quarterback position.

The second half of the regular season began with the Steelers hosting their cross-state rivals, the Philadelphia Eagles. The hotly anticipated game turned out to be a laugher.

The Steelers were methodical if unspectacular on offense, seemingly running the football at will, piling up 238 yards rushing on forty-eight attempts. Bradshaw was steady through the air, completing more than half his passes and throwing one touchdown against no interceptions. The Steel Curtain defense was brilliant yet again, limiting the Eagles to just 143 total yards of offense and forcing three turnovers, including an interception returned fifty-two yards by Mel Blount for the final score in a 27–0 shutout victory.

Week Nine was to be a real test for the Steelers, as they were scheduled to visit Cincinnati and play the second-place Bengals in what was being touted as a key game in determining which team would reign supreme in the division. It was a test the Black and Gold failed.

Bradshaw had a miserable game, completing just thirteen of thirty-five passes for 140 yards, and accounting for the Steelers' lone turnover with an interception.

Try as they might, Harris and the running game could not get the Steelers' offense over the hump, although they rushed for 161 yards and averaged over four yards per rushing attempt.

The Bengals won the game because quarterback Ken Anderson came up big in the game's biggest moments. He completed twenty of his twenty-two passes, and that helped overcome the Bengals' three fumbles. After a scoreless first quarter, the Bengals took a 10–0 lead and stretched it to 17–3 heading into the fourth quarter. A Preston Pearson touchdown narrowed the final score to 17–10, but the Bengals held on for a well-deserved victory.

Noll was now at a crossroads. Gilliam had been, at times, spectacular. Other times, his play had been poor. Through it all, he ignored game plans and broke team rules. Bradshaw, on the other hand, had performed no better. Desperate to find a solution at quarterback, Noll named veteran third-string quarterback Terry Hanratty as the starter for the team's Week Ten visit to Cleveland.

The Browns were just 3–6, but they had played the Steelers tough just four weeks before. They jumped off to a 3–0 lead in the first quarter until Hanratty completed a twenty-eight-yard touchdown pass to Shanklin. Field goals filled out the rest of the scoring in the first half, and the Steelers led 13–6 at the break.

Hanratty's touchdown pass proved to be one of the two completions he had the entire game. In fifteen pass attempts, he threw one more interception, three in total, than he did completed passes. Noll had to resort to Gilliam to come in for relief, but he proved just as ineffective, completing one of four passes.

Down 16–13 in the fourth quarter, the Steelers rallied for a 26–16 victory, thanks largely to a fourteen-yard fumble return for a touchdown by defensive back JT Thomas. The Steel Curtain defense had won the game, and while his team was 7–2–1, Noll was losing his patience with his underperforming offense.

First Gilliam, then Bradshaw, then Hanratty. Who was Noll going to turn to now?

Perhaps choosing the lesser of three evils, Noll settled on Bradshaw for the Week Eleven tilt against the New Orleans Saints at Tulane Stadium in New Orleans, the site for the upcoming Super Bowl just two months hence.

Receiver Frank Lewis opened the scoring, catching a thirty-one-yard pass from Bradshaw. Bradshaw, himself, scored on an eighteen-yard run in the second quarter, and rookie Swann scored on a brilliant sixty-four-yard punt return to stake the Steelers to a 21–0 lead in the third. Bradshaw closed the scoring with a one-yard pass to Larry Brown, and the Steelers won 28–7.

Throwing the ball, Bradshaw actually had a somewhat poor game. Sure, he threw for two touchdowns, but he also threw two interceptions on a day he completed just eight of nineteen passes for eighty yards. Where Bradshaw excelled on this particular afternoon was on the ground, where he rushed for ninety-nine yards on nine carries, giving the Steelers' offense an added dimension. Franco Harris led the way running the ball, gaining 114 of the Steelers' rushing total of 272 yards in what was a dominant victory.

Maybe, just maybe, the Noll and the Steelers had found their team identity, one built on a strong defense that forced turnovers and managed by a ball possession offense centered on running the ball and minimizing costly mistakes.

Just when things may have been figured out, the Oilers came into Three Rivers Stadium and defeated the Steelers 13–10 on a cold, windy day in Pittsburgh. It was a day to forget as quickly as possible.

The Steelers gained just eighty-four total yards against the cellar-dwelling Oilers and committed three turnovers. Bradshaw had a horrible game, throwing an interception, taking three sacks for a loss of thirty yards, and completing just six of twenty passes for sixty yards. Rather unbelievably, Hanratty was worse in relief, pitching two interceptions and throwing not a single completion in his five pass attempts.

In what felt like a season on the brink of collapse, the Steelers were still in first place in the division, sporting an 8–3–1 record heading off to Foxboro, Massachusetts, to take on the New England Patriots.

Bradshaw started the game, and Noll had him feature Harris and the running game. Harris gained 136 yards on twenty-nine carries, and Bleier tacked on another forty-two yards on twelve carries to pace the Steelers' offense. The game plan alleviated any pressure Bradshaw might have felt for needing to spark the offense, and it greatly minimized his penchant for turning the ball over. For his part, even though Bradshaw did throw a single interception, he otherwise played his role effectively, completing ten of sixteen passes for eighty-six yards.

While the offensive production might not have been anything to write home about, the Steel Curtain continued to shine. They held the Patriots to less than 200 yards and forced three turnovers in the Steelers' 21–17 victory. With the Bengals having lost their second consecutive game that same day, the win against the Patriots clinched the division crown ahead of their season-closing game against Cincinnati at Three Rivers Stadium the next Saturday.

Without much to play for other than pride, the Bengals ended up not putting up much of a fight. The Steelers opened the scoring with a five-yard touchdown pass from Bradshaw to Stallworth, and they never looked back on their way to a 27–3 victory. The Steelers pounded the ball on the ground, posting 171 yards rushing, and Bradshaw had a very good day, throwing two touchdowns against no interceptions, and completing eight of thirteen pass attempts for 132 yards. With the game in hand, Gilliam saw action, as well, and completed four of his eight passes for fifty-one yards.

With the victory, the Steelers closed out their regular season with a 10–3–1 record. Despite playing only twelve games, Harris once again broke the 1,000 mark, finishing the season with 1,006 yards and averaging an impressive 4.8 yards per carry. Four other players rushed for over 200 yards on the season, including Bradshaw with 224 yards, and Frenchy Fuqua tacked on another 156 yards for good measure. In total, the team posted 2,416 yards on the ground, second in the league to the Dallas Cowboys' 2,454 yards.

Of course, the cynic might say the Steelers needed to be effective on the ground during the 1974 season because of their struggles in the passing game. With three quarterbacks seeing action, and each starting at least one game, the team passed for just 2,154 total yards, completing only 43 percent of passes and throwing nearly twice as many interceptions as touchdowns.

The saving grace for the struggling offense was another superb season from the defense. The Steel Curtain surrendered just 3.6 yards per offensive play by their opponents, and for the season allowed just over 3,000 yards—by far the best in the league. They recorded fifty-two sacks, or nearly one out of every seven pass attempts, and forced forty-eight turnovers—twenty-five interceptions and twenty-three forced fumbles.

Heading into the playoffs, Noll knew he had the defense to clamp down the opposition. If he could get his offense to play effectively, controlling the ball on the ground and using an error-free passing game as a complement when needed, the Steelers would be in a strong position to make some noise in the postseason.

In the postseason, Gilliam would see spot action late in the club's first game. After that, he would spend just the 1975 season with the Steelers, appearing in four games, before being cut from the team. At the age of twenty-five, Gilliam's NFL career was over.

Gilliam's time in Pittsburgh was tainted by rumors of drug use, and in 1976, he was arrested in New Orleans on counts of possession of both a firearm and cocaine. While he was signed by the New Orleans Saints ahead of both the 1976 and 1977 seasons, he was cut before the season started both times.

Still trying to work his way back into the NFL, Gilliam knocked around several semi-pro football leagues, but never achieved the success he enjoyed as a standout collegiate player at Tennessee State. He gave a run at the new United States Football League (USFL) in 1983, first with the Denver Gold, who cut him, and then with the Washington Federals, with whom he stuck. Gilliam played in four games, starting two, throwing five touchdowns and ten interceptions. He was cut in training camp ahead of the 1984 season.

In interviews, Gilliam said he thought his demotion as the Steelers' starting quarterback and his eventual dismissal from the team were based on racism. However, it's not a point of view shared by his past Steelers teammates, who point to poor play on the field, departures from Noll's game plans, and drug use.

Gilliam's teammates thought his actions led to his career falling short of its once-promising potential. In an edition of HBO's *Real Sports with Bryant Gumbel* in February 2000, Bradshaw told interviewer James Brown about Gilliam, "He gave me my job back. It's not like I beat him out."

On December 16, 2000, Gilliam attended the final Steelers game played at Three Rivers Stadium. Days later, on Christmas Day, he tragically died of a cocaine overdose, four days shy of what would have been his fiftieth birthday.

After four decades of futility, the Steelers headed for the playoffs for the third consecutive year, and fans were optimistic about their chances. For the first round, the Black and Gold drew the Buffalo Bills, who had finished the season second in the AFC East Division at 9–5, earning the conference's wild-card spot in the postseason.

The Bills were led by running back OJ Simpson, who had become the first-ever to rush for over 2,000 yards when he accomplished the feat in 1973. With opposing defenses keyed on him throughout the 1974 season, he gained *only* 1,125 yards, but he still averaged a well-earned 4.2 yards per carry. Fullback Jim Braxton complemented Simpson in the backfield not only as an effective lead blocker but also as a running threat himself, having accounted for 543 yards on the ground and four rushing touchdowns, one more than Simpson.

With a strong running game that produced over 2,000 yards on the ground during the season, the Bills did not have to rely on quarterback Joe Ferguson, who attempted less than twenty passes per game, completing a little more than half, for an average of about 123 yards passing per game.

Both teams were going to approach the game with similar game plans: lean on the rushing game to control possession, minimize turnovers, gain an advantage in field position and depend on a quality defense.

Game day, December 22, dawned sunny and cold, but warm enough to have the previous week's snow be a non-issue, and fans turned out to Three Rivers Stadium in droves—another sellout crowd.

Blount returned the opening kickoff to nearly midfield, where Bradshaw and the offense took over. They pushed the ball deep into Bills' territory but had to settle for Gerela's short twenty-one-yard field goal to open the scoring.

The Bills weren't deterred. On their first possession, they marched the ball downfield. From the Steelers' twenty-two-yard line, Ferguson faked a handoff to Simpson on the left, rolled out to his right, and hit tight end Paul Seymour with a touchdown strike. The first quarter ended with the Bills leading 7–3.

Bradshaw took over on the Steelers' ensuing drive, both with his feet and his arm. On the drive's last play, with perfect protection from the line providing him seemingly all day to find a receiver, Bradshaw hit a streaking Bleier, whom he had faked a handoff to just seconds before, down the right sideline for a twenty-seven-yard touchdown completion, giving the Steelers their first lead of the game.

Ultimately, it would be all they needed.

On the Steelers' next possession, Bradshaw got Swan involved in the attack, first with an end around reverse good for a twenty-five-yard gain, then with a short pass in the left flat that Swan converted into a fourteen-yard gain down to the one-yard line. From there, Harris punched it in for the score, and with a missed PAT, the Steelers kicked off with a 16–7 lead.

With Simpson being bottled up by the Steel Curtain, Braxton caught most everyone by surprise and reeled off a thirty-yard run. Steelers safety Wagner, however, caused a fumble at the end of the play, and with linebacker Ham's recovery, the Steelers' offense was back in business.

The offense marched down the field, with Swann's diving thirty-five-yard reception at the Bills' four-yard line the highlight. Harris scored his second touchdown on the day from there, and the score swelled to 22–7.

But the Steelers weren't done. On their next possession, Bradshaw hit receiver Larry Brown with a beautiful twenty-nine-yard pass to set up another Harris touchdown plunge. With Gerela's extra point, the Steelers held a comfortable 29–7 lead going into the halftime intermission.

The Bills gave it one more push in the third quarter, putting together a nice drive of mostly short passes, culminated by Simpson's three-yard scoring reception of a Ferguson pass. From there, the Steelers concentrated on holding onto the football, burning up the clock, and advancing to the second round of the playoffs.

Gerela added a short field goal, and the Steelers were content to let the clock expire with the ball inches from yet another touchdown, leaving the final score to be 32–14.

Bradshaw had had an error-free day, and the rushing game pounded out 235 yards on the ground. The Steel Curtain had given up two touchdown drives but also forced two turnovers. In the end, the victory had been a comfortable one.

It was onto the AFC Championship Game. Any guess on who the opponent would be?

If you guessed the rival Oakland Raiders, you'd be correct. The game with a berth into Super Bowl IX on the line would be the teams' sixth contest against each other in just twenty-six months, and their third meeting in the sudden-death, win-to-advance playoffs.

The Steelers' 1973 season had ended, of course, with their defeat at Oakland in the divisional round of the playoffs. Then they had looked outclassed by the Raiders in losing their Week Three matchup 17–0. Still, they traveled out west for the game feeling optimistic about their solid rushing attack, improved quarterback play, and stout defense.

The Raiders had finished the regular season with a 12–2 record, tops in the AFC West. Then, they squeaked past the defending two-time Super Bowl champion Miami Dolphins in the first round of the playoffs courtesy of a Stabler touchdown pass to running back Clarence Davis in the final seconds, a catch memorialized by commentators as "The Sea of Hands" due to all the outstretched hands of Dolphins defenders in the area. The Raiders entered the game featuring a strong running game spearheaded by backs Hubbard, Banaszak, and Davis and a potent passing game led by the swashbuckling Stabler. They also had the home-field advantage of the Oakland-Alameda County Coliseum and their legendary fans in the "Black Hole."

The game started well for the Steelers as the Steel Curtain forced the Raiders to punt thanks to a Greene sack of Stabler on the quarterback's first passing attempt. However, after a booming punt by Guy, Swann fumbled when tackled on the return. The Raiders recovered the miscue and were sitting pretty on the Steelers' forty-one-yard line.

The Steel Curtain stayed impenetrable, and the Raiders had to settle for a forty-yard field goal by the forty-seven-year-old Blanda for the game's first score.

Trailing 3–0, the Steelers had no need to panic. The defense had proven it was up to the task of stopping Stabler and the Raiders' offense. For Bradshaw and the

Steelers' offense, it was imperative to chip away, slowly but surely, and eliminate any costly errors, like the Brown interception return for a touchdown that so dramatically changed the complexion of the previous year's playoff game on the same field.

After trading punts, the Steelers took over again at midfield as the first-quarter clock clicked down. Facing a long third down, Bradshaw helped his own cause by scrambling for a first down. Harris then pounded out a first down on the next third-down play. A short pass reception by Bleier on the next third down kept the chains moving and the drive going.

The drive then stalled, and Gerela came into the game for a short twenty-yard field goal attempt to tie the game. And . . . he missed, shanking his kick and pulling it badly to the left.

The Steelers had been relaxed and confident all week and had positioned themselves to tie the game. But they had failed. The question was, would it haunt them for the remainder of the game?

Unfazed, the defense, winning the line of scrimmage with Lambert and the defensive line, forced another three-and-out from the Raiders at the top of the second quarter. Thanks to a late hit penalty on Swann's punt return, the Steelers took possession at midfield.

On a third down, Bradshaw connected on a pass with tight end Larry Brown to move the yard markers and keep possession. The Steelers kept pounding away, leaning on the Raiders' defense and forcing their will on the pace of play. When the Raiders stiffened deep in their own territory, Gerela came out yet again for another short field goal attempt. This time, from twenty-three yards away, Gerela split the uprights to tie the game at 3–3. That score held up the rest of the first half.

Midway through the third quarter, Stabler got things going for the Raiders' offense for the first time in the game. He completed three short passes to move the ball into Steelers' territory. Then, he uncorked a beautiful thirty-eight-yard pass on a play-action fake to speedy wideout Cliff Branch for a touchdown and a 10–3 Raiders lead.

Once again, the Steelers would need to come from behind to earn a victory.

And, once again, there was no panic from Noll, Bradshaw, and the rest of the Steelers. They calmly went back to their game plan and continued blasting away with the running game. The offensive line repeatedly won their matchups, moving the line of scrimmage downfield, and Bleier broke off a couple of big gains. Then, Bradshaw converted a key third-and-ten with a strike to Stallworth to give the Steelers a first-and-goal from the eight-yard line.

On the first play of the fourth quarter, Harris blasted up the middle to score. With Gerela's PAT, the score was tied, 10–10. But the Steelers had very much controlled the game on both sides of the ball for much of the contest. Momentum was definitely behind the Steelers.

The previous year's playoff matchup had changed with Brown's key interception. This time around, the game-changing play was linebacker Ham's interception of Stabler, his second of the game, returning the ball not for a touchdown, but giving his team possession at the nine-yard line. When Bradshaw hit Swan on a slant pattern for a six-yard touchdown pass, the Steelers had their first lead of the championship game.

With the Raiders completely ineffective in running the ball against the Steel Curtain, a significant departure from their first meeting earlier in the season, they were forced to depend on Stabler's throwing arm. On cue, Stabler connected on a crossing pattern to Branch, and only Lambert's outstanding open field tackle on a world-class speedster prevented it from being a touchdown. Still, the forty-three-yard play advanced the ball to the twenty-four-yard line.

Stabler then found Branch on an out pattern on the left sideline, gaining another first down and moving the ball to the twelve. The Steelers held them from there and faced with a fourth down and four yards to go for a first down, six for a touchdown, Madden blinked and sent in Blanda for a short field goal attempt. Blanda nailed the twenty-four-yard attempt, narrowing the Steelers lead to 17–13.

Preston Pearson returned the ensuing kickoff to the Raiders' forty-nine-line, setting Bradshaw and company up with outstanding field position in which to burn time off the clock. After a three-yard run by Bleier, Bradshaw called his own number on a naked bootleg to his left. Carrying the ball in just his left hand, Bradshaw saw lots of green grass ahead of him. Only, he knocked the ball out of his hand with his leg, and his fumble bounced around on the field for several long seconds. Multiple Raiders defenders appeared to have great shots at a recovery. But saving the day for the Steelers was Bleier, who dove in and recovered the ball, maintaining Steelers possession. Despite rushing for ninety-eight yards and adding on another twenty-five receiving yards, the play was probably Bleier's biggest on the afternoon.

On the next play, third and eight, Bradshaw restored order by connecting with Swann on a first down completion. Another set of downs milked the clock down further, and after punting the ball away, the Raiders had the ball on their own twenty-yard line with just 3:41 left to play.

The Steel Curtain flexed its muscles again with a Lambert blitz, forcing Stabler to throw an incompletion on third down. With the ball so deep in their own territory, Madden decided to punt the ball away and see if the defense could stop the Steelers and get the ball back.

Just after the two-minute warning, Bradshaw attempted a pass on a third and eight from midfield. His incompletion deep downfield, intended for Swann, stopped the clock. The Raiders were going to get another opportunity to drive the length of the field for a come-from-behind victory for the second consecutive week.

The Steelers had depended on an outstanding defense for the past two seasons. The team's fate for the remainder of the 1974 season now lay in their capable hands once again. True to their nature, the defense rose to the occasion.

On the third play of the drive, Stabler, hurried by the pass rush, unleashed a deep throw down the center of the field, where JT Thomas intercepted it. He returned the ball to the twenty-five-yard line, and that was it for any Raiders threat. Harris sealed the deal with a twenty-one-yard scoring dash, and the Steelers won the AFC Championship, 24–13.

The Steelers were going to the Super Bowl, where they would play for their first NFL championship!

Chapter 15

A COMING-OUT PARTY IN THE BIG EASY

Super Bowl IX was to be played in New Orleans, Louisiana, and it was originally scheduled to be played at the Louisiana Superdome, a massive structure designed to cover more than thirteen acres with its steel frame footprint and destined to become the largest fixed dome structure in the world. However, during its construction, it was apparent that schedule overruns were going to prevent it from being completed in time for the January 12, 1975 game. As a result, the league was forced to move the game's location to Tulane Stadium on the campus of Tulane University, just a few miles away.

This would be the third Super Bowl played in the stadium, as Super Bowls IV and VI were played on the same field, at the time the home of the NFL's New Orleans Saints.

The Steelers' opponents in the championship game were the Minnesota Vikings, who were looking for redemption after their lackluster performance in the previous year's Super Bowl, a 24–7 stinker of a loss at the hands of the Miami Dolphins. The Vikings, who had finished the regular season with a 10–4 record, were powered by an often-spectacular offense and a stingy defense known by its memorable moniker, the "Purple People Eaters."

On offense, the Vikings' stars were veteran quarterback Fran Tarkenton and second-year running back Chuck Foreman, a true dual-threat as both a runner and a receiver coming out of the backfield—he actually led the team in receptions on the season with fifty-three, including six touchdown catches to add to his nine touchdowns scored on the ground.

Tarkenton, who would eventually be inducted into the Hall of Fame, was renowned for his scrambling abilities, making big plays out of seemingly lost causes by his antics in the pocket. His offensive line was anchored by right tackle Ron Yary and center Mick Tingelhoff, who would both go on to join Tarkenton as Hall of Famers.

The Purple People Eaters featured three future Hall of Famers as well—Page and Carl Eller on the defensive line and Paul Krause at the safety position. The Vikings posed a threat with their pass defense and had pressured opposing quarterbacks into throwing twenty-two interceptions. Their real strength, however, was bottling up opponents' rushing games, where they had limited foes to just 3.7 yards per carry.

After a week of practice at home in Pittsburgh, Noll and the Steelers went to New Orleans to finish game preparations, as customary. This wasn't Noll's first Super Bowl experience. He had been on Shula's Baltimore Colts staff as an assistant coach in Super Bowl III.

Those Colts had been a huge favorite to beat the upstart New York Jets of the AFL, who were led by Joe Namath. Namath, of course, famously predicted a Jets victory in the days leading up to the game, and sure enough, the Jets delivered the upset with a 16–7 victory.

Noll felt the Colts had been too restrictive with its players in the lead-up to that game, fostering a nervous anxiety that resulted in the team playing the game tightly. He was determined to not repeat that mistake, particularly in the city known as "The Big Easy."

Coach Noll's approach was much different from that of the hardline one adopted by Minnesota head coach Bud Grant. Grant had coached the Vikings in two previous Super Bowls, both rather uninspiring losses. In the lead-up to Super Bowl IX, he and his team were strictly business.

Pundits, prognosticators, and fans alike predicted a low-scoring Super Bowl as both teams had tremendous defenses—the Steel Curtain had surrendered only 189 points in the regular season, and the Purple People Eaters weren't far behind at 195. When dawn broke on Super Bowl Sunday, the weather looked to be another variable for both offenses to overcome.

A controlled climate under the roof of the Superdome would have been nice, as the game-time temperature was only 46° Fahrenheit, and the Astroturf playing surface was slick from an early-morning rain. To make matters worse, the whipping wind was strong and gusty. It was to be the coldest Super Bowl to date.

Still, over 81,000 fans flocked to the stadium, led largely by a huge contingent of long-suffering Steelers fans. The atmosphere in and around the stadium was more like a home game at Three Rivers than a game played at a neutral site.

Preston Pearson received a short opening kickoff into the wind and returned it to the thirty-six-yard line to get the game started. After two running plays produced very little, Bradshaw was sacked on third down. Stuffed on their first series, the Steelers were forced to punt away possession to the Vikings.

Tarkenton and his troops took over at their own eighteen-yard line, where he came out firing, connecting with receiver John Gilliam on a sixteen-yard completion. That was it for the possession though, as the Steel Curtain forced the Vikings to punt into the fierce wind.

Possession number two for the Steelers started again in good field position, on the forty-two-yard line. Bleier streaked up the field on an eighteen-yard scamper to push the ball into the Vikings' territory for the first time. However, penalties stalled the drive, and the Steelers once more punted possession away.

The Vikings could muster nothing of their own either. Foreman's first touch of the game resulted in a two-yard loss when Ham tackled him behind the line of scrimmage. The Steelers forced another punt, and they again took possession with good field position, this time setting up shop on the Vikings' forty-four-yard line.

This time around, Bradshaw converted a third down, connecting with receiver Larry Brown. But the Vikings' defense kept the Steelers from converting another third down. As a result, Noll sent in Gerela to attempt a thirty-seven-yard field goal. Gerela, however, hooked the ball wide to the left, and the game remained scoreless.

The Steel Curtain forced another three and out—three Minnesota offensive plays and then a punt. With the defense allowing next to nothing from the Vikings' offense, the Steelers had possession of the ball for the fourth time in the quarter.

On this drive, the Steelers started moving the ball a little thanks to the ground attack. First, Harris broke free for a fourteen-yard gain, and Bradshaw followed it up with his own eleven-yard run.

Still, the Steelers' offense could not punch it into the end zone, and Gerela entered the game to attempt a short field goal. On this attempt, a fumbled snap prevented holder Bobby Walden from cleanly placing the ball for a kick, and he was gobbled up by two Vikings on his desperate attempt to run for a score.

The first quarter confirmed the suspicions of a low-scoring Super Bowl, as it ended as it began, with a score of 0–0. The Steelers had given up only twenty yards, all through the air, and just a single first down to Tarkenton and his team. Minnesota's defense had prevented the Steelers from scoring, despite having ceded superior field position However, the Steelers' running game had broken off three good-sized gains on the way to posting sixty-one yards rushing.

The teams switched ends of the field for the second quarter, and Minnesota had its first opportunity with the wind at its back. Tarkenton took quick advantage by connecting with Foreman for a fourteen-yard gain. But still, the Vikings could not get the running game established. Holmes, Greene, and Greenwood were having their way with the Vikings' offensive line, and White, who had spent time with an illness in a New Orleans hospital in the days leading up to the game, was contributing more than his fair share too. After a near-miss interception by Russell, the Vikings were forced to punt once again.

The Steelers' ensuing possession began at their fifteen-yard line, by far their worst starting field position in the game. After a short run by Harris, Bradshaw uncorked a spiral in the direction of a streaking Stallworth, only to have the ball tipped away by defender Jackie Wallace to prevent an eighty-yard scoring play. The Vikings surely had to feel as though they had caught a break.

Bradshaw then connected with Swann for a first down, but the play was nullified by an offensive pass interference penalty. Repeating third down, Bradshaw handed the ball off to Bleier on a delayed draw play. Bleier blasted through a huge hole, but safety Jeff Wright punched the ball out of his grasp causing a fumble that bounced out to the twenty-four-yard line before being recovered by the Vikings.

After having managed next to nothing all day on offense, the Vikings' defense had set them up for a scoring opportunity.

The Steel Curtain continued to be impenetrable. After a short run and two incomplete passes, Grant was forced to send in his placekicker, Fred Cox, to attempt a field goal to open the scoring. Cox's thirty-nine-yard attempt was just wide of the right upright, and the game remained scoreless.

The Steelers began their ensuing drive well, with Bradshaw hitting Stallworth on a slant pattern for a nice twenty-two-yard gain. Crossing midfield before the drive was stopped, Walden, punting into the wind, pinned the Vikings deep in their own territory when Vikings rookie receiver Sam McCullum cradled the punt on his own six-yard line.

If McCullum had not fielded the ball, it appeared the ball would have gone into the end zone, resulting in a touchback and the ball being placed on the twenty-yard line. Instead, the Vikings' offense would be huddling up in the shadow of their own goalpost. McCullum's decision would therefore prove to be instrumental in the game's first score.

On second down from the ten-yard line, Tarkenton got crossed up on a handoff to running back Dave Osborn, and the ball bounced backward toward the goal line.

Tarkenton dived on it and skidded just inside the end zone, where White downed him for a Steelers safety.

Improbably, the first score of the game was a safety, but it was a just and well-earned reward for a Steelers' defense that had come out and dominated the game from the very beginning. The Steelers were ahead in Super Bowl IX, 2–0.

Per the rules, the Steelers received the ball after the scoring safety, fielding a free kick that went out of bounds at the Steelers' thirty-five-yard line. Once again finding themselves with good field position, Bradshaw, Harris, and team set out to rub salt into the Vikings' fresh wounds.

Three plays, however, netted the Steelers just one total yard as Wallace stuffed Stallworth for a loss on a third-down pass attempt. The Steelers were forced to punt once again, and Walden delivered a booming, low spiral against the wind, forcing McCullum to field the ball again deep in his own territory, where the Steelers special teams swarmed him at the twenty.

With time running out in the first half, Tarkenton put together the best Vikings drive of the afternoon. Blount was called for interference to gift the Vikings fifteen yards right away. On a rollout to the right, Tarkenton connected with Foreman for a nice gain. On the next play, Foreman got just enough on a run up the middle to get a first down. On the very next third down, Foreman made a juggling reception for a seventeen-yard gain and a first down at the Steelers' thirty-five-yard line.

Rather remarkably, three first downs in succession was a high-water mark for the Vikings, who had been the fifth highest-scoring team in the NFL over the course of the regular season, in the first half.

A four-yard run by Foreman advanced the ball, and then play stopped for the two-minute warning. The Vikings were threatening to take the lead in a game in which they had been convincingly outplayed.

When play resumed, Tarkenton, under pressure, completed a three-yard pass to tight end Stu Voight to move the ball slightly, but most importantly, stop the clock from running as the play ended out of bounds. The Vikings converted the third down on a two-yard dump-off from Tarkenton to Osborn.

On a first down drop back pass from the twenty-five-yard line, Tarkenton saw Gilliam flash open across the middle of the field. When the ball arrived at Gilliam at the five-yard line, so did Steelers safety Edwards, and the resultant collision forced the ball to sky straight upwards, where, seconds later, it fell into the hands of Blount for an interception.

The Steelers had stopped the Vikings on their best drive of the game thus far, and they went into the locker room at halftime with a slim 2–0 lead.

During his fourteen-year career in professional football, Mel Blount was often described as the prototypical cornerback for that era of the NFL. In truth, he would be considered the prototypical cornerback in today's NFL too.

Blount was tall and rangy, standing six feet, three inches with long arms. He was built solidly at 205 pounds, but his style of hitting and tackling made him seem like he was carrying an extra twenty pounds. In addition to his size, he was quick. Add to that his toughness, tenacity, and intelligence, and Blount was just the player to shut down opposing receivers.

Blount was born on April 10, 1948, in Vidalia, Georgia, where he grew up on an impoverished farm. As a teenager, he excelled in sports year around—football, basketball, track, and baseball—and earned an athletic scholarship to Southern University in Baton Rouge, Louisiana.

Despite being named to the All-America team at both safety and cornerback, Blount hung around in the 1970 NFL Draft until the third round, when the Steelers snatched him up with the fifty-third overall pick.

During his first two seasons on the team, Blount bided his time, sharing duties as the cornerback on the right side of the field. In his third season, 1972, he was the starting cornerback and throughout the entire season, he did not allow a single scoring reception.

His ability to lock down one entire side of the field allowed the Steelers to play a variety of man-to-man and zone coverage schemes, confusing opposing quarterbacks and giving the Steel Curtain a distinct advantage.

Blount was known for his aggressive, physical style of play, where he would step up to the receiver pre-snap on the line of scrimmage, and when the ball was snapped, explode his arms into his opponent's chest and bump him off stride as soon as he started running his pass pattern. It didn't get any better after that initial shot for the receiver either, as Blount had the speed and strength to be a general nuisance the entire rest of the play. When the NFL instituted its new illegal contact rule in 1978, prohibiting defenders from contacting receivers past the first five yards of the line of scrimmage, many referred to it as "The Mel Blount Rule."

Blount intercepted at least one pass in each of his fourteen seasons, fifty-seven in total, with a high mark of eleven during the 1975 campaign, when he was named the NFL's Defensive Player of the Year. Over his career, Blount earned All-Pro acclaim for four seasons and played in five Pro Bowls.

After his playing days, Blount served in the role of Director of Player Relations for the NFL from 1983 to 1990. He also founded the Mel Blount Youth Home to serve as a shelter and ministry for victims of child abuse and neglect, the first in Toombs County, Georgia, in 1983, and a second in Claysville, Pennsylvania, in 1989.

In 1989, Blount was inducted into the Pro Football Hall of Fame. In 1994, he was named to the NFL's seventy-fifth anniversary All-Time team.

The second half began with the Steelers kicking off. Just as Gerela was sweeping his right leg to strike the ball, his left foot slipped on the slick turf, resulting in an unintentional squib kick tumbling along down the middle of the field. In the scramble for the ball, Steelers reserve linebacker Marv Kellum emerged with the pigskin. Unexpectedly, and rather unbelievably, the Steelers had the ball on the Vikings' thirty-yard line.

After a run by Bleier gained nothing, Harris took a handoff and scampered up the middle, through a big hole in the line, cut to his left, and ran all the way to the six-yard line before getting pushed out of bounds.

First-and-goal for the Steelers!

On the next play, Vikings linebacker Wally Hilgenberg knifed through the line and dumped Harris for a three-yard loss. Undeterred, Bradshaw went back to Harris the very next play, a sweep around the left end. Harris, fleet-footed on the slick turf, streaked untouched into the end zone for a touchdown. Gerela added the extra point, and the Steelers led 9–0.

The Steelers had survived the Vikings' best offensive threat at the end of the half, a drive that could have easily put the NFC champs in the lead. Then, the Steelers had benefited from Gerela's miscue at the start of the second half. In short order, the Steelers had seized upon the opportunities presented to them and were in control of the game.

On the Vikings' first possession of the second half, they once again tried to establish a running game. Two consecutive plays stuffed for short gains proved once again it was going to be a futile effort. On third and long, Tarkenton hit Foreman with a short pass in the left flat, but Foreman lost his footing, slipping to the ground just short of a first down. On fourth down, Tarkenton attempted to draw the Steelers offside. Somehow, he succeeded in drawing offside penalties on *both* teams. Thinking better of going for it so deep in his own territory in what was still a two-score game, Grant had his punter Mike Eischeid kick the ball away yet again.

With the Steelers at the twenty-six-yard line, Bradshaw started the possession by handing the ball to Harris on an off-tackle run to the right side. It almost proved disastrous.

Harris bounded through the big hole and seemed destined for a large gain but fumbled at the conclusion of the play. With the ball at his feet, Vikings defensive end Page tried to pick it up. Players from both teams quickly converged and a pile formed, each player fighting for the ball. When the officials untangled the pile, Harris had the ball in his hands. A potentially game-changing turnover had been averted.

The Steelers continued to focus on controlling the ball, mixing rushing plays with short passes to move the chains and keep the clock ticking down. Across midfield, the Steelers faced another fourth down, and when Walden's punt tumbled into the end zone for a touchback, the Vikings were awarded the ball at their own twenty-yard line.

After an unusual play in which the Vikings were penalized for Tarkenton throwing two forward passes on one play, they started to move the ball. First, Foreman cracked off his longest run of the game, a twelve-yard gain. A few plays later, Tarkenton connected with Voigt on a twenty-eight-yard completion, the longest play from scrimmage for the Vikings.

Two plays later, In Steelers territory at the forty-eight-yard line, Tarkenton rolled to his left, looking for another big gain through the air. When he released it, though, a jumping White deflected the ball upward. The ball came down into the hands of Greene for an interception, the Steelers' second pick of the game.

On offense again, the Steelers proved to be in no hurry, pounding Harris into the Vikings on defense. On a third down, the Steelers escaped disaster once again, as a Bradshaw pass intercepted by linebacker Jeff Siemon was called back due to an offside penalty on the Vikings. With the turnover avoided and their lesson learned, the Steelers finished the quarter with little fanfare, keeping the ball on the ground.

For a player who had spent time hospitalized with an illness in the week leading up to Super Bowl IX, defensive tackle Dwight White made a significant contribution to the eventual outcome of the game. After having lost a reported twenty pounds due to his battle with the flu and pneumonia, White made impacts early in the game, late in the game, and all along in between.

On the Vikings' first possession, White made his presence and intent known by swallowing up running back Osborn on the Vikings' third snap of the game. In the second quarter, it was White who downed Tarkenton in the end zone for the safety and the game's first points. On the play that resulted in Greene's interception, it was White who tipped the ball after Tarkenton had uncorked his pass.

White had joined the Steelers when the club selected him in the fourth round of the 1971 NFL Draft with the 104th overall selection. He immediately earned a spot in the starting lineup, and his intensity on the field drove a fierce playing style, leading teammates to nickname him "Mad Dog."

Over his ten-year career in the trenches for the Steelers, he played in 126 games, intercepted four passes, and recovered seven fumbles. During his career, quarterback sacks were not an official statistic of the NFL, but even so, White is credited with fifty-five, including ten in his second year.

White earned two Pro Bowl honors in his career and was a key member of four Super Bowl-winning teams. He retired after the 1980 season, and he was named to the Steelers' All-Time team in 1982 and again in 2007.

Dwight White passed away June 6, 2008, from complications related to back surgery. He was just fifty-eight years old.

The fourth quarter began with bits of starts and stops in the action. First, a Bradshaw incompletion left a fourth down, and the Steelers chose to punt. Walden knuckled a short punt in an attempt to pin the Vikings deep in their own territory, but the wind pushed it back the opposite direction, and a fair catch left the ball on the twenty-three-yard line.

After a six-yard reception by Foreman, the Steel Curtain stood tall, stopping a run in its tracks and forcing a Tarkenton incompletion. On the Vikings' punt, Swann broke off a nifty return up the middle, positioning his offense with good field position once again, this time at their own forty-six-yard line.

Then, things began to get interesting.

Everyone in the stadium and the millions watching the NBC telecast expected the Steelers to play it close to the vest, rush the ball, and work on running the clock. So there was little surprise when Bradshaw handed the ball to Harris on a first down play.

Harris never got a good handle on the ball, though, and his fumble was recovered by safety Krause at the Steelers' forty-eight-yard line.

The Vikings offense now had possession, down just two scores, with plenty of time on the clock and the ball in great field position to mount a drive. Despite having been dominated for most of the game, the Vikings were still a threat.

Looking to strike quickly, Tarkenton dropped back and let loose a bomb down the right sideline, looking for receiver Gilliam. The ball fell to the turf, incomplete.

Then, late, a penalty flag flew onto the scene. A somewhat dubious pass interference penalty was called on Wagner, placing the ball on the Steelers' five-yard line.

The Vikings were just five yards from paydirt and closing the scoring gap to just two points. For one of the few times in the game, momentum was behind the team from the north.

On the next play, momentum turned on a dime and got behind the Steelers again. Foreman mishandled a handoff on a dive play up the middle. Greene gobbled up the ball, adding the recovered fumble to his interception from earlier, giving him a nice two-turnover haul for the game.

The Steelers had dodged a bullet and began their possession at the six-yard line. A Harris run to the right gave the Steelers a bit of room. But the Vikings' defense once again stood strong and forced another punt.

With the ball on the fifteen-yard line, Walden positioned himself just a touch closer to the line of scrimmage in a concession to the still strong wind. This time, Vikings linebacker Matt Blair streaked in from Walden's right side and blocked the punt. The ball bounced into the end zone where it was almost casually scooped up in stride by Terry Brown for a Vikings touchdown.

What the Vikings offense couldn't do moments before, the Vikings' special teams had accomplished. Momentum had flipped once again, as easy as a coin flipping through the air. Even as Cox's extra point attempt clanked off the left upright and fell to the ground, no good, the Vikings felt positive about trailing only 9–6 in a game where its offense up to that point had totaled well less than one hundred yards.

It was a whole new ball game. Ten minutes, thirty-three seconds remained. Which team was going to impose its will against the other and come out of Tulane Stadium with the victory?

What the Steelers needed was a long, sustained drive to run down the clock and salt away the game. They delivered in the form of an eleven-play, sixty-six-yard drive that took nearly seven minutes off the clock.

But the drive wasn't without its perilous moments. On the drive's first third down, Bradshaw connected with tight end Brown deep down the right side of the field. However, when he was tackled by Wallace and linebacker Roy Winston, the ball came free. Linebacker Siemon pounced on it and the officials ruled it as a recovered fumble, with Minnesota taking over possession on their twenty-eight-yard line. It was a giant break for the Vikings, and it appeared as though the Steelers were going to be on their heels.

The first two game officials on the scene, back judge Ray Douglas and field judge Dick Dolack, had ruled the play a fumble, with a subsequent recovery by the Vikings. Much to the relief of the Steelers and their fans, though, head linesman Ed

Marion correctly overruled their call, stating Brown was down by contact before the ball fell free of his hands.

The Steelers had dodged another potential bullet, and that ever-fickle momentum began to slip from behind the Vikings.

Two plays after the thirty-yard gain by Brown, Bleier broke off a seventeen-yard gain on a beautiful misdirection run that had fooled the aggressive pursuit of the Purple People Eaters, who had been fixated on Harris. On the next third down, needing five yards for a first down, Bleier went for six yards with a pass from Bradshaw to advance the ball to the five-yard line.

Two rushing plays netted very little, but on third down again, Bradshaw rolled to his right and rifled a pass into the arms of Brown four yards deep into the end zone for a Steelers touchdown. Gerela nailed the extra point, and the Steelers were now in firm control with a 16–6 lead. Only three minutes and thirty-one seconds remained before the Steelers would be crowned champions!

The Vikings, unable to move the ball consistently throughout the game, now needed two scores to either tie or take the lead. And they had little time to get that accomplished.

Determining no time was better than the present, Tarkenton dropped back and rolled to his left to pass on the Vikings' first play. He heaved a deep pass downfield intended for Gilliam. Safety Wagner stepped in front of the route, tipped the ball up in the air to himself, then cradled it for the interception.

Running out the clock in front of boisterous Steelers fans in the crowd, Bradshaw ran off seven consecutive plays, keeping the clock running down and forcing the Vikings to burn their allotment of timeouts. When the Steelers finally turned the ball over on downs, just thirty-eight seconds remained in Super Bowl IX.

Two plays later, and over forty-one years since Rooney, the Chief, had founded them, the Pittsburgh Steelers were the champions of professional football. Noll, who had turned the team into champions in just six seasons as the head coach, was carried off the field on the shoulders of his players.

Harris, who finished the game with thirty-four carries for a Super Bowl-record 158 yards and a touchdown, was named the game's Most Valuable Player. The Steel Curtain held the potent Vikings to just 119 total yards and forced five turnovers in the win.

The city of Pittsburgh heartedly celebrated the Steelers' first-ever championship—and just the city's ninth championship in any of the major sports leagues, joining the Pirates' four World Series titles (1909, 1925, 1960, and 1971), the Homestead Grays three Negro World Series titles (1943, 1944, and 1948), and the Pipers' lone ABA Finals title (1968).

This 1883 wood engraving of a Howard Pyle illustration depicts William Penn's meeting with colonists during his first trip to America. (Source: Library of Congress Prints and Photographs Division)

Andrew Carnegie, pictured sometime between 1865 and 1880. (Source: Brady-Handy Photograph Collection at the Library of Congress Prints and Photographs Division)

Published in 1892, these two drawings by Charles Mente; after photographs by Dabbs, Pittsburgh; depict the mob assailing the Pinkerton men on their march to the temporary prison downtown and barges burning on the river outside the plant. (Source: Library of Congress Prints and Photographs Division)

Photograph of the Pittsburgh skyline, possibly taken at Schenley Park, sometime between 1900 and 1920.
(Source: Detroit Publishing Company photograph collection at the Library of Congress Prints and Photographs Division)

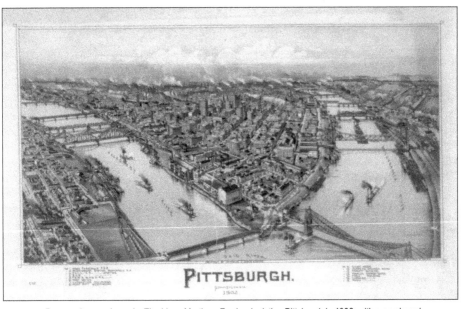

Panoramic map drawn by Thaddeus Mortimer Fowler depicting Pittsburgh in 1902, with a numbered
index at the bottom indicating points of interest, including major railroad stations, the post office,
Fort Pitt blockhouse, and the courthouse, as well as the Frick, Carnegie, and Park buildings
(Source: World Digital Library at Library of Congress Geography and Map Division)

This 1907 photograph shows the wetting and cooling of a bed of pig iron
in a blast furnace at a Pittsburgh mill.
(Source: H. C. White Co. at the Library of Congress Prints and Photographs Division)

A photograph looking down Sixth Avenue in downtown Pittsburgh, circa 1908.
(Source: Detroit Publishing Company photograph collection
at Library of Congress Prints and Photographs Division)

A Jones and Laughlin steel mill,
as photographed sometime between 1900 and 1915.
(Source: Detroit Publishing Company photograph
collection at the Library of Congress Prints
and Photographs Division)

Andrew Mellon, pictured between 1921 and 1923.
(Source: Harris & Ewing photograph collection
at the Library of Congress Prints and Photographs Division)

This 1938 photograph by Arthur Rothstein shows the hot, dusty
work of tapping a blast furnace in a Pittsburgh steel mill.
(Source: Farm Security Administration - Office of War
Information Photograph Collection at the Library of Congress
Prints and Photographs Division)

A Pittsburgh steel mill, as captured in a photograph taken in July 1938 by Arthur Rothstein. (Source: Farm Security Administration - Office of War Information Photograph Collection at the Library of Congress Prints and Photographs Division)

Steelers Hall of Fame defensive tackle Ernie Stautner walks on the sidelines during a 1962 game. Stautner's #70 is one of only two jersey numbers retired by the Steelers. (Sources: AP Photo/NFL Photos)

Chuck Noll [right] poses with Dan Rooney, general manager of the Steelers, January. 27, 1969, as he's announced as the Steelers' 14th head coach. (Source: AP Photo)

US Army PFC Robert "Rocky" Bleier recuperates from his combat injuries at the military hospital at Camp Oji in Tokyo, Japan, September 1, 1969. (Source: AP Photo/Henri Huet)

Steelers' running back Franco Harris eludes a tackle by Jimmy Warren of the Oakland Raiders on his 60-yard "Immaculate Reception" to score the winning touchdown in the AFC Divisional playoff game in Pittsburgh, Sunday, Dec. 23, 1972. (Source: AP Photo)

Ernie Holmes, Mean Joe Greene, Mike Wagner, JT Thomas, and Dwight White celebrate a safety after Vikings' quarterback Fran Tarkenton was downed in the end zone in the second quarter of Super Bowl IX in New Orleans, January 12, 1975. (Source: AP Photos/Charlie Kelly)

Steelers' wide receiver Lynn Swann dives to catch a pass during Super Bowl X in Miami, January 18, 1976. (Source: AP Photo)

Steelers' running back Rocky Bleier hauls in a 7-yard touchdown pass over Dallas Cowboys' linebacker DD Lewis to give the Steelers the lead in Super Bowl XIII in Miami, January 21, 1979.
(Source: AP Photo)

Mean Joe Greene is interviewed by former Oakland Raiders' head coach John Madden during media day ahead of Super Bowl XIV in Fullerton, California, January 16, 1980.
(Source: AP Photo)

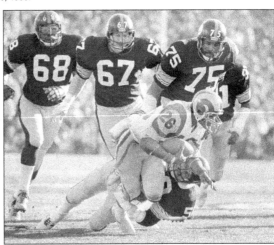

Steelers' linebacker Jack Lambert throws Los Angeles Rams' running back Wendell Tyler for 4-yard loss as Steelers' teammates LC Green-wood, Gary Dunn, and "Mean Joe" Greene converge on a play in Super Bowl XIV in Pasadena, California, January 20, 1980. (Source: AP Photo)

Co-author Tom O'Lenic with his brother, Tim, at Super
Bowl XLV in Dallas, Texas, February 6, 2011.
(Source: Tom O'Lenic)

A quote from Steelers' head coach Mike Tomlin, used as a motto in
the Steelers' locker room at Acrisure Stadium. (Source: Tom O'Lenic)

The Roberto Clemente Bridge, also known as the Sixth Street Bridge, spanning the
Allegheny River leading into downtown Pittsburgh, 2022. (Source: Tom O'Lenic)

Jim Baker holds the ball that Franco Harris caught
on the Immaculate Reception play. (Source: Tom O'Lenic)

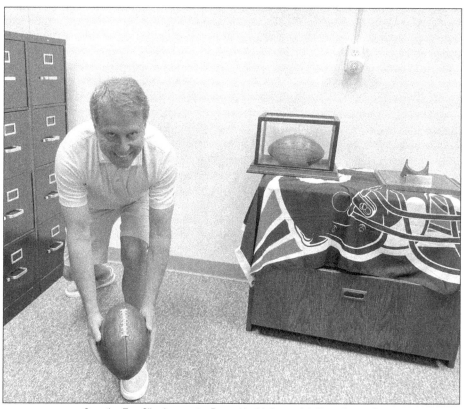

Co-author Tom O'Lenic recreates Franco Harris's Immaculate Reception catch
with the actual gameday football in Jim Baker's safe. (Source: Tom O'Lenic)

Chapter 16

A RETURN TO DOMINANCE

O n January 13, the day after the Super Bowl, the city of Pittsburgh turned out en masse to welcome and honor their returning gridiron heroes. As office workers settled into their desks in buildings throughout the Golden Triangle downtown, fans began lining the streets, braving the below-freezing temperatures.

State police officials estimated a crowd of 120,000 spectators lined the parade route in Gateway Center and along Liberty Avenue, Fifth Avenue, and Grant Street. Fans frolicked and danced and more than a few celebrated with spirits and drinks. In Market Square, the state liquor store had to close early, at the request of the police, because of the rowdy crowd growing a bit impatient waiting for the players.

Spectators made up their own amusement. The Frank Kalik Orchestra even performed from a second-story roof at the Carlton House Hotel.

Finally, in mid-afternoon, the first car appeared along the processional route, with the crowd lustfully cheering Bradshaw, with a barely visible, or noticed, Mayor Pete Flaherty in the back seat. Fireworks boomed from Point State Park.

After the cars containing the Steelers players, the true stars of the show, a significant gap developed before the first of the thirteen hastily commissioned floats. The crowd, unaware that more of the promised parade was still to come, filled the gap in the procession.

The floats were stranded on the Fort Pitt Bridge exit ramp, where they were discovered by the crowd. Before they were picked apart by fans seeking to take home a souvenir, the police re-routed the floats along Commonwealth Place and out of harm's way.

The crowd further up the route, unaware of the mess at the tail end of the procession, felt a bit . . . underwhelmed . . . and misled by the media who they felt had blown up this so-called parade into something it wasn't.

Most of the spectators went home. Those that remained crowded into nearby bars. Some bars only admitted regulars, and almost every bar reached capacity, with lines forming outside of doors.

Uniformed police patrolled the area, confiscating—and breaking with their nightsticks—open containers of alcohol on the street and trying to prevent any damage to local storefronts.

By the end of the night, over one hundred arrests had been made, most for public intoxication. It was substantially fewer than the night before, when rowdy revelers celebrating the championship wreaked havoc in the Golden Triangle, breaking at least eleven store windows. That night before, there had been 233 arrests and over sixty reported injuries.

Politically, the years-long Watergate saga was coming to an end, and a week and a half before the Steelers' triumph in Super Bowl IX, key Nixon administration officials John Mitchell, HR Haldeman, and John Ehrlichman had been found guilty of cover-up activities. They were sentenced in late February to prison terms that ranged from two and a half years to eight years.

Later in the year, in September, President Ford escaped injury in two separate assassination attempts on his life, both in California, over seventeen days. Neither attempt was based on either Watergate or the economy but on radicalized political views.

On the last day of April, the Vietnam War came to a conclusive end with the fall of Saigon. Communist forces from North Vietnam swept into the city, forcing the chaotic evacuation of the remaining Americans and the few fortunate South Vietnamese. The South Vietnam government was forced to surrender unconditionally.

In late spring, the unemployment rate in the United States hit nine percent, signaling the definitive and symbolic end of the country's post-World War economic boom. For context, consider there have been only four economic cycles with higher unemployment peaks: 10 percent in late 2009, 10.8 percent in November and December 1982, 14.7 percent during the 2020 COVID-19 pandemic, and 25 percent in 1933 at the height of the Great Depression.

The OPEC oil embargo had ended, but the price of crude oil continued to climb. In nominal values, the average price per barrel of crude oil had been $4.08 in 1973. In 1975, it averaged $13.95 per barrel.

Increased fuel costs had a ripple effect across the country and its communities. Businesses faced high transportation costs for both raw materials and finished goods. Likewise, consumers spent more of their disposable income on fuel, leaving less for other spending. Although economic history shows the multi-year recession ended in March 1975, its pain was still felt throughout the country.

Though they tried to hide it with optimistic statements to the financial press, corporate steel behemoths like U.S. Steel were feeling the pain too. U.S. Steel saw net income plummet 33.8 percent for the fourth quarter of 1975, contributing mightily to the yearly decline of 11.2 percent. Sales totaled 8.17 billion, down over 11 percent from that of the previous year. While accountants could still point to a profit, it was clear that steel was not a growth industry.

And the worst was yet to come.

For the Steelers, the months leading up to the 1975 season were quite tame, allowing the team to bask in its accomplishments. The 1975 NFL Draft didn't compare to the team's 1974 draft; for that matter, none ever have, either of the Steelers or those of other clubs.

As the reigning champions, the Steelers had the final selection of the first round, and with that pick, they chose Dave Brown, a defensive back out of the University of Michigan. Brown would appear in thirteen games in his rookie season and contribute most prolifically returning punts, where he averaged almost ten yards a return.

However, Brown's tenure with the Steelers would be cut short after just one season; he was selected by the Seattle Seahawks in the 1976 expansion draft. Brown then went on to become a fixture on the Seahawks' defense for eleven seasons, all spent as the team's starting right cornerback. In a career that would last fifteen full seasons in the NFL, Brown intercepted sixty-two passes, returning five of them for touchdowns. Additionally, he recovered twelve fumbles and recorded a safety.

Brown may not have reached his career achievements with the Steelers, but he was certainly an example of the Steelers' ability to recognize playing talent and the potential to make an impact in professional football.

Training camp opened, and subsequently closed, without a quarterback controversy this time around. Bradshaw had proven himself, particularly during the 1974 playoff run, as a more than capable starter. He was still prone to inaccuracy when throwing, but his rushing prowess added another dimension to the offense and complemented the backfield tandem of Harris and Bleier.

The regular season got underway for the defending champions on Sunday, September 21, on the road against the San Diego Chargers. They overpowered the overmatched Chargers from the opening kickoff.

Bradshaw was sharp, completing twenty-one of twenty-eight for 227 yards and two touchdowns, and the rushing game, led by Harris, piled up over 200 yards rushing. The defense was stellar, shutting out the Chargers and limiting them to just 146 yards in total offense while forcing four turnovers.

Despite winning the game 37–0, Noll didn't think his team had played as well as they could.

Week Two saw the Buffalo Bills return to Three Rivers, looking to avenge their playoff defeat from the past December. If it was redemption the Bills sought, it was redemption they received.

Offensively, Bradshaw had a day to forget, stumbling badly with unforced fumbles and throwing an interception. He got a quick hook from Noll and was replaced by Gilliam,

Defensively, the Bills blasted through the Steel Curtain, cutting through the vaunted defense like no team in recent memory. For the game, the Bills rushed for over 300 yards, led by Simpson's 277 yards. Simpson's eighty-eight-yard touchdown scamper in the third quarter spotted the Bills with a 23–0 lead, one they would comfortably hold until the final whistle, winning 30–21.

Humbled, the Steelers, as a team, brought it back to basics and set off on the rest of their schedule. And what a trip it was.

In their next three games, on the road against the Browns and then home against both the Broncos and the Chicago Bears, the Steelers outscored their opponents 96–18, winning 42–6, 20–9, and 34–3.

In the three-game stretch, the Steelers forced seven turnovers while committing just two of their own. Importantly, Bradshaw had not thrown an interception. In fact, his only interception of the season thus far had been a pick thrown in the Week Two loss to the Bills.

With their record at 4–1, the Steelers then traveled to Milwaukee to face the Green Bay Packers, coached by their legendary former quarterback, Bart Starr. After surrendering a two-yard touchdown by running back John Brockington to fall behind 6–3 in the second quarter, the Steelers responded immediately on a ninety-four-yard kickoff return for a touchdown by reserve running back Mike Collier.

From there on, it was old-school football at its best. The Steelers rushed the ball fifty-nine times for 248 yards, and Bleier was the primary workhorse, carrying the ball thirty-five times for 163 yards, both career highs. The Steel Curtain limited the Packers' offense to just eleven first downs, and the Steelers overcame three fumbles and scored last to win a nail-biter, 16–13.

The Week Seven contest was against the undefeated Bengals in Cincinnati's Riverfront Stadium. Once again, the Steelers started slowly, and after giving up a short field goal, trailed 3–0 entering the second quarter. Then, they scored twenty-three unanswered points to take a big lead into the fourth quarter. Highlights in that stretch included two touchdown receptions by Swann, the first from thirty-seven yards and the second from twenty-five yards, both on passes from Bradshaw.

Bengals quarterback Anderson put up big numbers in passing yards in the Bengals' desperate attempt to come back. However, the Steelers' defense picked off three interceptions and added four sacks. Bradshaw's short touchdown run in the fourth added some breathing space, and the Steelers walked off the Bengals' home field with a convincing 30–24 victory and a share of first place in the division.

L. C. Henderson Greenwood was born on September 8, 1946, in Canton, Mississippi, where he would grow up and live until he went off to college. He graduated from Arkansas Agricultural, Mechanical & Normal (Arkansas AM&N), later renamed the University of Arkansas at Pine Bluff, where, of course, he starred on the football field.

Greenwood was drafted by the Steelers in the tenth round of Chuck Noll's first draft with the club in 1969. By 1971, he ascended into the starting lineup, where he became a cornerstone defensive end of the Steel Curtain until he retired in 1981.

Greenwood was a tall defensive end, standing six feet, six inches tall, with a long wingspan, and he leveraged his length and strength to be a fearsome pass rusher. In his era, sacks were an unofficial statistic, but he was credited with leading the team in sacks on six different occasions, with a career-high of eleven in the 1974 season, on his way to a career total of seventy-eight.

To fervent and casual fans alike, Greenwood was known for wearing gold-colored cleats when he played, in an apparent attempt to allow spectators and television commentators to easily identify him.

Greenwood was a player that didn't need shoes to garner attention because his play on the field attracted plenty in its own right. Over his career, he was a six-time Pro Bowler and was named to NFL All-Pro teams in 1974 and 1975. He played on four Super Bowl-winning teams in Pittsburgh, and no fan will ever forget his four sacks of Roger Staubach in Super Bowl X.

Greenwood passed away in 2013 at the age of sixty-seven from kidney failure. He was buried in his hometown of Canton, Mississippi.

The Steelers started the second half of the 1975 season atop the AFC's Central Division with a 6–1 record, albeit with company. Their victory over Cincinnati the week before had finally dropped the Bengals from the ranks of the undefeated. However, somewhat surprisingly, the Houston Oilers were at the crowded perch atop the division with a 6–1 record too.

The Oilers were just in their sixteenth year of existence and their sixth in the NFL. They were a team on an upward trajectory, though, and had improved from 1–13 in 1973 to 7–7 in 1974. They rolled into Three Rivers Stadium with their only loss a tough two-point deficit against the Bengals in Week Three.

Steered by first-year head coach Bum Phillips, the Oilers' offense was directed by veteran signal caller Pastorini, and their balanced attack featured receiver Ken Burrough and running backs Ronnie Coleman and Don Hardeman. Defensively, the Oilers were led by veteran linemen Curley Culp and Elvin Bethea, along with rookie linebacker Robert Brazile.

The Steelers jumped out to a quick 10–0 lead in the first quarter, scoring on a short Gerela field goal and a short touchdown pass from Bradshaw to Swann. Coleman's three-yard touchdown run in the second quarter closed the gap, but only temporarily as Bradshaw's six-yard touchdown to Brown pushed the lead back up to ten points, 17–7.

There was no quit in the visitors from Texas, however. A forty-eight-yard field goal by Skip Butler and a one-yard touchdown run by Fred Willis deadlocked the two teams at seventeen into the fourth quarter. Bradshaw's third touchdown pass of the day, a twenty-one-yard strike to Stallworth, gave the Steelers the margin necessary to escape with a hard-earned 24–17 victory. With the win, the Black and Gold took sole possession of first place in the division.

Before a rematch with the Oilers on a *Monday Night Football* telecast, the Steelers first flexed their muscles at home against the Kansas City Chiefs. Starting slowly, the Steelers fell behind 3–0 in the second quarter. From then on, led by Bradshaw and his touchdown passes to both Swann and Stallworth, the club reeled off twenty-eight consecutive points to win, going away, 28–3. The defense was, again, fabulous, shutting down the rushing attack while also sacking Chiefs quarterbacks six times and intercepting two passes.

The rematch with the Oilers in the Houston Astrodome was a sloppy affair, with nine total turnovers, five committed by the Steelers. White got the scoring started on defense with a two-point safety, stopping Pastorini in the end zone. After Butler put the Oilers up 3–2 in the second quarter with a field goal, the Steelers took control.

First, Harris scored on a four-yard scamper. Then Bradshaw connected again with Swan for a touchdown, this one from eighteen yards out. At the half, the Steelers were up 15–3.

Gerela tacked on a field goal in the third, and Fuqua scored on a thirteen-yard run in the fourth to spot the Steelers a 25–3 lead. After a Burrough score on a bomb from Pastorini, the Steelers killed off the game with another Harris scoring run, this one from thirteen yards out. The win lifted the Steelers' record to 9–1 and clinched a playoff spot in the postseason.

Week Eleven, the Steelers visited New York to take on Namath and the Jets. It was an easy win. They intercepted four Namath passes, and Bradshaw threw two touchdown passes to stake the Black and Gold to a 20–0 lead. A fourth-quarter score by the Jets made the final a 20–7 Steelers victory.

The next two weeks had the Steelers homesteading against the division-rival Browns and Bengals, allowing them the opportunity to sweep the division in the regular season. The Browns came out swinging in their December 7 matchup, fired up to atone for their dismal Week Three showing.

After Browns running back Greg Pruitt scored on a one-yard run in the second quarter, disaster struck the Steelers when, on the ensuing kickoff, returner Collier fumbled the ball without being hit. Browns rookie Willer Miller scooped up the ball and jogged in untouched for a touchdown, giving the Browns a 17-7 lead.

From there, the Steelers set out methodically to capture control of the game as the overall talent disparity played to their advantage. Harris ran for 103 yards, pushing him over 1,000 yards for the third time in his career. Bradshaw threw two touchdowns to Swann in the third quarter, and Harris' eight-yard touchdown run in the fourth, his second scoring run of the game, completed the scoring in a 31-17 victory.

The last chance for a loss in the division came the very next week when the Bengals visited, bringing their 10–2 record with them. The Steelers jumped out early and never looked back, winning 35–14 and preserving a perfect record in the Central Division.

The 1975 season finale saw the Steelers travel out west to play the Los Angeles Rams. While the game would mean very little with respect to setting the field for the playoffs, it was still a matchup of titans, and the Rams had an 11–2 record and a stout, strong defense. In fact, combined, the Rams and Steelers had allowed fewer points in the season than eleven individual teams had.

As dominant as the Rams' defense was, the Rams' offense had sputtered early in the season. Then, quarterback James Harris righted the ship and made the Rams a well-balanced machine.

Harris was injured though, and his backup, Ron Jaworski, was under center to compete against the Steelers. Jaworski didn't get much done against the Steel Curtain, despite Noll resting many of his starters in the second half. Still, Jaworski engineered a drive in the fourth quarter, when it mattered, and scored himself on a five-yard quarterback draw.

Bradshaw also sat out the second half, and the Steelers never got their offense clicking. Harris rushed for over one hundred yards, but four turnovers on offense stymied any chance to sustain drives. While the Steelers lost 10–3, they had played tough against a good team and had rested many of their stars to protect against possible injury. They returned to Pittsburgh healthy and ready for another important playoff run.

The Steelers completed the 1975 season with a 12–2 record and rather comfortably won the AFC Central Division crown over an eleven-win Bengals team and a ten-win Oilers team—the first time three teams from one division had recorded ten or more victories in a single season. Along the way, they had outscored opponents 373–162.

Now in his sixth season, Bradshaw had continued his progression as a starting quarterback with his best year yet. He completed nearly 58 percent of his passes and threw for eighteen touchdowns, both career highs. Just as important, he had limited his interceptions, tossing only nine, for a career-low 3.1 percent of his pass attempts. For his play, Bradshaw was awarded his first Pro Bowl berth.

Harris, too, had a big year, setting career-highs of 262 rushing attempts, 1,246 rushing yards, and ten rushing touchdowns. He continued to develop as a dual-threat back, catching passes out of the backfield as he recorded career-high receiving totals of twenty-eight catches for 214 yards and another touchdown. Harris was named to his fourth consecutive Pro Bowl and also earned All-Pro recognition.

From the offensive side of the ball, Swann, tackle Jon Kolb, and center Ray Mansfield were also included on the 1975 All-Pro team.

Perhaps no other indicator of the Steelers' strength over the course of the season was more leading than the honors received by its defensive team members. Eight members of the starting eleven on defense earned Pro Bowl honors. All-Pro honors went to the entire defensive line of Greene, Holmes, White, and Greenwood; the entire linebacker corps of Lambert, Ham, and Russell; and three-quarters of the defensive backfield, Blount, Wagner, and Edwards.

For good measure, kicker Gerela and punter Walden also graced the All-Pro roster.

Without question, the 1975 Steelers had been one of the NFL's best-ever teams in the regular season. But would they hold up in the playoffs?

In the first round of the playoffs, the Steelers hosted an explosive and vastly improved Baltimore Colts team, offensively built around quarterback Bert Jones and running back Lydell Mitchell, Harris's collegiate teammate at Penn State. In the regular season, the Colts had scored an average of just over twenty-eight points a game, second best in the entire year.

The Colts had been dismal in 1974, enduring a 2–12 campaign. Interestingly, the 1975 season started similarly. After winning their season opener against the Bears, the Colts then turned around and promptly lost their next four games in succession, leaving them with a 1–4 record. Then, they turned it around in a big way and reeled off nine consecutive victories to close the season. They rolled into Three Rivers Stadium with a 10–4 record and plenty of confidence.

On the Colts' first possession of the game, however, Jones, having narrowly avoided a sack attempt by White that nearly took off his helmet, scrambled to make the most out of the play. Getting tackled by JT Thomas, Jones suffered an injury to his throwing arm.

The Steel Curtain was not kind to Jones's replacement, Marty Domres, a seven-year pro out of Columbia. Late in the first quarter, Ham picked off a Domres pass, giving Bradshaw and the offense the ball on the Steelers' thirty-nine-yard line.

On the first play of the possession, Bradshaw connected with Lewis on a thirty-four-yard completion deep down the middle. Three plays later, Harris stormed in from the eight-yard line and the Steelers had a 7–0 lead.

In the second quarter, Bradshaw threw an egregious interception, with Colts cornerback Lloyd Mumphord the only player in the vicinity of the throw. Mumphord snapped off a fifty-eight-yard return to set up his offense on the Steelers' nineteen-yard line.

Soon thereafter, Domres found receiver Glenn Doughty alone in the end zone for a five-yard scoring completion. It would be one of only two completions on the day for Domres, but it was enough to level the score at 7–7.

Early in the third quarter, the Colts converted a Harris fumble into a field goal and, despite not having the services of Jones, led the game 10–7.

The Steel Curtain continued to clamp down on the Colts. Try as the Colts might, they could not get their running game going against Greene and company—for the afternoon, they ran the ball forty-one times for a paltry eighty-two yards.

With the running game going nowhere, Domres tried to get something going with the passing game. Deep in Colts' territory, he threw an ill-advised pass into a pack of three Steeler defenders. Blount picked the pass off, returning the ball to inside the Colts' ten-yard line. That play proved to be the turning point of the game.

Bleier broke two tackles and scooted into the end zone, and the Steelers quickly had a 14–10 lead. When Bradshaw scored on a two-yard run in the fourth, the Steelers bumped their lead up to 21–10.

Seeing the Colts' season coming to an end, Jones reentered the game and produced his share of anxious drama for Steelers fans. He hit Doughty down the left sideline for a fifty-eight-yard catch and run and had the Colts threatening to narrow the score.

Then, from the Steelers' three-yard line, Ham knocked the ball out of Jones's hand as the quarterback was about to unleash a pass. The bouncing ball was scooped up by Russell, and the thirty-four-year-old linebacker ran it back the entire way, ninety-three long, torturously slow yards, for the final score of the game. After the game, Ham quipped perfectly, "I couldn't tell if he [Russell] was running for a touchdown or running the clock out."

The Steelers had won 28–10, and it was a deserved victory. The defense had done its job and had benefited from Jones missing more than half the game. On offense, Harris had a great day rushing, carrying the ball twenty-seven times for an impressive 153 yards. But he had lost two fumbles, too, and in total, the Steelers' offense had committed five turnovers.

The Steelers were advancing in the playoffs, but they knew they had opportunities to improve upon their level of play. Their next playoff game would be for the AFC Championship and an invitation to Super Bowl X. Their opponent, almost naturally, would be the Oakland Raiders.

Jack Ham was born on December 23, 1948, in Johnstown, Pennsylvania, about an hour's drive east of Pittsburgh. For college, he stayed relatively close to home and played football at Penn State. There, in his first two years as a starting linebacker, the Nittany Lions were undefeated. After his senior year, in 1970, Ham, as his team's co-captain, was named to the All-America team.

The Steelers selected Ham in the second round of the 1971 NFL Draft, with the thirty-fourth overall selection. As a rookie with the team, he immediately stepped into the starting lineup.

Ham's biggest strengths were his speed and football-playing instincts. He had the quickness to cover receivers and the hustle to cover deep down the field as well. Plus, when his instincts took over, he could get anywhere he needed to be on the field.

Over his twelve-year career, spent entirely with the Steelers, Ham displayed a flair for making the big, dramatic plays. His career statistics include fifty-three take-aways—twenty-one recovered fumbles and thirty-two interceptions. Incidentally, those fifty-three turnovers represent the most in NFL history by a player who did not play defensive back.

Ham earned first-team All-Pro honors six times, and from 1973 to 1980, he was named to eight straight Pro Bowls. And he played for four Super Bowl-winning championship teams.

In 1988, Ham was inducted into the Pro Football Hall of Fame. Two years later, he was inducted into the College Football Hall of Fame. Never one to be outshone, in 1999, Ham was ranked number forty-seven on *The Sporting News's* list of the 100 Greatest Football Players.

On January 4, 1976, coach John Madden led his Oakland Raiders into Three Rivers Stadium for yet another postseason showdown with the Steelers. It was the fourth consecutive year the two teams had met in the playoffs, and for the second straight year, it was for the right to represent the AFC in the Super Bowl.

The Raiders had recorded another great regular season, finishing 11–3, atop the AFC West Division. Offensively, they were led by the same cast of characters—Stabler, Branch, Biletnikoff, Hubbard, Banaszak, and Davis. Defensively, they featured a new 3-4 defense forced, in part, by injuries to the defensive line. Within that structure, their new addition at linebacker, Ted Hendricks, fit in wonderfully with established Raiders veterans like Sistrunk, Thoms, Villapiano, Brown, Tatum, and Atkinson.

The two teams knew each other very well.

The day dawned cold for the 1:00 p.m. kickoff, with twenty-degree temperatures and twenty-mile-an-hour winds pairing for a windchill factor of just two degrees. Footing was to be slick on the frozen turf at Three Rivers. The wind and cold would make handling the ball difficult. The visitors from California, who had never won a playoff game on the road, were decided underdogs, as the Steelers were favored by nearly a touchdown.

The weather led both teams to try to establish a running game, and the first half featured a hard-hitting game between two hard-nosed teams. The Steelers tried to get Harris going, but Hendricks and Villapiano would have none of it, limiting Harris to just twenty-four yards on eleven first-half carries.

Bradshaw picked up the slack with regards to moving the ball in the first half. Surprisingly nimble after having suffered a knee sprain against the Colts the week before, Bradshaw moved and found receivers open downfield. However, those drives came to premature ends when Bradshaw threw three first-half interceptions.

The Raiders also tried to move first with the running game. For their efforts, they had equally futile results.

The Raiders featured long-time Pro Bowlers Upshaw and Shall on the left side of their line, so it made sense they tried there first, away from Greene, Greenwood, and Ham stationed to Stabler's right. But there were no weak links in the Steel Curtain on either side.

Because of two Tatum interceptions, the Raiders had good field position in the first quarter but were unable to score. Forced to rely more on the passing game to move the ball, Stabler turned the ball over when Wagner made a diving interception.

Gifted good field position from Wagner's forced turnover, Bradshaw led the Steelers to within Gerela's range, and the kicker converted a thirty-six-yard field goal attempt for the only score of the first half.

The weather had definitely affected the play of both teams in the first half. Footing was treacherous, and slips and slides caused many plays to end before they really got going. Frozen hands and fingers dropped a lot of balls.

That experience of the first half, though, didn't help out in the second half. The third quarter alone featured a combined five turnovers between the two teams.

After a Davis fumble was recovered by Lambert at the Steelers' thirty-yard line, one of his three recovered fumbles on the afternoon, Bradshaw led the team on its best sustained drive of the game.

The drive covered seventy yards in just five plays and was culminated by Harris's twenty-five-yard scamper around the left side and down the frozen sideline. Early in the fourth quarter, the Steelers led, 10–0.

Playing in an almost desperate state, the Raiders took to the air, and Stabler delivered the best Raiders drive in return. Three consecutive receptions by tight end Dave Casper ate up large chunks of yardage. Stabler then polished off the drive with a fourteen-yard strike to receiver Siani who got just beyond the goal line for a touchdown.

With plenty of time left, the Raiders were back in the game, trailing just 10–7.

On the Raiders' next possession, however, with the chance to tie or even take the lead, Greenwood's tackle of Hubbard forced a fumble, which Lambert recovered on the Raiders' twenty-five yard line.

Three plays later, Bradshaw hit Stallworth, who had jumped in front of a slipping Neal Colzie, with a twenty-five-yard touchdown pass. A fumbled snap scrubbed the Gerela's extra point attempt, but the Steelers had put the game seemingly out of reach, leading 16–7, with less than half a quarter to play.

However, in possession of the ball and running out the clock, Harris fumbled, and the Raiders recovered on their own thirty-five-yard line. Remarkably, it was the seventh Steelers turnover of the game, and it gave the Raiders one last-gasp chance to take a victory.

With the game clock ticking away, Stabler hurried the Raiders downfield and into Steeler territory.

With the Raiders facing a third down and without any timeouts remaining, Madden, figuring his team needed nine points to just tie the game, sent in Blanda to attempt a forty-one-yard field goal. Blanda nailed it, the forty-eight-year-old's longest field goal of the year. The Raiders would have one last chance to win the game if they could recover an onside kick.

Every person in attendance at Three Rivers—players, officials, and fans alike—knew an onside kick was coming, and the slippery turf proved to be a willing accomplice. Ray Guy squibbed a kick to his left, the ball sliding around on the ground. Mishandled by Steelers receiver Reggie Garrett, the kick was recovered by Hubbard on the Raiders' forty-five-yard line.

Fifty-five yards away from a score and with just seven seconds remaining, Stabler heaved a pass deep down the left side of the field where Branch leaped and caught it. However, Blount tackled him promptly in the field of play at the fifteen-yard line, and time duly expired.

The Steelers, despite turning the ball over a mind-boggling seven times, won the game, 16–10. Once again ending the Raiders' season, they were advancing to Super Bowl X, where they would look to defend their championship against the Dallas Cowboys.

The Super Bowl came to life as part of a merger agreement in 1966 by the NFL and the AFL. The idea was a simple one: have the best team from each league compete for a championship.

It was originally called the "AFL-NFL World Championship Game," and the first edition featured the Kansas City Chiefs and the Green Bay Packers. Lamar Hunt, the owner of the Chiefs, often referred to the championship game discussed in the merger meetings as the "Super Bowl." He believed his inspiration in doing so probably stemmed from his kids playing with a bouncy Super Ball toy.

Leading up to the first championship game in January 1967, league owners voted to call the game the AFL-NFL World Championship Game. But, as Hunt kept referring to it as the Super Bowl, the media took his cue and ran with it.

Still not satisfied, the NFL worked through a variety of potential names before the second game, but by that time, the genie was out of the bottle. Although the second game was still, officially, the AFL-NFL World Championship Game, it was more commonly referred to as the Super Bowl.

The NFL stopped fighting against it leading up to the third game when it became officially known as the Super Bowl.

Of course, it's common practice to place Roman numerals rather than the year at the end of the words "Super Bowl" to identify one game from another. Those Roman numerals were officially added for the fifth edition of the game, played in 1971.

As of 2022, every team in the NFL has played in at least one Super Bowl, except for the Cleveland Browns, Houston Texans, Jacksonville Jaguars, and Detroit Lions. Twenty of the league's thirty-two franchises have won the Super Bowl.

Chapter 17

SHOWSTOPPER SWANN STEALS THE SHOW

Super Bowl X was scheduled for January 16, 1976, at the Orange Bowl in Miami, Florida. It was to be one of the first major sporting events in the year-long celebration of the American bicentennial. In fact, each team's jersey featured a commemorative patch with the bicentennial logo.

The Steelers' opponents were the Dallas Cowboys, who had been the first wild card team from the NFC to advance to the Super Bowl. The Cowboys were one of the country's most popular teams—they weren't quite "America's Team" yet, as they would eventually be known, but they were working in that direction.

The Cowboys were helmed by head coach Tom Landry, and they had completed the season with a 10–4 record, finishing second in the NFC East Division to the St. Louis Cardinals.

On offense, the Cowboys were led by quarterback Roger Staubach, a former Heisman Trophy winner from Navy. Staubach engineered an offense that racked up over 5,000 yards during the regular season, third-best in the league.

The Cowboys' rushing attack featured several running backs, with Robert New-house leading the way. Staubach's targets for passes included receivers Drew Pearson and Golden Richards, tight end Jean Fugett, and a familiar name for Steelers fans coming out of the backfield in veteran running back Preston Pearson. Pearson had been cut by the Steelers just before the season had started when Noll kept rookie Collier on the roster. Landry and the Cowboys quickly snapped him up after they had lost both Calvin Hill and Walt Garrison to injuries.

Defensively, the Cowboys were solid in all aspects of the game. The defensive line featured tackle Jethro Pugh in the middle and rookie Ed "Too Tall" Jones at end. The linebacker corps was centered by veteran mainstay Lee Roy Jordan at middle linebacker. The veteran defensive backfield included Mel Renfro at cornerback and Cliff Harris and Charlie Waters at safety positions—together, the defensive backs had accounted for fourteen interceptions.

The Cowboys had started the regular season with four straight victories. Since that quick start, though, they had been a bit streaky. However, they closed the regular season by winning five of their last six, including their final two games to qualify for the playoffs. Once in the playoffs, they dispatched the Vikings on the road in the divisional round. Then, in the NFC Championship game, they dismantled the Rams, also on the road, to earn the franchise's third Super Bowl appearance.

A seven-point underdog, the Cowboys nevertheless were poised to present a significant challenge to the Steelers.

In the days leading up to the Super Bowl, most pundits felt as though Swann would be unable to play. He had suffered a severe concussion in the AFC Championship Game on a heavy, but unpenalized, collision with the notoriously hard-hitting Atkinson. His replacement, Stallworth, went on to make the game-winning catch.

Swann's concussion was severe enough to warrant a two-day stay in the hospital. It also kept him from participating in most of the Steelers' practices leading up to the game, and in those practices he did attend, he only performed relatively minor workouts.

In an attempt to perhaps intimidate, but certainly to add doubt in Swann's mind about suiting up and playing, Cowboy safety Harris mentioned in interviews that while he would never intentionally look to hurt someone in a game, if a receiver was in his area, he would certainly go after him with all he had. Mind game tactic or not, it didn't sway Swann from competing.

The Cowboys won the coin toss and elected to receive the opening kickoff. Fielding Gerela's kick in the field of play, the Cowboys immediately unleashed a bit of trickery in the form of a reverse. Pearson caught the kick, started to his right, and just when all the Steelers set off in that direction, he handed the ball off to linebacker Thomas "Hollywood" Henderson sweeping around the left side. Henderson returned the kickoff forty-eight yards before Gerela chopped him out of bounds at the Steelers' forty-four-yard line.

On the play, Gerela injured himself, badly bruising his ribs. Immediately, after the game's first play, the Steelers knew their kicking game would be compromised for the remainder of the afternoon.

With the big play on the kickoff, the Cowboys had an early edge in momentum. The Steel Curtain immediately made amends and rectified the situation. On the Cowboys' first play from scrimmage, Staubach took the snap and rolled to his right. Greenwood was not fooled by any imagination and stripped Staubach of the football. It was recovered by center John Fitzgerald, and the Cowboys retained possession. But the Steelers' defense had made a statement from the get-go. If the Cowboys were going to win the ballgame, it would take more than gadget plays and trickery.

The Cowboys were forced to punt, and possession transferred to Bradshaw, Harris, and company for the first time. Big runs by Harris and Bleier carved out a first down, but then the drive stalled and the Steelers sent in the punt unit. That's when disaster struck.

Walden, perhaps distracted by a fierce Cowboys rush from his right side, inexplicably fumbled the snap. By the time he gathered it in, a pack of Cowboys swarmed him on the twenty-nine-yard line. The first big break of the game had gone the Cowboys' way.

Staubach wasted no time in striking. On the Cowboys' first play, he faked a handoff to Pearson sweeping to the right, took a deep drop, and fired a strike to receiver Drew Pearson running across the middle of the field. Pearson caught the ball in stride, with speed, and easily scampered past Russell to score. With Toni Fritsch's extra point, the Cowboys had a 7–0 first-quarter lead.

That touchdown was the only first-quarter touchdown scored against the Steelers' defense the entire season. The team now had a hole to dig themselves out of in the season's most important game.

The Steelers started their next possession with good field position at their own thirty-two-yard line. Four straight rushes, two each by both Harris and Bleier, netted the Steelers a first down, twenty yards and ball on the Cowboys' side of midfield. Then, on second down, Bradshaw dropped straight back and threw deep down the field to Swan, who made a leaping catch on the right sideline and advanced the ball to the Cowboys' sixteen-yard line.

Still establishing a rushing game, the Steelers pounded two more running plays to push the ball to the seven-yard line. Then, with three tight ends on the field and lining up for an apparent run to get the first down, Bradshaw resorted to a little misdirection of his own.

Guard Gerry Mullins, who had lined up as a tight end, went into motion ahead of the snap, moving toward his left. As he approached Bradshaw, the quarterback took the snap, with Mullins attacking the interior of the Cowboys' line as if a run up the middle was imminent. Bradshaw, however, tucked the ball in, rolled to his right, and hit tight end Randy Grossman, who was alone behind the fooled Dallas defensive secondary, in the end zone.

Working through his injury, Gerela barely got his extra point attempt over the crossbar and inside the left upright to tie the score 7–7. Interestingly, Super Bowl X was the first Super Bowl to feature first-quarter scores by both teams.

With their third possession, Staubach looked to establish the Cowboys' rushing game. He mixed rushes with Newhouse and Doug Dennison and broke things up with a nine-yard completion down the middle to tight end Fugett.

It was a nice drive, and the Cowboys entered scoring position inside the Steelers' twenty-yard line. Facing a fourth and inches, Landry and Staubach went for it, and Dennison delivered with a run off the left tackle for a first down.

Two rushing attempts later, with the ball resting on the Steelers' fourteen-yard line, time expired in the first quarter. The teams switched sides of the field, deadlocked 7–7.

Lining up their twelfth play of the drive to open the second quarter, the Cowboys were penalized before the snap. Facing a third-and-fourteen from the Steelers' nineteen-yard line, Staubach positioned himself in shotgun formation, where he stood five yards behind the center to better set up a passing play. He had ample time to throw, but his pass was nearly intercepted by safety Edwards. The Steelers had missed a chance to force a key turnover, but they had stopped a productive Cowboys drive.

On the next play, Fritsch split the uprights with his thirty-six-yard field goal, and the Cowboys moved ahead 10–7.

The Steelers then set off on a drive of their own. Bradshaw split carries with Bleier and Harris and even scrambled himself for a first down on a third-down run. After another leaping catch by Stallworth, however, the Cowboys stood strong at their own thirty-six-yard line.

Facing a fourth down, the Steelers knew they were not in the field goal range of the injured Gerela. And, despite the Cowboys' success in moving the ball on offense so far, Noll had confidence in his league-leading defense to hold down the fort if required. So the Steelers decided not to punt and instead set their sights on earning a first down.

Bradshaw faked a run up the middle to Bleier and dropped back to pass. He spotted an open Harris streaking down the right sideline. However, as Harris cradled in the throw, he was met by the Cowboys' Harris, who knocked the ball loose. The incompletion halted the Steelers' drive and gave possession back to the Cowboys.

Another big play had just barely slipped through the Steelers' grasp.

The Steelers' defense quickly validated Noll's decision by forcing the Cowboys to punt on their first three-and-out of the game.

Rookie Brown returned the punt to the Steelers' twenty-two-yard line, where Bradshaw took over once again. A short Bleier run, an incomplete pass, and the first sack of the game, by Randy White and Harvey Martin, provided the means for a subsequent three-and-out possession for the Steelers.

What had started out as a wide-open, back-and-forth affair had settled down into an exchange of punts and a field position game.

With a little over eight minutes remaining in the half, Staubach and the Cowboys took over at their own forty-eight-yard line, in great position to add to their tally before the break. After a nine-yard reception by Preston Pearson, Staubach nearly turned the ball over when he fumbled the snap on second down. He quickly recovered his miscue, and on third down, the Cowboys converted when Staubach connected with Pearson on a seven-yard completion down the left sideline.

After a two-yard run by Newhouse and an incompletion, the Cowboys faced a critical third-and-eight to keep their drive going. Staubach took the snap out of the shotgun formation, eluded a near sack by Greenwood, scrambled around for a few more seconds, then heaved a pass to reserve running back Charley Young, who worked the ball down the right sideline to the Steelers' twenty-yard line. The Cowboys were threatening to extend their lead.

Challenged, the Steelers' defense held strong. On first down, Russell trapped Newhouse behind the line of scrimmage for a three-yard loss. Greenwood then burst through the line on second down and sacked Staubach for a loss of twelve yards. Not to be outdone, White got in on the show the very next play and sacked Staubach, setting the Cowboys back another ten yards. In three plays, the Steelers' defense had pushed the ball from their twenty-yard line to their forty-five-yard line. Looking like they would at least have an attempt at a field goal and three points just a minute and a half before, the Cowboys were now forced to punt.

An excellent punt by Cowboys punter Mitch Hoopes buried the Steelers at their own six-yard line with 3:47 left in the first half. On first down, Bradshaw handed off to Bleier, who swept around the left side and found a bunch of Cowboys defenders in his way on a hard-earned two-yard run. Harris then got bottled up on second down, gaining another two yards to set up a third-and-six.

That third-down play would prove to be one of the most memorable plays in Super Bowl history.

Bradshaw took the snap and, facing a Cowboys blitz, dropped back to his goal line. From there, he heaved a pass with all his might down the center of the field in the direction of Lynn Swann. Swann had his defender, Mark Washington, beat, but the pass was just slightly underthrown, letting Washington catch up. At the fifty-yard line, Swann soared into the air, and as Washington collided with him, tipped the ball upwards. Then, keeping his eyes laser-focused on the ball, Swann brought in the pass just as he hit the field. Somehow, the sure-handed receiver kept a hold of the ball as he hit the turf, securing one of the greatest catches ever seen in the Super Bowl.

The next week, Swann's catch was immortalized with a stunning image on the cover of Sports Illustrated. The Heinz Kluetmeier photograph captured Swann's athletic ability and focus to become a truly iconic representation of Super Bowl history.

But the play wasn't even over yet. Swann probably should have been marked down by contact with Washington at the Cowboys' forty-three-yard line. But, with no whistle being blown, Swann got up and scampered to the thirty-seven-yard line before being tackled by Renfro.

After the fifty-three-yard completion, Bradshaw wasted no time in attacking again. On the next play, Bradshaw dropped back and let go a pass deep down the middle, again intended for Swann. This time, a diving Swann just missed getting his hands on the ball at the six-yard line.

After the near miss, Bleier banged the ball up the middle for a seven-yard gain. Harris then pounded out a first down with a four-yard run, and the Steelers called timeout with 1:10 on the clock and the ball on the Cowboys' twenty-six-yard line.

A scrambling Bradshaw hit Brown with a pass to advance the ball to the nineteen-yard line and put the Steelers in scoring position. From there, the drive stalled, and Noll sent in Gerela for a thirty-six-yard field goal attempt. However, Gerela's injury reared up again, and he hooked his kick, missing it to the left.

An entertaining first half ended one play later. The Cowboys had controlled the time of possession, holding the ball for eighteen minutes. The Steelers, thanks to two acrobatic catches by Swann, held an advantage in yards gained: 194–98. However, the Cowboys led where it mattered, on the scoreboard, by three points, 10–7.

Lynn Swann was born on March 7, 1952, in Alcoa, Tennessee, but wasn't there for long. At age two, Swann and his family moved to San Mateo, California. Growing up in the Bay area, Swann played football and ran track. In his senior year, in 1970, Swann won the state title in the long jump, defeating Randy Williams, who himself would go on to win a gold medal in the event at the 1972 Olympic Games.

Attending the University of Southern California, Swann excelled both in the classroom and on the gridiron, where he played for head coach John McKay. In addition to being a key contributor on the 1972 national championship team, Swann was also named to the All-America team.

A first-round pick of the Steelers in 1974, Swann led the NFL with 577 punt return yards as a rookie, a club record and the fourth-highest total in league history up to that point.

Swann ascended to the starting lineup in 1975, his second season with the Steelers, and he immediately shined. In the regular season, he caught forty-nine passes for 781 yards and led the league with eleven touchdown receptions.

While his second regular season in the NFL was a tough act to follow, Swann did just that in the playoffs, and his feats in that postseason proved to be the stuff of legends. We've only covered half of his legendary exploits in Super Bowl X.

Over the entirety of his nine-year professional football career, all with the Steelers, Swann played in 116 games and totaled 336 career receptions for 5,462 yards and fifty-one touchdowns. He also had eleven rushing attempts for seventy-two rushing yards and a touchdown, as well as sixty-one punt returns for 739 return yards and a touchdown. He was a Pro Bowl selection three times, named to the All-Pro team on three occasions, and was selected to the NFL's 1970s All-Decade Team.

After his playing career ended, Swann served on the President's Council on Fitness, Sports, and Nutrition from 2002 to 2005. And, in 2006, Swann made a go at politics, challenging for the governor of Pennsylvania as the Republican Party nominee.

Lynn Swann was inducted to the Pro Football Hall of Fame in 2001, one year before his fellow 1974 draftee and long-time receiving corps running mate, John Stallworth.

After both teams made halftime adjustments, the game resumed with the Cowboys kicking off to the Steelers. Bradshaw and company could do nothing, however, and after three plays they punted on fourth down.

The Cowboys took their first possession of the half again with great field position, this time beginning at their own forty-two-yard line. Two running plays netted little. On third down, and again from the shotgun formation, Staubach took the snap, dropped back, and let fly a pass down the right side in the direction of receiver Richards. The pass was picked off, however, by cornerback Thomas, and he ran back a brilliant return thirty-five yards to the Cowboys' twenty-five-yard line. It was the first turnover of the game, and it flipped the field position battle from the Cowboys' favor to that of the Steelers.

Harris took handoffs on three consecutive plays to earn a first down and move the chains. Then, Bradshaw was tackled on a keeper behind the line of scrimmage for a short loss. On second down, facing a stout, blitzing rush from the Cowboys, Bradshaw fired the ball out of the end zone for an incompletion, living to fight yet another play. That third-down play, however, resulted in an incompletion when Cowboys defender Washington broke up a pass intended for Swann at the goal line.

Gerela came into the game to attempt a thirty-three-yard field goal, which he missed left once again. After the play, the Cowboys' Harris got in Gerela's face and started mouthing off. Lambert came to the defense of his kicker and threw Harris to the ground. It was an offense that could have been penalized, and it could have even resulted in an ejection of Lambert from the game. Luckily for the Steelers, the referees let bygones be bygones, and the Cowboys were awarded possession of the ball on their twenty-yard line.

The Cowboys grounded out a first down on two running plays. But, on the next series of downs, Lambert stopped Staubach on a scramble just short of a first down at the forty-yard line. Brown fielded a good Hoopes punt and advanced the ball to the Steelers' twenty-four-yard line to set up the Steelers' offense.

Harris plowed through the middle for a short gain on first down. Then, Bradshaw, mixing things up a bit, dropped back and fired a pass in the right flat, along the sideline, in the direction of Swann. Swann, just coming out of his break, barely had time to see the ball. Still, he spun around and cradled it in for a catch and a twelve-yard gain for a first down.

The drive soon faltered. Facing a third down and short yardage, Bradshaw looked to catch the Cowboys' defense by surprise with a pass over the middle. It fell incomplete, however, and the Steelers were forced to punt.

With 4:06 left in the quarter, the Cowboys took over on their own eighteen-yard line. Three running plays just squeaked out a first down, but punishing tackles by the Steelers defenders, led by the frenetic play of Lambert, something that had been going on all game, gave the distinct impression that the Steel Curtain was well in control.

Two plays later, the Cowboys got another first down on a short catch by Newhouse on the left sideline. Then, on a first-down scramble by Staubach, Newhouse was hit with a fifteen-yard clipping penalty that set the Cowboys back to their own twenty-six-yard line.

All that hard work fighting against the Steelers' defense was negated with one toss of the referee's flag.

The Steelers held from there, stopping Preston Pearson from reaching the first-down marker on a third-down reception. The conservatively played quarter ended.

Six total possessions, three by each team, concluded with an interception, a missed field goal, and three punts, with a fourth punt ready to open the fourth and final quarter. The score remained 10–7 in favor of the Cowboys.

Jack Lambert was having a great Super Bowl, flying around the field, making tackles and constantly inspiring his teammates. It wasn't a surprise, as the second-year player did the same every game.

Lambert burst onto the scene as a rookie, starting every game, and he, with his mustache and fierce grimace highlighting his missing front teeth, soon became an iconic image of the hard-nosed Steelers and, in many ways, the NFL during that era.

John Harold Lambert was born on July 8, 1952, in Mantua, Ohio, near Akron, on the outskirts of Cleveland. As far as those missing teeth were concerned, Lambert lost those during a high school basketball practice. As a young man growing up he was particularly sensitive about those missing teeth.

On the football field, Lambert was a quarterback in high school before switching to defensive end at Kent State. And, thanks in part to Mick Jagger and the story related previously, he made the transition to starting middle linebacker while in college.

Lambert may have grown into being the prototypical linebacker of his era, but he didn't have the prototypical body of a middle linebacker coming out of college. He was on the tall side for a middle linebacker, listed at six-foot-four. But Lambert was relatively slender for the position. For the majority of his career, he was listed at 220 pounds, although reports have him as light as 200 pounds coming out of college.

When middle linebacker Henry Davis, a Pro Bowl selection with the Pittsburgh Steelers in 1973, became injured, Lambert was placed in the starting lineup as a bit of a stop-gap measure. From there, he never looked back. Lambert went on to be named Rookie of the Year, and he was a central part of the Steelers' commanding defense. In his first postseason, particularly against the Raiders in the AFC Championship Game in Oakland, Lambert was a dominant force.

Lambert proved to be a tackling machine over the course of his career. According to the Steelers media guides, he averaged just under 150 tackles per season over his first decade in the league.

Over his career, Lambert recorded nearly 1,500 tackles, with over 1,000 of them being credited as solo tackles. He was also adept at falling back into pass coverage, as his twenty-eight interceptions attest. Beginning in his second year, Lambert ran off nine consecutive seasons being named to the Pro Bowl, and he won the Defensive Player of the Year award in 1976, his third season.

Jack Lambert was inducted into the Pro Football Hall of Fame in 1990.

The back-and-forth first half was followed up by a conservative, defensively-minded third quarter. Both teams had poked and probed on both sides of the ball, looking for advantages to exploit. It was time for both teams to make their moves to become Super Bowl champions.

On the first play of the fourth quarter, rookie Brown mishandled the Hoopes punt, resulting in a scramble inside the Steelers' twenty-yard line. Luckily for the Black and Gold, Thomas recovered, preventing the Cowboys from receiving a fortuitous break and a very real opportunity to extend their lead. The Steelers had dodged a proverbial bullet.

On the first play of their position, Bradshaw dropped back and scrambled around until he found Harris wide open on the right sideline. The crowd erupted as he sprinted for an apparent go-ahead score. However, as Harris was still romping along about thirty yards from paydirt, the whistle blew. Just after he caught the ball, Harris had stepped out of bounds to avoid a diving attempt by Cowboys Dave Edwards to break up the play. Still, Harris' twenty-six-yard reception, his first and only reception of the game, advanced the ball to the forty-three-yard line.

The Cowboys had dodged their own bullet just one play after the Steelers had.

Feeling frisky, Bradshaw took the next snap, dropped straight back, and uncorked a deep pass in the direction of an open Stallworth downfield. The pass fell just beyond Stallworth's outstretched arms inside the Cowboys' twenty-yard line. While the pass was incomplete, it was the second play in a row where Steelers receivers had found plenty of open space.

The Steelers drive then stalled as first, Harris was stopped behind the line of scrimmage, and then, Bradshaw was sacked for a big loss by rookie defensive tackle Randy White on third down. After a booming fifty-seven-yard Walden punt, the Cowboys took over on their nineteen-yard line.

Heading the same direction as they had in the first quarter when they tried a reverse on the opening kickoff, the Cowboys reached into their bag of tricks again on first down. Staubach handed the ball to Preston Pearson, who took a couple of steps up the middle before swiveling around and pitching the ball back to Staubach for a flea-flicker pass. Staubach had his eyes deep downfield on a streaking Drew

Pearson, but his receiver was blanketed in close coverage by Thomas. Under a heavy pass rush and forced to cut his losses, Staubach pulled down the ball and ran before getting swamped by Furness and Lambert.

Denison ran for next to nothing on second down, and Holmes then pressured Staubach into a sack by White and Furness to force fourth down. The Steel Curtain was taking control. Despite being down 10–7 on the scoreboard, the entire Orange Bowl felt as though the Steelers' defense was imposing its will against the Cowboys.

On the very next play, the Steelers took another giant step forward.

Standing at his goal line to field the snap, punter Hoopes was met with a heavy rush up the middle by reserve running back Reggie Harrison. Jumping high, Harrison blocked the punt. The ball careened out the back of the end zone, resulting in a safety and two points for the Steelers, who would also receive the ball on a free kick.

Even though they still trailed by a point, there was no doubt that momentum was now squarely behind the Steelers.

Collier fielded Hoopes' free kick on the next play at the Steelers' thirty-yard line and immediately sprinted up the middle of the field. With a wall of blockers escorting him, he advanced the ball into Cowboys' territory, finally being tackled at the forty-five-yard line.

The Steelers then struck out to make a further impression on the ground. Harris sandwiched two runs around a Bleier run to gain a first down. After Bleier was stopped short on first down, Bradshaw ran a keeper around the right end, gaining eight yards before fumbling—luckily fumbling out of bounds.

On third-and-one at the twenty-yard line, Bradshaw collided with Harris in the backfield during the handoff. Harris clawed forward but was downed just shy of the first-down marker.

Facing a fourth down and one yard to go at the nineteen-yard line, Noll called on the injured Gerela to attempt a thirty-six-yard field goal. Gerela had already missed from thirty-three and thirty-six yards in the game. But, with the wind at his kicker's back, Noll gave Gerela one more opportunity.

Gerela seized the moment, splitting the uprights to give the Steelers their first lead of the ballgame, 12–10.

Adding a bit more fuel to the Steelers' fire, Preston Pearson subsequently dropped the kickoff but fell on it at the Cowboys' fifteen-yard line to retain possession. With 8:32 left in the game, Staubach came back onto the field, trailing for the first time and desperate to get something—anything—positive going.

Taking a deep drop on first down, Staubach rifled a pass down the middle of the field toward Drew Pearson. Tracking Staubach's eyes the entire way, Wagner stepped in front of the intended receiver and intercepted the pass, taking the ball all the way down to the six-yard line. Once again, the Steelers' defense had delivered a devastating blow.

Three runs, one each by Bleier, Bradshaw, and Harris, who had to recover his own fumble, moved the ball to the two-yard line. Facing fourth down, Noll turned once more to his kicker. Gerela made good on his nineteen-yard attempt, upping the Steeler lead to five, 15–10.

Despite having been dominated by the Steelers for most of the second half and darn near every second of the fourth quarter, the Cowboys still only need one score to win.

A big loss on a sack by Greenwood on second down pushed the Cowboys back. When a short reception by running back Young fell short of first-down yardage, the Cowboys had to punt once more.

The Steelers' grasp on a Super Bowl X victory was getting ever tighter.

Looking to run off some clock, Bradshaw handed the ball to Harris on two consecutive runs up the middle. Facing third-and-five from their own thirty-six-yard line, the Steelers needed a first down to continue their possession and milk down the clock.

They got a lot more.

Bradshaw took a deep drop, avoided a blitzing D. D. Lewis, and spied Swann streaking down the center of the field on a post pattern, Washington trailing behind him. Bradshaw, just before he was leveled by defensive end Larry Cole, rifled a perfect pass, hitting Swann in stride at the five-yard line, where Swann corralled the ball and sauntered into the end zone. The sixty-four-yard touchdown pass essentially put the game away, and it put an exclamation point on Swann's remarkable game. His four spectacular catches for 161 total yards and a touchdown would earn him the game's Most Valuable Player award.

The Cowboys weren't done quite yet, though. Staubach connected with Drew Pearson on a thirty-yard completion to advance the ball past midfield. Preston Pearson then caught a pass and pushed the ball down to the thirty-two-yard line before stepping out of bounds. On the next play, however, White ushered in the two-minute warning with another sack of Staubach.

On the first play back from the break, Staubach found receiver Percy Howard alone on the left side of the end zone after Blount misstepped and fell on the play. The touchdown and Fritsch's extra point kept the Cowboys in the ballgame, cutting the deficit to just four points, 21–17, with 1:48 left to play.

The Cowboys' best chance for a miraculous come-from-behind victory resided in an onsides kick. Mullins of all players, an offensive guard, swallowed up the kick and the Steelers held possession.

On the touchdown pass to Swann, Bradshaw had suffered a concussion and had been taken back to the locker room for further evaluation. In his place stood Hanratty, seeing his first action in quite some time. Circumstances dictated the Steelers would run the ball, and the Cowboys brought their entire defense forward to stop the rush. Three straight Steelers runs were stopped cold, and the Cowboys called timeouts after each play.

Perhaps fearful of a repeat fumbled snap by Walden, Noll eschewed a punt and instead had Hanratty hand the ball off to Bleier on fourth down. The Cowboys stuffed the play, stopping him well short of the first down marker. With 1:22 remaining in Super Bowl X, the Cowboys would have one last chance, taking possession on their thirty-eight-yard line with no timeouts remaining.

Staubach took the first snap of the drive and scrambled for eleven yards and a first down. Then, Preston Pearson brought in a twelve-yard reception for another first down. Both plays had ended in the field of play, however, keeping the clock running.

The clock was under twenty seconds by the time Staubach took the snap out of the shotgun formation. A low snap fooled Staubach, and he fumbled around trying to gain control of the ball. He finally grabbed the ball, eluded a sack, and started to run up the field when he stopped and fired a deep pass to Drew Pearson downfield, near the goal line.

The Orange Bowl crowd collectively shouted in excitement; Cowboys fans in anticipation, Steelers fans in anxiety. But the pass was overthrown, allowing everyone—players included—to catch their breath.

With twelve seconds left, Staubach heaved a deep pass to the right corner of the end zone in the area of Howard, where Edwards jumped with the receiver and knocked the pass down for an incompletion.

With three seconds left on the clock and the ball placed at the thirty-eight-yard line, the Cowboys had one last play to pull out a victory.

Staubach's desperate pass into the end zone was deflected and fell into the hands of Edwards for an interception to seal the Steelers' victory.

With their win in Super Bowl X, the Steelers had become the third team to win back-to-back Super Bowls. For the Chief, it had taken forty-one years to win his first championship. It had taken just one more year to add a second title.

The winner of the Super Bowl is awarded the Vince Lombardi Trophy, named in honor of the legendary coach of the Green Bay Packers, who, incidentally, coached the winners of the first two Super Bowls.

The trophy Lombardi and his team received was inscribed with "World Professional Football Championship." It wasn't named after Lombardi until after his death in 1970. The first Vince Lombardi Trophy was presented to the Baltimore Colts after their victory over the Dallas Cowboys in Super Bowl V.

The design of the trophy was sketched by Tiffany & Co. Vice President Oscar Riedner during a 1966 lunch with NFL Commissioner Pete Rozelle. Tiffany has produced each of the trophies since its inception.

The Vince Lombardi Trophy is made entirely of sterling silver and depicts a football in a slanted position, like upon a tee ready for a kickoff, on a three concave-sided pedestal. Standing twenty-two inches tall, the trophy weighs seven pounds.

Originally, the trophy was presented inside the winning team's locker room, but that lacked any appeal to the tens of thousands in attendance at the game. Perhaps taking a cue from the National Hockey League and its presentation of the Stanley Cup on the ice, the NFL began on-field presentations of the Vince Lombardi trophy at Super Bowl XXX in 1996.

Unlike the NHL's Stanley Cup, however, the Super Bowl-winning team maintains permanent possession of the Vince Lombardi Trophy. Soon after the trophy is presented, it's reclaimed and sent back to Tiffany's to engrave the names of the participating teams, the date, game location, and the game's final score. Then, it's back to the team for their display.

Except for one Vince Lombardi Trophy, that is. That very first Lombardi-named trophy from Super Bowl V does not reside with the Colts franchise in its current location of Indianapolis, Indiana. Rather, it sits in the city of Baltimore, which retained the trophy as part of its legal settlement with the team after they relocated to the Midwest in 1984.

The Pittsburgh Steelers are tied with the New England Patriots as the team with the most Vince Lombardi trophies with six apiece. The Dallas Cowboys and the San Francisco 49ers are nipping at their heels with five trophies each.

Chapter 18

CLOSE, BUT NO CIGAR
FOR THE CHIEF & THE STEELERS

The Steelers returned from Super Bowl X in Miami at the absolute summit of professional football. It was quite a turnaround from what local fans had grown accustomed.

Consider the beginning of Noll's tenure just seven seasons before, in 1969, when his first Steelers football team finished the year with a 1–13 record. In the four seasons between 1972 and 1975, the Steelers had lost only twelve regular season games against forty-three victories. In the ten seasons previous to 1972, the Steelers had just forty-six wins.

What used to take a decade now took four years!

In the four seasons between 1972 and 1975, the Steelers had won three division titles, seven playoff games against just two losses, and two consecutive Super Bowl championships. Plus, there was a distinct feeling around both the Steelers' offices and the town that things were just getting started.

In the 1976 NFL Draft, the Steelers selected tight end Bennie Cunningham out of Clemson with their first-round pick, the twenty-eighth overall selection. Then, they added offensive tackle Ray Pinney out of the University of Washington in the second round. Both players would become regulars in the starting lineup over their long careers with the Steelers.

Ten picks after selecting Pinney, still in the second round, the Steelers, recognizing a need to improve the depth of their quarterbacking corps behind Bradshaw, selected Mike Kruczek out of Boston College with the forty-seventh overall pick.

In addition to the marquee top-three selections, the Steelers also added defensive lineman Gary Dunn from the University of Miami, Florida in the sixth round. Dunn would eventually play in 156 games over eleven seasons for the Steelers, another example of the team's insightful, value-added draft selections in later rounds of the annual draft.

In today's NFL, it's become almost a tradition for the defending Super Bowl champions to open the season at home, in a nationally-televised game in prime time. Back in the 1970s, that wasn't the case. The defending champion's first game was just another game in the league's overall schedule.

It was that lack of fanfare that saw the 1976 NFL season open up for the Steelers on the road, facing off against none other than . . . the Oakland Raiders. This bitter, hard-fought rivalry had grown over the past four seasons to be the league's biggest and best rivalry, surpassing that of the Cowboys and Redskins, the Raiders and Chiefs, and the Packers and Bears. Not only had each of the four previous seasons seen the Steelers and Raiders match up in the playoffs, but they had also met three times in the regular season. The Steelers held a 5–2 edge in those seven combined contests.

On a sunny Sunday afternoon in mid-September, the Steelers took the field against their well-known foes. Stabler, of course, was quite familiar with the Steelers' defense, and he looked to keep them guessing by mixing short passes and runs to both sides of the field. He also looked to strike deeper when the opportunities arose.

In the first quarter, Stabler found a bit of success and moved into Steelers territory. But there, the drive stalled, and the Steelers kept the scoresheet clean by blocking a Fred Steinfort field goal attempt.

Still later in the first quarter, Stabler again found success against the Steelers by continuing with the same game plan. He scrambled for a big gain and hit Branch on another long gain. But, as the Raiders entered scoring territory, Steelers safety Edwards made a leaping interception of a Stabler pass intended for Branch in the end zone. Once again, the Steelers' defense left the field with the score still knotted 0–0.

Bleier then sparked the best drive of the young game so far by the Steelers, breaking off a couple of solid runs and hauling in a twenty-four-yard completion from Bradshaw to move into Raiders territory. But, after a nice run off the right tackle, Bleier coughed up the ball, and the Raiders recovered the fumble.

The first quarter ended with the Raiders continuing to move the ball well. The score was still, however, 0–0.

Stabler picked up at the start of the second quarter exactly where he had stopped in the first. He connected with Branch on another good gain to the Steelers' thirty-one-yard line. After another first down was secured by running back van Eeghan, Furness sacked Stabler to give the Steelers a little breathing space.

The sack didn't faze Stabler one bit. Using a clever pump fake directed to the middle of the field to momentarily freeze the Steelers' defensive backs, Stabler connected with his tight end, Casper, open at the four-yard line. Casper easily sidestepped Edwards at the two-yard line and sauntered into the end zone for a touchdown. After moving the ball surprisingly easily against the Steelers, the Raiders had finally scored to carve out a 7–0 lead just a couple of minutes into the second quarter.

The Raiders touchdown seemed to wake up the Steelers, on both sides of the ball. Taking a page from the Raiders' offensive game plan, the Steelers began moving the ball. Harris and Bleier gained big chunks of yardage on rushing plays, and Bradshaw mixed it up with a completion to Swann. However, when the drive stalled at the two-yard line, Gerela's short field goal attempt was blocked, negating the Steelers' best drive of the game so far.

After stopping the Raiders, the Steelers again took possession deep in their own territory with just a few minutes remaining in the half. Bradshaw got things started immediately with a flare pass out of the backfield to Bleier, who scampered up the left sideline for a twenty-four-yard gain. At the two-minute warning, Bradshaw, under pressure and scrambling to his left, just got a pass off in the nick of time to Stallworth, who got another first down.

With ninety seconds left in the half, Bradshaw dropped back but couldn't find a receiver downfield. Blessed with great protection by his offensive line, he had the time to find Harris wide open in the left flat. Harris cradled in the reception and ran the ball all the way to the Raiders' six-yard line. Bleier subsequently punched it in from the two-yard line and the Steelers drew even at 7–7 as the first half ended.

The third quarter saw much the same as the second had. Edwards brought down his second interception of the game when he hauled in a deep Stabler throw down the right sideline, intended for Davis. Ham got an interception of his own when he secured a tipped ball along the same sideline, directly in front of an exasperated coach Madden.

The only score of the third quarter was a spectacular score at that, and it was the Steelers who came up with it. With the ball at his own thirty-seven-yard line, Bradshaw completed a pass to Harris, who started rumbling up the field. When Tatum began to wrap him up around the legs for what was to be a sure tackle, Harris spied Stallworth alone to his left. As he was headed to the ground in Tatum's grasp, Harris lateralled the ball to Stallworth, who then galloped to the end zone for a touchdown to complete the play. With that score, the fourth quarter would start with the Steelers up, 14–7.

The Steelers upped their lead early in the fourth quarter when Bradshaw connected with rookie wide receiver Theo Bell, who had been a fourth-round pick in the draft, on an eleven-yard touchdown pass.

Feeling the game slip away, Stabler and the Raiders' offense looked to respond. They methodically grounded out first downs, both with the run and the pass. Once in scoring territory, the "Snake," Stabler, struck with a pass just over the outstretched fingertips of a leaping Thomas and into the waiting hands of Biletnikoff in the end zone. The twenty-one-yard touchdown pass narrowed the score to 21–14 in favor of the Black and Gold.

Not to be outdone, the Steelers' offense again showed its mettle. Bradshaw connected a couple of times with Stallworth to advance the chains. Harris finished the drive with a three-yard rush up the middle for a touchdown, and the Steelers, with their formidable defense stepping on the field, had a seemingly comfortable fourteen-point lead.

On the ensuing Raiders possession, Blount stepped in front of a Stabler pass intended for Branch for an interception, the fourth Raiders turnover of the day. With field possession inside the Raiders' twenty-yard line, the Steelers had the game firmly in their grasp.

Rivalries like the Steelers and Raiders of the mid-1970s don't become sources of legendary folklore, however, without true gut-check performances. In that regard, the Raiders did not disappoint.

The Raiders forced a Harris fumble and recovered, putting the ball back into the hands of Stabler. Casper made a juggling catch of a pass that could have easily been Stabler's fifth interception of the game, gaining twenty yards. Then, Stabler went right back to Casper for another big gain down the left sideline.

Stabler, facing a fierce pass rush like he had the entire drive, found Biletnikoff again on the right side. Then, Stabler and the Raiders benefited from a facemask penalty on Furness that negated an important sack.

Banaszak surprised the Steelers' defense with a draw play run, moving the ball to the ten-yard line. From there, Stabler connected once again with Casper along the back of the end zone for a touchdown. The Raiders were mounting a comeback and had narrowed the score to 28–21.

The Raiders' defense then penned the Steelers deep in their own territory. Forced to punt with 1:55 on the clock, the Raiders partially blocked Walden's punt, recovering the ball on the Steelers' twenty-nine-yard line.

The sold-out crowd at Oakland-Alameda County Coliseum was in a loud frenzy. They quieted down again, though, as Stabler threw three consecutive incomplete passes, bringing up a fourth-and-ten. It was a make-or-break play in the ballgame.

The Raiders made it. Stabler eluded a strong pass rush, slipping out of an almost sure sack, and found Branch on the left side of the field. Branch caught the ball and then turned on his world-class speed, streaking all the way across the field to the right side, where Wagner made a diving stop, wrapping up Branch's ankles and tackling him at the two-yard line.

Wagner's touchdown-saving tackle proved all for naught on the next play, however, as Stabler faked a handoff to a diving Davis up the middle and bootlegged to his left, running untouched into the end zone for a touchdown. With fifty-nine seconds left in the game, Steinfort's extra point tied the game, 28–28.

Looking to avoid an overtime period, brought into the rulebook by the NFL in 1974 in an attempt to eliminate games ending in a tie, the Steelers took to the air. It was there that disaster struck.

Defensive tackle Dave Rowe deflected a Bradshaw pass, and the ball fell into the hands of linebacker Willie Hall for an interception. The Raiders took over possession at the Steelers' twelve-yard line, already well within scoring range. With just twenty-one ticks remaining on the clock, Steinfort kicked a twenty-one-yard field goal to complete the Raiders' comeback.

Rather inexplicably, the defending Super Bowl champions had surrendered a fourteen-point lead in the fourth quarter. Twice! For the game, the Raiders, despite the four interceptions from Stabler, gained 440 yards and totaled twenty-eight first downs. Licking their wounds, the Steelers made their way back to Pittsburgh with the taste of a bitter defeat in their mouths.

Perhaps feeling the effects of a post-Raiders hangover, the Steelers came out flat against the Browns the next weekend at their home opener, trailing 14–0 at the intermission. Four forced fumbles by the defense, 221 yards rushing on forty-five carries, and two Bradshaw touchdown passes to Stallworth provided the fuel for the Steelers' eventual 31–14 victory.

The Steelers then stumbled the next week at home against the Patriots, fumbling the ball seven times on the way to losing six of them. As a result, they lost the game, 30–27.

Week Four, they visited Minnesota for a rematch of Super Bowl IX with the Vikings. Again, the Steelers' offense turned the ball over six times, with Bradshaw accounting for four of those turnovers with interceptions. Leading 6–0 after one quarter, the Steelers eventually succumbed under the undue pressure put upon them by their own offense, losing 17–6.

The Steelers had opened the season with their strongest roster ever, looking to become the first NFL franchise to win three consecutive league titles since the 1965–1967 Green Bay Packers, who had also accomplished the feat between 1929 and 1931. Instead, the Steelers had lost three of their first four games, as they continued their road trip to Cleveland and a rematch of their second-week encounter.

Sure enough, just as Steelers' fans thought things couldn't get worse, they did.

The Steelers lost the game to their divisional rivals 18–16. But it was worse than that. On a fourth-quarter play with his team leading, 18–10, Browns' defensive end Joe "Turkey" Jones broke through the line on a pass play. He grabbed Bradshaw up high, above the waist, and drove him back five yards when the official's whistle signaled the end of the play. Standing behind Bradshaw with his arms still clasped around him, and either not hearing the whistle or not adhering to it, Jones spun to his right and corkscrewed Bradshaw into the ground, head first.

Bradshaw bounced off the turf at Municipal Stadium with the back half of the top of his helmet, causing his neck to bend alarmingly.

Medical facilities weren't commonplace at stadiums in the 1970s, and certainly not in older stadiums like Municipal Stadium. Bradshaw spent the rest of the game outside of the locker room, immobilized by being strapped to a door that had been removed from inside the locker room. After the game, he was transferred, door and all, to the Steelers' airplane for the short trip to Pittsburgh, where Bradshaw received medical care at a hospital.

Bradshaw had suffered a spinal contusion. According to interviews, Bradshaw didn't begin to have feeling in his extremities until two days later, Tuesday, when his toes began to tingle. Having waived both Hanratty and Gilliam from the roster, the Steelers were forced to push rookie Kruczek into the starting lineup.

Their season on the brink, the Steelers were in dire straits. But there was too much of the season yet to play for the 1–4 Steelers to give up on the 1976 season. If they were to right the ship, so to speak, they were going to have to do it with a rookie quarterback under center. And so, they set off to do just that.

The recipe for playing with a rookie quarterback is fairly straightforward. First, you tighten up the screws and play good defense. The Steelers had proven they were capable of being the elite defensive squad in the NFL.

Second, you protect your young quarterback by relying on a solid run game. With the Steelers' offensive line and the tandem of Harris and Bleier in the backfield, the Steelers felt they had that point covered as well.

Finally, you keep things close to the vest with regard to playcalling, focusing on gaining positive yards but absolutely emphasizing the minimization—if not the complete elimination—of turnovers. In their first five games of the season, the Steelers had been guilty of turning the ball over a staggering nineteen times, almost an entire season's worth. Noll and his staff set out to remedy that.

So how did the Steelers rebound with rookie Kruczek at the offensive helm? Well, they started reeling off victories with their first-year signal caller and never looked back.

The streak started with a 23–6 victory over the Bengals at Three Rivers Stadium, where Harris led a 201-yard team rushing effort with 143 yards of his own on a heavy diet of forty-one carries.

Then, the defense did something extraordinary. Behind Lambert and company, the Steelers' defense reeled off three consecutive shutouts of their opponents. In those three games—against the New York Giants, the Chargers, and the Chiefs—the Steelers outscored their opponents 95–0 and pushed their record to 5–4.

During those three shutouts, the Steelers' defense forced thirteen turnovers, more than making up for the four committed by their own offense, and added fourteen sacks. It was the best run of defensive excellence in the league in memory.

Bradshaw came in off the bench against the Chargers, just three weeks after suffering his injury and, rather remarkably, scored a touchdown on a one-yard run in the fourth quarter. He then started the next week in the Week Nine tilt in Kansas City against the Chiefs.

The defense's scoreless streak ended the next week when the Dolphins visited Three Rivers Stadium. But, still, Yepremian's forty-five-yard field goal in the third quarter was the only blemish on the scoreboard. The kick snapped a streak of eighteen consecutive scoreless quarters for the vaunted Steelers' defense.

In a Week Eleven matchup at home with the Oilers, the Steelers jumped out to a 12–0 lead before something truly rare happened. Oilers quarterback John Hadl connected with speedy wideout Ken Burrough on a sixty-nine-yard touchdown pass. It was the first touchdown scored against the Steelers since the third quarter of the second Browns game in Week Five, on October 10.

After twenty-two consecutive quarters over a month and eleven days, the Steelers had finally surrendered a touchdown. The Oilers would go on to add one more touchdown in the fourth quarter, closing out the scoring in a 32–16 Steelers victory. Unbelievably, that would be the final touchdown scored against the Steelers for the remainder of the regular season.

After a hard-fought 7–3 win over the Bengals in Week Twelve at Cincinnati, the Steelers then went on to finish the season with shutout victories over the Tampa Bay

Buccaneers and the Oilers. Since that fateful day in Cleveland on the shores of Lake Erie, the Steelers had run off nine consecutive victories en route to a 10–4 record and another AFC Central Division crown.

Let's review that recipe laid out just after Bradshaw's injury. First up, the defense needed to stand tall. In the nine-game win streak, the Steelers gave up a total of twenty-eight points, or three less than they surrendered in the Week One loss to the Raiders. That's simply as good as it gets in the modern era of professional football.

For the season, the Steelers held their opponents to less than ten points a game on average, finishing first in the league in points allowed. The defense also led the league in rushing yards allowed, total yards allowed, and first downs against.

As far as running the ball, the veteran backfield of Harris and Bleier excelled, with each running back gaining over 1,000 yards, becoming only the second backfield duo to accomplish that feat in NFL history. Harris rushed for 1,128 yards on 289 carries, while also catching twenty-three passes out of the backfield for another 151 yards. Bleier rushed for a career-high 1,036 yards, averaging an eye-popping 4.7 yards a carry. As a receiver, he one-upped Harris by hauling in twenty-four receptions for 294 yards.

As a team, the Steelers rushed for nearly 3,000 yards, easily leading the league. They also scored thirty-three touchdowns on the ground, with Harris accounting for fourteen, to lead the league in that category as well.

With regards to turnovers, during the nine-game win streak to close out the regular season, the Steelers committed just twelve turnovers.

For his part, Kruczek threw only three interceptions in his eighty-five passing attempts. And, while he didn't throw a touchdown pass, Kruczek did help his own cause by rushing for two touchdowns of his own, on his way to tacking on 106 yards rushing for the season.

Regarding Kruczek, the most important statistic of the 1976 regular season was his record as a starting quarterback. In his six starts in place of Bradshaw, Kruczek steered the Steelers to six victories.

Kruczek's 6–0 result was an NFL record for the best start for a rookie quarterback. His mark stood the test of time for nearly thirty years until it was broken, coincidentally enough, when the Steelers' own Ben Roethlisberger went 13–0 as a starter his rookie season of 2004.

Franco Harris had felt awful about his fourth-quarter fumble deep in Raiders' territory in the season opener. Not only had it stopped a potential scoring drive for the

Steelers, but it had also injected life into a moribund Raiders team and proved to be the catalyst for their come-from-behind victory.

From that point on, Harris had played well, carrying, in large part, the Steelers' offensive attack—something to which his teammates, coaches, and fans were quite accustomed.

Harris had burst onto the scene as a rookie in 1972, rushing for 1,055 yards on his way to winning the Offensive Rookie of the Year Award. After being limited to just 698 yards in an injury-saddled sophomore season, Harris then ran off six consecutive 1,000 yards-plus seasons, the 1976 season being the third of the bunch.

In addition to his rushing prowess, Harris was a legitimate multi-threat back, as he was a dependable receiver coming out of the backfield. Remember, it was Harris' sure-handed catch literally off the top of his shoes that made the Immaculate Reception a reception in the first place.

Some NFL fans might remember Harris for dodging tackles on sweeps around either end by slyly slipping out of bounds. And he certainly saved himself a lot of punishment by doing just that on many occasions. But it's important to note Harris usually slipped out of bounds after a rush of four, five, six, or more yards.

It's also important to note that when he ran between the tackles, Harris standing six-foot-two and weighing 230 pounds, brought a load with him. Ask any defender in the era—Harris was a tough out and a difficult runner to take to the ground.

His physicality was also on display as a blocker for his running mate, Bleier. In college, Harris was primarily a blocking back for his teammate Lydell Mitchell, who would himself go on to star in the NFL with the Colts. Harris relished his role as a blocker, a relatively rare trait in star running backs both then and now, and he contributed mightily to Bleier's success running the ball.

Harris played twelve seasons for the Steelers before ending his career with a single season in Seattle. When he hung up his cleats, he had rushed for 12,120 yards, caught passes for another 2,287, and scored an even one hundred touchdowns.

Harris, of course, was a key contributor on four Super Bowl championship teams. With his workman-like performances in those four Super Bowl appearances, he still holds records for both the most career Super Bowl rushing attempts—101— and most career Super Bowl rushing yards gained—354.

At the conclusion of the 1976 season, Harris was recognized by the league with its prestigious NFL Man of the Year Award, now known as the Walter Payton NFL Man of the Year Award, for excellence on and off the field.

Franco Harris was inducted into the Pro Football Hall of Fame in 1990.

What's in a number?

A great number of professional sports teams, particularly those with long histories, have the established practice of retiring the numbers worn by their legendary players. The honor is intended to immortalize the player by making the number unavailable for any future player to wear it.

It's all a rather informal process, and each team decides for itself how to go about the honor. For example, some teams allow a number to be re-issued only if the honored player—or his family—gives permission.

The first number ever retired by a team in a professional sports league was Ace Bailey's number six, retired by the Toronto Maple Leafs hockey club in 1934.

In baseball, the New York Yankees have made retiring numbers something of an art form. Throughout its distinguished history, the team has retired twenty-three numbers. Or rather, they've retired twenty-two numbers of twenty-three players, as they retired number eight, that worn by both Yogi Berra and Bill Dickey, in the same ceremony on July 22, 1972. Every single-digit uniform number with the club has been retired.

As Shakespeare once famously wrote, "I am ill at these numbers." No, not *that* Shakespeare, the one Rooney drafted in the first round of the 1936 NFL Draft. This time, we're referring to the Bard of Avon himself, the English playwright who wrote that line in Act Two of *Hamlet*.

For the Pittsburgh Steelers professional football franchise, only two numbers have been officially retired, and neither of them is Franco Harris's 32, although no player has worn that number since Harris left the team. The Steelers' only officially retired uniform numbers are the 75 of Mean Joe Greene and the 70 of Ernie Stautner. Harris's 32 is set to be retired during a ceremony on December 23, 2022, marking the fiftieth anniversary of the Immaculate Reception.

Ernest Stautner was born on April 20, 1925, in Cham, in the Bavarian region of Germany. When he was three, his family immigrated to East Greenbush, New York. After Stautner served in the United States Marine Corps during World War II, he enrolled at Boston College, where he was a four-year starter as both an offensive and defensive tackle. Multi-faceted, he also kicked on kickoffs and extra point attempts.

The Steelers selected Stautner in the second round of the 1950 NFL Draft with the twenty-second overall selection. Over his fourteen-year career with the Steelers, Stautner distinguished himself as one of the best linemen of his era, with nine Pro Bowl honors being proof points.

Stautner personified toughness, and he was not only the cornerstone of some exceptional defensive teams, he was also very much a team leader. In fact, at the end of his career, Stautner served as a player-coach for the Steelers.

In 1964, his first year in retirement as a player, Stautner's number 70 became the Steelers' first retired number. In 1969, his first year of eligibility, Stautner was inducted into the Pro Football Hall of Fame.

After his career as a player, Stautner remained in the game with a distinguished coaching career, including a long stint as the Dallas Cowboys' defensive coordinator, a role he held from 1973–1988. Stautner was on the Cowboys' sideline, opposite the Steelers, in Super Bowl X and Super Bowl XIII.

The Steelers kicked off the 1976 postseason by facing off in the first round with the Colts for the second consecutive year, although this time in Baltimore at old Memorial Stadium. Under the guidance of head coach Ted Marchibroda, the Colts had finished the year with an 11–3 record and the AFC East Division title.

The Colts featured the league's highest-scoring offense, led by Jones at quarterback and Mitchell at running back. Not only had Mitchell rushed for 1,200 yards on the season, but he had also led the team in receptions with sixty. The Colts were poised to test the tough Steelers' defense.

On the Steelers' first possession, Bleier badly sprained a toe, limiting his play. For the afternoon, he carried the ball just one time. His injury didn't slow down the Steelers much in this game though.

Bradshaw was in good form throughout the afternoon, and he opened the scoring in the first quarter with a seventy-six-yard touchdown pass to Lewis. Gerela, nursing a groin injury, missed the extra point, leaving the Steelers with a 6–0 lead.

After a field goal by Gerela pushed the lead to nine, the Colts responded with a touchdown of their own on a seventeen-yard Jones touchdown pass to receiver Roger Carr. It was the first touchdown scored against the Steelers in the first quarter the entire year.

The Steelers never flinched. They scored on their first three possessions, and their fourth possession ended only when reserve running back Harrison lost a second-quarter fumble at the Colts' two-yard line. After the Colts' score, the Steelers ran off seventeen points to extend their lead to 26–7 at the intermission.

The third quarter was scoreless, but the Steelers continued to wear down an overmatched Colts defense. In the fourth quarter, the Black and Gold sandwiched touchdowns around another Colts' touchdown, and they were driving at the Colts' three-yard line when the clock mercifully expired with the Steelers on top 40–14.

Interestingly, even as Gerela made two field goal attempts, his groin injury was adversely affected by the cold winter day. In a concession to the injury, Noll replaced Gerela on kickoffs with Walden and, rather remarkably, longtime Steelers center Mansfield. After the Steelers' final touchdown, a ten-yard scamper by Harrison, Mansfield successfully kicked the extra point. It was Mansfield's first point scored in his illustrious fourteen-year NFL career.

The Steelers racked up twenty-nine first downs and 526 total yards of offense in dominating the game. But, in addition to Bleier's toe injury, Harris had suffered severely sprained ribs early in the third quarter, knocking him out of the remainder of the game. Questions about the two backs' availability for the AFC Championship Game in one week's time muted any Steelers celebration.

The Steelers' opponent in the conference championship game was to be none other than the Oakland Raiders. The matchup would mark the fifth consecutive year the two teams squared off in the playoffs and the third straight year where the winner would earn a Super Bowl berth. Those five playoff games, with the sudden death nature of playoff games, boosted the fierce rivalry to stratospheric levels.

After defeating the Steelers in the season opener, the Raiders had gone on to complete a tremendous season, the only blemish on their record a Week Four loss on the road at New England. Along the way to a 13–1 record, they had also done the Steelers a favor by defeating the Bengals in Week Thirteen, a result that elevated the Steelers to atop the Central Division. If the Bengals had won that game, they would have won the division, and they, rather than the Steelers, would have advanced to the playoffs.

As their reward for opening the door for the Steelers to get into the playoffs, the Raiders now had to defeat the Steelers to advance to the Super Bowl. Although the Raiders had appeared in every AFL or AFC championship game save two since 1967, they had only appeared in one Super Bowl, a 33–14 loss to the Packers in Super Bowl II.

Fortunately for the Raiders, they took to the field without having to face either of the Steelers' two 1,000-yard rushers. Both Harris and Bleier would not play a single down due to their injuries suffered the week before against the Colts.

The Raiders opened the scoring with a thirty-nine-yard field goal by Earl Mann, who had replaced Steinfort mid-way through the season. Then, linebacker Hall made a diving interception of a Bradshaw pass that deflected off the hands of Fuqua, returning it to the Steelers' one-yard line. From there, Davis punched it in for the score, and with the extra point, the Raiders had a 10–0 lead early in the second quarter.

The Steelers responded with what would prove to be their best drive of the game. The eight-play drive spanned seventy-five yards, and it was capped when Harrison covered the final three yards for a touchdown. Mansfield, once again, hammered through the point after touchdown. The Steelers had reduced the deficit to just three points.

Not to be outdone, Stabler then led the Raiders on a sustained drive of their own. Against the vaunted Steelers' defense, the Raiders marched downfield on a fourteen-play drive, getting solid gains on rushes by Davis, Van Eeghan, and Banaszak. When Stabler connected with backup tight end Warren Bankston on a wide-open four-yard pitch and catch for a touchdown, the Raiders secured a 17–7 advantage they would take into halftime.

In the third quarter, Stabler led another sustained Raiders drive, mixing in a big completion to Branch with steady gains by his running backs. Stabler finished off the drive with a five-yard touchdown pass to Banaszak, and the Raiders entered the final quarter with a 24–7 lead.

Playing without their starting running backs proved to be too much of a handicap for the Steelers. While Harrison and Fuqua had sparks of success here and there, Bradshaw could never get the running game going. Forced to go to the air, the Raiders' defensive backs played well, keeping Swann, Stallworth, Cunningham, and the rest of the Steelers' receivers blanketed in coverage and always in front of them.

In the fourth quarter, Bradshaw and the offense just could not come through with the clutch plays to convert on key third and fourth downs. Gaining possession of the ball on downs, and with reserve quarterback Mike Rae in the game for an injured Stabler, the Raiders concentrated on keeping the ball on the ground and winding down the clock.

The final Steelers' possession ended deep in Raiders' territory as the game clock expired. Raiders fans swarmed the field to celebrate their team's victory and a long-awaited return appearance in the Super Bowl.

The 24–7 loss was a bitter pill for the Steelers and their fans to swallow. After an incredibly rocky start to the season in defense of their back-to-back league champions, they had rallied behind a historically dominant defense. Lambert is still convinced the 1976 Steelers team was the best one on which he played.

If Harris and Bleier had been healthy and played in the game, would it have been enough to swing the outcome? It's a topic that still makes for compelling barroom debate, even today.

Two weeks later, the Raiders went on to defeat the Vikings 32–14 in Super Bowl XI, providing Madden his first and only NFL title. Oh, what might have been were it not for a set of bruised ribs and a sprained toe?

John Madden faced the Steelers just one more time in his storied coaching career, in a regular-season game the very next year, 1977. He subsequently retired from coaching after the 1978 season.

Over the course of his ten years as a head coach, all with the Raiders, Madden amassed a record 103–32–7, posting a .759 winning percentage. That winning percentage is the highest of anyone who has coached one hundred or more games in the NFL, including Vince Lombardi.

As successful as Madden was as a coach, he was perhaps even more successful as an announcer. His unrivaled enthusiasm and "everyman's" approach to the game made him incredibly popular as an analyst, a role he served for twenty-nine years, earning sixteen Sports Emmy Awards. Almost synonymous with the NFL, his eponymous video game for computers and gaming consoles has been an annual best-seller since its debut release in 1988.

For all his contributions to the sport, including his incredible success as head coach, Madden was enshrined in the Pro Football Hall of Fame in 2006.

Chapter 19
DEBTS COME DUE

There wasn't a single death blow to the US steel industry. Neither was the industry's demise a case of a death by a thousand paper cuts. Rather, it was something in between.

And, truth be told, accounts of the "death" of the steel industry have been, repeating the famed words of American comedian W. C. Fields, greatly exaggerated.

The steel industry in America still exists. In fact, according to Statista, 87 million metric tons of steel were produced in the United States in 2021, producing a projected $110 billion, a 21 percent increase in value from the year previous. But steel producers in the United States are nowhere near the top of the global industry.

Globally, annual steel production increased from 971 million tons in 2003 to 1.86 billion tons in 2020. On the world stage, China was the leading steel producer in 2019, accounting for more than 50 percent of the world's production.

A great many factors conspired to doomed Pittsburgh's dominant position in the steel industry. And a lot of it may have been doomed by Pittsburgh's early start in producing steel.

Being a first mover in most any marketplace can be advantageous. But, over time, competitors catch up, and new entries into mature markets benefit from new technologies and more efficient methods.

Look at mobile phones, for instance. The United States was plagued by outdated legacy infrastructure as mobile communication technology advanced by leaps and bounds. For years, the country's consumers looked at users overseas with envy for what they could do with their mobile phones. Some countries that were late entries into telecommunications leapfrogged generations of older technologies almost completely. Their investments in telecommunications started with high-tech solutions and completely bypassed older technology that required significant infrastructure investments in towers and wires.

Examples also abound concerning building infrastructure. At one time, LaGuardia airport in New York was a crown jewel in the world of aviation. Today, it doesn't hold a candle to airports like Dubai International Airport.

Pittsburgh was not a first mover in iron and steel production. However, the city's first steel mills were fast followers, spurred on by the country's westward expansion and beneficiaries of wartime boosts in demand. Afforded the capital from many years of profitable production, established mills quickly adopted new methods to make better quality steel more efficiently and less expensively. But still, they were very labor-heavy in their production.

The steel industry and its labor have experienced a long, complex, and contentious relationship over its history.

The labor movement has long roots in American history, as it was born alongside the United States. Both the labor movement and the collective union of the states were stoked, in part, by the same ideals of social equality.

The earliest recorded labor strike occurred in 1768 when journeymen tailors in New York protested wage reductions. Sustained trade unions began in 1794 when Philadelphia shoemakers created the Federal Society of Journeymen Cordwainers.

Following in the footsteps of the shoemakers, no pun intended, local unions sprouted throughout major cities during the first Industrial Revolution. As businesses grew, many, if not most, looked to exploit cheap immigrant labor. The unions fought to defend their skilled trades and contest ever-elongating workdays and work weeks.

The early history of organized labor was strife with legal confusion. The young country was, naturally, largely devoid of case law, and debate sprang on the applicability of, oddly enough, English common law. Several court cases centered on the arguments of whether the illegality of conspiracies to raise wages was properly applied.

The legal matter was settled once and for all with *Commonwealth v. Hunt*, the landmark 1842 case in the Massachusetts Supreme Judicial Court that ruled labor combinations were legal provided they were organized for a legal purpose and used legal means to achieve their goals.

By the mid-nineteenth century, unions began to burst out of their contained cities and take on national and, along with their fellow trade workers in Canada, international designations. However, despite manufacturing facilities springing up across the country, including, of course, Pittsburgh, industrial workers made up very little of organized labor unions, whose membership catered to more skilled crafts.

Labor reform grew alongside trade unionism. At the time, they were separate and distinct. Trade unionism focused on workers' immediate needs and relied heavily on the tactics of strikes and boycotts. The labor reform movement, marked by organizations like the National Labor Union that launched in 1866, had broader, far-reaching objectives, aimed at creating a more cooperative commonwealth rather than a simple higher current wage.

During the 1880s, those two movements merged when the Knights of Labor enlisted large numbers of workers looking to improve their immediate working conditions.

Feeling threatened, the national trade unions joined together in December 1886 to form the American Federation of Labor (AFL), and it immediately put to rest the notion of labor reform for good. Led by Samuel Gompers, the AFL borrowed from the Marxist view that trade unionism was the central instrument to prepare the working class for revolution through self-organization along occupational lines and a focus on job equity to provide workers a fair and just future.

Gompers and the AFL advocated craft or trade unionism, which restricted membership to wage earners and grouped those workers into local unions based on their trade or craft. This marked contrast to labor reformers—like the Knights of Labor, who sought to develop community-based organizations open to wage-earning workers and others, including employers—easily won in the worker-dominated court of public opinion.

Gompers was a fervent believer in economic reform over less trustworthy political reform in securing workers' rights and welfare. Idealistically, Gompers knew laws could change with the political winds, but what workers fairly earned in the economic marketplace would be long-lasting.

However, Gompers was also a realist, and he knew political activism would, at times, be inevitable. Regarding politics, Gompers championed a nonpartisan path where organized labor would develop and socialize its own independent political agenda.

By the turn of the twentieth century, big business had grown weary of the AFL's dynamic and explosive growth and had started to use the country's new anti-trust laws as a legal basis for court-issued injunctions against strikes and boycotts. It reached a tipping point for Gompers and the AFL in 1906 when nonunion employers sued the hatters' union and each of its individual members for treble damages in compensation for losses suffered in a union boycott.

Looking to secure the rights of organized labor to engage in economic action, Gompers and company jumped feet first into the deep waters of politics, launching wide-reaching, comprehensive campaigns to elect union members or otherwise labor-friendly candidates to political offices across the country. While its power has waned recently, that singular organized labor tactic ultimately shaped the country's local and national political agenda for generations.

In 1876, the Amalgamated Association of Iron and Steel Workers (AA) was formed to represent skilled iron and steelworkers. Its membership was concentrated west of the Allegheny Mountains, and the union negotiated national uniform wage scales on an annual basis. It also aimed to improve general working conditions, including the regulation of working hours, workload levels, and work speeds.

On January 1, 1882, the AA engaged in a strike at the Homestead Steel Works, an important manufacturing plant for the Carnegie Steel Company located in Homestead, Pennsylvania. The nearly three-month-long strike was a vicious affair, with violence perpetrated by both sides.

In 1889, the union struck at the Homestead plant once again after negotiations for a new three-year collective bargaining agreement failed. Striking workers seized support from the neighboring town. Remember, at the time, most every citizen could trace their livelihood to the industry. If you didn't work at a mill, your customers of the business you did work for worked at the mill.

Backed by the town, the strikers drove off a trainload of strikebreakers that management had transported in. When the sheriff's office showed up with hundreds of newly sworn-in deputies, the union countered with thousands of riled-up townspeople.

Eventually, the union conceded to wage cuts, but labor essentially ran the plant, making it impossible for the company to maximize output to the plant's capacity.

Those two strikes eventually led to the seminal moment that forever shaped labor relations in the Pittsburgh-area industry.

Homestead Steel Works was a critical key manufacturing plant for the Carnegie Steel Company. After it had installed an open-hearth system in 1886, the plant had been able to produce steel suitable for structural beams. More importantly for the company, it also provided the means to produce armor plate for the United States Navy, which was then, as it is now, rather infamously known to pay much higher prices for premium products.

Henry Frick was in operational control of the company at the time, and he was determined to break the union at Homestead. Carnegie, his mentor and boss, had always been publicly favorable to organized labor. But he was convinced by Frick to eliminate the union and basically start the operational foundation of the plant over again.

Frick and the union leadership began negotiating in February of 1892, well ahead of the June 30 expiration of the existing collective bargaining agreement. The steel business was booming, and the union, which represented over 20 percent of the nearly 4,000 workers at the plant, asked for an increase in wages to offset the concessions made three years before. Frick immediately countered with a 22 percent *decrease* in wages.

You can see where the entire endeavor was destined to go.

Eventually, Frick initiated a partial lockout on June 28. The next day, he locked the union out of the entire plant. The plant became a fortress, with a barbed-wire fence, sniper towers, and water cannons at the entrances. Strikers referred to the plant as "Fort Frick."

The AA, of course, publicly renounced the company for initiating a lockout before the labor contract's expiration. They called for a strike, and the Knights of Labor, which represented the mechanics and transportation workers at the plant, agreed to walk out alongside the AA. Additionally, workers at Carnegie plants in Pittsburgh, Duquesne, Union Mills, and Beaver Falls also struck as a symbol of coalition.

In response to the fortress-like plant, the strikers took on a military demeanor of their own, patrolling the Monongahela River, which ran alongside the plant, and establishing picket lines with twenty-four-hour shifts. Rather remarkably, the strikers even kept keen surveillance at both ferry docks and the train station. If strangers could not provide an appropriate explanation for why they were in town, they were promptly escorted out of town. Even members of the working press were subject to having their credentials allowing free passage revoked if their stories were too unfavorable toward the union membership.

The situation got worse from there. Frick, determined to break the union, had posted ads for workers from St. Louis to Boston. It's even been reported that he placed ads in Europe, of all places. With strikers driving off non-union workers, the company sought protection from law enforcement to bring supervisors into the plant, followed by strikebreakers.

Strikers, however, easily outnumbered sheriff's deputies, and they rebuffed their efforts with ease.

With Frick intent on opening the plant on July 6, company attorney Philander Knox arranged a plan to get a force of 300 agents of the Pinkerton National Detective Agency into the plant by way of the river. Many of the agents were newly hired, uncertain of what tasks lay ahead for them. Each was armed with a rifle and a badge that, according to accounts in *The Wheeling Daily Intelligencer*, read, "Watchman, Carnegie Company, Limited."

The skirmish between the strikers and the Pinkertons began downriver, where a boat of strikers took several shots at two barges filled with agents as they were towed to the plant. Strikers on the boats returned and alerted the plant, whereupon their compatriots blew the plant's whistle at 2:30 a.m. to alert the rest of the town. Startled awake, thousands from the town descended on the plant.

The Pinkertons attempted to land at 4:00 a.m., and by all accounts, chaos broke loose. The crowd tore down the fence, and strikers and their families stormed into the plant. First, stones were thrown. That quickly changed to gunfire.

Accounts vary as to which side started shooting at the Homestead Steel Works plant. Regardless, shots flew in both directions. The Pinkertons shot into the crowd, killing two and wounding eleven. The crowd fired into the barges full of Pinkertons, also killing two and wounding another twelve. The initial firefight then ended, and both sides of the conflict dug into fortified positions.

Word of the conflict spread quickly. In Pittsburgh, steelworkers gathered in the streets, listening to reports. In quick time, they armed themselves and began to trek toward Homestead.

At 8:00 a.m., the Pinkertons made another attempt at disembarking, and both sides resumed shooting. Many of the newly recruited agents retreated to the barge furthest from the shore. More seasoned agents took up positions to fight off any advances from the crowd.

Later in the day, strikers attempted to burn the barges out from underneath the Pinkertons. They first tried a raft full of oil-soaked lumber, but that fire burned out before reaching the barges. Later, a railroad flatcar loaded with barrels of oil was ignited and sent down the rails to where the barges were docked, only to stop at the edge of the water and burn out harmlessly.

Looking to end the hostilities, Union leadership attempted to get the Sheriff's office to convey a message to Frick seeking a meeting. Frick declined, thinking the longer the violent stalemate continued, the more likely the state's governor would intervene with the militia, an outcome he deemed to be more favorable to his side.

By afternoon, the strikers had an estimated force of 5,000 men, many of whom were armed. With the cover of darkness and the element of surprise both long gone, and essentially trapped and facing insurmountable odds, the Pinkertons waved a white flag to surrender.

Outgoing AA Union President William Weihe argued to the crowd to make way and let the agents flee. In return, he was shouted down by the angry crowd. Hugh O'Donnell, who worked in the plant and was the head of the union's Strike Advisory Committee, led calls to have the Pinkertons arrested for murder and jailed.

Agents, guaranteed their safe passage out of town by O'Donnell, surrendered their arms and disembarked from the barges. To cross the grounds of the plant, the Pinkertons had to walk through a gauntlet of angry strikers and their families, and that mob let their feeling be known, hurling not only insults, but rocks too. Several agents were beaten into unconsciousness.

Into town, the Pinkertons were marched, toward the opera house that was to serve as a temporary jail. Through the town, more agents were beaten, and eyewitness accounts by the media turned the press' sympathies away from that of the strikers.

Sheriff William H. McCleary and Weihe met that night to agree upon a transfer process, and in the early hours, after midnight on July 7, a special train took the Pinkertons to Pittsburgh. At Pittsburgh, state officials claimed the agents were not to be arrested, a statement made with the full concurrence of the union's attorney. At 10:00 that morning, another special train whisked the agents out of Pittsburgh for good.

Even after a dramatic day and a half, the drama wasn't over.

Governor Robert E. Pattison had been elected largely due to Carnegie's influence. But he had not sent in the state militia; he knew Homestead was a union town and its population would be aligned with the strikers. The last thing the governor wanted was a battle between his troops and the townspeople, who were, after all, voters as well.

On July 12, the troops finally arrived. O'Donnell sought to welcome the troops and pledge the union's cooperation. The militia commander, Major General George R. Snowden, hastily rebuked him, making it clear he was in the Carnegie Steel camp and was returning the property to its rightful owners.

More than 4,000 soldiers displaced the striking picketers, and by mid-morning, company officials were back on the job. Two thousand additional troops camped on a hill overlooking the city and plant.

Frick promptly found able and willing strikebreakers, and the company quickly built an on-site infrastructure to accommodate them. When the mill's furnaces were reignited on July 15, some striking workers attempted to storm the plant and extinguish them. State militia fought them off, injuring six with bayonets attached to their rifles.

Frick had won the battle, but he hadn't won the war. He knew he couldn't keep the plant operating with replacement workers living on site. He needed a permanent solution, but he was steadfast in refusing to negotiate with the union, even spurning a request from Whitelaw Reid, the Republican candidate for vice president, who stated the conflict was hurting the political party.

Then, on July 23, Alexander Berkman, a New York anarchist with no ties to either organized labor or the steel industry, broke into Frick's office and shot and stabbed him in an unsuccessful attempt to kill him. Media accounts of the attempted murder were the last straw in undermining any public support for the union, and it ultimately caused the collapse of the strike.

O'Donnell, seeing no way out, proposed that if they were to get their jobs back, workers would concede to the lower wage rate. For his efforts, he was relieved from his position as committee chair. On August 12, the company announced the plant was operating at full capacity with 1,700 workers.

Union members were defeated, and a great many made difficult decisions to support their families. Picket lines were crossed regularly, and on October 13, the militia was recalled, ending its three-month occupation.

Frick had broken the union, but it wasn't like workers and their families forgot his ruthless—and at times, shameful—tactics. And it wasn't like conditions that helped create unions in the first place didn't continue to exist.

Four years later, in 1896, Frick had to suppress an organizing drive at Homestead. In 1899, Frick resorted to ordering the Homestead plant to shut down to effectively quelch another threat after workers had formed a union lodge.

Following Frick's lead, de-unionization efforts continued across the industry, and by 1900, not a single steel plant in Pennsylvania was unionized. Plants in other states held on until 1903 before succumbing.

Before the Homestead strike, the AA union had over 24,000 members. By 1909, membership had declined to 6,300. In 1936, the AA was taken over by the Steel Workers Organizing Committee. Six years later, in 1942, the two organizations disbanded to form the United Steelworkers.

The United Steel, Paper and Forestry, Rubber, Manufacturing, Energy, Allied Industrial and Service Workers International Union, better known as the United Steelworkers or the USW, is headquartered in Pittsburgh, with members in the United States, Canada, and the Caribbean.

As you can tell from its proper name, the union represents workers in a wide range of industries. It may have started with primary and fabricated metals, but it now includes workers in chemicals, glass, paper, rubber, tires, transportation, utilities, and container industries, among others. It even includes pharmaceuticals, health care, and, in quite the departure from its roots, call centers.

Members of the United Steelworkers refer to themselves, and are most often referred to as, "Steelworkers." The singular word and its uppercase treatment are significant, as it identifies workers related to the union, as opposed to non-union steelworkers. It's an important distinction because, despite Frick's best efforts at the tail end of the nineteenth century, a great amount of the US steel industry was unionized, including the nation's biggest facilities, like U.S. Steel's Gary Works in Gary, Indiana.

Relationships between management and organized labor are often strained, and that's common across most every industry and trade profession. Unfortunately, in some of the most physically-demanding trades, those relationships have, at times, involved violence. Regardless of which side perpetrated the violence, the actions are never forgotten.

Steelworkers never forgot, and certainly never forgave, the violent interactions they had with management during the industry's formative years in America. In turn, they didn't make things easy for management and the companies for which they worked. Of course, that, over time, didn't exactly make things easier for themselves either.

But the relationship between the parties was, and to a great extent is still, complex. Steelworkers, for the most part, knew their jobs were difficult and dangerous, and yet they still showed up at the plant. Millwork, for the longest time, was stable work, and it provided for the workers' families.

Repeated tales have been passed down generationally from mill families, each with a familiar refrain of the family patriarch sternly stating, "My son will not work at the mill!" While it was good enough for dad and provided for the family, Father was doing so in order for his children to go elsewhere, into different professions.

Some offspring left; others stayed. But the mills continued on, and the workers continued to walk through the front gate and go to work.

As much as some steelworkers hated the mill, they also protected it. Recall the Donora Smog and what happened when the first investigators descended onto the scene. They were reportedly driven off by armed millworkers.

The millworkers knew the plant was largely—if not solely—culpable for the environmental disaster that left so many townspeople dead and hospitalized. But they also knew the mill was the literal lifeblood of the town, and that they, and their families, were dependent on the regular paycheck.

Dr. Dave Lonich and Brian Charlton, two conceptual historians in Donora, often say the local plant workers "traded a lifestyle for a livelihood." The mill provided for families and the community. In return, the community protected the mill.

Protected the mill to an extent, that is. In this case, the enemy of your enemy wasn't your friend, but rather an outsider. Outsiders needed to mind their own. What happened in the mill was between the company and its workers.

No quarter was to be lightly given as the American steel industry started to slump severely between 1974 and 1985. Post-war, the productivity of legacy US mills was problematic compared to new rivals, particularly the new steel-producing concerns in both Japan and Germany, built, in part, by reconstruction assistance from the countries of the Allied war effort. New mills had new technologies and processes, and they produced more steel while taking on a lower cost structure. In the United States, one of the biggest costs was that of labor associated with production methodologies and technologies.

Simply, wages, benefits, and pension costs severely hamstrung the American steel industry's effort to better manage costs to compete globally. Labor costs weren't the only factor, of course. But labor would again be a hot point issue as firms looked to competitively stand their ground.

This book doesn't attempt to offer a comprehensive look at the labor issue within the steel industry, as those books already exist. For those interested in the topic, perhaps the best writeup is *And the Wolf Finally Came: The Decline and Fall of the American Steel Industry*, by John Hoerr. Hoerr does an excellent job of investigating and reporting on the crippling labor conflicts of the 1980s. Do yourself a favor and pick it up.

Chapter 20

TURNOVERS LEAD TO A SHIFT IN POWER

The ending of the 1976 season at the hands of the Raiders in the AFC Championship Game on December 26 was a bitter pill for the Steelers to swallow. The season had not started well, that's for certain, what with a 1–4 record and a starting quarterback in the hospital with a severe spinal contusion. But, from that point on, the Steelers, and in particular its defensive unit, were sublime.

It bears repeating the magnificence of the Steelers' defensive performance over the last nine games of the 1976 regular season. They produced five shutouts and limited their nine opponents to just twenty-eight total points.

For context on that twenty-eight points, consider that twelve years later the Redskins scored thirty-five points against the Broncos in the second quarter of Super Bowl XXII. Thirty-five points in a single quarter!

Granted, those thirty-five Redskins points represent a Super Bowl record that still stands, but it also came in the Super Bowl against an AFC champion that entered the game a three-point favorite.

During the 1976 season, the Steelers leaned heavily on their rushing game as Bradshaw fully recovered from his injuries. They developed into a dominant rushing team. Then, just like that, their rushing game practically disappeared in the lopsided divisional playoff game against the Colts.

First, Bleier went down with his toe injury, on the same foot he severely injured in Vietnam. Then, Harris went down with bruised ribs. Next in line, Fuqua suffered an injury of his own.

All three of those injured running backs missed practice leading up to the Raiders game. Only Fuqua managed to play against Oakland, and he was severely limited. Harrison was the only healthy running back left on the roster.

The Steelers were forced to go into the game without their most trusted offensive threats. It had a two-fold effect, for Noll had to rely almost solely on Bradshaw and the passing game, and Madden and the Raiders knew they could concentrate on defending the pass as they didn't fear the crippled Steelers ground game.

Heading into the offseason, the Steelers couldn't help but think what might have been without those injuries to Bleier and Harris in the blowout victory against the Colts.

Offseason activity began with the 1977 NFL Draft, where the Steelers selected linebacker Robin Cole out of the University of New Mexico in the first round with the twenty-first overall selection. Cole would go on to a twelve-year NFL career, with eleven of those spent in Pittsburgh.

Other notable draftees of the class of 1977 were defensive end Tom Beasley, receiver Jim Smith, guard Steve Courson, linebacker Dennis "Dirt" Winston, and quarterback Cliff Stoudt. All in all, a very sound draft of players who would contribute to several Steelers teams.

The Steelers went into the summer of 1977 with some good vibes. They had a potential third-straight championship season the year before derailed perhaps only by key injuries, and they had filled their roster with a number of good, young ballplayers.

That, however, might have been the highlight of the entire year, for soon the Steelers found themselves in a seemingly constant swirl of turmoil.

Remember Lynn Swann's incredible Super Bowl X performance? He nearly missed that game with a concussion suffered two weeks before in the AFC Championship Game against the Raiders. Raiders safety Atkinson had delivered a big blow, and Swann's concussion sent him to the hospital for two days.

In today's NFL, with its concussion protocols designed to minimize head injuries and their long-term effects, Swann most likely wouldn't have been allowed to suit up for Super Bowl X. But, suit up he did, and Swann subsequently delivered a performance for the ages.

The very next game Swann played in, however—the 1976 season opener at Oakland—he again faced off against Atkinson, and once again, he suffered a concussion. On that September afternoon, Atkinson had hit Swann on the back of the head with a blow clearly against the rules of football, but one that was ultimately not penalized by game officials.

Noll, having seen his star receiver suffer two serious head injuries in two consecutive games against the same opponent and player, was apoplectic in his post-game press conference, referring to Atkinson as part of the "criminal element" of football he would like to see excised from the game.

NFL Commissioner Rozelle was less than pleased with both the play and the press conference, fining Atkinson $1,500 for his hit and Noll $1,000 for his remarks.

Atkinson was more displeased, and it had nothing to do with his fine. Atkinson felt Noll's remarks labeled him a "criminal," which he considered libelous. In response, Atkinson brought forth a lawsuit seeking up to $2 million in total damages, including punitive damages.

All of that came to a head in July 1977 as Atkinson's case went to court in California. Rather predictably, the trial was a bit of a circus sideshow.

Atkinson's chief attorney, California State Assemblyman Willie Brown—not the same Willie Brown who had a Hall of Fame career as a cornerback playing alongside Atkinson—argued not only that the comment would diminish Atkinson's potential value as a player, but that Noll, with three years of law school under his belt, fully knew that before he made his comments.

For his part, Raiders manager and general partner, Al Davis, never one to shy away from making bombastic statements in public, testified that Atkinson's trade value had been forever diminished and that his career would most likely be shortened because game officials would forever more examine his play with undue scrutiny.

Noll's attorney, James MacInnes, told the court that Noll's description was, in fact, accurate, in that Atkinson's action was a clear rules violation. As for "criminal element," he argued the phrase was no more demeaning than other labels attached to Atkinson, like "dirty," and as a player who delivered "cheap shots." As for future earnings, MacInnes argued that Atkinson had not lost, but rather gained additional publicity and notoriety.

The trial lasted ten days, and the first witness called was Noll, who testified for nine hours. Four hours after the jury went into deliberations, it returned with a verdict in favor of Noll and the Steelers.

Oh, but the drama wasn't over.

On the stand, Noll was asked about players other than Atkinson whom he might classify as players who, on occasion, play outside the rules. Film clips were even shown featuring hits from Noll's own players. Among others, Noll mentioned Greene and Blount in his assessment.

Blount was already unhappy with the Steelers. About ready to enter his eighth year, and at the height of his career with two successive Pro Bowl nods and the Defensive Player of the Year Award in 1975, Blount wanted to be paid much more than his $50,000 annual contract. He had already stated he wasn't going to return to the team under those contractual terms.

Getting called out by Noll by name on the stand only furthered Blount's resolve and then some. Blount filed his own lawsuit against his head coach, Noll, suing for $5 million in compensatory damages and another $1 million in punitive damages for being grouped into the "criminal element" label. During the Atkinson trial, Blount told reporters, "There's no chance at all that I'll play for the Steelers under Noll."

Generally speaking, statements made under oath during trials are considered privileged for the purposes of libel law. Blount wasn't going to win his case, and he eventually withdrew it. That resolution, however, didn't make Blount any happier.

As it was, Blount missed fifty-six days of training camp leading up to the 1977 season. Lambert and Edwards also held out of camp seeking renewed contract talks.

Heading into the 1977 regular season, all was not well with the Pittsburgh Steelers.

The 1977 season opener saw the San Francisco 49ers visit Three Rivers Stadium on a beautiful September night for a game nationally televised on ABC's *Monday Night Football*. Against an overmatched opponent, the Steelers flexed their muscles for the prime-time audience.

Harris sandwiched two Gerela field goals with his two touchdowns, one in the second quarter, the other in the fourth, on his way to an even one hundred yards rushing on the night. Bradshaw connected with Stallworth on a fifteen-yard pass to close the scoring in a convincing 27–0 shutout victory.

It would appear that the Steel Curtain was picking up where it left off the season before, despite the rocky lead-up to the campaign. The defense racked up four sacks and three turnovers while limiting the 49ers to 101 total yards of offense.

If you had sauntered into a Pittsburgh watering hole after the game and bet people that it wasn't going to get any better than that in the 1977 season, you'd likely have gotten a lot of takers. If you had, you would have made a lot of money.

The Steelers fell back to reality the next week when their archrivals—and defending Super Bowl champions—the Oakland Raiders visited Three Rivers. In many ways, the game was typical of the Steelers versus Raiders matchups of recent years.

The Raiders played conservatively, concentrating on running the football and minimizing any mistakes that would create momentum for the Steelers in front of their faithful home crowd. On the day, they rushed for 140 yards, although it took them forty-six carries to do so.

The Steelers found better success running the ball, rushing for 152 yards on thirty-one carries. But they self-destructed with turnovers, losing three interceptions and two fumbles.

The Raiders didn't turn the ball over, and that's how they won. Three second-quarter field goals by Mann spotted them a 9–0 lead going into halftime. The Raiders then tacked on a fourth-quarter touchdown on an eight-yard run by Van Eeghan to push the score to 17–0.

Only Bradshaw's forty-three-yard touchdown pass to Cunningham prevented a shutout, and that score was very much a case of too little, too late. The outcome of the game left little doubt that a new pecking order had been firmly established in the AFC, and the Steelers were no longer at the top.

That Raiders game would prove to be the final game between the two teams in the 1970s. They played eleven times during the decade, with five tilts coming within the high-stakes realm of the playoffs. The Raiders held the edge in those games with six total victories. In the five playoff games, the Steelers held a 3–2 advantage.

For the second year in succession, the Steelers had split their first two games and started 1–1. The Steelers then split their next two games, a 28–14 win at Cleveland followed by a 27–10 defeat at Houston.

In what would develop into a season of lowlights, the Houston game might have been the lowest of them all. The Oilers burst out to the lead with a trick-play forty-four-yard touchdown pass from running back Ronnie Coleman to Burrough. After that, the Steelers went into the half with a 10–7 lead, courtesy of a Gerela field goal and a short Bleier plunge.

Then, the wheels fell off. For the game, the Steelers committed nine turnovers, including six interceptions, four by Bradshaw and two by backup quarterback Tony Dungy. Yes, that would be the same Tony Dungy who would later coach the Indianapolis Colts and Peyton Manning to a Super Bowl championship before pivoting into television and being a studio analyst for NBC's *Sunday Night Football* telecast.

The Steelers' turnover total could have easily reached double digits for the game were it not for recovering two of their five fumbles. On top of the ball-handling miscues, the Steelers were also flagged for ten penalties.

The Oilers scored the last twenty points to win going away, 27–10.

The Steelers then won two games at home, against Cincinnati and a rematch against Houston, before losing two straight games on the road, at Baltimore and Denver. Sitting at 4–4, the Steelers were in a three-way tie for second place in the division behind the surprising Browns. More importantly, several problematic trends were becoming evident.

First, the Steelers were turning the ball over in an alarming manner. For the season, they had already turned the ball over thirty-four times, an unacceptable total for any team looking to contend for a title.

Second, the defense was perhaps beginning to show its age a bit. That or they showed what happens when a large portion of a defensive squad holds out of training camp in contract disputes. The defense had only forced twenty-one turnovers after eight games, and while in some games, they were effective at taking the ball away—one game with six turnovers, another two games with five—they were equally as ineffective in others—three games with zero takeaways.

More importantly, the defense was generally giving up a lot of yards and first downs, at least in comparison to recent seasons past. And, of course, they were giving up a great many more points, although much of that blame fell to the offense and its turnovers.

Lastly, the team continued to face distractions, as it had all summer and autumn. In October, backup cornerback Jimmy Allen quit the team, like some kid might do in junior high school. Sure, he changed his mind the next day and came back, but it still signaled that much was amiss with this edition of the Steelers.

Then, before the Denver game on the first Sunday in November, Edwards left the team because he was unhappy with the recently renegotiated contract he had signed just months earlier. He, too, returned, right after the loss to the Broncos.

If the Steelers were to make anything out of the 1977 season, they needed to snap out of their slump quickly. And there would prove to be no better time than Week Nine when the first-place Browns visited Three Rivers Stadium.

On a cold, blustery day in Pittsburgh, the two teams put on an entertaining, barn-burning game for the sold-out crowd.

The Browns opened the scoring with a Don Cockroft forty-four-yard field goal in the first quarter, to which the Steelers quickly responded with a thirty-nine-yard Bradshaw-to-Swann touchdown pass that gave the Black and Gold the lead.

In the second quarter, the Steelers then reeled off three straight touchdowns—a two-yard run by Bleier, a thirty-eight-yard reception by Stallworth, and a sixteen-yard run by Harris—to take a seemingly commanding 28–3 lead into the halftime intermission.

The Browns scored the only third-quarter points on a five-yard Cleo Miller touchdown run to narrow their deficit to eighteen points. But the Steelers opened the fourth-quarter scoring with a nine-yard Bradshaw touchdown pass to Stallworth.

At that point, the Browns, behind quarterback Dave Mays, went on a tear. Mays connected with running back Larry Poole on three fourth-quarter touchdown passes to scare the dickens out of the Steelers and their home crowd. Time expired though with the Steelers on the victorious side of a thrilling 35–31 game.

The victory against the Browns was the first of what proved to be a four-game win streak, with the Steelers prevailing over the Cowboys, Jets, and Seahawks in succession.

The streak ended in a Week Thirteen loss at Cincinnati. As the Browns had faded after their loss to the Steelers, the Steelers' 17–10 defeat at the hand of the Bengals left those two teams in a tie atop the Central Division. With 8–5 records, the only way either team would earn a spot in the playoffs would be with a divisional crown. The final week of the regular season was a must-win occasion if either the Steelers or Bengals wanted to advance to the postseason.

The Steelers' season-ending opponent was the San Diego Chargers, in an afternoon game at venerable San Diego Stadium. Desperate to win, the Steelers came out and played . . . like they weren't desperate to win.

The Chargers played just well enough in the first half to squeak out a 9–0 lead on a short touchdown run and a mid-range field goal. The Steelers' defense was carrying the load for the team, and on the afternoon, pretty much handled the Chargers.

On offense, the Steelers struggled mightily. In the third quarter, they finally got on the scoreboard on a one-yard run by reserve back Sidney Thornton. Later in the third, they took the lead on a twenty-seven-yard field goal by Gerela.

The Steelers held on to win a tight 10–9 game, and coupled with the Bengals' crushing 21–16 defeat at the hands of the Oilers, advanced to the postseason as AFC Central Division champions. It was the Steelers' fourth consecutive divisional crown, fifth in the last six seasons.

Despite earning a playoff berth, the Steelers weren't expected to make much noise. The power struggle for AFC supremacy had shifted. The other teams in the AFC to make the playoffs were the Broncos, Raiders, and Colts. The Steelers had played each of those three teams in the 1977 season and had lost all three games by a combined score of 68–35.

The Steelers allowed 243 points to opponents in 1977, or 105 more than the season previous, falling to seventeenth in the twenty-eight-team league. They also surrendered 4.2 yards per play to opponents, up from 3.8 in 1976. Where the defense continued to excel was in creating interceptions, where they led the league with thirty-one.

The offense also led the league in a category, and that was in fumbles lost, where they totaled twenty-eight. Adding on the quarterbacks' combined twenty-one interceptions, the Steelers had the ignominious distinction of leading the NFL in turnovers.

Individually, Harris again posted another 1,000-yard season, rushing for 1,162 yards and eleven touchdowns. For his results, he was named to the Pro Bowl, as well as recognized as an All-Pro.

Joining Harris with Pro Bowl nominations were Swann, Greene, Ham, and Lambert.

The Steelers reward for earning a playoff berth was a return trip to Denver for a Christmas Eve rematch with the Broncos, winners of the AFC West Division crown with a 12–2 record.

Over the first three quarters, the Broncos scored three touchdowns to take the lead in the ballgame, only to have the Steelers gallantly fight back to score touchdowns of their own to tie the game. When Brown scored on a one-yard pass from Bradshaw early in the fourth quarter, it knotted the game at twenty-one.

Just as turnovers had affected the outcome of so many games during the regular season, they proved to be the undoing of the Steelers and their 1977 campaign.

Bradshaw threw two fourth-quarter interceptions, both by linebacker Tom Jackson, who in retirement later grew to more widespread fame as a storied ESPN pro football analyst. The Broncos took care of business the rest of the way, pulling away to a 34–21 victory that mercifully ended the Steelers' tumultuous season.

The 1977 season was the final season with Ernie Holmes, a charter member of the Steel Curtain, in a Steelers uniform.

Earnest Holmes was born July 11, 1948, in Jamestown, Texas, where he grew up on his family's farm in the far eastern part of the state near Louisiana. After high school, Holmes went on to play collegiately at Texas Southern University.

The Steelers selected Holmes in the eighth round of the 1971 NFL Draft. Other notable Steelers players selected that year included Lewis, Ham, Mullins, and Larry Brown.

Holmes was often overshadowed in his career, playing on the line alongside Greene, Greenwood, and White, each of whom was honored with multiple Pro Bowl selections and was the subject of storied Super Bowl exploits. However, Holmes was a key figure in the success of so many dominant Steelers' defenses.

Holmes would garner a lot of attention from opponents' offensive lines, freeing up linebackers like Ham and Lambert to clean up with tackles, and paving the way for Greenwood and others to rush the quarterback. And perhaps no Steeler played with such a fierce, reckless abandon than Holmes, who his Steelers teammates often characterized as "crazy."

Holmes was a character, sporting a haircut in the shape of an arrow pointing straight ahead, a style he said was intended to point him directly at opposing quarterbacks. His time off the field was marked by police chases, shooting at law enforcement officials, an arrest for cocaine possession, and stories of wild nights of drinking.

Nicknamed "Fats" throughout his career, Homes' girth contributed to his exit from the Steelers, as the club thought his constant weight issues were adversely affecting his play. As a result, he was traded to New England ahead of the 1978 season, where he finished his seven-year career in the NFL with a final season.

After his playing career, Holmes took to professional wrestling, where he appeared in WrestleMania 2. He also dabbled in acting, appearing in an episode of *The A-Team* and the movie *Fright Night*.

Ernie Holmes passed away on January 17, 2008, a victim of a single-car rollover accident in which he was driving.

Chapter 21

BRADSHAW BLOSSOMS AS RUST BELT APPEARS

During World War II and the years that immediately followed, the steel industry experienced a long period of growth. Not only was steel needed for the war effort, but it was also required for reconstruction afterward, and there was a lot of reconstruction to complete. Additionally, in the United States, a strong economy fueled a construction boom across the country, and steel was in great demand.

Over the decades that followed, though, new plants came online throughout the world, introducing new technologies and new methods. However, there was a tendency in North America to stay the current path. Steel is an incredibly capital-intensive industry, and new investments might well be put off if continuous improvements could be made to run more efficiently and cost-effectively.

Beginning in the 1970s, the decisions made by the US steel industry began to catch up to them. After steel production in the United States peaked in 1973 at 111.4 million tons, it steadily decreased to 97.9 million tons by 1978. Then, the bottom fell out of production, and by 1984, domestic production of steel was just 70 million tons.

Back in the 1970s you might recall, the industry, steered in part by the government, economists, and Wall Street financiers, greatly over forecasted the worldwide demand for steel in the 1980s. They ended up missing the mark by upwards of 50 percent, as the steel industry unexpectedly began competing not only within itself, but with aluminum, plastics, and ceramics manufacturers as well. Consumers could discover this themselves as they noticed the abrupt change in materials used by automobile makers.

Throughout the 1970s though, the investment by US steelmakers in new equipment fell roughly 25 percent as compared to the decade before. Domestic producers also generally turned their back on new methods, like the basic oxygen furnace— also known as BOF, Linz-Donawitz steelmaking, or the oxygen converter process. Invented by a Swiss engineer and first commercialized in Austria, the BOF process was increasingly used around the world. Back in America and in Pittsburgh, it was more often an open-hearth process.

The lapse in production technology wasn't a new phenomenon. In 1960, oxygen converters were responsible for 3.4 percent of US steel production, as compared to 11.6 percent in Japan. Five years later, in 1965, US producers lagged behind even more, with oxygen converters making up 17.4 percent of US production versus 55 percent of Japanese production. The manufacturing cost advantage of oxygen converters could be as high as $10 per ton. Over time and at scale, it proved to be a significant savings and source of capital for investing in further innovation.

There were small segments of innovators in the domestic industry, most notably the "mini-mills," the relatively small-scale mills that produced steel from scraps in electric furnaces instead of smelted ore. Those mini-mills grew as the legacy mills shrunk, increasing their domestic market share to 16 percent in 1982. Four short years later, it ballooned to a 23 percent market share.

For the big legacy producers, investments, or rather the lack of investments, over time caught up to them. In Hoerr's book, he writes that US companies invested roughly 0.6 percent of revenues in research and development, while those in Japan invested three times as much, or 1.8 percent. There are multiple reasons American companies didn't invest in technology, but, ultimately, it came down to available funds, and those funds were more scarce to American producers due to earlier marketplace competition and . . . a much higher labor wage structure.

According to the report "Great Lakes States: Trouble in America's Industrial Heartland," by 1980, almost 25 percent of American steel production was the output of outdated, inefficient machinery and methods. It's little wonder that in that same year, Japanese steel makers accounted for 16 percent of the global production of steel versus that of the United States' 14 percent.

Outdated methods and machinery, of course, meant a continued dependence on increasingly expensive labor. In a 1984 article in *The New York Times*, it was reported that Japanese manufacturers produced a ton of steel with 8.25 hours of labor, compared to 11.5 hours for plants in the United States.

If that wasn't enough to turn the competitive tide in favor of Japan, consider that, according to estimates by the Bureau of Labor Statistics' Office of Productivity and Technology quoted in that same *Times* article, members of the United Steelworkers were getting paid more than $22 an hour, including benefits. Their Japanese counterparts were being paid $12 an hour.

Simply, US steel producers had to use more people-hours at a significantly higher wage scale. Estimates in the *Times* article pegged the cost of producing steel in American mills in 1984 at a range of between $350 and $550 per ton, or as much as $150 per ton more than steel produced in Japanese mills.

Japan wasn't the only international competitor taking a bite out of the US industry. Producers in Taiwan, South Korea, and Brazil had the same advantages as their Japanese peers.

Ill-prepared to compete globally, American steel producers faced no other option than to retrench. The domestic industry needed to get its act together if it were to survive, and it was destined to be a long, difficult transition.

It started with costs and capacity. It made no sense to make more steel that was more expensive than its competitors and lose more money, forcing fewer investments going forward. In an act of self-survival, it would have made sense for labor and management to attempt to work together, for the common betterment. Instead, they more often went at each other's throats.

Even within the union, there was considerable infighting. Union leaders who publicly endorsed concessions were often swiftly labeled as sellouts looking out for their self-interests.

In short time, nothing could prevent the inevitable plant closures.

The American Iron and Steel Institute estimates the US steel industry accounted for 512,000 jobs in 1974, down from a peak of 650,000 in 1953. From 1974 to 1980, employment dropped to 399,000. Then, from 1980 to 1984, it fell another 40 percent to 236,000 jobs.

In that same four-year time period in the Pittsburgh area alone, the number of steelworkers fell from 90,000 to just 44,000. In addition to those steelworkers, Hoerr suggests another 50,000 manufacturing jobs in other industries were lost in the region.

Beginning in 1980, U.S. Steel began shuttering its worst plants in terms of production efficiency. Over eight painful years, the company cut its industrial workforce from 75,000 to 20,000. Salaried workers weren't spared along the way. Those ranks were slashed from 30,000 employees to just 5,000. The father of one of the authors of this book was one of the many casualties in 1981.

However, amidst all the economic turmoil associated with the city of Pittsburgh's legacy steel industry and the very real hardship felt by Pittsburghers and others in western Pennsylvania, the Steelers marched onward. Their professional football team, a source of civic pride, gave yinzers something tangible to grasp ahold, take strength, and steel their resolve.

The fact the Steelers and their fans were disappointed by the team's 1977 campaign spoke volumes as to changed expectations. A 9–5 record and a playoff berth may well have generated bedlam in the 1960s. In the late 1970s, after the best run of success in the franchise's history, it was viewed as a disappointing year.

A change for the entire NFL came into effect for the 1978 season. The traditionally interminable six-game preseason was shortened to just four games, allowing the fourteen-game regular season to be expanded to sixteen games. Furthermore, an additional wildcard entrant was added to the playoff format of each conference, expanding the field from four teams to five, or ten total for the entire NFL.

But that wasn't all. Two key rules were instituted, both with the intent of freeing up the capabilities of offenses. The first rule, familiarly known as "The Mell Blount Rule," prohibited defenders from contacting receivers more than five yards past the line of scrimmage.

The second rule allowed offensive lineman to use their hands in blocking, something that would greatly aid them in protecting the quarterback on passing plays. Football fans everywhere, of course, extolled the virtues of the changes and eagerly looked forward to the season.

The 1978 NFL draft would not produce any stars for the Steelers, but three of their first four draft picks—defensive backs Ron Johnson and Larry Anderson and punter Craig Colquitt—would each play at least five years for the club.

Finally, with the problematic offseason of 1976 well behind him, Noll started his tenth year at the helm, moving him ahead of Walt Kiesling as the team's longest-tenured head coach. However, his coaching staff did suffer some turnover. Defensive coordinator Bud Carson moved to the Rams, and offensive line coach Dan Radakovich, credited with much of the success of the Steelers' vaunted rushing game, moved onto the 49ers.

In addition to welcoming rookies from the draft class, the roster also saw a few key departures. Notably, Holmes was gone. But so too were the disgruntled Edwards, traded to the Chargers, and Lewis, traded to the Bills.

The Steelers opened up the 1978 season, the team's forty-sixth in the NFL, on September 2 in Buffalo, where they squared off with the Bills. Behind three touchdowns, the Steelers held a 21–0 lead before their old teammate, Lewis, finally broke the ice for the Bills when he hauled in a twenty-two-yard touchdown pass. Still, behind the coolly efficient play of Bradshaw, the Steelers won easily, 28–17.

Now in his ninth season, Bradshaw was truly coming into his own. The new rules, of course, allowed him to be a more effective passer. Then again, the rules were the same for every quarterback. Very specifically to Bradshaw, he was concentrating on passing more, scrambling less, and all the while, taking much less punishment to his body and avoiding injury.

After the season-opening victory, the Steelers blitzed through the next six games, including key divisional wins against the Browns, twice, and the Bengals, once. The Steelers won rather handily in each of the games, save the first Browns matchup on Week Four, at Three Rivers Stadium. On that occasion, the Browns, undefeated at that point in the season, forced the game into sudden death overtime tied at 9–9. Bradshaw put to rest any Cleveland designs on an upset when he engineered a walk-off victory with a thirty-seven-yard touchdown pass to tight end Cunningham.

The seven straight victories to open the season was the best start in the franchise's history, and it would stand as such for the next forty-two seasons, until the 2020 team opened with eleven consecutive victories.

The defense had played well, limiting four of its seven opponents to ten points or less and forcing seventeen total turnovers. The offense was doing its job, too, scoring twenty-eight or more points in five of the games—and generally presenting a balanced attack between the rushing and passing efforts.

The only real cause for concern was the loss of Cunningham, who injured his left knee in the Week Six victory over the Falcons in Pittsburgh. Up to his injury, Cunningham was enjoying an outstanding season in his third year, hauling in sixteen receptions for more than twenty yards per catch, tops of any tight end. To replace Cunningham, Noll turned to fifth-year tight end Randy Grossman, who had only three catches through the first six games.

Week Eight saw the Houston Oilers come to Pittsburgh, featuring their exciting rookie running back Earl Campbell, the Heisman Trophy winner from the year before at the University of Texas. Campbell had burst onto the scene for coach Bum Phillips's Oilers and showed the Steelers and their home crowd what all the fuss was about.

Campbell scored on three short touchdown runs and averaged nearly four and a half yards per carry during the game. Quarterback Pastorini was effective in mixing in the passing attack to keep the Steelers' defense off balance. In the end, it was too much for Bradshaw and his two touchdown passes to Swann to overcome, and the Oilers put the first blemish on the Steelers' record with a 24–17 victory.

The Steelers responded by winning their next two games, also at home, against the Chiefs and the Saints to lift their record to 9–1 ahead of traveling out west to take on the Los Angeles Rams.

With the Rams' record standing at 8–2, the game was a premier matchup between two of the best teams in the league. Both teams set out to impose their will on their opponent.

The Rams' defense, led by two Youngbloods, Jim and Jack, no relation to one another, as well as Fred Dryer and Jim "Hacksaw" Reynolds, played a spirited game, shutting down Harris and Bleier cold.

The Steel Curtain defense was effective, too, although a bit less spectacularly than the home team. Nonetheless, they were ending drives and keeping their team in the game.

The first half ended with the score it had started with, 0–0.

In the second half, the Steelers struck first blood, scoring a third-quarter touchdown on a fourteen-yard Swann reception of a Bradshaw pass. Before the quarter ended, though, the Rams had clawed through for a field goal, making the score 7–3 in favor of the Steelers heading into the final quarter.

The Rams pulled out a hard-earned, come-from-behind victory in the end though, scoring a touchdown on a ten-yard pass from quarterback Pat Haden to receiver Willie Miller. The loss dropped the Steelers' record to 9–2. It would be the final time they tasted bitter defeat that season.

The Steelers got back to their winning ways the next Sunday at home against the hapless Bengals, who stumbled into Three Rivers with a 1–10 record. But, the Steelers' win sure wasn't easy.

The Bengals turned the ball over five times and were flagged for five penalties, and they *still* outplayed the Steelers in almost every facet of the game. Bradshaw threw four interceptions and the Steelers fumbled the ball four times, thankfully only losing one.

After Chris Barr put the Bengals in front with a twenty-nine-yard field goal in the first quarter, the Steelers responded with a one-yard Bleier run in the second. Barr kicked another field goal for the Bengals to send the game into halftime with the Steelers holding a narrow 7–6 lead.

That's exactly how the game ended. The Steelers had escaped with a victory, but after producing just fourteen points and committing eight turnovers in two games, the offense was definitely mired in a slump.

Bradshaw and his running mates got better the next week at Candlestick Park against the 49ers. Bradshaw connected with Swann for two touchdowns, and Stallworth for another. After a 24–7 victory, the Steelers were ready to go to Houston for a Week Fourteen rematch with Campbell and the Oilers.

Sitting at 9–4 and two games behind the Steelers in the Central Division, the Oilers had to repeat their Week Eight win if they were to have any hope of wresting the division title out of the Steelers' grasp. The Steelers, led by their defense, would have none of it.

The teams traded field goals in the first half, the first one by Gerela in the first quarter, then one by Fritsch in the second to go into halftime at a 3–3 stalemate. The second half was all Steelers, with Gerela adding a short field goal in the third quarter and Bradshaw connecting with Stallworth on a short touchdown pass in the fourth.

In the Steelers' decisive 13–3 victory, they limited the Oilers to just nine first downs and allowed only eighty-one yards rushing and 164 yards in total offense. Safety Donnie Shell ended Campbell's game early with a massive shot directly in the bruising back's ribs, causing Houston's rookie sensation to be helped off the field.

The victory over the Oilers pushed Pittsburgh's record to 12–2, and it clinched their fifth consecutive AFC Central Division title.

The Steelers then ran off victories in their final two regular-season games. In a 35–13 victory over the Colts, Bradshaw threw three touchdown passes and Harris had two touchdown rushes. In the season finale in Denver against the Broncos, Bradshaw threw two touchdown passes after Harris opened the scoring with a rushing touchdown, and the Steelers exerted some degree of revenge for the previous year's playoff defeat with a 21–17 win.

The Steelers ended the regular season with a conference-best 14–2 record, ensuring it would play all of its playoff games at Three Rivers Stadium in front of their boisterous crowd. It also meant they had a first-round bye to rest and recuperate.

Bradshaw had his best season as a professional in 1978, completing over 56 percent of his passes for what was at that point a career-high 2,915 yards. Additionally, he threw a career-high twenty-eight touchdown passes against twenty interceptions. For his play and his leadership, Bradshaw was selected as the NFL's Most Valuable Player.

Harris once again ran for over 1,000 yards, the sixth such occasion in his seven-year career. Swann again led the team with sixty-one catches and eleven touchdowns, and Stallworth added another nine touchdowns from his forty-one receptions.

Over the final ten games of the season, Grossman developed into one of Bradshaw's most trusted mid-range targets, and he ended the season with thirty-seven catches at over twelve yards a pop.

The Steelers' defense once again allowed the fewest points in the league at just 195, and they didn't allow a single first-quarter touchdown. They also forced forty-eight turnovers, with the previous year's backup quarterback, Dungy, leading the team with six interceptions after being converted to defensive back.

In total, ten players were named to the Pro Bowl squad, a full 25 percent of the AFC's forty-player roster. Those ten were Bradshaw, Swann, Webster, Greene, Ham, Harris, Greenwood, Lambert, Shell, and Blount.

All-Pro honors were bestowed to Bradshaw, Webster, Swann, and Ham.

The Steelers' first opponent in the playoffs ended up being the Broncos, the team they had defeated two weeks before to complete the regular season. It was also a rematch of the playoff game the year before that had eliminated the Steelers and launched the Broncos to eventually play in the Super Bowl.

The Broncos had lost Super Bowl XII to the Dallas Cowboys, 27–10, in a game they were never really in. They hadn't suffered too much from a Super Bowl hangover, though, as they went through their season in a fairly steady manner to finish 10–6, once again tops among the AFC West Division.

Offensively, the Broncos were led by thirty-five-year-old veteran quarterback Craig Morton, and they featured a running attack by committee, with six backs rushing for over 300 yards on the season and a sixth who checked in just below with 296 yards.

The strength of the Broncos still remained their fierce "Orange Crush" defense, led by Pro Bowlers Lyle Alzado, Randy Gradishar, Bill Thompson, Louis Wright, and Jackson, he of the two interceptions in the 1977 playoff game. The Broncos' defensive unit had finished second only to the Steelers in points allowed with 198. The divisional playoff game was shaping up to be a defensive struggle of a game.

The Broncos opened the scoring in the first quarter with a thirty-seven-yard Jim Turner field goal. The Steelers got that score back and then some when Harris found the end zone later in the quarter on a one-yard run. The point after touchdown attempt, however, was no good, so the Steelers led only 6–3.

In the second quarter, Harris provided a little buffer with his eighteen-yard touchdown run, and with that extra point made, the Steelers pressed to a 13–3 advantage.

Meanwhile, the Steel Curtain was feasting on the Broncos' offense, generally making life miserable for Morton. In Denver's first five possessions, the Steelers surrendered a total of forty-nine total yards. More importantly, on the four possessions after their first, the Broncos had only moved fourteen yards. The Steelers' defense forced the hand of Broncos head coach Red Miller, who summarily replaced Morton with third-year backup quarterback Norris Weese to spark his offense.

With a third-quarter score of 19–10—advantage Steelers—Greene made a play on special teams that pretty much ended any Broncos' hopes of pulling off the upset. On a twenty-nine-yard field goal attempt by Turner to close the deficit to just a single score, Greene got his hands on it and blocked the attempt.

From there, the defense continued to clamp down. In the fourth quarter, Bradshaw connected with both Stallworth and Swann on long touchdown passes to allow the Steelers to comfortably pull away to a 33–10 victory.

The Steelers had utterly dominated a pretty good football team in the Broncos. The defensive unit held Denver in check, allowing only 218 total yards, with six sacks and two forced turnovers. On offense, the Steelers chalked up 425 yards, with Stallworth leading the way with ten receptions for 156 yards and his fourth-quarter touchdown.

Next up in the AFC Championship Game would be a familiar foe in the Oilers, their divisional rival who had split their regular-season series with a victory on the home turf of Three Rivers Stadium.

In 1978, Steelers center Mike Webster was voted to his first Pro Bowl. It would be the first of seven consecutive Pro Bowl nods, with an eighth to follow after a single season break.

"Iron Mike" Webster was part of the Steelers' legendary 1974 draft class when he was selected in the fifth round out of Wisconsin. Over his first two years, he was an understudy to veteran center, and occasional place kicker, Mansfield. In Webster's third season, he ascended into the Steelers' starting lineup, where he was a mainstay, anchoring the offensive line for thirteen years.

Webster was born on March 18, 1952, in Tomahawk, Wisconsin. In college, he was considered the best center in the Big Ten, a conference known at the time for its teams' ability to run the football in rough and tumble games.

When Webster became the Steelers' starting center in 1976, he began a streak of 150 consecutive games of starting in one of the most physically demanding positions on the gridiron. He struck a memorable presence on the field, with his gigantic, muscular arms pushing the short sleeves of his jersey to their very limits.

At the tail end of his seventeen-year career in the trenches of professional football, Webster played two seasons for the Chiefs. Considered by most to be the best ever to play his position, Webster was enshrined in the Pro Football Hall of Fame in Canton in 1997.

Unfortunately, despite all his on-field accomplishments, it is perhaps Webster's post-football life for which he is most remembered. After retirement, Webster suffered from amnesia, dementia, and depression, along with acute bone and muscular pain. As a result, he lived erratically, bouncing around locations and disappearing for long stretches of time without contact with friends and family.

Eventually, Webster's teenage son took care of him. On September 24, 2002, at just fifty years of age, Webster died of a heart attack.

After his death, Webster was diagnosed with chronic traumatic encephalopathy, or CTE, a neurodegenerative disease. Diagnosable only after death, Webster was the first former NFL player to be diagnosed with the condition. Upon examination, Webster's brain tissue exhibited the same type of damaging scarring as that of some boxers and others who suffer from repeated blows to the head. A portion of Webster's story is portrayed in the 2015 motion picture *Concussion*, starring Will Smith.

After Webster's post-death medical examination, his estate filed suit against the NFL, contending he was disabled at the time of his retirement, and, therefore, owed disability payments under the NFL's retirement plan. In 2005, a federal judge ruled in favor of the Webster estate. A year later, the US Court of Appeals affirmed the decision.

On January 7, 1979, the Steelers hosted the Oilers in a frigid afternoon game at Three Rivers Stadium. At kickoff, the temperature was twenty-five degrees, and the steady breeze made the windchill factor feel like sixteen degrees.

The weather conditions didn't do either team any favors, but it probably affected the visiting Oilers more as they were a southern-based team that played their games indoors in a domed stadium.

On the Three Rivers Stadium turf made slick by freezing rain, the weather had a definitive impact. Remarkably, the two teams combined to fumble the ball eleven times in the first half alone. Despite the messy affair, the Steelers dominated the game from the outset.

The Steelers scored first on Harris's seven-yard touchdown run to culminate a fifty-seven-yard scoring drive. On the next possession, Ham recovered a fumble deep in Oilers' territory, leading to a fifteen-yard touchdown run by Bleier.

Just like that, the Steelers had a commanding lead at 14–0.

The Steelers' scoring streak was temporarily interrupted when the Oilers' Fritsch converted on a short nineteen-yard field goal in the second quarter. Soon afterward, the Steelers put away any notion the outcome of the game should be in doubt.

After another Oilers fumble led to a twenty-nine-yard touchdown reception by Swann, the Oilers promptly fumbled away the subsequent kickoff. Stallworth then hauled in a seventeen-yard touchdown reception to boost the score to 28–3 in the waning moments of the first half.

But, the half wasn't over yet. On the Oilers' possession, they fumbled once again. Gerela blasted home a thirty-seven-yard field goal to finish a Steelers explosion of seventeen points in just fifty-four seconds of game time. At 31–3, the game was essentially over.

The teams played the second half in a manner that somewhat suggested they just wanted to get the game over with on this wet, miserable, freezing day. Bleier became so chilled in the second half he was sent to the locker room to warm up and prevent possible hyperthermia.

The Steelers' defense again drove the Oilers to self-destruct the rest of the way, forcing four more turnovers in Houston's six second-half drives. For the game, the Oilers suffered through nine turnovers while gaining just 142 yards of total offense.

Ham delivered one of the best statistical games by a defender in playoff history. He accounted for three Oilers turnovers that resulted in seventeen Steelers points. He finished the afternoon with five tackles, a sack, a forced fumble, two fumble recoveries, and an interception.

Before the halftime intermission, the Oilers' Campbell ran the ball to Ham's side of the field on ten occasions. The result of all that effort was eleven measly yards. For the game, Campbell, who was named both the Offensive Player of the Year and the Offensive Rookie of the Year, finished with sixty-two yards rushing on twenty-two carries.

The Steelers had won the AFC Championship 34–5, their third conference title in five years, and were advancing to Super Bowl XIII. Their opponents at the game to be held in the Orange Bowl in Miami would be the Dallas Cowboys, the defending champions who would be playing in their third Super Bowl in four years.

Chapter 22

WHEN CAT IS SPELLED M-V-P

The Dallas Cowboys entered Super Bowl XIII as the NFL's defending champions, having rather easily dispatched the Denver Broncos the year before. While they were the same team the Steelers faced in Super Bowl X, executing primarily on the same offensive and defensive schemes, the current edition of their club featured some new personnel.

Wily veteran Staubach continued to engineer the offense, but he had an exciting new weapon to deploy in second-year running back Tony Dorsett, a native of Aliquippa, Pennsylvania. The 1976 Heisman Trophy winner while playing at the University of Pittsburgh, Dorsett had been the Cowboys' first-round pick in the 1977 NFL draft in large part due to Landry and the Cowboys' front office recognizing the impact Harris and Bleier had on the outcome of Super Bowl X.

Dorsett had paid immediate dividends, rushing for over 1,000 yards and winning Offensive Rookie of the Year honors in the Cowboys' championship-winning season. As a follow-up, his 1978 campaign had been even better, with 1,325 yards rushing, another 378 yards receiving, and nine total touchdowns.

Staubach's favorite receiver continued to be ex-Steeler Preston Pearson, running patterns out of the offensive backfield, and he led the team with forty-seven receptions on the year, most of them converting key third downs. To press the ball further down the field, Staubach looked in the direction of second-year receiver Tony Hill, as well as trusted veteran, Drew Pearson. And, of course, tight end Billie Joe DuPree continued to be a key target in the middle of the field.

The abundance of talented weapons afforded to Staubach allowed the Cowboys to amass 5,959 yards of total offense, second best in the league. Additionally, they had led the league with 384 points scored.

On defense, the Cowboys continued to run their "Flex" package, and they featured a great many players familiar to the Steelers and their fans, including Jones and Harvey Martin on the line, Lewis at linebacker, and Waters and Harris as safeties.

However, since Super Bowl X, defensive tackle Randy White had developed from a spot-duty rookie contributor to a dominating force in the middle of the defensive line. In fact, both he and Martin shared the Most Valuable Player Award in Super Bowl XII.

Together, the Cowboys led the league in the fewest rushing yards allowed and were second in total yards allowed and third in scoring defense, surrendering just 208 points on the season.

The Cowboys had endured a streaky start to defending their championship, and when they lost consecutive games in the ninth and tenth weeks, their record stood at 6–4. They then reeled off six straight wins to close out the regular season with a 12–4 record and the NFC East Division title.

In the divisional round of the playoffs, the Cowboys had squeaked past the Atlanta Falcons in a come-from-behind victory. Backup quarterback Danny White, in relief of a shaken up Staubach, directed the Cowboys to two second-half scores to secure the win.

Staubach returned for the NFC Championship Game a week later in Los Angeles. After a scoreless first half, Staubach led the team on three successive touchdown drives to take a commanding lead. Flamboyant linebacker "Hollywood" Henderson then put the game on ice with a sixty-eight-yard interception return for a touchdown. Shutting out the Rams 28–0, the Cowboys advanced to their fifth Super Bowl—and their third appearance in the Super Bowl in the last four years.

Super Bowl XIII would feature the NFL's two best teams, and it would be the first Super Bowl rematch between teams who had contested a previous Super Bowl. The rematch would again take place in Miami's Orange Bowl, only this time on a natural grass field that had replaced the stadium's worn, slippery artificial turf.

The first Super Bowl to be played in a prime-time evening slot on the east coast had been Super Bowl XII, the previous year. Super Bowl XIII followed suit, and the buildup to the game, both over the two weeks since the conference championship games as well as the afternoon leading up to the game, had the crowd at a fever pitch. The Super Bowl had arrived as an American sports institution, and it now surpassed any other event, including the World Series and heavyweight title bouts in boxing.

A great amount of the pre-game hype had been generated by the Cowboys' Henderson. Before the NFC Championship Game against the Rams, Henderson had boasted that the Cowboys would shut out the Rams. Not only had he and his teammates delivered on that statement, but Henderson's touchdown return of his interception also proved to be the crowning moment.

Relishing the attention, Henderson talked leading up to Super Bowl XIII like Muhammad Ali would talk leading up to a boxing match. He made national headlines by questioning Bradshaw's intellect, saying, "Bradshaw couldn't spell 'cat' if you spotted him the *c* and the *a*."

Steelers players had never been shy about speaking honestly and forthrightly with the media. Still, they didn't follow suit and play Henderson's hype game. With a veteran roster led by the likes of Greene and Bradshaw, they set out to make their statements on the field of play.

January 21 was a temperate—albeit windy and drizzly—Florida winter day, just about perfect for a football game. Both teams took advantage of the opportunity, and it made for a spellbinding watch for fans there and around the world.

Gerela got things going with the opening kickoff, returned by the Cowboys' Butch Johnson to his twenty-eight-yard line, where they would begin with the game's first offensive possession.

Dorsett started his day with a nine-yard sweep around the left end. On second down, he electrified the crowd with a sixteen-yard sprint up the middle, gaining a first down and advancing the ball into Steelers' territory at the forty-seven-yard line.

After Newhouse was stopped cold by Lambert, Dorsett broke off another long run, this time around the right end. When he was finally forced out of bounds, he had scampered thirteen yards to give the Cowboys a first down at the Steelers' thirty-four-yard line.

Dorsett had carried the ball on three of the Cowboys' first four plays and had gained thirty-eight yards against the Steelers' stellar defense. Then, inexplicitly, the Cowboys attempted to get fancy, and it came back to bite them.

On first down, Drew Pearson went in motion ahead of the snap, moving from the right side to the left. At the snap, Staubach handed off to Dorsett, who took off to his left. After a few steps, Dorsett attempted to hand the ball to a reversing Pearson, who had designs on pitching back to Staubach for a look downfield.

Pearson never got a good handle on the ball, and it fell to the turf, where defensive end John Banaszak recovered the ball at the forty-seven-yard line for the Steelers. After a shaky first few plays, the Steelers had been somewhat gifted a big play to steady their ship.

After Harris was bottled up on the Steelers' first two offensive plays of the game, Bradshaw, under heavy pressure from a Cowboys' blitz, connected with Stallworth across the center of the field. The twelve-yard gain kept the drive going.

After an incompletion and a short run by Bleier, Bradshaw was once again faced with a long third down. Once again, Bradshaw converted the opportunity, threading his throw just beyond the outstretched fingers of Waters to connect with Grossman on a ten-yard pass to move the ball to the Cowboys' twenty-eight-yard line.

On the next play, Bradshaw again dropped back to pass, and upon seeing Stallworth break free beyond the Dallas secondary, lobbed a gentle pass to his receiver along the left boundary of the end zone. Stallworth cradled in the reception just as the Cowboys descended upon him for the opening score of the game. With Gerela's extra point, the Steelers had jumped out to a 7–0 lead.

Both offensive teams had enjoyed success in moving the ball, a somewhat surprising development considering the pedigree of each defense. The Cowboys, however, had produced a self-induced turnover, and the Steelers had wasted no time to pounce.

On their next possession, the Cowboys again moved the ball downfield, with the biggest play being a third-down reception by Johnson that covered twenty-six yards and pressed the ball to the Steelers' forty-two-yard line.

The Steel Curtain stopped the promising Cowboys drive with two consecutive sacks. First, after escaping a blitzing Lauren Toews, Staubach was corralled by Furness for a big twelve-yard loss. On the very next play, White chased down Staubach for another ten-yard loss.

After the Cowboys' punt, Bradshaw got to cooking again. On a third-and-five from his own thirty-five-yard line, Bradshaw found Harris out of the backfield for a twenty-two-yard gain and a first down. On the very next play, Bradshaw threw a strike to Swann on the right sideline, gaining another thirteen yards.

The offensive line was giving Bradshaw time to throw the ball, and his accurate throws were beginning to shred the Cowboys' secondary. At the Cowboys' thirty-yard line and driving, Bradshaw looked for more on the next play.

That pass, however, went strangely astray. Facing a blitzing defense, but not much pressure in the pocket, Bradshaw threw a looping pass out to his left that was easily intercepted by linebacker Lewis. With a gift in his hands, Lewis rumbled past the thirty-five-yard line to give the Cowboys some breathing room.

The Steelers' defense stood strong, forcing the Cowboys to give up possession on the first three-and-out of the game. A poor White punt—in addition to being the backup quarterback to Staubach, White also handled punting duties—gave the Steelers excellent field position at their thirty-eight-yard line as they attempted to put a stamp on the first quarter.

However, in facing a third down and a heavy pass rush, Bradshaw was stripped of the football from behind by Martin. The fumble bounced up the field to the forty-one-yard line, where "Too Tall" Jones recovered for the Cowboys.

After Newhouse got a couple of yards on a first-down run, Staubach went for broke, going deep downfield to Drew Pearson in the end zone. Safety Shell recovered quickly, though, and broke up the play for an incompletion.

On the next play, Staubach attempted to strike again, and this time, he was successful. With plenty of time to throw after his line had picked up a Steelers' blitz, he connected with receiver Hill, who had beaten Shell on a down-and-out pattern toward the left sideline. Turning upfield at the sideline, Hill then breezed by Blount who had his back turned while covering his receiver, Drew Pearson, man-to-man downfield.

The Cowboys had struck back on the final play of the first quarter. With the score tied 7–7, the two teams traded sides of the field to begin the second quarter.

As we've covered, the Steelers enjoyed a long period of sustained success on the playing field because, in large part, they chose wisely in the annual draft. That hadn't always been the case, as the team had a history of trading draft picks for veteran players. However, the abrupt change in direction had been developed from a very conscious decision.

By Super Bowl XIII, Dan Rooney, the oldest son of the Chief, was the chief executive of the ball club. He and his brother, Art Rooney Jr., the head of the Steelers personnel department, had a long-held belief in building the team through the draft. In fact, the roster had just three players on it—Gerela, reserve tight end Jim Mandich, and reserve defensive back Ray Oldham—who had started their careers with other teams.

The Steelers, from the front office to the field, were really one big family.

It wasn't just the draft that built the roster, either. It was also finding the proper gems who slipped through the draft entirely.

One such player was Banaszak, who recovered Drew Pearson's first-quarter fumble in Super Bowl XIII. Banaszak was a tough gamer but unheralded throughout his football career—he went unrecruited out of high school and undrafted out of college.

The Steelers, though, saw promise in the defensive lineman and signed him to the roster as an undrafted free agent in 1975. By 1978, he had ascended into the starting lineup, where he shared time with White. In the process, he became an instant fan favorite, with a banner reading "The Banaszak Bunch," complete with signatures of some 70,000 fangs, hung in Three Rivers Stadium.

Between high school and college, Banaszak served in the United States Marine Corps on active duty from 1969–1971. And on the football field, both in practice and in games, he was a blue-collar, lunch-pail-toting type of player, putting in honest, hard work on a daily basis. It was an ethos that matched perfectly with that of the Pittsburgh community, who embraced him as one of their own.

Interestingly, Banaszak was from another hardscrabble town, Cleveland, where he grew up in a house of fervent Browns fans. It's been reported that when Banaszak phoned home to tell him the Steelers had signed him, his father, disgusted he was speaking to a Steeler, hung up on him. In short time, however, the elder Banaszak acquiesced and became part of Steeler Nation as a devoted member of the Banaszak Bunch.

The rousing start of Super Bowl XIII didn't let up in the second quarter.

The Steelers started their next possession on their own twenty-seven-yard line, whereupon Bradshaw quickly found Grossman in the left flat for a ten-yard gain and a first down.

Harris then carried the ball three times in succession, probing the left side of the offensive line, pushing the ball forward to the forty-eight-yard line and another first down.

With good field position, Bradshaw wanted to test the Dallas pass defense. On first down, he threw an incompletion in the middle of the field, setting up a long second down. On second down, Bradshaw rolled to his right and nearly threw an interception, but Cowboys safety Waters just wasn't able to get a handle on his pass.

Then, on third-and-ten, Hollywood Henderson backed up his pre-game talk a bit. After taking the snap, Bradshaw collided with Harris in the backfield, knocking the ball from his grasp. Bradshaw, however, scooped the ball up while on the run and continued to roll to his right, looking to unload a pass downfield. That's when Henderson wrapped him up for what looked to be a simple sack.

Henderson stood up Bradshaw but, before he spun him to the ground, his fellow Cowboys linebacker, Mike Hegman, came upon the scene and ripped the ball out of Bradshaw's grasp. From there, it was a simple thirty-seven-yard rumble into the end zone for a touchdown.

The Steelers had just committed their third straight offensive turnover, and the Cowboys had taken advantage once again by scoring their second touchdown. With the successful point after touchdown, the Cowboys now led 14–7, with 12:08 left in the half.

Not only had the Steelers fallen behind, but Bradshaw looked to be in some distress on the sideline, nursing his left shoulder that had been driven into the ground by Henderson.

Bradshaw, however, didn't miss a play. And on the Steelers' next possession, he struck quickly. After Harris ran twice for five yards, Bradshaw again called a passing play.

Bradshaw took a deep, ten-yard drop and found Stallworth open on the right side. Stallworth brought in the reception and immediately slipped a tackle from Cowboys defensive back, Aaron Kyle. Stallworth then headed upfield, but not at full speed, waiting for both Swann and Grossman to run interference with blocks. As his teammates crossed his path, Stallworth planted off his right foot and slanted toward the middle of the field, unleashing all of his speed.

By the Cowboys' forty-yard line, Stallworth was free and clear, with nothing but green grass in front of him until he reached the gold- and black-painted end zone. The seventy-five-yard touchdown pass was a speedy response to the Cowboys' unexpected defensive score, and after Gerela's extra point, the score in Super Bowl XIII was tied, 14–14.

Energized by the quick score to tie the game, the Steel Curtain then picked an apt time to flex its muscles. On first down, Banaszak stuffed Newhouse for a four-yard loss. On second down, Ham lassoed Dorsett, who had started the game gashing the Steelers for big gains, for a three-yard loss on an attempted sweep around the right end.

On third and long, Staubach dropped back to pass and faced a Steelers rush from all angles. Greene knocked the ball free with his left hand on the sack, and the bouncing ball was nearly recovered by Furness. The Cowboys eventually recovered the loose football at their own thirteen-yard line but were forced to punt.

Bell fielded another short punt, and the Steelers' offense was again set up in great field position at the Cowboys' forty-eight-yard line.

With the momentum clearly behind the Steelers, Bradshaw looked to pounce quickly. On first down, he connected with Swann on a catch-and-run that gained twenty-six yards to the Cowboy's twenty-two-yard line.

"Too Tall" Jones helped temporarily stem the tide when he bottled up Harris for a big eight-yard loss on first down. But Henderson gave it right back on the next play, getting flagged for defensive holding, with the penalty giving the Steelers a first down at the twenty-five-yard line.

After an incompletion and a two-yard gain by Harris, Bradshaw again faced a long third down. On this occasion, Hegman got to Bradshaw for a sack and a big eleven-yard loss that dropped the Steelers all the way back to the thirty-four-yard line.

That loss of yardage proved to be painfully critical, as Gerela's subsequent fifty-one-yard field goal hit the left upright and bounced away, no good, keeping the score tied at fourteen.

The Cowboys took over on their own thirty-four-yard line and Staubach immediately got them driving. Dorsett got it started with a nifty five-yard run off the left tackle. Then, after Newhouse was stuffed on a rush at the line of scrimmage, Staubach, working out of the shotgun formation the Cowboys favored on passing downs, connected with Preston Pearson on an out pattern to the right side. Pearson's seven-yard gain gave the Cowboys an important first down.

On first down, Staubach executed a play-action fake, fooling the Steelers' coverage into thinking it was a running play, and found Hill open for an eleven-yard catch and another first down on the Steelers' side of midfield at the forty-four-yard line. That play brought the half to the two-minute warning.

On the first play after the break, Staubach evaded a Steelers' blitz and just barely got the ball out to Dorsett in the flat, who turned it into another first down at the Steelers' thirty-two-yard line.

After the play, Dorsett and Johnson got into a scuffle, with Dorsett pushing the ball into Johnson's face mask. Both players were assessed unsportsmanlike penalties, offsetting one another and leaving the ball exactly where it was spotted. But the altercation seemed to fire up the Steelers' defense.

On the next play, Staubach took a deep drop and fired a pass down the center of the field for Drew Pearson, in the middle of a pack of Steelers' defenders. Blount stepped in front of the throw, intercepting the pass, and returned the ball to the twenty-nine-yard line, where he was positively leveled by DuPree on the tackle. DuPree was flagged for unnecessary roughness, allowing Bradshaw and the offense to take possession at the forty-four-yard line, with 1:41 left on the clock to get another score on the board before the intermission.

Following a ten-yard penalty on guard Mullins, Bradshaw quickly got the yardage back and then some by connecting twice with Swann. First, on a wide receiver screen on the right side, Swann caught a short pass and then dodged, weaved, and broke tackles on a magnificent run to complete a twenty-nine-yard pass play. On the very next play, Bradshaw again spotted Swann downfield, and his trusty receiver gathered in the pass on a leaping reception for another twenty-one yards gained.

Forgoing a timeout, the Steelers ran up to the line of scrimmage to get a play off quickly, hoping to catch the Cowboys off-guard. Bradshaw did find an open Harris on the right side, but the ball slipped through the back's hands for an incompletion that stopped the clock.

On the next play, Harris made up for his rare gaffe by rushing the ball down to the seven-yard line. On the play, Harris became the all-time leading rusher in Super Bowl history. He would add to that total, of course, and it's a record he holds today.

After a Steelers' timeout, on a third-and-one play, Bradshaw took the snap and rolled to his right. Just before he got to the sideline boundary, he threw the ball while still on the run, targeting the pass to Bleier, who was between two Cowboys' defenders in the end zone. Bleier jumped up in front of linebacker Lewis to grab the football, falling onto his back in the end zone for the go-ahead touchdown.

Sports Illustrated subscribers would open their mailboxes the next week to find a photo of Bleier's catch immortalized on the cover. The seven-yard touchdown catch spotted the Steelers to a 21–14 lead at the half.

The first half of Super Bowl XIII was played at a frenetic pace, with the action moving up and down the field and big plays causing frequent swings in momentum. Coming out of the locker rooms at the end of the halftime intermission, it appeared both teams looked to slow the pace by playing good defense and getting the game to the final quarter, where they could settle the championship debate once and for all.

Rookie reserve defensive back Larry Anderson gave the Steelers good field position to open the second half by returning the kickoff to the thirty-nine-yard line. But, from there, the Cowboys bottled up Harris on his first-down run, creating a four-yard loss. After a Bradshaw incompletion, a third-down reception by Bell wasn't close to a first down. With a three-and-out series to start the half, the Steelers were forced to punt the ball away.

Staubach led the Cowboys' first possession of the second half from their own fifteen-yard line. They got one first down courtesy of a holding penalty against Shell. Then, after being penalized themselves for delay of game, Staubach got another first down on a ten-yard scamper.

After a one-yard run by Dorsett and another Staubach scramble for seven yards, reserve back Scott Laidlaw was met at the line of scrimmage by linebackers

Cole and Lambert on his third-down run. Their short drive brought to an end, the Cowboys punted.

On the Steelers' second possession, they moved backward. First, Harris lost three yards. After Bleier got two of those yards back on a second-down run, the Steelers were then penalized five yards for illegal procedure. On a third and long, Bradshaw threw incomplete, intended for Swann.

Following the second three-and-out possession to start the half, Colquitt punted into the wind. The Cowboys' Johnson fielded the short punt and managed a nice return, pushing the ball to the Steelers' forty-two-yard line and setting up Staubach with great field position.

On the first play, the Cowboys tried to trick the Steelers once again. Dorsett took the handoff, and as he got to the line of scrimmage, he turned and lateralled the ball back to Staubach, who fired a deep pass downfield to a well-covered Hill. The flea-flicker pass hadn't fooled the Steelers.

Not to be deterred, Dorsett gained four yards around the right end to set up a third down and six. Out of the shotgun formation, Staubach then hit Preston Pearson with a clutch throw, moving the ball down to the Steelers' twenty-nine-yard line.

Three running plays—two Dorsett rushes around a Laidlaw run—gained the Cowboys another first down at the eighteen-yard line and sustained the drive.

Staubach threw incomplete on first down. Then, on second down, the Cowboys ran a perfect play to counter the Steelers' blitz, and Dorsett popped a draw run for an eight-yard gain. If it weren't for Shell's saving tackle, Dorsett would have surely scored.

That set up a third-and-two from the Steelers' ten-yard line. The Cowboys lined up in a heavy formation, with thirty-eight-year-old veteran Jackie Smith joining DuPree in a two-tight-end alignment.

Taking the snap, Staubach faked a handoff up the middle, and as he turned around on his drop, he found Smith all alone in the end zone. Not wanting to overthrow his wide-open receiver, Staubach took a little off his throw, forcing Smith to go low and slide for the catch. Somehow, on the biggest stage and under the brightest lights of his distinguished sixteen-year career, the ball bounced right out of Smith's hands for an incompletion.

Smith had spent the previous fifteen years with the St. Louis Cardinals, and this was his first opportunity to play for a team with legitimate Super Bowl aspirations. Smith, who had 480 receptions over his career, is in the Pro Football Hall of Fame. But his dropped pass in Super Bowl XIII is unfortunately what most football fans might remember of his long, productive, and well-decorated career.

From the outset until the very end, the play had the look of a sure touchdown to tie the game, yet the Steelers had made a grand escape. Rafael Septien converted a short twenty-seven-yard field goal attempt to close Dallas' deficit to four, but the Cowboys weren't in a celebratory mood. They knew they had let a golden opportunity fall, literally, through their fingertips.

On their third possession of the third quarter, the Steelers finally earned their first first down, when Bradshaw, on a third-and-six and scrambling under pressure to his right, connected with Bell over the middle for a gain of twelve yards.

The next set of downs went by quickly. Bradshaw threw two incompletions, and on third down, White sacked Bradshaw for a loss of three yards, the fourth sack of Bradshaw in the game. Colquitt, kicking into the wind for the final time as the quarter ticked down, uncorked a big punt, a fifty-two-yarder. But, the Cowboys' Johnson reeled off a twenty-one-yard return to give the Cowboys the ball at their twenty-eight-yard line.

Dorsett gained two yards on a first-down run to the thirty-yard line, and that's where the third quarter ended.

The fourth quarter began with a Staubach incompletion on a pass intended for Drew Pearson. Pearson was still catchless on the day, shadowed flawlessly by rookie defender Johnson, who was the only rookie in the starting lineup for either team.

On the next play, however, Dorsett cradled a third-down screen pass and slipped upfield for a thirteen-yard gain to the Cowboy's forty-three-yard line, earning a new set of downs. That set of downs proved to be ineffective.

On first down, Dorsett got wrapped up by Lambert for no gain. Then, Laidlaw, on a delayed draw, gained five yards on second down before he was brought down by Ham. Then, on third-and-five, Green batted down a Staubach pass for an incompletion and a forced fourth down.

White's second punt—his first was nullified by a penalty—into the steady breeze was a good one, pinning the Steelers on their fourteen-yard line where they'd try to reignite their offense that had failed to sustain drives on any of their three second-half possessions thus far.

After a Harris two-yard run and an incompletion thrown by Bradshaw, the Steelers faced a long third down attempt deep in their own end of the field. On that third-down play, Bradshaw found Grossman, who craftily ran his pattern to be just past the yardage marker needed for a first down. Despite being covered well by the Cowboys' Harris, Grossman pulled down the catch and moved the sticks.

It was an important first down for the Steelers, as it allowed them the opportunity to control more of the game, something that had been slipping away toward the Cowboys for most of the second half.

On first down from the twenty-six-yard line, Bradshaw connected with Swann, who went down to his knees to catch the low throw—a thirteen-yard completion and another first down.

Harris then took a pitch to the left side and rushed for five yards, moving the ball to the Steelers' forty-four-yard line. Then, Super Bowl XIII got a bit controversial.

On second down, Bradshaw took the snap, dropped back, and threw early to avoid the Cowboys' blitz, lobbing a high pass downfield in the direction of Swann. By the time the ball arrived downfield, however, both Swann and defender Benny Barnes were lying on the Orange Bowl turf at the Cowboys' twenty-two-yard line.

The officials immediately threw a flag and signaled pass interference on Barnes. Barnes and the Cowboys were irate. Television replays showed the contact between Swann and Barnes could have been called incidental, resulting in no penalty. But it was a close play, and it could have also been correctly called a penalty during live action.

It was a fifty-fifty call. In this case, it was a penalty on the Cowboys, and it resulted in a first down at the Cowboys' own twenty-three-yard line.

Incidentally, the game official who threw the flag for the penalty on Barnes was none other than Fred Swearingen. Does that name ring a bell? It should, as Swearingen was the referee at the center of the controversy in 1972's Immaculate Reception game.

After a short completion to Swann and a short run by Harris, the Steelers faced another third down play, this time from the Cowboys' seventeen-yard line. On the snap, Bradshaw dropped back to pass and was immediately swallowed up by Henderson, who eventually spun him to the ground all the way back to the thirty-yard line.

However, during the play, players and fans alike could clearly hear the shrill of the referees' whistles. The referees had blown the play dead and flagged the Steelers for delay of game. The penalty against the Steelers was actually a saving grace. It pushed the ball back five yards, but it nullified what would have been a big sack and an even bigger loss of yardage. Plus, it gave the Steelers another chance to run a play.

As the referees marked off the penalized yardage, Harris and Henderson were involved in an animated discussion. Harris was uncharacteristically upset and went back to the Steelers' huddle and asked for the ball on the next play. It turned out Harris would ultimately get in the last word.

On the next play, a third-and-nine with 7:17 left on the game clock, Bradshaw took the snap and, forgoing what most thought would be a pass, instead handed the ball to Harris. Harris flashed his speed, bursting through a hole in the line and heading straight upfield. A couple of Cowboys just barely got hands on him around his ankles, but Harris easily broke through to the end zone and a twenty-two-yard touchdown run.

One player who had a great opportunity of stopping Harris downfield had been Waters, but his path to Harris was blocked by an official. You can probably guess who that official was. Of course, it was Swearingen. It proved to be yet another point of contention raised by Cowboys' players and fans after the game.

Regardless, with Gerela's extra point, the Steelers led 28–17 and were closing their grip around another Lombardi trophy.

On the ensuing kickoff, Gerela's plant leg slipped, and he unintentionally got off a short, squib-type kick for the second time in his Super Bowl history. The ball bounced downfield into the hands of defensive tackle White, who was playing the game with a cast protecting his broken thumb.

White mishandled the ball, and when Dungy hit him, the ball popped loose. It appeared the Steelers recovered, but a big scrum broke out, with a pile of players from both teams fighting for the ball. After a long minute or two, the referees signaled Pittsburgh's ball, and the player who came up with the ball at the bottom of the pile was second-year linebacker Dirt Winston.

With the ball on the Cowboys' eighteen-yard line, Bradshaw looked to strike immediately and seal the Cowboys' fate. Bradshaw threw a perfect pass over the Cowboys' Harris that Swann jumped to catch before sliding down through the end zone for the touchdown.

After the catch, Swann ran over and jumped into the arms of tackle Ray Pinney, who held him up in the air, the index finger on Swann's right hand extended, telling the world the Steelers were number one. Gerela's extra point after the Steelers' second touchdown in just seventeen seconds of game action extended the Steelers' lead to 35–17.

A clipping penalty on the Cowboys during the kickoff return left the ball on their eleven-yard line. Everything, it seemed, was going against the Cowboys, and Steelers fans were beginning to celebrate. Maybe some of the Steelers' players on the sideline were celebrating too.

With there being no question of surrender, the Cowboys buckled up and got to work. Dorsett got them started with a seven-yard reception. Then, Banaszak threw a wrench into the plans, planting Staubach with a sack.

Facing a third-and-eleven, Staubach converted with an eighteen-yard scramble to gain a new set of downs at the twenty-eight-yard line. On the next play, he finally connected with Drew Pearson, gaining seventeen yards on the receiver's first catch of the game, and moving the ball to the forty-five-yard line.

Dorsett then broke off a twenty-nine-yard run on a draw play to get the ball deep into Steelers' territory. The Cowboys were gaining big chunks of yardage, but, at the same time, they were also burning precious seconds off the dwindling play clock.

Under a heavy rush on the next play, Staubach got the ball away at the last moment, passing to his tight end DuPree along the left sideline and stopping the clock. From the sixteen-yard line, Staubach then found Drew Pearson again, and that completion moved the ball to the seven-yard line.

On the eighth play of the drive, Staubach threw a short completion in the right flat to Dupree, and the big tight end beat both Johnson and Wagner to the goal line for a touchdown. With the extra point, the Cowboys had narrowed the score to 35–24 with 2:27 remaining in the game.

The Steelers' celebrations—from fans and players alike—were still going on, but they were a bit more muted.

With everyone expecting an onside kick, Septien and the Cowboys executed one perfectly, with rookie defensive back Dennis Thurman recovering the kick on the Cowboys' side of midfield, at the forty-eight-yard line.

After an incompletion, Staubach connected with Drew Pearson on a twenty-two-yard gain on a play that ended at the two-minute warning.

Coming back from the break in play, Furness got the Steelers' fifth sack of the day on Staubach, pushing the Cowboys' offense back to the forty-yard line. Dorsett then caught a short pass to the right, but Ham, the only defender between Dorsett and a big gain, expertly gathered him up and dropped him for just a two-yard gain, setting up a third-and-eighteen for the Cowboys.

Staubach then went for the end zone but overthrew Hill, his intended target. It set up fourth-and-eighteen, and the Cowboys needed a huge play to keep their championship dreams alive.

Staubach and Drew Pearson came up with that big play. Taking a deep drop on the snap, Staubach fired long, deep down the center of the field to his receiver, who leaped right in front of Wagner for the catch, Pearson's fourth of the quarter. Wagner stopped him at the thirteen-yard line.

Dorsett took a short catch on the next play down to the four-yard line. Then, after an incompletion, Staubach found Johnson all alone in the back of the end zone for another touchdown. Septien's extra point closed the score to 35–31, with the four-point spread representing the difference in points when the Cowboys had to settle for a field goal rather than a Smith touchdown reception.

The Cowboys had one last-gasp effort left in them, and that was a second onside kick attempt. This time, Septien knuckled a kick straight ahead, and Bleier scooped it up securely for the Steelers.

All that was left was for the Steelers to run out the final twenty seconds on the game clock. Bradshaw dutifully performed that task with two kneel downs.

The Steelers had won Super Bowl XIII with a 35–31 victory over the Dallas Cowboys. In doing so, they became the first franchise to win three Super Bowls.

Most observers thought Super Bowl XIII was the best Super Bowl played up to that point. In winning, the Steelers' thirty-five points were the most points scored in a Super Bowl.

In his nine-year career, Terry Bradshaw had never thrown for either 300 yards or four touchdowns in a game. He accomplished both of those feats in Super Bowl XIII. For his performance, Bradshaw was named the game's Most Valuable Player.

Bradshaw also got the last word in on Hollywood Henderson when he remarked, "Can he spell M-V-P?"

Chapter 23

STEEL CITY GIVES WAY TO THE CITY OF CHAMPIONS

I t's not entirely fair to trace the domestic steel industry by examining just one company, U.S. Steel, but that's what you get when you name your company U.S. Steel and your headquarters dwarfs all other buildings in downtown Pittsburgh.

The U.S. Steel Tower, also known as the Steel Building, took over four years to construct and was officially completed on September 30, 1971, at a cost of over $50 million. Standing 841 feet tall, the sixty-four-story building cast a towering shadow over the rest of the Pittsburgh skyline, whose previous tallest building had been the forty-four-story Gulf Building.

In the initial planning stages, it was rumored that company executives had the hubris to consider building what would have been at the time the world's tallest building. Common sense apparently snapped them out of those grandiose plans, and they settled on a design that would mark the tallest building on the continent outside of New York and Chicago.

That, of course, has changed over the past fifty years as newer, taller buildings have been erected. But as it is, the U.S. Steel Tower is still the tallest building in Pittsburgh and the fifth-tallest in Pennsylvania.

The tall building and the lofty corporate name became a proxy and somewhat symbolic barometer of sorts for the entire domestic steel industry. How U.S. Steel performed was generally reflective of how most traditional, legacy producers fared.

In 1975, U.S. Steel reported a net income of $559.6 million on sales of $8.17 billion. By 1979, profits had turned to losses—the company reported a net loss of $279 million on sales of $12.9 billion.

In 1978, sales hit $11 billion, but the net income was only $242 million. More importantly, the company's non-steel businesses, namely its transportation and utility subsidiaries, were responsible for 27 percent of total sales and a staggering 86 percent of the company's operating income. The year's results signaled danger on the short-term horizon. U.S. Steel wasn't making its money on steel.

In 1980, the business started shrinking. In that year, U.S. Steel shipped just 17.2 tons of steel, an 18 percent drop from a year previous, and the lowest total for the company since 1961. Sales fell to $12.5 billion, although net income returned at $504 million.

Early in the Reagan Administration, U.S. Steel and other steel concerns won substantial tax breaks as part of the federal government's plan to help them compete against lower-cost importers. Ostensibly, those savings in taxes were meant for the companies to invest in modernizing their mills and production processes.

U.S. Steel and other producers had different thoughts on the matter. Understanding, in general, the downward outlook for steel, they stayed away from further investments to shore up their steel production. Rather, they abruptly shifted capital away from their main lines of business to diversify into higher growth, more profitable industries.

In the case of U.S. Steel, it was evidenced by the January 1982 acquisition of Marathon Oil, where U.S. Steel collaborated with Marathon executives to fight off a hostile takeover bid from Mobil. Part of the offer for Marathon was a cash investment of $1.4 billion, a large part of which consisted of U.S. Steel's tax concession funds.

U.S. Steel was, in a manner of speaking, getting out of the steel business. Not completely, of course, but its investment strategy showed exactly where the company thought the future lay. That year, U.S. Steel reported a loss of $361 million, and it reported its lowest amount of steel shipments since 1938. Operating loss for the dead-on-arrival steel line of business was pegged at $852 million.

U.S. Steel was no longer, first and foremost, a steel company. In late 1986, the company recognized the fact it was a very different company than that of its roots, and it changed its name to USX Corporation, with principal operating units in energy, steel, and a diversified portfolio of businesses.

With steel companies seeing greener pastures elsewhere and pushing their investments in that direction, mills closed, and with them, their high-paying skilled manufacturing jobs. In the eight years between 1979 and 1987, it has been estimated that Pittsburgh and the surrounding area lost between 125,000 and 135,000 manufacturing jobs.

The steel industry and its related businesses may have been suffering, but that wasn't the case in the rest of the country. The nation's gross domestic product (GDP) continued to rise. On top of that, the Reagan Administration's policy of deficit spending fueled an employment boom in many sectors of the economy and a great number of geographies. Between 1982 and 1987, over thirteen million jobs were created in the United States.

But there weren't enough new jobs created in western Pennsylvania to offset the damaging impact of the steel industry's decline. It's been estimated that a full 10 percent of the jobs in Pittsburgh in 1980 had been in the steel industry.

With jobs hard to come by, many Pittsburghers faced no other choice than to relocate. In 1950, Pittsburgh reached its peak population of 676,806, making it the twelfth-largest city in the United States. By 1980, the population had shrunk to 423,938, the thirtieth-largest city in terms of population. By 1990, the population stood at just 370,139, making Pittsburgh the forty-second-largest city in the country.

Large numbers of Pittsburgh's unemployed left, with a great many relocating to the booming "Sun Belt" in the southern United States. Pittsburgh, on the other hand, had joined hand-in-hand with its steel-producing brethren Gary and East Chicago, Indiana, and Cleveland and Toledo, Ohio, to form the nation's "Rust Belt."

Through the decline of the steel industry, the mill closures, the layoffs, and the mass exodus, a great many more Pittsburghers stayed than left. They were determined to stay at home and stick it out.

But, those yinzers needed hope. More than ever, they needed heroes. In 1979, their professional sports teams obliged.

The Steelers entered the offseason leading up to the 1979 regular season in a familiar spot as Super Bowl champions. With their previous experience, they understood the task at hand in trying to repeat as champions, from the players in the locker room to the executives in the front office.

In the disappointment of the 1977 season, there was widespread belief around the league that perhaps the Steelers' roster was getting a little long in the tooth, with age and injury beginning to catch up to so many great players. The Steelers, of course, did have a veteran roster, but Dan Rooney and his staff, with Noll as the ultimate decision-maker, had carefully infused new talent into the team with players like Shell, Cunningham, Bell, Johnson, and others.

In the 1979 NFL Draft, the Steelers looked to add new young players to their roster, and they drafted a sound class that included, surprisingly to some, two running backs, Greg Hawthorne and Russell Davis, with the club's first and third picks. On one hand, the draft picks weren't surprising, as the running back position is a notoriously tough position, and players' productivity tends to drop once they hit thirty years of age, if they're fortunate to even hit that mark as a player in the first place. Harris and Bleier, the Steelers' trusty tandem at running back, would be entering the season ages twenty-nine and thirty-three, respectively.

In addition to the two running backs, the Steelers added linebacker Zack Valentine, receiver Calvin Sweeney, and Matt Bahr, a placekicker from Penn State who was earmarked to take over for Gerela.

The roster heading into the season would consist of players who had been developed by the Steelers, either drafted by the club or signed as undrafted free agents. A full forty players on the roster were draft choices, speaking to the Steelers' ability to get valuable contributors in later rounds of the draft.

Also entering the season, the Steelers had a bit of a new personality as a team. Throughout the decade, they were known as a defensive ballclub, and rightly so with the historically good defenses they had presented. They were also known to feature a grinding running attack, rushing the ball relentlessly with a strong backfield duo and offensive line.

Now, they were also known as an explosive passing team. The new NFL rules instituted in the 1978 season had sparked offenses throughout the league. But perhaps no one took better advantage than Bradshaw, who had delivered the best season by far in his now well-tenured career. With MVP honors in both the regular season and the Super Bowl, and with a receiving corps featuring Swann, Stallworth, Bell, Cunningham, Grossman, and now Sweeney, the Steelers were threats to score from almost anywhere on the field.

The Steelers opened their 1979 campaign on September 3, visiting the Patriots in the first *Monday Night Football* telecast of the season. And while they gave the national television audience an exciting game, it was perhaps a bit too close, too exciting, for the Steelers and their fans.

The Patriots drew first blood on a four-yard touchdown reception from quarterback Steve Grogan to his tight end, Russ Francis, in the first quarter. In the second quarter, the Steelers countered the Patriots with a two-yard scoring run by running back Thornton, who started in place of an injured Bleier. Importantly though, Bahr's extra point attempt was no good.

Bahr had been drafted in large part due to the highly erratic seasons Gerela produced in both 1976 and 1978. Needless to say, it was an inauspicious debut by the young rookie.

From there, the remainder of the second quarter was all Patriots, with the scores coming from two short field goals by John Smith, the first from thirty-one yards, the second from thirty-two yards. The Patriots led at the half, 13–6.

After a scoreless third period, the Steelers finally got the tying touchdown, again courtesy of Thornton, who hauled in a twenty-one-yard scoring pass from Bradshaw. Bahr's point after tied the game at thirteen.

Unable to settle the game in regulation time, the two teams went to overtime. In the extra stanza, Bahr delivered with a game-winning forty-one-yard field goal, allowing the Steelers to escape with a 16–13 victory. Bahr had gone from goat to hero in one game's time—it turned out to be a well-enough debut after all.

With the opening week under their belts, the Steelers then welcomed the Oilers to Three Rivers Stadium, and they gave the visitors from Texas a belting at that.

The Steelers picked up where they left off in last winter's playoff game, forcing turnovers and pouncing on the Oilers from the start. Thornton scored two more touchdowns, again both on the ground and through the air, and the Steelers stormed out to a 38–0 lead in the fourth quarter. A late Guido Merkens touchdown reception from reserve quarterback Gifford Neilson was the only blemish on the Steelers' eventual 38–7 victory.

In the game, the defense bottled up Campbell, limiting him to just thirty-six yards rushing on sixteen attempts. In total, the Oilers mustered only 124 yards of offense and turned the ball over six times.

Any win over a divisional opponent is a big win, and the win against the Oilers, a legitimate playoff contender, put the Steelers a game up in the standings over them, tied with the Browns atop the division with a 2–0 record.

The Steelers won the next two games, on the road in St. Louis and at home against Baltimore, but they weren't easy—and may have hidden some negative trends.

Against the Cardinals, the Steelers fell behind early and trailed 21–7 in the fourth quarter. A twenty-yard Bahr field completed a seventeen-point fourth-quarter rally to win, 24–21. In the victory, the Steelers had overcome seven total fumbles, two of which they lost. Combined with two Bradshaw interceptions, the Steelers won a tight ball game despite losing the turnover battle with the Cardinals 4–1.

In Week Four, the Steelers had to mount a comeback on three different occasions in the game. A fourth-quarter touchdown pass from Bradshaw to Cunningham paved the way for a 17–13 victory. Again though, the Steelers had won a tight game despite losing the turnover battle, 4–2.

Pittsburgh's sloppy play caught up with them the next week, Week Five, on the road against intrastate rival Eagles. Once again, the Steelers turned the ball over four times, to only two for the Eagles, and it was too much to overcome as the Eagles held on for a 17–14 win.

The loss dropped the Steelers into a logjam for first place in the division, alongside both the Browns and Oilers. A showdown for at least a portion of the division lead was the backdrop for the next week's game at Cleveland.

Led by Bradshaw and Harris, the Steelers snapped out of their turnover funk. Bradshaw threw two first-quarter touchdown passes, one to Cunningham and the other to newfound touchdown-scoring machine Thornton, to spot the Black and Gold a fourteen-point lead. Harris added another touchdown to extend the lead to 21–0, still in the first quarter.

Another Bradshaw touchdown pass, this one a fourteen-yard reception by receiver Jim Smith, extended the Steelers' lead to twenty-seven points in the second quarter.

Down so much, so quickly, Browns quarterback Brian Sipe was forced to throw, and throw he did. Sipe ended up throwing for five touchdowns on the day, but he could never claw the Browns' deficit any closer than thirteen points.

In the fourth quarter, on a third-and-one rushing play up the middle, Bleier broke through the line of scrimmage and saw nothing in front of him but the well-worn grass of Municipal Stadium. That and the dirt baseball diamond that took up one end of the multi-use field. Bleier went all the way for a touchdown, seventy yards, for the longest run of his career.

Thornton's one-yard touchdown run in the fourth completed the scoring in the Steelers' 51–35 victory. Importantly, the Steelers had turned the ball over just once, while forcing the Browns into five turnovers of their own. Six games into the season, the Steelers stood atop the Central Division with a 6–1 record, and with their propensity for turnovers seemingly behind them, they looked ready to go on a tear.

The winless Bengals hosted the Steelers, and abruptly put any thoughts of going on a tear to a halt. Also, any thoughts of stopping the torrid flow of turnovers were squelched too.

The Steelers opened the scoring with a Bahr field goal from forty-six yards away. The Bengals responded in the first quarter with a seven-yard touchdown pass from Anderson to Dan Ross. And from that point on, the Steelers handed the game to the Bengals, quite literally.

On the afternoon, the Steelers turned the ball over a staggering nine times, seven by fumble. In the second quarter, the Bengals scored three touchdowns off three Steeler fumbles in just two minutes.

First, after a Stallworth fumble, running back Pete Johnson scored from a yard out. Then, Anderson fumbled the resulting kickoff, which Howie Kurnick dutifully scooped up and returned twelve yards for the second touchdown. On the next possession, Harris fumbled, and that turnover was picked up by linebacker Jim LeClair and returned for the third touchdown.

The Bengals would eventually go up 34–3 before surrendering a fourth-quarter touchdown from Bradshaw to Stallworth on the way to a 34–10 victory. Humbled, the Steelers were sent home licking their wounds with a long week ahead before hosting a good Denver Broncos squad.

On Monday night, October 22, the Broncos came into Three Rivers with the same 5–2 record as the Steelers, and they were looking to test themselves as AFC contenders against the defending champs. It was a test they wouldn't come close to passing, at least not on that night.

Swann, having missed the previous two games nursing a sore hamstring, opened the scoring in the first quarter with an eleven-yard touchdown reception from Bradshaw. The Broncos, with their first series, responded with a touchdown of their own when receiver Haven Moses hauled in a Morton pass at the thirty-five-yard line, bounced off a collision, and ran into the end zone to complete a sixty-four-yard play.

From there, it was all Steelers. Harris scored twice, and Thornton scored twice more. Finally, rookie running back Anthony Anderson salted it away with a ten-yard touchdown run, his first touchdown as a professional.

After suffering through their worst loss since a 29–3 drubbing by the Oilers in 1971, the Steelers had turned around and trounced the Broncos, 42–7, the worst loss for the Broncos in eleven years.

At the halfway point of the season, the Steelers' record stood at 6–2, good enough for first place in the AFC Central Division.

The Steelers weren't the only ones making news in Pittsburgh in October of 1979. Not by a long shot.

In fact, the Steelers weren't the only championship team playing in Three Rivers Stadium. They were joined there by their baseball brethren, the Pittsburgh Pirates.

Led by first baseman Willie "Pops" Stargell, right fielder Dave Parker, third baseman Phil Garner, center fielder Omar Moreno, and pitchers Jim Bibby, John Candelaria, Bert Blyleven, and Kent Tekulve—among others—the Pirates had stormed through the regular season with a 98–64 record, edging out the Montreal Expos by just two games to win the National League East.

After sweeping the Cincinnati Reds in three games to win the NL pennant, they faced off against the Baltimore Orioles in the World Series, the first time the Pirates had appeared in the "Fall Classic" since winning it in 1971.

In the first game of the series, played in Baltimore, the Orioles exploded for five first-inning runs and held on to win 5–4. The next day, however, the Pirates evened up the ledger by scoring in the ninth inning when catcher Ed Ott scored on pinch hitter Manny Sanguillén's two-out single to right field.

Gaining a valuable split of games on the road, the Pirates returned to Three Rivers Stadium to play in front of capacity crowds of over 50,000 people. Despite the local support, however, the Pirates dropped two consecutive games to fall into a three-games-to-one hole to the Orioles.

Game Five of the series was a must-win game for the Pirates, and veteran pitcher Jim Rooker, filling in the rotation due to injury, came up big, retiring the first ten batters he faced and limiting the Orioles to just one run over five innings. The Pirates' bats perked up late, powering across seven runs over the last three innings, and the Pirates staved off elimination with a 7–1 victory.

That game, Game Five of the 1979 World Series, was the final World Series game played in Three Rivers Stadium and, for that matter, remains the last World Series game played in Pittsburgh.

Still down three games to two, the Pirates traveled to Baltimore to play the deciding games.

Candelaria pitched a gem in Game Six, tossing six shutout innings. Tekulve mopped up with three shutout innings of his own for a save in the 4–0 Pirates victory that forced a deciding Game Seven.

In front of President Jimmy Carter—who threw the ceremonial first pitch—the Orioles kicked off the scoring in Game Seven when second baseman Rich Dauer hit a home run in the bottom of the third inning. From there, it was "Pops" and the Pirates.

Stargell ignited the comeback with a towering two-run home run in the sixth inning to give the Pirates the lead. Two insurance runs in the ninth inning pressed the Pirates' advantage to 4–1. Tekulve finished the game with his third save in the series, and the Pirates completed their comeback, winning the World Series title.

Enduring images remain from that Pirates season and their World Series triumph. The Pirates' boxy, striped stovepipe hats gave the team a distinctive look. And the close-knit team made an impression across the country, with its theme song, Sister Sledge's disco anthem, "We Are Family," providing the memorable soundtrack.

The Steelers began the second half of their 1979 schedule against the opponent with which they closed out the previous season. The Dallas Cowboys were coming to town in a rematch of Super Bowl XIII nine months earlier.

In the NFL Films' production of its highlights of the Cowboys' 1978 season, narrator John Facenda opened with the introduction, "They appear on television so often that their faces are as familiar to the public as presidents and movie stars. They are the Dallas Cowboys, 'America's Team.'" During the telecast of their season-opening game against the Cardinals, CBS announcer Pat Summerall repeated the description, and the nickname stuck. The Cowboys' were becoming "America's Team."

Steelers fans had a different description. They picked up on Banaszak's description of the "Dallas Cry Boys," a reference to remarks made by some after the Super Bowl placing blame for the loss on the what-ifs. You know, like what if Barnes wasn't called for interference? What if Waters hadn't been shielded by the referee? What if Smith hadn't dropped the apparent touchdown pass?

The Cowboys trotted onto the field at Three Rivers sporting a 7–1 record and looking for a modicum of revenge. A regular season victory wouldn't salve the wounds of a Super Bowl loss, but it would go a long way to progressing their season for another shot at the title.

Unlike the explosive Super Bowl game featuring wide-open offenses, the rematch was a defensive struggle all day long.

After a scoreless first quarter, Harris broke through on a one-yard touchdown run to provide the Steelers with a 7–0 lead. The Cowboys finally broke through with a Septien field goal from thirty-two yards out to narrow the score to 7–3 at halftime.

The Steel Curtain was dominant all day. The Cowboys sustained only three drives the entire afternoon. Aside from Septien's second-quarter field goal, there was another missed field goal and a fourth-down incompletion in the end zone that ended the third and final drive.

The Steelers put the game out of reach in the third quarter when Harris took advantage of a miscommunication along the Cowboys' defensive line and burst forty-eight yards for his second touchdown of the afternoon.

Staubach, constantly battered throughout the game, was replaced by Danny White in the second half. Even so, the Steelers limited the Cowboys to less than 300 total yards in the game and prevented them from scoring a touchdown for the first time in 106 games, dating back more than seven seasons. With a physically convincing 14–3 victory, the Steelers moved to 7–2 on the season.

The Steelers had their way the next two games, with big victories over the Redskins, 38–7, and the Chiefs, 30–3.

In the game against the Redskins, Bradshaw threw four touchdown passes, two to Stallworth, and threw for over 300 yards. However, in the victory, Thornton, who had emerged as both a running and receiving threat while spelling Bleier, suffered a significant ankle injury.

Against the Chiefs, the defense was outstanding, limiting Kansas City to 127 yards of total offense and just eight first downs while forcing three turnovers. Bradshaw threw another three touchdown passes to ease the Steelers to victory and push their record to 9–2.

The Steelers had reeled off four consecutive wins since their debacle in Cincinnati and took to the road to visit the 8–3 San Diego Chargers. There, in Week Twelve, the Steelers delivered another debacle.

The Chargers were an explosive team, named "Air Coryell" for the playcalling of their coach, Don Coryell, and quarterbacked by future Hall of Famer, Dan Fouts. The Steelers' defense, however, was up to the task and performed their role fairly well.

Throughout the afternoon, they kept Fouts primarily in check, limiting him to less than 50 percent passing and just 137 yards. He did throw two touchdowns, but the Steelers' defense also picked him off twice, with both Johnson and Lambert getting interceptions.

It was the Chargers' defense that had the unexpected leverage in the game. San Diego's defensive line dominated the trenches, limiting the Steelers to just sixty-six yards on twenty-nine carries. Forced to try to move the ball through the air, Bradshaw had a horrible game, throwing five interceptions, with linebacker Woodrow Lowe returning one seventy-seven yards for a third-quarter touchdown.

The Steelers fell behind early, and with eight total turnovers in the game—yes, eight—they were never able to get back in the game. The Chargers won easily, 35–7, and handed the Steelers their third road loss of the campaign.

Home cooking got the Steelers back in the win column in both of the next two weeks. In the first game, Week Thirteen against the Browns, it didn't come easy, though.

The Steelers fell behind 10–0 early against the Browns and had to claw their way back the entire ballgame. Every time the Steelers inched a little closer, the Browns came back to push the lead out further.

Finally, the Steelers scored the final ten points in the fourth quarter to tie the game and send it into overtime. In the extra period, Bahr connected on a thirty-seven-yard field goal to power the Black and Gold to a hard-earned 33–30 win.

In Week Fourteen, the Steelers had their way with an over-matched Bengals team, winning 37–17. Swann had a big game, posting a monstrous stat line of five catches good for 192 yards and two touchdowns, from fifty-eight and forty-two yards out. Harris and Bleier added touchdown runs, and Bahr knocked through another three field goals.

The victory over the Bengals set up a showdown with the Oilers the very next week, this time down South in the Houston Astrodome, in a game featured nationally on *Monday Night Football*.

The game was a typical hard-hitting intra-divisional tilt, and it was played in front of a loud and raucous Oilers crowd, lending even greater drama to the telecast.

In a scoreless first quarter, the Oilers' defense shut down the Steelers' attack on all fronts. The Steel Curtain, though, was doing much the same against Campbell, Pastorini, and the Oilers.

The Oilers finally broke the scoreless tie when Pastorini hit receiver Burrough with a twenty-five-yard touchdown pass in the second quarter. Then, in the third quarter, the two teams traded field goals.

Fritsch kicked another field goal in the fourth to give the Oilers a 13–3 lead. It was then the Steelers struck back with their best drive of the game. It ended with a touchdown by Swann on a nine-yard run on a wide receiver reverse, the ball going from Bradshaw to Bleier first, then Bleier to Swann, and his run to the end zone.

The Oilers answered promptly with a four-yard touchdown run by Rob Carpenter behind an excellent block by Campbell, making the score 20–10. The Steelers closed the gap to just three points when Stallworth hauled in a thirty-four-yard pass from Bradshaw for a touchdown.

With a little over a minute to play, the Steelers needed an onside kick to stay in the game. They looked to have secured one last chance to win the game when Anderson recovered the onside kick from Bahr.

The officials, however, ruled the ball did not travel the requisite ten yards to allow the kicking team to recover. Television replays seemed to show contradictory evidence that the ball had traveled over ten yards. But this was well before the NFL instituted replays to overturn or confirm on-field decisions.

As a result, the Steelers were penalized and forced to kick again. This time around, Oilers tight end Mike Barber made the recovery. With that, the Oilers ran out the clock on their 20–17 victory.

The Oilers' victory put them in a tie with the Steelers for the AFC Central Division crown heading into the final week of the season. If both teams won their final game, the Steelers would win on the fourth level of the tie-breaking criteria, net points in division games. However, that was predicated on both teams winning. If the Oilers could defeat the Eagles at home, then the Steelers would need to beat the Bills at Three Rivers Stadium to win the division.

The 7–8 Bills came into Three Rivers Stadium on December 16 to close out the regular season, and the Steelers did not greet them with holiday season hospitality. The defense set the tone early, and the Steelers steadily pulled away, despite turning the ball over four times.

The Steel Curtain took away the running game completely, surrendering just seventy-eight yards on twenty-four rushing attempts. In total, they allowed just eight first downs and 156 yards of total offense.

Offensively, the Steelers scored a touchdown in every quarter, starting with Swann's fifth of the season in the first quarter. Harris added two rushing touchdowns, his tenth and eleventh rushing touchdowns on the season. Plus, Thornton returned, scoring on a third-quarter run, his sixth rushing touchdown of the season, along with four additional scores through receptions.

The Steelers won handily, 28–0. And combined with the Oilers' surprising loss at home to the Eagles, there was no need for any tie-breaking calculations. The Steelers had won their sixth consecutive AFC Central Division title and headed into the playoffs looking to defend their Super Bowl title.

No self-respecting story about how the Steelers saved Pittsburgh would be complete without a mention of how a . . . fish . . . also saved Pittsburgh.

The Fish That Saved Pittsburgh is a sports fantasy/comedy motion picture released on November 6, 1979, by United Artists. Directed by Gilbert Moses, the film featured basketball legends Julius Erving—in a starring role—Kareem Abdul-Jabbar, and Meadowlark Lemon. From the entertainment world, it featured James Bond III, Stockard Channing, Jonathan Winters, and Debbie Allen among its cast.

Shot on location in Pittsburgh, the film revolves around the fictional Pittsburgh Pythons professional basketball team, whose long losing streak and lackluster roster make them the less-than-lovable losers of the city.

Desperate to turn around the fortunes of his favorite team, ball boy Tyrone Millman (Bond) turns to the only remedy he thinks is powerful enough—astrology. Psyched at the prospect, he goes to astrologer Mona Mondieu (a role initially cast with Cher but played by Channing when Cher dropped out at the eleventh hour) with his idea. Collaborating, they develop their conceptual framework to build out the team's roster with players of the same astrological sign as the team's star player, Moses Guthrie (Erving).

If you guessed the astrological sign was Pisces, you got it right!

The eclectic roster of Pisces-born players blossoms together, and with the help of Mondieu's readings, the newly renamed Pittsburgh Pisces turn things around and develop championship aspirations.

According to IMDb, the movie grossed $8,281,246 worldwide at the box office. However, over time, the movie had developed a sort of cult-like following, in large part to its groovy, disco-era-influenced wardrobes and soundtrack, which included two songs recorded by The Spinners specifically for the film.

The Fish That Saved Pittsburgh is available for streaming on a variety of digital platforms.

The Steelers finished the 1979 season with a 12–4 record, but all had not been well. True, they had the NFL's highest-scoring offense, and that unit had gained more yards than any other team. And true, their defense was still among the league's best, allowing the second-fewest yards on the season and finishing fifth in points allowed.

Despite that, the Steelers had been a mediocre team on the road, posting a 4–4 record as the visiting club. In addition, they had those two dreadful road games against the Bengals and the Chargers.

Troubling still, the Steelers' offense had turned the ball over fifty-two times. They rather equally distributed those turnovers, too, with twenty-six coming on Bradshaw interceptions.

For success in the postseason, it would be important to play at home and hang onto the football.

Benefiting from a bye in the first round, the Steelers ushered in the playoffs two weeks after the regular season finale, hosting the Miami Dolphins on December 30 at Three Rivers. The Dolphins had earned their way into the playoffs by posting a 10–6 record and winning the AFC East Division.

The Steelers jumped on the Dolphins early, scoring touchdowns on their first three possessions in the first quarter. First, Thornton continued his fantastic season with a one-yard plunge. The second touchdown came on a seventeen-yard pass from

Bradshaw to Stallworth. Finally Swann closed out the scoring in the quarter with a twenty-yard touchdown reception from Bradshaw.

Bradshaw's touchdown pass to Swann was his twenty-ninth touchdown pass in the postseason, and it established a new NFL record. Up 20–0 in the first quarter, in front of their boisterous home crowd, the Steelers coasted the remainder of the game.

The Dolphins were limited to just twenty-five yards on the ground, on twenty-two rushing attempts. The Pittsburgh attack was well-balanced, gaining 159 yards on the ground and 230 through the air. Despite three turnovers, the Steelers came away with a relatively easy 34–14 victory, advancing to their sixth AFC Championship Game in the last eight years. Their opponents would be their division rivals, the Houston Oilers, who with a backup quarterback had upset the Chargers the day before, 17–14.

The Steelers had, of course, split their season series with the Oilers, with each team winning at home. The Oilers were built in the image of their tough Texan head coach, Bum Phillips. On offense, they rode the strong legs of Earl Campbell, who had led the league in rushing with 1,697 yards, earning the Most Valuable Player and Offensive Player of the Year awards. The Oilers' defense was ranked seventh in the league, and they led the league in takeaways, a potentially dark omen for the Steelers and their penchant for playing loose with the football.

The good news for the Steelers was the game was at Three Rivers. The better news is that once again the Pittsburgh winter weather was not accommodating for a southern team that played in a domed stadium.

Game day was cold, windy, and icy. In addition to facing a tough, physical opponent, each team would also have to face the unyielding elements.

The Steelers began the game by receiving the opening kickoff, and they immediately started driving. Bradshaw used passes to Stallworth and rushes with Harris to move into Oilers territory. That's when disaster struck.

Defensive back Vernon Perry, who had four interceptions of Fouts the week before, stepped in front of a Bradshaw pass intended for Cunningham for an interception, and started running the other direction. Perry didn't stop until he crossed the goal line seventy-five yards later for a touchdown. Less than three minutes into the game, the Oilers held a 7–0 lead.

The Steelers punted after their next possession, and the Oilers took over. Pastorini was playing with broken ribs, an injury that had kept him out of the Chargers game the week before. He was wearing a flak jacket under his uniform, a protective form of padding that in future years would be worn by almost every quarterback in football, from high school to the professional ranks.

Campbell wasn't able to get much on two carries, and the Oilers' possession was ended when Greenwood sacked Pastorini on third down.

With the ball a third time, the Steelers finally put their mark on the scoreboard. The key play of the drive was a twenty-five-yard scramble by Bradshaw on a third-and-fourteen play. The resulting play kept alive the drive, which ended with a Bahr twenty-one-yard field goal.

The Oilers then took off on their own march down the field, aided by a Pastorini screen pass to fullback Tim Wilson that went for forty-one yards. Early in the second quarter, Fritsch kicked a short field goal to extend the Oilers' lead, 10–3.

Bradshaw responded with the Steelers' first possession of the second quarter and spirited the team down the field, opening up the Oilers' defense with receptions to Bleier, Harris, and Swann. Bradshaw's sixteen-yard touchdown pass to Cunningham allowed the Steelers to draw level at 10–10.

The Steel Curtain was having its way with Campbell, shutting the big back down completely. But Pastorini was finding success, and it looked like the Oilers had something going until receiver Mike Renfro fumbled away a reception, with Blount recovering.

Benefiting from the turnover, Bradshaw drove the Steelers downfield again. His scoring toss to Stallworth, a twenty-yard completion, gave the hometown Steelers their first lead of the game, 17–10. That's where the score stood when the first half ended.

For most of the third quarter, the teams traded the football, and the Oilers squandered a couple of good opportunities. First, the Oilers couldn't take advantage of a fumbled punt by Bell. Then, on an apparent fourth-down conversion, they were penalized for delay of game and ended up having to punt the ball away.

Then, with just 1:30 left in the third quarter, a play took place that very much ushered in change throughout the NFL.

Driving deep in Steelers territory, the Oilers had a first-and-goal at the six-yard line. Pastorini took the snap and floated a gentle pass to Renfro in the back right corner of the end zone. Renfro caught the ball with his right foot on the turf in bounds and his left foot scraping the ground in front of the orange pylon marking the corner of the end zone.

While the Oilers looked to celebrate a touchdown, the officials on the field converged for a discussion. Referee Jim Tunney ruled the play as an incomplete pass, the ruling being that Renfro's second foot was out of bounds, nullifying the apparent touchdown.

Naturally, the Oilers' sideline was incensed, protesting the call. If the NFL had replay, the call on the field—an incomplete pass—would have likely been overturned, with the play ruled a touchdown. That singular play, maybe more than any other, ushered in the league's use of instant replay to rule on close plays.

Regardless, the play was ruled an incomplete pass. The Steelers' defense stiffened, and the drive ended with an Oilers' field goal. Importantly, instead of a deadlock at 17–17, the score was 17–13 in favor of Pittsburgh.

The fourth quarter proved to be all Steelers. The tide turned for good when Bradshaw connected with a sliding Swann to just barely get a first down on a third-and-twenty play, a play that seemed to take a little heart out of the Oilers' defense. After a long, clock-burning drive, however, the Steelers couldn't find the end zone and had to settle for a thirty-nine-yard field goal by Bahr, pressing their advantage to 20–13.

Down just a single score, Pastorini began another drive. That drive ended when receiver Merkens fumbled after making a twelve-yard reception. Blount forced the fumble, and Shell pounced on it to end any threat.

From there, all Bradshaw and the Steelers had to do was run out the clock. Bleier put the game on ice, bringing in two catches for first downs to keep the drive—and the clock—ticking. Then, on third-and-goal, he ran the ball in from the four-yard line for a touchdown with less than a minute remaining on the clock.

Despite the controversy surrounding the Renfro call, the Steelers, holding Campbell to just fifteen yards on seventeen carries, were well-deserved victories, taking a 27–13 victory and a berth in Super Bowl XIV two weeks later in the Rose Bowl in Pasadena, California.

Chapter 24

CEMENTING A LEGACY OF GREATNESS

T he Steelers' opponent in Super Bowl XIV was the Los Angeles Rams, and it marked the first Super Bowl where one of the participants was playing in its home market—the Rose Bowl in Pasadena, just ten miles from Los Angeles. The Rams, led by head coach Ray Malavasi, had an interesting journey to the Super Bowl. In the middle of the season, they had endured a three-game losing streak, including lopsided losses to both the Cowboys and the Chargers. They corrected course, however, and won five out of six, including four in a row, before dropping their season finale at home against the New Orleans Saints.

Taking advantage of a relatively weak division—the Saints, Falcons, and 49ers were a collective 16–32 on the season—the Rams managed to win the NFC West with a 9–7 record. As such, they went into the postseason as an uncertain entity.

That changed when they traveled to Dallas and beat the Cowboys 21–19. Quarterback Vince Ferragamo, who started just the sixth game of his professional career, threw three long touchdown passes, the shortest covering thirty-two yards. His fifty-yard touchdown pass to receiver Billy Waddy with 2:14 left in the game was the game-winner to complete their improbable comeback victory.

In the NFC Championship Game, the Rams flew cross-country to Tampa Bay to play the Buccaneers. In just their fourth year of existence, the Bucs had shaken off the stigma of going 0–26 at the dawn of the franchise to win the NFC Central Division with a 10–6 record.

To write that the game was a defensive struggle would be an understatement. The Rams' defense, in particular, rose to the occasion, limiting the Bucs to just 177 yards of total offense and harassing Tampa Bay's quarterbacks into a collective five completions in twenty-seven attempts.

After a scoreless first half, the Rams managed enough offense to get three short Frank Corral field goals on the board. That was more than enough on the afternoon, as the Rams won 9–0 to advance to their first Super Bowl.

Throughout the season, the Rams had performed solidly in all aspects of the game, despite not being exceptional in any. They featured a well-balanced offense, tending slightly toward the rushing game once Ferragamo ascended to the starting lineup in Week Twelve, replacing injured quarterbacks Pat Haden and Jeff Rutledge.

The Rams' rushing attack was led by halfback Wendell Tyler, who had rushed for 1,109 yards—at a league-leading clip of 5.1 yards per carry—and scored nine touchdowns on the season. He was joined by fullback Cullen Bryant and savvy veteran back Lawrence McCutcheon.

The receiving corps was represented by wide receiver Preston Dennard, who led the team with forty-three receptions. The Rams' backs featured heavily in the passing game, with both Tyler and Bryant each catching over thirty passes on the season.

On the other side of the ball, the Rams featured many of the same players who had led an outstanding defensive unit for several seasons, including defensive end Jack Youngblood, named to his seventh consecutive Pro Bowl and playing in the postseason on a broken leg. Fred Dryer was also on the line, and linebackers Jim Youngblood and "Hacksaw" Reynold patrolled right behind them. In addition, third-year player Nolan Cromwell was making an impressive name for himself all over the field as an exceptional free safety.

Heading into the Super Bowl, the Rams' defense posed a significant threat to the Steelers. There was one proof point that said it all. In Week Ten, on the road at Seattle, the Rams held the Seahawks to minus seven yards of total offense—a negative seven yards! That tally remains an NFL record. And it was against no slouch of an offensive team, either. Despite being shut out by the Rams, 24–0, over the season, the Seahawks scored the fourth most points in the league and finished seventh in total yards gained.

The Steelers were heavy favorites to defeat the Rams, but they weren't taking their opponents lightly. Historically, the Rams held an advantage in the matchup between the two teams with an all-time record of 12–1–2 against the Steelers. More importantly, though, were two recent victories, a 1975 10–3 win and a 1978 10–7 win, both against Steelers teams that would go on and eventually win the Super Bowl.

A Super Bowl-record crowd of 103,985 spectators jammed the Rose Bowl on a beautiful, sunny southern California winter day to watch which team would claim supremacy as NFL champions.

The Rams received the opening kickoff, and after a short kick, began their first possession in good field position, at their own twenty-nine-yard line. The Steelers promptly forced a three-and-out possession, and the Rams were forced to punt.

A nice forty-three-yard punt by the Rams' Ken Clark was extended even further with a fifteen-yard clipping penalty assessed against the Steelers. With that, Bradshaw and the offensive unit started their day at their own twenty-one-yard line.

After Harris was bottled up and stopped on a one-yard gain on first down, Bleier burst through a hole in the middle on a trap-blocking play to ramble ten yards and earn the Steelers' initial first down.

Then, the Steelers almost repeated the set of downs; only this time, Bleier was just inches short of a first down after a nine-yard gallop on second down. Harris subsequently hammered a third-down rush for a yard's gain and a first down, extending the Steelers' drive.

After Bleier was stuffed on a first-down carry, the Steelers struck for their first big play of the ballgame. Bradshaw, attempting his first pass, found Harris open down the middle of the field. After the catch, Harris rambled all the way to the Rams' twenty-six-yard line for a gain of thirty-two yards.

The Rams' defensive line stiffened, and on third-and-eight, Bradshaw overthrew a pass to Swann in the end zone for an incompletion that stalled the drive. Bahr cleaned up with a forty-one-yard field goal to open the scoring, and the Steelers held a 3–0 lead with 7:31 remaining in the first quarter.

On the kickoff, Bahr tried to catch the Rams' special teams napping and booted a high, looping, but very short kick to the right side of the field, looking for a Steelers' defender to run under it for a successful onside kick. The tricky ploy failed, however, and the Rams took over with great field position at their own forty-one-yard line.

Wendell Tyler got things going for the Rams. On first down, he caught a pass out of the backfield for a six-yard gain. Then, on second down, he swept to the left, made a couple of cuts and broke a few tackles, and ran all the way down to the Steelers' fourteen-yard line. His thirty-nine-yard run was the longest against the Steelers the entire season, and only Shell's tackle saved a likely touchdown.

The Rams set out to make that tackle a moot point. First, McCutcheon carried three straight times for eleven total yards, setting up a first-and-goal at the three-yard line. From there, Tyler carried twice to push it to the one. Finally, Bryant took a handoff and blasted into the end zone for a touchdown, the first rushing touchdown ever scored against the Steelers in a Super Bowl. With Corral's PAT, the Rams jumped out to a 7–3 lead.

The Steelers immediately set out to respond. Larry Anderson returned the kick forty-five yards to set up Bradshaw at the Steelers' forty-seven-yard line. On the first play, Harris finally broke free on a rushing play, plowing ahead for a gain of twelve yards and pushing the ball into Rams' territory.

Bleier had short runs in front of and behind an eight-yard Cunningham reception to move the chains once again. On the last play of the quarter, Bradshaw hit Swann with a twelve-yard completion to advance the ball to the Rams' eighteen-yard line.

When play resumed after the teams traded ends of the field, Bradshaw rolled to his right and fired a pass to the center of the field, finding Cunningham for a thirteen-yard reception that moved the ball to the five-yard line.

On first-and-goal, Harris was tripped up after a one-yard gain. Stallworth then made a leaping catch at the one-yard line but just couldn't get past Rod Perry and Bob Brudzinski for the score. Finally, Harris took a third-down pitch and swept around the right end, untouched, for a touchdown. Bahr's extra point put the Steelers back in front, 10–7.

In a topsy-turvy start to Super Bowl XIV, the Rams responded with a long scoring drive of their own.

The drive began with three rushing plays, two by Tyler on first and third down, that gained fourteen yards and a first down at the Rams' thirty-three-yard line. Ferragamo then followed that up with his third completion in three attempts, a screen pass to Tyler, which the running back turned into an eleven-yard gain and another first down.

After a four-yard run by Bryant, Ferragamo connected with McCutcheon on a sixteen-yard completion to move the ball into Steelers' territory, where it was first down at the thirty-six-yard line.

After Cole stuffed McCutcheon for a two-yard loss, the Rams caught a big break, courtesy of the officials. On second down, Ferragamo, reading the Steelers' blitz, lofted a pass down the right side intended for receiver Waddy. Shell made contact with the intended receiver with his elbow while the ball was in the air, moving Waddy off his route a little. The official saw it as a pass interference penalty, and the result was a twenty-yard mark off of yardage.

On first down at the eighteen-yard line, Bryant gained eight yards on a shifty run off right tackle. On the next play, Greene met Tyler in the backfield, and when the back broke free, he was summarily dropped by Winston and Thomas for a loss of three.

Facing a third-and-six, Ferragamo dropped back and lined a pass to receiver Rod Smith, free at the back of the end zone. The receiver wasn't able to come down with the catch, resulting in Ferragamo's first incompletion of the game. On fourth down, Corral's thirty-one-yard field goal tied the game, 10–10, with 7:21 left in the first half.

Anderson had another huge kickoff return, running the ball to the Steelers' forty-five-yard line before being upended by Corral, the last line of defense between Anderson and the end zone. The Steelers, however, weren't able to take advantage of the great starting field position, and after a three-and-out possession, they punted for the first time in the game.

Starting at their twenty-yard line, the Rams weren't able to move the ball, and after a three-and-out of their own, were forced to punt back to the Steelers. Bell returned the ball to the Steelers' thirty-seven-yard line to set up Bradshaw for a final scoring drive of the half.

However, it didn't turn out that way. On the first play of the Steelers' possession, Bradshaw's pass off a play-action fake went directly to Rams' defensive back Dave Elmendorf, who returned the interception to the Steelers' thirty-nine-yard line.

Instead of the Steelers possessing the ball for a final scoring drive of the half, it was now the Rams' ball and their opportunity.

Cole sacked Ferragamo for a ten-yard loss on first down, and Ferragamo's second-down pass fell incomplete. On third down, however, Ferragamo completed a pass to Bryant good for twelve yards and left head coach Malavasi with a decision to make at the two-minute warning.

With the ball on the thirty-seven-yard line, the Rams were at the far end of Corral's field goal range—in fact, his thirty-one-yard field goal earlier had broken a streak of nine straight missed field goal attempts from longer than thirty yards. In addition, Corral was nursing an injured right arm, hurt when he made his touchdown-saving tackle on Anderson.

Gambling, Malavasi decided to go for it on fourth down. Ferragamo rewarded his coach's faith in him with a ten-yard completion to Waddy for a first down.

On first down, Ferragamo then hit tight end Terry Nelson for a thirteen-yard gain and another first down. After two incompletions on passes into the end zone, Banaszak broke through the Rams' pass protection and sacked Ferragamo on third down.

Corral came through big in the clutch, blasting a forty-five-yard field goal just inside the right upright to give the Rams their second lead of the game, 13–10, with just fourteen seconds left on the clock.

Pittsburgh's starting safeties in Super Bowl XIV were Donnie Shell and JT Thomas. Not playing in the game, however, was veteran safety Mike Wagner, who had missed the last half of the season with a hip injury.

All three safeties enjoyed fantastic NFL careers.

JT Thomas was the least-decorated of the three players with just one Pro Bowl nod during his career, at the end of the 1976 season. Still, Thomas had a nine-year playing career, not counting his missed season in 1978 due to the blood disorder, Boeck's sarcoid.

James Thomas Jr. was born on April 22, 1951, in Macon, Georgia, where he grew up. Upon graduation from Florida State University, Thomas was drafted by the Steelers in the first round of the 1973 NFL draft, with the twenty-fourth overall selection.

Thomas became a starting left cornerback, opposite Blount, his second season, in 1974, and he locked down that side of the field for four seasons, collecting twelve interceptions and recovering two fumbles, one of which he returned for a touchdown.

After sitting out the 1978 season, Thomas returned to the club for the 1979 season, shifting his position to free safety, where he played for three seasons. Thomas finished his career with one final season with the Denver Broncos. He retired after the 1982 season with twenty career receptions in his 125-game career.

Michael Wagner was born June 22, 1949, in Waukegan, Illinois, and played his collegiate football at Western Illinois University, earning NAIA All-America honors in 1969.

In the 1971 NFL Draft, the Steelers selected Wagner in the eleventh round, the 268th overall selection that year. At first, the Steelers didn't know what to do with Wagner and tried him at wide receiver. In due time, he shifted to safety, where he definitively found his calling.

Wagner became a starter in his rookie season and instantly became a contributor all over the field, from sideline to sideline. His eight interceptions led the league in 1973, and he was named to the Pro Bowl at the conclusion of the 1975 and 1976 seasons.

Injuries curtailed Wagner's seasons in 1977 and 1979, but he came back to again feature prominently in his final season, 1980. Over his ten-year career, all spent with the Steelers, Wagner amassed thirty-six interceptions and five fumble recoveries. A member of four Super Bowl-winning teams, Wagner intercepted passes in both Super Bowls IX and X.

Donnie Shell was born on August 26, 1952, in Whitmire, South Carolina, where he grew up. In his senior year at Whitmire High School, Shell starred as a linebacker on a defense that did not surrender a touchdown the entire season.

After playing collegiately at South Carolina State University, Shell went undrafted in 1974. The Steelers signed him as a free agent, and he ended up playing fourteen years in the NFL, all with the Steelers.

Shell played strong safety, which often required him to play close to the line of scrimmage to keep opponents' rushing games in check. His strong, physical tackling allowed him to excel in the role.

He also had responsibilities in pass coverage, and Shell was a demon in coverage, with an instinctive nose for the football. Shell twice intercepted seven passes in a season, both in 1980 and 1984. Throughout his career, Shell intercepted fifty-one passes and recovered nineteen fumbles. He also scored four defensive touchdowns.

Shell earned five consecutive Pro Bowl nods from 1978 to 1982, and in three of those years, he was named first-team All-Pro. Having played 201 games in a Steelers' uniform, Shell is fourth all-time on the club's list, behind only Ben Roethlisberger, Mike Webster, and Hines Ward.

Donnie Shell was inducted into the College Football Hall of Fame in 1998. In 2020, Shell was inducted into the Pro Football Hall of Fame as part of its Centennial class.

The Steelers received the second-half kickoff, and once again, Anderson busted out a fantastic return, affording the offense good field position at the thirty-nine-yard line. Trying to get Swann into the ballgame, Bradshaw opened the series by deftly avoiding the Rams' rush and connecting with his receiver for a four-yard gain. On the next two downs, Bleier and Harris each banged up the middle of the line to get the ball just past the first-down marker.

Harris gained four yards on another tough run off right tackle as Bradshaw attempted to lure the Rams' defenders up toward the line of scrimmage. Then, Bradshaw struck deep.

Dropping back at the snap, Bradshaw had a clean pocket until the very last moment. Stepping up, he threw deep for Swann. At the five-yard line, Swann leaped high between two Rams' defenders to cradle the ball and tumble into the end zone. The forty-seven-yard touchdown pass gave the Steelers their third lead of Super Bowl XIV.

But, once again, the Rams fought back.

Ferragamo and the Rams' offensive unit took possession at their twenty-three-yard line. After a short run by Tyler and an even shorter reception by Bryant, Ferragamo decided to test the Steelers deep on third down.

With plenty of time to throw, Ferragamo heaved the ball downfield in the direction of Waddy. Waddy leaped over Johnson to snare the ball, completing a fifty-yard reception.

Looking to build upon the big catch, the Rams' next play was a trick play, a halfback pass. Ferragamo handed the ball to McCutcheon, who started running what looked to be a sweep around the right end. After a few steps, though, McCutcheon threw the ball on the run to receiver Ron Smith, who snagged the ball and bounced off Thomas and into the end zone for a touchdown.

The Rams' response to Swann's touchdown had been a quick-striking, four-play touchdown drive of their own. Corral missed the extra point, but the Rams had still moved out front, 19–17.

Taking over at their twenty-eight-yard line, on second down Bradshaw ran the same play that had sprung Harris to his long catch-and-run in the first quarter. This time, it was good for a fourteen-yard completion, and it moved the ball to the Steelers' forty-four-yard line.

Scrambling to his right on the next play, Bradshaw threw across his body toward the center of the field, and the pass was nearly picked off by Cromwell, who would have easily returned it for a touchdown if he had held on. It was, perhaps, a foreshadowing of what was to come.

After a false start penalty, Bradshaw completed a pass to Swann on the left side. Swann soared high on the reception, but when defender Pat Thomas hit him, there was a five-foot drop for Swann to hit the Rose Bowl turf.

The completion had gained six yards and left Bradshaw with a third-and-eight. It also left Swann on the sidelines for the remainder of the game, having been shaken up when the side of his head banged off of the field.

On the next play, Bradshaw threw deep down the left sideline, but he had finally pressed his luck too far. Safety Eddie Brown intercepted the pass, and before he was tackled, lateralled the ball to Thomas, who advanced it to the Rams' thirty-eight-yard line.

The Steelers survived the turnover by forcing a quick three-and-out possession from the Rams. Ken Clark's punt went out of bounds at the Steelers' twenty-seven-yard line, where Bradshaw and company again went to work.

After two Harris runs netted four yards, Bradshaw again connected with his back on a pass down the center of the field, and after the catch, Harris rambled all the way to the Rams' forty-nine-yard line, completing a twenty-yard play.

Harris ran for two yards on first down, and Thornton followed with a four-yard gain on second down. Facing a third-and-four, Bradshaw, lining up under center, noticed the Rams had no middle linebacker in their formation. Seeing an opportunity, Bradshaw took a quick snap and barreled forward for five yards and a first down.

Dropping back on the next play, Bradshaw fired a strike down the center of the field to Thornton, who made the catch for a twenty-two-yard completion that moved the ball into scoring position at the Rams' sixteen-yard line.

Harris couldn't gain any ground on a sweep to the right, and Thornton couldn't move forward on a second-down rushing attempt. On a third-and-ten, Bradshaw threw a pass into a crowd at the five-yard line. The ball bounced high into the air before falling into the hands of Perry for Bradshaw's third interception of the game.

The Rams had survived a ten-play Steelers' drive without surrendering any points or the lead. One play later, the third quarter ended. As the teams changed directions on the field one last time, the Rams stubbornly held a 19–17 lead.

On the ensuing series, Toews and Furness brought down Ferragamo for a seven-yard loss on second down, the Steelers' third sack of the game. Deep in his own territory, Ferragamo handed off to Bryant on a third-and-long, and the big fullback almost got the first down, rumbling for fourteen yards. Short of the distance required, the Rams were forced to punt.

Clark's booming fifty-nine-yard punt pushed returner Jim Smith back inside his twenty-yard line, where he slipped several tackles in running the ball out to the twenty-five.

On first down, Harris, who had been bottled up most of the game on rushing attempts, gained just two yards. Then, a second-down screen pass attempt to Thornton fell to the ground, incomplete.

On third-and-eight, Bradshaw took a deep drop and was once again protected well by his offensive line. Spying Stallworth streaking deep downfield, Bradshaw unleashed a long pass. The ball just flew by the outstretched fingertips of a leaping Perry and settled into the arms of Stallworth at the thirty-yard line. From there, the speedy receiver easily scored. The seventy-three-yard touchdown pass gave the Steelers their fourth lead of the unexpectedly back-and-forth game. After Bahr's extra point, the Steelers led 24–19.

On the ensuing kickoff, the Rams tried a reverse, much like the one the Cowboys pulled off on the opening kickoff of Super Bowl X. This time, however, the Steelers weren't fooled, and they dropped returner Jim Jodat at the Rams' own fourteen-yard line.

Faced with poor field position, the Rams tried to use Tyler and the ground game to get some space between them and their goal line. After a four-yard gain on first down, however, linebacker Toews forced Tyler backward on a run to the left side. Tyler reversed course, but by that time the rest of the Steelers had caught up to him and swarmed him down to the ground at the nine-yard line.

On third-and-long, and passing from the shadow of his own end zone, Ferragamo went for broke, throwing deep down the field to receiver Preston Dennard. Johnson had it covered all the way, though and had a better shot at catching it. Johnson did not bring down the interception, but the incompletion did bring up a fourth down.

With 10:11 left to play in the game, the Steelers took over at the Rams' forty-six-yard line, looking to salt the game away. The Rams' defense had other thoughts, however, and standing up strong against the running game, forced the Steelers into a three-and-out and the second Steelers punt of the game.

Punter Colquitt did his job, keeping the Rams pinned in their own territory, this time at the sixteen-yard line. Ferragamo, too, did his job well on first down, connecting with Dennard on a twenty-four-yard completion to get the Rams to more neutral territory at their forty.

Ferragamo went right back at Dennard, connecting with him for an eight-yard gain before Blount drove him headfirst into the turf on the tackle. Tyler then burst through the middle for another eight yards and a first down in Steelers' territory at the forty-four-yard line.

After Tyler slipped for a loss of two and Ferragamo threw an incompletion, the Rams faced a difficult third-and-twelve. It wasn't too much for Ferragamo, though, as he connected with Waddy on a fourteen-yard gain to move the chains once again.

Down a single score, the Rams were moving the football.

Making just the seventh start in the biggest game of his career, Ferragamo had played exceptionally well. His next pass, however, proved to be one he would like to have back.

Looking for receiver Smith running a slant across the field, Ferragamo let loose his throw. He hadn't seen Lambert, though, who, upon reading a pass from the start of the play, used his speed to drop back deep in the center of the field. Lambert, who had recorded six interceptions during the regular season, intercepted the ball and returned it to the twenty-nine-yard line.

With 5:24 left on the clock, Bradshaw and the offense were given another opportunity to put the game out of reach. This time, they delivered, due in no small part from, once again, Stallworth.

With the Steelers facing a third-and-seven with four minutes left in the game, the Rams faced a critical play to get the Steelers' offense off the field and return possession to Ferragamo and their own offense.

Needing to convert the third down, Bradshaw dialed up the same play on which he had connected with Stallworth for the go-ahead touchdown earlier in the quarter. Again, Stallworth made an incredible catch on a well-thrown ball, bending backward to bring the ball in over his shoulder.

The forty-five-yard reception moved the ball to the Rams' twenty-two-yard line. More importantly, it seemed to take the wind out of the Rams' sails.

On second down, Bradshaw, with Swann and Bell out of the game with injuries, threw to Smith in the end zone. The pass fell incomplete, but the officials ruled pass interference on Rams' defender Thomas. By rule, the ball was placed on the one-yard line.

Bleier was stood up at the one on first down, and the two-minute warning sounded soon afterward. On second down, Harris was stopped short of the goal line, but the clock kept ticking down, forcing the Rams to call their first timeout.

On third down, Harris finally broke through for his second touchdown of the game, plowing through both Jim Youngblood and Thomas at the goal line to put the game out of reach. Bahr's PAT made the score 31–19.

Facing almost insurmountable odds, Ferragamo and the Rams were not about to give up their title dreams. Ferragamo first scrambled for eight yards. On second down, he made an excellent play after initially tripping over Greene, who had dived into the play before the snap, offsides. Refusing to fall down, Ferragamo stumbled his way to his left before righting himself and firing a twenty-eight-yard completion downfield to Drew Hill at the Steelers' thirty-yard line.

On third down on the next series, Thomas rushed in on a safety blitz, sacking Ferragamo for the fourth time of the day, and leaving the Rams with a fourth-and-eighteen to keep their dreams alive. Ferragamo's pass to Waddy fell incomplete, though, and the Steelers took possession on downs with only thirty-nine seconds left.

Bradshaw took the honors of cradling the ball and downing himself, and the clock kept ticking until it expired on the Steelers' 31–19 victory in Super Bowl XIV. It was the Steelers' second consecutive Super Bowl triumph and their fourth in six years. They had truly established themselves as the first dynasty in the NFL's Super Bowl era.

Despite tossing three interceptions, Bradshaw, who was fourteen of twenty-one for 309 yards and two touchdowns, was named the Super Bowl's Most Valuable Player for the second consecutive year.

Super Bowl XIV was the second Super Bowl where the Steelers had to come from behind in the fourth quarter to win the game, the first being Super Bowl X when they had trailed the Cowboys 10–7.

Most pundits had the Steelers heavily favored in Super Bowl XIV, and many expected the Steelers to win handily. Bettors in Las Vegas declared the Steelers ten-and-a-half-point favorites. They may have eventually won by twelve points, but the Steelers never had it easy. Super Bowl XIV remains the only Super Bowl in history where the lead changed hands seven times between the two teams.

Chapter 25

ALL GOOD THINGS COME TO AN END

oday, it's common for championship sports teams to visit the White House. While the practice dates back nearly 160 years, a White House visit hasn't always been a tradition.

The earliest visit on record is August 30, 1865, when President Andrew Johnson hosted the Brooklyn Atlantics and Washington Nationals baseball teams. President Ulysses S. Grant welcomed the first professional sports team in 1869 when the Cincinnati Red Stockings baseball club paid a visit. The first World Series victors to visit the White House were probably the 1924 Washington Senators, hosted by President Calvin Coolidge the next year.

Professional football was the laggard of the sports. The first Super Bowl championship team to visit the White House was the Steelers, who joined their fellow champion Pirates to pay a visit to President Jimmy Carter on February 22, 1980.

In the unique dual ceremony, Pittsburgh Mayor Richard Caliguiri presented Carter with both a Pirates baseball cap and a Terrible Towel. In his remarks, the president singled out both the Pirates' fallen hero Clemente and the Steelers' Bleier for their actions off the playing field—Clemente for his relief efforts for Nicaragua and Bleier for his military service in Vietnam.

In speaking of the Pirates, Carter mentioned brotherhood, cooperation, common purpose, friendship, and a team spirit built on "We Are Family." To the Steelers, the president spoke of the same spirit, along with the unity, courage, commitment, and ability to not only reach success, but sustain success over time.

In a telling nod to the importance of the two ball clubs to the community, Carter closed his remarks with the following:

"Art Rooney's Steelers and Dan Galbreath's Pirates have now established some great traditions, not only of winning games, not only of winning championships in athletic events, but of teamwork off the field as well. What they have done has united a community, has united a region of our nation and has aroused the admiration of every American who's interested in sports, interested in courage, interested in achievement, interested in cooperation and teamwork, interested in the spirit of patriotism and the value of a close family relationship."

Between Super Bowl XIV and the White House visit, the Pittsburgh Penguins professional hockey club changed their colors to adopt the black and gold of that of the Steelers and Pirates.

Founded in 1967, the Penguins had played in a number of variations of a blue-and-white uniform. In adopting black and gold, they would make Pittsburgh the only city that had all its professional sports teams share the same color palette in their logos and uniforms.

However, it wasn't easy for the Penguins. In changing their uniform colors, they had to overcome a formal objection from the Boston Bruins, who had worn black-and-gold uniforms for more than fifty years. Needless to say, the Bruins' protest was summarily dismissed by the National Hockey League.

The new colors, however, didn't pay immediate dividends, as the visiting St. Louis Blues spoiled the great reveal, defeating the Penguins 4–3 on the night of January 30, 1980.

Later in the season, the Bruins exacted a bit of revenge by eliminating the Penguins from the postseason, winning the first-round matchup three games to two.

Between the 1982–1983 and 1987–1988 seasons, the Penguins did not qualify for the Stanley Cup Playoffs. But they had uncovered a special gem when they drafted Mario Lemieux with the first overall selection in the 1984 NHL Entry Draft. Lemieux had an immediate impact on the Penguins, the entire league, and the city of Pittsburgh.

Mario Lemieux was born on October 5, 1965, in Montreal, Quebec, Canada, where he began playing hockey at age three in his basement. When the basement proved too small, his father built a rink in the front yard for Mario and his two older brothers.

Lemieux was a phenom in junior hockey, breaking records the likes of those of the legendary Guy Lafleur. It was no surprise the Penguins chose him with the first selection of the draft.

The Penguins weren't good and seemed to be in a constant flux of financial turmoil and the subject of relocation rumors. The club declared bankruptcy in 1975, and finances suffered more as the team played to an average of fewer than 7,000 fans per game at the Civic Arena, less than half of capacity.

With the signing of Lemieux, the Penguins changed all that. Lemieux made his NHL debut on October 11, 1984, against the Boston Bruins. On his very first shift, he stole the puck from eventual Hall of Fame defenseman Ray Bourque and scored a goal with his first NHL shot. After that, the goals kept coming.

Lemieux became the first rookie to win the NHL All-Star Game's Most Valuable Player Award on his way to a forty-three-goal, one-hundred-point season. However, It took until his fifth season, 1988–1989, for Lemieux and the Penguins to earn their way into the Stanley Cup Playoffs.

In that year, Lemieux exploded for 199 total points—eighty-five goals and 114 assists. On New Year's Eve 1988, against the New Jersey Devils, Lemieux became the only player in NHL history to score a goal in all five possible game situations in the same game—at even-strength, on the power-play, shorthanded, by a penalty shot, and on an empty net.

Behind Lemieux's leadership, the Penguins won the Stanley Cup after both the 1990–1991 and 1991–1992 seasons. The next season started strongly, too, until Lemieux shocked the sporting world when, on January 12, 1993, he announced he had been diagnosed with Hodgkin's lymphoma, a blood cancer. He subsequently missed two months of the season while undergoing aggressive radiation treatments.

Upon Lemieux's return, the Penguins won an NHL-record seventeen consecutive games on their way to their best regular-season record ever. Unfortunately, the season ended when the New York Islanders upset them in the second round of the Stanley Cup Playoffs.

The Penguins would not win another Stanley Cup with Lemieux as a player, but that didn't mark the end of Lemieux's story with the Penguins.

The Penguins had spent money hand-over-fist to build a contending club around Lemieux in the early 1990s, and facing a growing mound of debt to various creditors, management asked Lemieux and other star players to defer their salaries. In time, Lemieux became the team's biggest creditor.

In 1998, the Penguins declared bankruptcy, and in 1999, the club appeared destined to be relocated. Then, Lemieux came in with a novel proposition. Promising to keep the team in Pittsburgh, he proposed the majority of his debt be converted to equity in the team, with him as the controlling interest. When the bankruptcy court approved it, Lemieux became the majority owner of the team and assumed the posts of president, chairman, and chief executive officer of the Penguins.

Then, he added the role of player too. Lemieux came out of retirement and played five more seasons before injuries and age forced him to hang up the skates at the conclusion of the 2005–2006 season, his only season playing alongside another young phenom, rookie Sydney Crosby.

With Lemieux as owner, Crosby took over the role of one of the NHL's best players. After the 2008–2009 regular season, Crosby led the team in claiming another Stanley Cup victory, giving his boss, Lemieux, his first as team owner. Crosby and the Penguins repeated the feat in both 2015–2016 and 2016–2017.

In 1993, the year he was diagnosed with Hodgkin's lymphoma, Lemieux created the Mario Lemieux Foundation to fund medical research projects. Over time, that foundation has supported several community health causes, including the Mario Lemieux Center for Blood Cancers at the UPMC Hillman Cancer Center.

Lemieux finished his career with a staggering 1,409 points in 1,108 games played—517 goals and 892 assists. The Hockey Hall of Fame waived its three-year waiting period to immediately induct Lemieux upon his first retirement in 1997. When he returned as a player in 2000, he became only the third-ever Hall of Famer to play after his induction into the Hall.

In 1980, Pittsburgh, while still very much in the throes of economic upheaval, was being referred to as "the City of Champions." The citizens embraced their sporting heroes and held them close to their hearts as a source of restored civic pride after having had that pride bruised and battered for a handful of years.

The Steelers went into the 1980 NFL Draft intent on reloading for another deep playoff run. In the first round, they selected Mark Malone, a quarterback out of Arizona State, to be the heir-apparent to Bradshaw at some point. They also addressed their aging defensive line by taking two linemen in the second round, Bob Kohrs, a teammate of Malone's in college, with the thirty-fifth pick, and John Goodman with the fifty-sixth pick. Both would end up playing five seasons with the Steelers.

In the same draft, the Steelers also uncovered two longtime contributors in the deep rounds. In the sixth round, the club selected tackle Tunch Ilkin with the 165th overall pick. Ilkin would eventually play in 176 games over thirteen seasons with the Steelers, earning Pro Bowl honors twice.

In the eleventh round, the Steelers selected running back Frank Pollard with the 305th overall selection of the draft. Pollard would play nine seasons for the Steelers, starting sixty-five of his 111 games, rushing for nearly 4,000 yards, and scoring twenty touchdowns.

The Steelers started the season well, beating the Oilers at home and the Colts on the road. Then, their penchant for offensive turnovers returned to haunt them, and again it occurred at Cincinnati against the hapless Bengals.

In that Week Three matchup, the Bengals opened the scoring in the first quarter when Bengals defensive back Ray Griffin returned a Bradshaw interception twenty-eight yards for a touchdown. The Steelers would claw their way into the lead in the second quarter and hold it for much of the game. But, in the end, their six turnovers, which didn't include another three fumbles they managed to recover themselves, were too much to overcome. The Bengals came from behind in the fourth quarter to win 30–28.

The Steelers rebounded with two straight wins to bump their record to 4–1. But injuries were catching up with the aging stars on the roster. Swann and Stallworth were out of the lineup. Other regulars would start dropping as the season progressed. Bradshaw, Harris, Thornton, Hawthorne, Smith, Bell, Grossman, and Cunningham became offensive contributors who missed at least one game due to injury.

The defensive unit didn't escape the injury bug either. Lambert, Winston, and Cole all missed games at the linebacker spot. On the defensive line, Greene and Greenwood battled nagging injuries.

Age and injury caught up with the Steelers in Week Six, and again it was against the Bengals. After storming out to a 17–0 halftime lead at Three Rivers, the Bengals held on to win, 17–16, the difference coming on a missed PAT by Bahr in the third quarter.

That loss ignited what proved to be a three-game losing skid for the Steelers. The middle game of that streak was the very next Sunday when the Raiders invaded Pittsburgh.

The Raiders had started their 1980 campaign with a 2–3 record and had won the week before against San Diego to level their record coming into Three Rivers Stadium. This Raiders' ball club was coached by Tom Flores and quarterbacked by veteran reclamation project, Jim Plunkett.

On a cool Pittsburgh evening, the two teams put on an exciting show for the national *Monday Night Football* audience. They combined to score seventy-nine points on the night, the most ever to that point in the eleven-year history of *Monday Night Football*. Together, the two teams put up 857 yards of total offense, and five of the ten touchdowns covered thirty-four yards or more.

The Raiders, however, pulled away late to win 45–34. Each team left with identical 4–3 records. But, whereas the Raiders would eventually go on a tear and win the Super Bowl after qualifying as a wildcard playoff team, the Steelers' season took a different turn.

The next week, with Bradshaw sitting out, the Steelers lost their third consecutive game, again giving up a fourth-quarter lead. This time, the Browns scored thirteen unanswered points in the final stanza to escape with a 27–26 victory.

At the halfway point of the season, the Steelers stood at 4–4, one game behind the Browns and the Oilers in the AFC Central Division race.

With their backs to the wall, the Steelers then ran off three straight victories, all very close games. In the first two games, at home versus the Packers and on the road against the Buccaneers, the Steelers held leads and survived fourth-quarter comebacks. In a Week Eleven rematch with the Browns, the Steelers flipped this script.

After jumping out to a 7–0 lead in the second quarter on a Jim Smith ten-yard touchdown reception from Bradshaw, the Browns scored thirteen straight points to take a 13–7 lead into the fourth quarter.

Late in the game, the Steelers had a chance to take the lead from inches away, but Smith dropped an easy touchdown pass from Bradshaw. On the next play, the Steelers turned the ball over on downs when Grossman couldn't get into the end zone.

But the Steelers had one last chance. At the Browns' three-yard line, Bradshaw looked for ages for an open receiver until he finally spotted Swann in the clear. His three-yard touchdown pass with eleven seconds remaining was the difference in a 16–13 come-from-behind Steelers' victory.

The win, the Browns' eleventh consecutive loss in Pittsburgh, kept the Steelers in the playoff picture, one game behind the Oilers.

The next week, however, the Steelers' playoff chances took a severe hit when they traveled to Buffalo and were outplayed by the Bills in a 28–13 loss. Pittsburgh's offense was stymied most of the game, particularly the running game, which accounted for just eighty-four yards. Meanwhile, quarterback Joe Ferguson threw three touchdown passes to pace the Bills.

With their record at 7–5, it was becoming clear that the Steelers needed to win the division title if they were to make the playoffs and have another opportunity to win three consecutive Super Bowls.

In Week Thirteen, they took care of business against the Dolphins, winning 23–10 to set up a showdown the next weekend at Houston.

The Oilers had lost two in a row, including the week before at home against Cleveland, and entered the game with the same record as the Steelers at 8–5. Both teams were looking up in the division at the surprising Browns, who were one game ahead of each with a 9–4 record.

Simply, the loser of the Week Fourteen game would be effectively—if not mathematically—eliminated from playoff contention.

The Astrodome was packed with a noisy crowd for the special Thursday night game, and the close nature of the game made it critical for each team to play error-free. Unfortunately for fans of the Black and Gold, it was the Steelers who too often made mistakes.

The Steelers had five turnovers in the game, against just one for the Oilers. The biggest was a fumble by Harris on a pitch by Bradshaw in the fourth quarter with the Oilers up 3–0. Harris tried to pick up the ball instead of falling on it but just couldn't get a handle on it. Oilers linebacker Greg Bingham eventually fell on it, recovering the ball at the Steelers' thirty-three-yard line. Five plays later, Fritsch hit a short field goal to extend the Oilers' lead to 6–0.

With seven minutes remaining, the Steelers were still within a single store. The 6–0 score stood until the final whistle blew, though, and it marked the first time the Steelers had been shut out since the Raiders performed the trick in 1974.

The loss left the Steelers with an 8–6 record. Most importantly, the Steelers were in third place in the division, one game behind the Oilers and two games behind the Browns, with just two games remaining.

In the home finale in Week Fifteen, the Steelers scored fourteen fourth-quarter points to come from behind to defeat the Chiefs. Bleier's eleven-yard touchdown run closed the scoring on a 21–16 victory.

The Steelers closed out the 1980 season visiting San Diego to take on the Chargers on *Monday Night Football*. The outcomes of the Sunday games had eliminated the Steelers from the playoff race. But the Chargers had an AFC West Division title to play for.

The Steelers looked out of whack early when, after a successful first drive, Bahr missed a short twenty-six-yard field goal. His counterpart on the Chargers, Rolf Benirschke, kicked three of his eventual four field goals in the first half to spot the Chargers a 9–3 lead.

In the second half, Chargers quarterback Dan Fouts played well, and the Chargers led by a comfortable sixteen points until Bradshaw connected with Cunningham on a sixteen-yard touchdown pass on the final play of the game to make the final score 26–17.

The 1980 Pittsburgh Steelers finished with a 9–7 record, good for only third place in the Central Division, and broke a six-year streak of division titles. In missing the playoffs, the Steelers had their eight-year streak of postseason berths snapped.

The 1980 Steelers, though, were a story of what could have been. They lost two games by one point each and another game by two points. In two of those losses, they had given up double-digit leads in the fourth quarter.

The offense proved its potency, finishing the season as the sixth-ranked unit in yards gained. However, its forty-two turnovers were too much to overcome.

The defense, despite Pro Bowl nods for Shell, Lambert, and Ham, fell precipitously from its heights of recent years, finishing fifteenth in points allowed and twelfth in total yards allowed. Additionally, the defense managed just eighteen sacks over the sixteen-game regular season.

The 1980 season marked the final season for two Steelers legends. Rocky Bleier announced during the season that he intended to retire. By doing so, he experienced an emotional send-off at the Steelers' final home game, the Week Fifteen victory over the Chiefs. In Bleier's final game at Three Rivers Stadium, he scored the game-winning touchdown on his eleven-yard run. The sold-out crowd gave him a standing ovation then, as well as when he was substituted out of the game with seven seconds to play.

Mike Wagner, too, had decided to retire, but he kept his decision to himself. He retired after the season, on January 7, 1981, and said at his informal press conference at Three Rivers, "I really feel Rocky deserved everything he got, and I didn't want to say, 'I'm retiring too.' Rocky is the heart and soul of what Pittsburghers love about football and the Steelers."

Wagner closed out his career with another typically strong season, second on the club with five interceptions and third in tackles, with ninety-nine. Bleier played in every game, rushing for 340 yards—second highest on the team—at an average of 4.4 yards per carry, and catching twenty-one passes for another 174 yards.

Chapter 26

TRANSFORMATIONS FOR CITY & TEAM

Thanks to NFL Films and CBS Sports, the Dallas Cowboys were America's Team. But the Steelers had their own sovereign nation, "Steeler Nation." For that, they, too, had NFL Films to thank.

The term *Steeler Nation* was coined by narrator Facenda in the NFL Films-produced highlight reel of the Steelers' 1978 season.

The Steelers, of course, followed the baseball Pirates, and the early years of Steelers football were mediocre at best. But, with the rise of the team's fortunes in the 1970s, the Steelers' popularity within the local fanbase skyrocketed. Today, there's no question of the most popular team in the region. Western Pennsylvania is Steelers Country.

In 2007, Turnkey Sports & Entertainment released its Team Brand Index, built upon an eighteen-month marketing survey that examined the local popularity of the then 122 major professional sports teams in North America. The Steelers were ranked number one in terms of the strongest team brand in any local market.[7]

Steeler Nation extends far beyond western Pennsylvania. As some Pittsburghers moved during the collapse of the local economy, their team affiliation moved along with them. Others around the country adopted the Steelers through their hard-nosed play and sustained competitive relevance.

In 2022, various sources reported the size of NFL fanbases, and the Steelers placed third, behind the Cowboys and the Patriots.[8,9,10] One quantifiable metric is the number of Facebook fans of each team. The Steelers come in third there, too, with nearly six million, trailing, again, Dallas and New England.

The Cowboys and the Patriots have much bigger populations in their metropolitan area—Dallas has 7.5 million in population, Boston 4.9 million, and Pittsburgh only 2.3 million. In terms of "fans per capita," the Steelers dwarf all other teams.

One point of evidence of popularity and support can be drawn from ticket sales for Steelers' games. The Steelers have sold out every game for fifty years, beginning with the September 17, 1972 season opener against—you might have guessed already—the Oakland Raiders.

Prior to the 2007 season, Steeler Nation gained a new citizen with the introduction of a mascot, Steely McBeam. Steely was introduced as part of the team's seventy-fifth-anniversary celebrations.

For that anniversary, the Steelers had a diamond jubilee weekend ahead of their *Monday Night Football* game with the Baltimore Ravens (the original Cleveland Browns franchise). On the night before the game, the Steelers hosted a banquet and gala at the David L. Lawrence Convention Center.

The master of ceremonies that night was Steve Sabol, president of NFL Films. Sabol said it well that evening when he stated, "The Steelers don't need a mascot. Their fans are their mascot. There were Gerela's Gorillas, Franco's Italian Army, Lambert's Lunatics, and people dressed up like bumble bees. You don't need a mascot when you have fans like that."

The Steelers entered the 1981 offseason motivated to return the club to the top echelon of the NFL, a spot to which it—along with all of Steeler Nation—had grown accustomed. In the 1981 NFL Draft, the Steelers took some swings, and they came up with a collection of both hits and misses.

In the first round, they chose Keith Gary, a defensive end out of Oklahoma, with the seventeenth overall pick. Gary ended up having a six-year career in which he was credited with twenty-five sacks.

Second-round pick Anthony Washington, a defensive back, and third-round pick Rick Donnalley, a center, both played only two seasons with the Steelers, however.

While those two high picks ended up being misses, the Steelers once again redeemed themselves in the middle rounds. In rounds six and seven, they selected linebackers Bryan Little and David Hinkle, each of whom would become fixtures in the starting lineup and enjoy twelve-year careers in Pittsburgh.

With an aging corps of star players, led by the likes of Greene, entering his thirteenth season in the NFL at the age of thirty-five, the team adopted a classic rallying cry. With Super Bowl winners traditionally gifting players rings to commemorate their championship seasons, the Steelers' veterans had enough—four—to fill the fingers of one hand. So the club adopted the motto, "One for the thumb in '81."

Super Bowl rings are given out by teams to more than just players. Others in the organization typically receive rings as well. Although, they're not always the *same* ring.

Super Bowl rings have always been opulent. But modern-day Super Bowl rings are just downright garish, jammed packed with diamonds and other precious stones. For example, the Tampa Bay Buccaneers ring from Super Bowl LV contains 319 diamonds.

According to Bankrate.com, the NFL allocates about $5,000 per ring to each Super Bowl champion. Therefore, in the last twenty years or so, teams have looked to save some costs by issuing different "levels" of rings, with B- and C-level rings issued to front office personnel.

In July 2008, citizens of Steelers Nation had a unique opportunity to purchase two different Steelers Super Bowl rings from an era before different levels of rings sprung up. A former team employee put them up on an eBay auction. The Steelers' Super Bowl IX ring sold for $32,751. The Super Bowl X ring sold for just a bit more, closing at $34,100.

Fans noticed a peculiarity with the Super Bowl IX ring. On the side of the ring are engravings of the games that made up the Steelers' playoff journey that season. Oddly, the final score of the first-round victory over Buffalo is incorrect.

The Super Bowl IX ring reads, "Steelers 32, Bills 6." The true final score, however, was 32–14, in favor of the Steelers.

So the ring was a fake, right?

Not so fast.

Jostens, the Minneapolis-based jeweler who manufactured the rings, checked its original molds stored in its vault. Sure enough, the mold reflects the incorrect score.

In thirty-four years, no one had ever noticed.

Gulf Oil, with its Mellon family roots, was a significant Pittsburgh institution for much of the twentieth century, and its namesake building dominated the city's skyline until the U.S. Steel Building was erected. In 1979, the company was number nine on the Fortune 500 list. Just six years later, in 1985, as a reflection of the Pittsburgh-area economy, Gulf Oil ceased to exist as an independent company.

While Gulf technically merged with Standard Oil of California in 1985 to form Chevron, it was, in effect, an acquisition. The headquarters of the new organization was established out west. Left in the wake was the loss of a great number of high-level corporate and PhD-level research positions. Estimates in 1985 suggested the stroke of the pen on the merger agreement negatively impacted up to 1,900 high-paying Gulf Oil positions.

Losses weren't, of course, isolated to just one organization. Reflective of the ripple effect that occurs in all such situations, consider the plight of a group like the Pittsburgh Symphony Orchestra. In the ten years before Gulf Oil's departure, the organization had received almost $800,000 of corporate support from Gulf. That windfall boost was immediately lost.

Other Pittsburgh institutions faced similar situations to that of Gulf Oil. Koppers Company was a locally-based global chemical and materials company until it was snatched up in a hostile takeover in 1988 by British conglomerate Beazer. Later in the year, Koppers Industries was created by local management as a smaller, more streamlined domestic enterprise.

Koppers, while it remained in name, was a much smaller company, with fewer employees and a smaller economic impact on the city during its early, formative years. Over time, it successfully grew its core business, and in 2006, Koppers went public with its initial public offering. But the transition of the company in the late 1980s was another thorn in the side of the city's economy.

Rockwell International, a Pittsburgh corporate citizen since the 1930s, also left Pittsburgh in 1988, moving its headquarters to California. Only a couple of hundred headquarters jobs were affected, but the loss of another high-profile company was further symbolic of the blight.

Pittsburgh and its citizens were discovering themselves at a crossroads. The economic downturn wasn't limited to just blue-collar industrial and manufacturing jobs. White-collar office workers were negatively impacted as well.

Pittsburgh didn't have a choice in undergoing its deindustrialization transformation. Industries were shrinking, if not going away completely. It was fight or flight time. Some, of course, flew, and Pittsburgh and its metropolitan area shrank in terms of population. Those who stayed to fight knew the future had to be something different from the past. How different, nobody knew for certain.

This book suggests a theory that bounced around the mind of one of its authors for at least twenty-five years. What was different about Pittsburgh from its Rust Belt cousins, like Detroit and Cleveland, that allowed it to come out of its deindustrialization and transform itself into a prosperous, healthy "New Economy" city? What braced the city for a disruptive change—gave it the strength to unite, persevere, and persist?

In the author's mind, it was the Steelers and the club's indelible mark as a central thread that is the cultural tapestry of Pittsburgh and western Pennsylvania. Those other cities might have professional football teams, but they weren't champion-ship-level teams that galvanized their communities as a source of civic pride. But, of course, the Steelers had plenty of help along the way.

A foundation of change and deindustrialization transformation rested in Pitts-burgh's long-standing strength in academia and higher education. Carnegie Mellon University—a legacy of the steel barons of yesteryear—the University of Pittsburgh, and Duquesne University are all prestigious schools that have enjoyed high rankings on lists of national undergraduate and graduate schools for generations.

CMU and Pitt grew over the years, in large part, to suit the needs of the steel industry. But, as the long, drawn-out collapse of the industry became evident, they both pivoted and redirected their research and academic visions in the direction of different sciences and technologies. The fruits of those efforts were subsequently delivered by pulling the local market toward high-tech fields.

Along the way to making waves in high technology, a little something was invented in 1982 that has, in many ways, fundamentally changed the way humans communicate today. On September 19 of that year, Carnegie Mellon professor Dr. Scott Fahlman invented the first emoticon, a little pictorial representation of facial expressions using characters like punctuation marks and the like, as a shortcut to expressing feelings or reactions. His first emoticon was the "smiley," :-). Emoticons grew to include emojis, and by 2015, humans were sending over six billion emoti-cons a day.

When the Pittsburgh Works of the Jones and Laughlin Steel Corporation—J & L, or, as yinzers said, "jane el"—stopped its operations on the site in 1981, some viewed opportunity among the despair. Ownership of the property bounced around a bit until it landed in the hands of the Urban Redevelopment Authority (URA) of Pittsburgh

With assistance from the Regional Industrial Development Corporation of Southwestern Pennsylvania, the URA won a highly-competitive federal grant that allowed the 1985 development and construction of what is now the Pittsburgh Tech-nology Center. The Center proved to be just one shining example of Pittsburgh's transformation, a byproduct of an alliance built across politics, business, academia, and civic leaders.

Pittsburgh was building the foundation on which to pivot its economy, moving from a Rust Belt has-been to a "Brain Belt" pioneer with established roots in science, technology, engineering, and math, or STEM.

In 2015, *WalletHub* sought to determine the best markets for STEM profession-als, comparing the country's one hundred largest metropolitan areas across nineteen metrics. Pittsburgh ranked seventh overall, trailing only Seattle, Austin, Boston, Madison, Minneapolis, and Atlanta, and notably above San Francisco, which slotted itself into eighth.[11]

How important was Pittsburgh's pivot in the mid-1980s? Consider that same *WalletHub* study of the top 1000 STEM markets placed fellow Rust Belt cities Cleveland forty-sixth, Buffalo forty-eighth, and Detroit ninety-first.

The Steelers opened their 1981 campaign at home against the Chiefs in front of a sold-out Three Rivers Stadium crowd, eager to put the disappointment of the previous year behind them. When the Steelers opened the scoring on an eighteen-yard touchdown pass from Bradshaw to Swann, it appeared to be a good omen. However, when rookie placekicker David Trout missed the ensuing PAT, it ushered in an omen that wasn't nearly so positive.

The Chiefs were coming into the game off an 8–8 season the year before, but they were forced to start Bill Kenney at quarterback in place of an injured Steve Fuller. It was an ideal scenario upon which the Steel Curtain had feasted for a decade.

Not this time around. Kenney and the Chiefs overcame three separate deficits to take an early fourth-quarter lead, benefiting greatly from Steelers' gifts, including another missed PAT by Trout, four lost fumbles out of a total of seven, and an interception.

Despite their sloppy play, the Steelers were still in the game. When Bradshaw connected with receiver Jim Smith on a forty-one-yard touchdown pass, the Steelers held a 33–30 lead with 7:12 to go.

The defense forced the Chiefs to punt, providing the opportunity for the Steelers' offense to run out the clock. They worked masterfully in that endeavor, moving the ball to the Chiefs' twenty-eight-yard line while forcing the visitors to burn all their timeouts.

Then, as the two-minute warning approached, blitzing Chiefs linebacker Frank Manumaleuga hit Bradshaw just as he was in the process of handing off. The Chiefs' Thomas Howard silenced the home crowd by scooping up the fumble in stride and bolting sixty-five yards for a touchdown to put the Chiefs up front once more with just 1:59 remaining on the clock.

Instead of milking the clock, the Steelers were then forced to drive the length of the field to win the game. That drive ended, however, when Chiefs' safety Gary Barbaro intercepted another Bradshaw pass, the Steelers' seventh turnover of the afternoon.

The Steelers' sloppy play was too much to overcome, and they lost the season opener, 37–33.

In Week Two, the Dolphins exposed the Steelers with a convincing 30–10 victory on *Monday Night Football*. The 1981 Steelers were a far cry from the teams just a couple of years before, and it was going to take marked improvement to get into playoff contention.

The Steelers rolled off four consecutive wins to head into a Week Seven matchup with the Bengals in Cincinnati's Riverfront Stadium, with first place in the division on the line. The Bengals left no doubt which was the better team on the afternoon, cruising to a 34–0 fourth-quarter lead before surrendering a score—a Bradshaw-to-Smith touchdown pass—to the Steelers.

The Steelers played hard, gritty football in winning four of their next six to head into a Week Fourteen *Monday Night Football* game in Oakland against the Raiders with an 8–5 record. But, being two games behind the Bengals in the division standings, it was an almost must-win game for the Black and Gold.

Unfortunately, on the Steelers' first possession of the second quarter, Bradshaw broke his right hand, his throwing hand, when he hit the helmet of Raiders' linebacker Rod Martin on the follow-through of a pass. Malone kept the Steelers in the back-and-forth game, but a fifty-three-yard punt return for a touchdown by the Raiders' Ted Watts proved too much to overcome. The Steelers lost the game 30–27 and limped home to face the Bengals the next week.

Malone came through with a steely performance in place of Bradshaw, but the Bengals proved to be too much once again, winning 17–10 and eliminating the Steelers from playoff contention for the second straight year. The next weekend, veteran tight end Dave Casper delivered a merciful close to the Steelers' 8–8 season when he hauled in his third touchdown of the game with 1:51 remaining.

There would be no final one for the thumb in '81 to mark Greene's final season before retiring. Furthermore, by missing the playoffs rather convincingly for a second year running, it was clear that a changing of the guard at the top of the NFL had occurred. The Steelers no longer reigned.

The 1982 season marked the Steelers' fiftieth season of professional football, and it got off to a rousing start, first with a 36–28 victory at Dallas, followed up by a thrilling 26–20 overtime victory over the Bengals at Three Rivers Stadium.

Then, the air was taken out of the ball, so to speak, as the NFLPA walked out on strike—something the steelworkers in western Pennsylvania knew too well as a labor tactic.

When the season resumed two months later, the Steelers dropped three out of five games, suffering two shutouts in the process. The first shutout occurred in Seattle in Week Four, where the Steelers committed five turnovers on the way to being blanked 16–0. After stomping the Chiefs 35–14, the Steelers were then pummeled by the Bills in Buffalo, 13–0, in a game where they could muster only ninety-six yards of total offense, including a negative two through the air.

The next week, they scored against the Browns, at least, but they still lost 10–9, a loss that left their record at 4–3.

Behind big games by Bradshaw and Harris, though, the Steelers capped their nine-game regular season with two big victories at home over the Patriots, 37–14, and the Browns, 37–21. With a 6–3 record on the abbreviated season, the Steelers earned a home playoff game against the San Diego Chargers.

The Steelers' return to the postseason didn't end well. Chargers quarterback Dan Fouts connected with tight end Kellen Winslow for two fourth-quarter touchdowns to give the Chargers a 31–28 come-from-behind victory.

That January 9, 1983 loss would be the last playoff game played in Three Rivers Stadium for ten years. Two days later, Lynn Swann retired after a nine-year career full of highlights that get replayed to this day. One month later, Jack Ham, citing his inability to fully recover from his 1979 foot injury, announced his own retirement after twelve years with the Steelers.

Later that spring, in the 1983 NFL Draft, the Steelers passed on local product Dan Marino, a decorated quarterback out of the University of Pittsburgh, to select Texas Tech defensive tackle Gabriel Rivera. To say that decision haunted the Steelers for a great number of years would be a tremendous understatement. The Chief reminded his sons of the error of their ways regularly.

Terry Bradshaw had always been a tough gamer at quarterback. He was big and strong, and he played the position physically. In 1982, the wear and tear on his body caught up to him. But he still played every game.

After injuring his right elbow in training camp, Bradshaw required a cortisone shot to play each week. Once the Steelers had been bounced from the playoffs, he underwent surgery to repair it. His recuperation caused him to miss the beginning of the 1983 campaign.

In Bradshaw's place stood Stoudt, and while entering his fourth year in the league, he had appeared in only fourteen games, with just one previous start. As could be expected, the young quarterback struggled.

After losing their 1983 season opener at home in a seven-turnover debacle, the Steelers reeled off nine wins in their next ten games, including seven in a row, to stand at 9–2. Then, they suffered three straight losses, the second a 45–3 thrashing by the Detroit Lions on Thanksgiving Day.

For Week Fifteen, the Steelers drew a Saturday date at New York's Shea Stadium to take on the Jets, and the club welcomed Bradshaw back to the starting lineup. Seeing his first game action of the season, Bradshaw came out gunning.

He opened the scoring with a first-quarter seventeen-yard touchdown pass to receiver Gregg Garrity to give the Steelers a 7–0 lead. In the second quarter, however, when throwing a ten-yard touchdown pass to Calvin Sweeney, Bradshaw felt his surgically-repaired elbow give way.

Bradshaw's second touchdown pass of the game would be his last pass thrown in the NFL. His injury overshadowed the Steelers' 34–7 victory.

Despite losing the final game of the season to the Browns in Cleveland, the Steelers' 10–6 mark was good enough to win their first AFC Central Division title since 1979. Their reward was a bye week in the first round of the playoffs before heading west to take on the Raiders, now playing in Los Angeles, yet one more time.

The Steelers, with Stoudt at quarterback, jumped out to a 3–0 lead on a seventeen-yard field goal by Gary Anderson in the first quarter. Still in the first quarter and deep in his own end of the field, Stoudt threw an interception to Raiders' cornerback Lester Hayes, who returned it eighteen yards for a touchdown. The Raiders never looked back in a one-sided 38–10 victory.

The Steelers' season had ended, while the Raiders continued on, capping their strong play three weeks later with a resounding 38–9 victory over the Redskins in Super Bowl XVIII.

In March, Mel Blount announced his retirement after playing fourteen seasons with the Steelers. Over his career, Blount was a five-time Pro Bowler, a two-time first-team All-Pro, four-time second-team All-Pro, and NFL Defensive Player of the Year in 1975.

He wasn't the only Steeler star to call it a career. Having come back too soon from his elbow injury, Terry Bradshaw also retired ahead of the 1984 season. Along with Tom Brady, Bradshaw is remembered as one of the best big-game quarterbacks in the history of the NFL, leading the Steelers to four Super Bowl championships, six

AFC championship games, and eight straight playoff appearances, compiling a 14–5 record in those playoff games.

At the start of the 1984 season, the Steelers handed the reins of the offense to quarterback David Woodley, and his first touchdown pass for the Black and Gold was an eighty-yard completion to the exciting rookie receiver, Louis Lipps. Unfortunately, not only did the Steelers lose their season opener, but Lambert also dislocated his toe on the very first series of the game, an injury that would plague him throughout the season.

The 1984 campaign saw the Steelers bang around at about the .500 mark for most of the season. A highlight came on October 14, in Week Seven, when they defeated the San Francisco 49ers 20–17 in Candlestick Park. It was to be the only loss suffered by the 49ers over the season, one which culminated with their triumph in Super Bowl XIX.

The Steelers clawed their way to two games over .500 with a Week Ten victory over the Oilers and finished the year with a 9–7 record and another division title. In the divisional round of the playoffs, they upset a 13–3 Broncos team in Denver by a score of 24–17, scoring the last fourteen points in the come-from-behind victory.

With a surprise berth in the AFC Championship team, the Steelers traveled to Miami to take on second-year star Marino and his Dolphins. Marino, who won the league's Most Valuable Player Award, showed the Steelers exactly what they missed out on in the 1983 draft. He completed twenty-one of thirty-two passes for 421 yards and four touchdowns on the afternoon, leading the Dolphins to a 45–28 victory.

In July, still hampered by the toe injury that caused him to miss eight games of the 1984 season, Jack Lambert retired after eleven years with the Steelers. Five years later, when Lambert was inducted into the Pro Football Hall of Fame, he said: "I was so fortunate to have played on some of the greatest teams of all time and arguably the greatest defense ever assembled. And finally, how fortunate I was to play for the Pittsburgh fans—proud and hard-working people that love their football and their players. If I could start my life all over again, I would be a professional football player, and you damn well better believe I would be a Pittsburgh Steeler."

In 1985, the Steelers lost four of their final five games to post a 7–9 record and miss the playoffs. It was the first losing season for the Steelers in fourteen years.

The year 1986 proved to be even worse. After losing six of their first seven, they stumbled to a 6–10 record on the season. The 1987 Steelers posted a winning record, going 8–7 for the year. At the season's conclusion, however, Stallworth announced his retirement, having caught 537 passes and scored sixty-three touchdowns over his remarkable fourteen-year career.

On August 25, 1988, less than two weeks ahead of the Steelers' season-opening game, Art Rooney Sr. died at age eighty-seven at Mercy Hospital, eight days after suffering a stroke in his Three Rivers Stadium office. The next day, a burial mass was conducted at St. Peter's Church, where 1,500 people paid their respects to the Chief. Rooney was buried at the North Side Catholic Cemetery in Pittsburgh, next to his wife of fifty-one years, Kathleen, who had passed away in 1982.

Perhaps playing on emotion, the 1988 Steelers opened the season with a 24–21 victory at home over the Cowboys. They then lost six in a row and ten out of eleven on the way to a 5–11 season, their worst record since 1969.

The year 1988 was the first—and still only—season since the AFL-NFL merger that the Steelers finished last in their division. It was also the last call for Mike Webster in a Steelers' uniform after fifteen seasons of suiting up for the club. Webster would finish his distinguished career with two additional seasons with the Chiefs.

Chuck Noll started his twenty-first season as head coach in 1989 with a young roster in an attempt to break out of the doldrums of four disappointing seasons and get back into contention. The season, however, probably could not have started any worse.

The Steelers were walloped at home in their season opener against the Browns, losing 51–0, the worst defeat in the franchise's history. It didn't get much better the second week either, as they lost to the Bengals 41–10.

They righted the skid the following week, but the team still struggled to reel off a string of wins. At the end of Week Ten, the Steelers' record stood at just 4–6, last in the Central Division.

It took until the final week of the season, a win against the Buccaneers in Tampa, for the Steelers to qualify for the playoffs. Their clutch three-game win streak to close the regular season allowed them to clinch the final playoff spot.

In the first round of the playoffs, the club traveled to Houston to take on the Oilers in what proved to be an exciting game. The Steelers led most of the game, only to see the Oilers come back and take a fourth-quarter lead. A two-yard touchdown run by running back Merril Hoge, however, got the Steelers tied and sent the game into overtime.

In the extra period, kicker Gary Anderson booted a fifty-yard field goal to clinch the win and quiet the Astrodome crowd.

The divisional round of the playoffs the next week saw the Steelers visit the Broncos at Mile High Stadium in Denver. Again, Noll coaxed a solid game out of the Black and Gold, and they nearly pulled off the upset before losing 24–23 on a one-yard plunge by running back Mel Bratton with just 2:22 remaining in the game.

The Steelers outperformed expectations in 1989 and made a solid run in the playoffs. For his coaching results, Noll was named the NFL's Coach of the Year for, remarkably, the only time in his coaching career. It would prove to be, however, the final team that Noll guided into the postseason.

Chapter 27

A NEW ERA

huck Noll coached two more seasons after 1989 but never again made the playoffs. In 1990, the team started 1–3 and didn't score an offensive touchdown in the process. Fifth-year quarterback Bubby Brister rallied the club to finish the season 9–7 but came up just shy of a playoff berth when the team lost to the Oilers in the final game of the regular season.

Noll's 1991 Steelers suffered through an early four-game losing streak to drop their record to 3–6. They were never able to put together a winning streak to recover and finished the season with a losing record of 7–9.

Four days after the end of the season, on December 26, Noll retired, stepping down from his position as head coach of the Steelers after twenty-three years. His final two games coached were 17–10 victories over divisional rivals Cincinnati and Cleveland.

Noll finished his career with a coaching record of 193–148–1 in the regular season. In the postseason, he posted a 16–8 record with, of course, four Super Bowl championships.

Noll had changed the Steelers' fortunes, beginning with his savvy drafting, something that started with the selection of Greene soon after he accepted the head coaching role. It reached its apex with the unbelievable 1974 draft class of four Hall of Famers.

Noll and the Steelers had always found talent in the middle and late rounds of the draft, but he had a poor record of first-round selections from 1975–1991. Only one of those first-rounders, Hall of Fame cornerback Rod Woodson, drafted in 1987, would become a definitive star in the league.

Poor tops of the draft eventually caught up with Noll and the Steelers, as they reached double digits in wins only once in Noll's last twelve years—1983's 10–6 record. In four of Noll's final seasons, the Steelers had losing records.

With all of Noll's success, it wasn't easy for fans to accept that the time was right to retire and hand the helm over to a new coach. But Steeler Nation quickly learned

Noll hadn't left the cupboard bare for a new coaching staff. In addition to Woodson, Noll had brought in players like Hoge, Neil O'Donnell, Barry Foster, Dermontti Dawson, John Jackson, Greg Lloyd, and Carnell Lake, all players who would make up the core of the Steelers' next championship-contending teams.

On January 21, 1992, Bill Cowher was hired to take over for Noll as head coach of the Steelers. Cowher was a local product, born and raised in the Pittsburgh suburb of Crafton. At Carlynton High in Carnegie, Cowher excelled in football, basketball, and track and took his talents to North Carolina State after graduation.

As a professional football player, Cowher spent five seasons in the NFL, three with Cleveland and two with Philadelphia, playing mostly on special teams as a reserve linebacker. Prior to the 1985 season, Cowher, realizing his limitations as a player, moved into the coaching ranks, joining the staff of Marty Schottenheimer in Cleveland.

When Schottenheimer moved on to Kansas City, Cowher went with him, and there he served as the Chiefs' defensive coordinator for three seasons. His total apprenticeship as a professional football coach had been just seven seasons.

Cowher was just thirty-four years old when he took over as the Steelers' fifteenth head coach, and he immediately achieved results. His first team won the division with an 11–5 record and clinched home-field advantage in the playoffs. And while it was eventually all for naught as the Bills ousted the Steelers with a 24–3 win in the divisional round, the stage was set for success, and Cowher was recognized as the NFL's Coach of the Year.

In 1993, Cowher again led the Steelers to the playoffs with a 9–7 record, in large part to Woodson's outstanding season that earned him the Defensive Player of the Year Award. However, the team was once again bounced from the playoffs after just one game, an overtime 27–24 defeat in Kansas City.

It was linebacker Lloyd's turn to win the Defensive Player of the Year award in 1994, and that Steelers team went 12–4. They also broke out of the first round of the playoffs after they defeated the Browns handily, 29–9. However, in the AFC Championship Game the very next week in Three Rivers Stadium, the Steelers couldn't hold a 13–3 third-quarter lead against the Chargers. Quarterback Stan Humphries threw two forty-three-yard touchdown passes to squash the Steelers' attempt to return to the Super Bowl.

The 1995 Steelers won their first two games, but then lost four of five to fall to a record of 3–4. Then, they reeled off an eight-game winning streak before losing to the Packers 24–19 in the season finale at Green Bay. With a record of 11–5, they won the division title and hosted the Buffalo Bills in a playoff game.

The Bills were a star-studded team led by quarterback and Pittsburgh native Jim Kelly, featuring great players like Thurman Thomas and Bruce Smith. They had played in four consecutive Super Bowls, losing them all, before having their streak broken the year before when they had missed the playoffs.

The Steelers ended any thoughts of a Bills' return to the Super Bowl by jumping out to a quick 20–0 second-quarter lead. After a fourth-quarter Thomas touchdown reception from Kelly closed the gap to just five, the Steelers salted the game away with two Bam Morris touchdown runs to win 40–21.

That victory put the Steelers into their second consecutive AFC Championship Game, again at home, but this time against the surprising Indianapolis Colts (the Colts had relocated to Indianapolis in 1984). In an exciting, hard-hitting game that wasn't settled until the very last play, the Steelers came from behind on four occasions to either tie or take the lead. Morris's one-yard touchdown plunge provided the difference in the Steelers' 20–16 victory. For the first time in sixteen years, the Steelers were headed back to the Super Bowl.

Super Bowl XXX matched the Steelers with the Cowboys, and both teams aimed to add a fifth Vince Lombardi Trophy to their trophy case. Doing so would tie the San Francisco 49ers for the most Super Bowl championships—the 49ers had won their fifth just the year before.

The game would prove to be the first loss suffered by the Steelers in a Super Bowl, with the difference lying in turnovers. Dallas won the turnover battle 3–0, and converting turnovers into touchdowns, they won the game.

Cowboys' cornerback Larry Brown, a former twelfth-round draft pick, intercepted quarterback Neil O'Donnell twice in the second half on his way to being named the game's Most Valuable Player. With the Cowboys leading 13–7 midway through the third quarter, Brown victimized O'Donnell with his first interception, returning it forty-four yards to the Steelers' eighteen-yard line. Shortly after, Emmitt Smith scored on a one-yard touchdown run to stretch the Cowboys' lead.

In the fourth quarter, O'Donnell led a furious comeback attempt by the Steelers, cutting the score to 20–17. Brown then ended all Pittsburgh hopes with his second interception, returning it to the Steelers' six-yard line. Smith's four-yard rushing touchdown finished the scoring in the Steelers' disappointing 27–17 defeat.

The Steelers won division crowns again in 1996 and 1997, and each year, they won their first playoff game. At the end of the 1997 season, they advanced once again to the AFC Championship Game but lost to the Broncos 24–21 at Three Rivers to miss out on a return trip to the Super Bowl, a game the Broncos would go on to win two weeks later.

The Steelers then finished off the 1990s with two losing seasons, going 7–9 and 6–10. They started the new millennium with a 9–7 record but narrowly missed out on qualifying for the playoffs for the third straight season. In the 2000 season finale on December 24, the Steelers defeated the Chargers 34–21. It would mark the final Steelers game at Three Rivers Stadium.

Pittsburgh has a long history in medical research, and it's particularly known as a major center for immunological research, or the study of the human body's immune system. It began its ascent in the field almost eighty years ago.

Upon the creation of the University of Pittsburgh School of Medicine in the early 1900s, chancellor Samuel McCormick, modeling the institution after top medical schools in the United States, began recruiting accomplished researchers for faculty positions. Soon, the university opened a new medical school building and forged relationships with both St. Francis and Mercy hospitals.

William McEllroy was elected dean by the medical school faculty in 1938, and he immediately worked to establish Pitt Med as a first-rate research institution. World War II, however, delayed his plans.

At the end of the war, McEllroy and the school benefited greatly from the influx of funds from industrialists and philanthropists as a key part of the first Pittsburgh Renaissance. McEllroy was an integral force in steering a portion of new endowments to fund a university-wide interdisciplinary research program known as the Division of Research in the Natural Sciences. With that McEllroy set off on recruiting researchers from around the country.

Recognizing virology as a promising field that could lift the national status of Pitt Med, McEllroy fundraised for virus research, and in 1946, he secured funds from the National Foundation for Infantile Paralysis (NFIP) to start the school's Virus Research Laboratory. Needing a director for the new laboratory, McEllroy convinced a young assistant professor of immunology at the University of Michigan School of Public Health to lead the charge—his name was Jonas Salk.

Starting in 1947, Salk aggressively built the laboratory from, literally, below ground—the lab was just two basement rooms with one technician in Municipal Hospital. Seeing the benefits of funding, Salk agreed to the tedious study of typing poliovirus, and the NFIP provided large grants. In short time, the laboratory expanded to take up two floors of Municipal Hospital, and Salk, now a full professor, started hiring associates.

At the end of the typing study in 1951, Salk's laboratory concluded there were three types of poliovirus. And, with that discovery, the team pivoted its efforts into producing a vaccine. Salk decided to pursue a killed-poliovirus vaccine instead of an attenuated-virus vaccine favored by most other scientists.

Another Pitt Med researcher, William McDowall Hammon, the chair of the Department of Epidemiology and Microbiology at the Graduate School of Public Health, was also pursuing a vaccine. An experienced polio researcher recruited from the University of California, Berkeley, McDowall steered clear of both killed-virus and attenuated-virus vaccine research and concentrated his efforts on passive immunization through gamma-globulin injections containing polio-resistant antibodies.

McDowall's NFIP-funded studies from 1951–1952 showed promise in passive immunization to fight polio. However, the produced immunity was only temporary, and gamma-globulin was scarce.

In 1953, Salk completed his first human trials of the killed-virus vaccine. In 1954, a national field trial was conducted with over 1.8 million children. On April 12, 1955, the overseer of the trial, Thomas Francis, declared the polio vaccine to be safe and effective.

The polio vaccine shot Salk into the rarified orbit of celebratory scientists. Later in 1955, he received both the Congressional Gold Medal and a Presidential Citation. The following year, he received the Albert Lasker Clinical Medical Research Award.

In 1963, Salk left Pitt Med to head his Salk Institute for Biological Studies in La Jolla, California. But he left an indelible mark in Pittsburgh as a major research center for the medical sciences.

From 2020–2021, the University of Pittsburgh received $597.8 million in funding from the National Institutes of Health (NIH), which went to 1,193 projects. According to the NIH's annual report, Pitt ranked eleventh in funding and fifth in the number of awards for the year.

Healthcare and medical research continue to lead the way in Pittsburgh, as the University of Pittsburgh Medical Center organizations and the Allegheny Health Network top the list of employers in the region.

Ahead of the 2001 season, the Steelers moved into their comfortable new digs at Heinz Field, their new stadium. Ground had been broken on the new stadium in 1999, and it was completed after the implosion of Three Rivers in February.

The sparkling new stadium differed tremendously from Three Rivers in that it was not designed to be a multi-purpose stadium. No longer did the Steelers and Pirates have to share a stadium that was not ideal for their particular use.

Heinz Field was built for $281 million and stands along the Ohio River in the North Shore neighborhood. Not to be one to shy away from the community's roots, the stadium used over 12,000 tons of steel in its construction.

Perhaps energized by their new home, the Steelers' three-year absence from the playoffs was broken by the outstanding 2001 team, led by Defensive Rookie of the Year Kendrell Bell at linebacker, Kordell Stewart at quarterback, and Jerome Bettis at running back. After losing their opener in Jacksonville against the Jaguars, the Steelers rolled off twelve victories in their next thirteen games and finished the season with a 13–3 record.

In the first round of the playoffs, the Steelers handled the Baltimore Ravens, their heated division rivals, 27–10. That set them up to host the AFC Championship Game the next week.

With a berth to Super Bowl XXXVI on the line, the Steelers welcomed the New England Patriots into Heinz Field, a team led by a rookie quarterback named Tom Brady. Brady had taken over the starting position when Drew Bledsoe had been injured in the second week of the season, and he had led them to an 11–5 record and the AFC East title.

With the Patriots leading 7–3 late in the first half, courtesy of a fifty-five-yard punt return touchdown by Troy Brown, Brady injured his leg and had to leave the game. Bledsoe came on in relief and threw an eleven-yard touchdown pass to David Patten to press the lead to 14–3 entering halftime.

It was to be the only offensive touchdown scored by the Patriots on the afternoon. Still, it proved to be enough.

The Patriots put the first second-half points on the board with a return of a blocked field goal for a touchdown. Stewart then tried to lead a come-back effort, but his two interceptions in the final three minutes killed any chance at a rally. The Patriots won, 24–17, and they would go on to upset the (now) St. Louis Rams two weeks later to win their first Super Bowl championship.

Again, the Steelers had come oh-so-close to the Super Bowl. It was Cowher's third loss in the AFC Championship Game in his ten years as head coach.

Ahead of the 2002 season, the NFL realigned its divisional structure. The Steelers were placed in the AFC North Division, along with the Ravens, Bengals, and the new Cleveland Browns, who had joined the league as an expansion club for the 1999 season. The Steelers went 10–5–1 on the season, with the tie coming in Week Ten against the Atlanta Falcons when neither team could score in overtime.

Champions of the AFC North, the Steelers hosted the Browns for the Wild Card playoff round and dispatched them in a thriller. Down twelve points in the fourth quarter, quarterback Tommy Maddox led a comeback effort. When running back Chris Fuamatu-Ma'afala scored on a three-yard run with only fifty-four seconds remaining, it lifted the Steelers to a 36–33 triumph.

For the divisional round of the playoffs, the Steelers traveled to Tennessee, where the Oilers had relocated in 1997 and renamed themselves the Titans. It proved to be another thrilling game, but the Steelers fell short this time around, losing 34–31 when Titans kicker Joe Nedney converted on a short field goal in overtime.

In 2003, the Steelers suffered a spate of injuries as they stumbled to a 6–10 record in a season where they did not win two games in succession. As of this writing, it remains the last Steelers team to close a season with a losing record.

A big reason for the long number of consecutive winning seasons after 2003's dismal record can be traced back to the 2004 NFL Draft, where the Steelers selected quarterback Ben Roethlisberger out of Miami, Ohio with the eleventh overall choice. Undoubtedly a future Hall of Famer, Roethlisberger played eighteen years for the Steelers, retiring after the 2021 season with over 64,000 passing yards and 418 touchdown passes.

As a rookie, Roethlisberger started the 2004 season as the third-string quarterback, serving the traditional rookie's apprenticeship behind starter Maddox and backup Charlie Batch. Then, in the second game of the season, Maddox injured his elbow. With Batch limited with a knee injury, the Steelers turned to Roethlisberger as their starter.

In his first game starting at quarterback, Roethlisberger threw an interception on *his first pass of the game*. Not to be deterred, "Big Ben" led the team to victory. In fact, he led the Steelers to victory in each of the thirteen games he started before getting injured in the penultimate game of the season.

In relief, a healthy Maddox led the team to victory in the finale, a 29–24 victory over the Bills, to close the regular season with a 15–1 record. It remains the best record in franchise history.

With a two-week break before the first playoff game, Roethlisberger got healthy enough to start the divisional playoff game against the Jets. His four-yard touchdown pass to receiver Hines Ward with six minutes remaining forced overtime, and when kicker Jeff Reed converted a thirty-three-yard field goal in the extra stanza, the Steelers escaped with a 20–17 victory.

The next week, the Steelers hosted the AFC Championship Game for the fifth time in eleven years—this time again against the Patriots, who they had defeated 34–20 in Week Eight of the regular season. In the game though, the veteran Brady outplayed the rookie Roethlisberger, who threw three interceptions, including one returned eighty-seven yards for a touchdown by safety Rodney Harrison, in a 41–27 defeat. The Patriots would go on to win Super Bowl XXXIX.

For the fourth time in eleven years, the Steelers had painstakingly lost an AFC Championship Game at home. In three of those four losses, the winner had gone on to win the Super Bowl.

After the disappointment in the way the 2004 season ended, the Steelers set off to reload. In the first round of the 2005 NFL draft, they selected tight end Heath Miller out of the University of Virginia in the first round with the thirtieth overall pick. He would immediately become another weapon for Roethlisberger to target.

The Steelers began the 2005 campaign well, and just past the halfway mark of the regular season, they had a 7–2 record and were tied with the Bengals for the division lead. Then, they lost a 16–13 overtime game in Baltimore that started a three-game skid. Standing at 7–5, the Steelers were in danger of missing the playoffs.

They righted the ship the next week at home against the Chicago Bears in Week Fourteen and added another three victories to end the season on a four-game win streak. With an 11–5 record, they qualified for the playoffs with the sixth and final seed.

In their first-round matchup, they had to travel to Cincinnati and take on the division champion Bengals. After falling behind 10–0 in the first quarter, Roethlisberger engineered a comeback victory with three touchdown passes. The Steelers' 31–17 victory advanced them in the playoffs.

Being the sixth seed, the Steelers then had to travel to Indianapolis to take on Peyton Manning and the 14–2 Colts, winners of the AFC South Division. The Steelers dominated the game for fifty-five of the sixty minutes. Then, the last five minutes got downright exciting.

The Steelers led 21–10 when All-Pro Steelers safety Troy Polamalu made a diving interception of a Manning pass at mid-field. The turnover, with 5:26 remaining on the clock, would have allowed the Steelers to run precious time off the clock. However, referee Pete Morelli overturned the interception call and possession reverted to the Colts.

Manning quickly moved the Colts downfield, and Edgerrin James scored on a three-yard run. Manning then connected with Reggie Wayne for a two-point conversion to narrow the score to 21–18.

Pittsburgh was forced to punt on their ensuing possession. But the defense held, and their fifth sack of the game forced the Colts to turn the ball over on downs at their own two-yard line with 1:20 on the clock.

The game appeared to be over, and disgruntled Colts fans were flocking toward the exits. All that changed on the very next play.

On first down, Roethlisberger handed the ball off to the normally sure-handed Bettis, but "the Bus" fumbled when he was hit by Colts linebacker Gary Brackett before he could get into the end zone.

Colts cornerback Nick Harper scooped up the ball and took off on what was in all probability going to be a game-winning touchdown return.

Roethlisberger, never the most fleet of foot, even as a young player, backpedaled as Harper sprinted down the field. Faked out by a Harper move, Roethlisberger spun around and tumbled. On his way down, Roethlisberger's right hand grabbed Harper's right ankle just enough to make the tackle on the Colts' forty-two-yard line.

Franco Harris had the Immaculate Reception. Roethlisberger had his game-saving shoestring tackle.

"Once in a blue moon, Jerome fumbles," said Roethlisberger. "Once in a blue moon, I make a tackle. They just happened to be in the same game."

Manning still had a last chance. He completed two passes to move the ball to the Steelers' twenty-seven-yard line, setting up a forty-six-yard field goal attempt by Colts kicker Matt Vanderjagt to force the game into overtime.

Vanderjagt's attempt was wide right of the upright, and the Steelers escaped Indy with a 21–18 victory.

The next week, the Steelers traveled to Denver to take on the Broncos in the AFC Championship Game. The Broncos had earned their way there with a 13–3 regular season record and 27–13 victory over the defending Super Bowl champion Patriots in the divisional playoff round.

This time, the Steelers would give their fans a much less anxious time. They scored three second-quarter touchdowns to take a 24–3 lead into the intermission. At the end of the game, the score stood 34–17 in favor of the Black and Gold.

With three straight postseason victories on the road, the Steelers had earned a berth to Super Bowl XL at Ford Field in Detroit.

Super Bowl XL took place on February 5, 2006, in the Detroit Lions' new facility, Ford Field, which had opened before the 2002 season. The Steelers' opponents were the Seattle Seahawks, who were playing in the franchise's first Super Bowl in their thirty-year history.

The Seahawks had started the season 2–2 before reeling off a team-record eleven consecutive victories on a way to a 13–3 record and the NFC West title. Playing both of their playoff games at home, the Seahawks easily dispatched both the Redskins and the Carolina Panthers to get to Detroit.

Coached by Mike Holmgren, who had coached the Green Bay Packers to victory in Super Bowl XXXI, the Seahawks featured the league's top-scoring offense. Quarterback Matt Hasselbeck directed a solid passing game, and running back Shaun Alexander earned Most Valuable Player honors after rushing for 1,880 yards and scoring twenty-eight touchdowns, twenty-seven on rushes.

Defensively, the Seahawks featured just one Pro Bowler, rookie middle linebacker Lofa Tatupu. However, the Seahawks led the NFL with fifty quarterback sacks.

When the Steelers were introduced as a team, they sent thirty-three-year-old veteran running back Bettis out first, acknowledging the future Hall of Famer was playing his last game and doing so in the Super Bowl being played in his hometown.

Despite the two potent offenses, the first quarter got off to a slow start, with each of the first four possessions ending with punts. Thanks to both a short punt and a good punt return, the Seahawks began their third possession at midfield. After two pass completions, Hasselbeck hit receiver Darrell Jackson in the end zone for an apparent touchdown to give the Seahawks the lead. The play, however, was called back due to an offensive pass interference penalty called on Jackson.

Later in the series, the Seahawks were forced to settle for a forty-seven-yard field goal by Josh Brown, and they took a 3–0 lead with just twenty-two seconds remaining in the first quarter. It was a first quarter that saw Roethlisberger complete just one pass for one yard, with the Steelers failing to gain a single first down.

The Steelers' offense didn't start the second quarter any better and were forced to punt after a three-and-out possession. After a Seahawks' punt, the Steelers sustained a drive for the first time, but that possession ended when a Roethlisberger pass was intercepted by Seattle safety Michael Boulware at the Seahawks' seventeen-yard line.

The defense again bailed the Steelers out, delivering a three-and-out of their own and forcing the Seahawks to punt once again. Again, the Steelers drove into Seahawk's territory.

With a penalty and a sack, though, the Steelers faced a third down with twenty-eight yards to go for a first. On the play, Roethlisberger was forced to scramble but still managed to find Ward for a thirty-seven-yard gain. It was the longest third-down conversion in Super Bowl history.

On a third-down play after the two-minute warning, Roethlisberger faked a handoff and dove into the end zone for a touchdown. With the score, the Steelers took a 7–3 lead into halftime.

The Steelers received the second-half kickoff, and almost immediately struck a decisive blow. On the second play from scrimmage, running back Willie Parker broke through the line and sped off for a seventy-five-yard touchdown run, the longest run in Super Bowl history. With that, the Steelers held a 14–3 lead.

Seattle moved the ball again, but when the drive stalled, Brown missed a field goal from fifty yards away, his second long miss of the afternoon—just before the first half ended he had missed a fifty-four-yard attempt.

Looking to put the game away, Roethlisberger and the offense drove fifty-four yards to reach the Seahawks' six-yard line. But, on the next play, Seahawks defensive back Kelly Herndon picked off a Roethlisberger pass and returned it seventy-six yards to give the Seahawks a new breath of life at the Steelers' own twenty-yard line.

Two plays later, Hasselbeck's sixteen-yard touchdown pass to tight end Jerramy Stevens cut the Steelers' lead to just 14–10.

The game settled down a little after the spurt of big plays, and the teams exchanged punts—two from the Steelers, one from the Seahawks. As the third quarter came to a close, the Seahawks had advanced the ball to midfield after starting on their two-yard line.

It was all to play for in Super Bowl XL as the fourth quarter started.

In the final quarter, the Seahawks continued their long drive, advancing to the Steelers' nineteen-yard line. Then, Hasselbeck again connected with Stevens on an apparent eighteen-yard completion to move the ball to the one—the word "apparent" being an important qualifier. On the play, Seattle tackle Sean Locklear was flagged for holding, and the ten-yard penalty negated the play and the Seahawks' go-ahead score.

Three plays later, Steelers cornerback Ike Taylor intercepted Hasselbeck to eliminate the threat. With a penalty called on Hasselbeck on the tackle, the Steelers took possession with great field position at their forty-four-yard line.

Four plays later, the Steelers ran a trick play, calling a wide receiver reverse, one in which Roethlisberger first pitched the ball to Parker, who swept to his left and handed off to receiver Antwaan Randle El running in the opposite direction.

If Randle El had run the ball, that would have been tricky enough. But he didn't. Randle El, who played quarterback in college, threw a perfect pass on the run, hitting Ward in stride for a forty-three-yard touchdown pass.

The play was the first time a receiver threw a touchdown pass in the Super Bowl. With Reed's conversion, the Steelers held a 21–10 lead with just 8:56 remaining in the contest.

On their next possession, the Seahawks drove briefly before being held up by the Steelers' defense just past midfield. After Seahawks punter Tom Rouen punted into the end zone, the Steelers took possession at their twenty-yard line, looking to finish off the game.

Pittsburgh leaned heavily on Bettis, who had seven of his fourteen rushes on the game during the possession. The Steelers milked over four minutes off the clock and forced the Seahawks to call all three of their timeouts. Still, when the Seahawks took over on their own twenty-yard line, they had just under two minutes in which to work a miraculous comeback.

The Seahawks' comeback never materialized, however. After driving into scoring territory, Seattle ended up turning the ball over on downs when a Hasselbeck pass to Stevens fell incomplete.

A Roethlisberger kneel-down was the final play of the game, and when time expired, the Steelers had a 21–10 victory in Super Bowl XL. The franchise finally had its fifth Super Bowl championship, or one for the thumb.

The Steelers had won the game despite losing the turnover battle, turning the ball over twice to the Seahawks' single turnover. Additionally, Roethlisberger, who became the second-youngest quarterback to start a Super Bowl and the youngest to win it, completed just nine of twenty-one passes for only 123 yards.

The differences in the game were the two explosive touchdown plays and Taylor's interception deep in scoring territory. The game's Most Valuable Player was Ward, who caught five passes for 123 yards and scored a touchdown.

Finally, after so many close calls and could have, should have, and would have opportunities, Cowher had succeeded in obtaining the crown jewel of his coaching career.

In the offseason leading up to the 2006 season, Roethlisberger was involved in a motorcycle accident in downtown Pittsburgh. Not wearing a helmet, he suffered a broken jaw and nose, in addition to a deep laceration on the back of his head. His various injuries required seven hours of surgery at Mercy Hospital.

The injuries set back Roethlisberger's conditioning, but he did manage to participate in most of training camp and part of the preseason schedule. Right after the preseason though, Big Ben required an emergency appendectomy, which caused him to miss the season opener, a 28–17 win over the Dolphins engineered by backup quarterback Batch.

Through his various ailments and surgeries, Roethlisberger reportedly lost fifteen pounds and wasn't in peak physical condition. He returned in Week Two but was ineffective against the Jaguars in Jacksonville, throwing two interceptions in the Steelers' 9–0 shutout loss.

The Steelers lost five of their next six games, including an overtime loss in Atlanta in Week Seven, where Roethlisberger got roughed up even more, seemingly affecting his play for several more weeks. The team suffered losses in the next two games. At the midpoint of the season, the defending Super Bowl champions had just a 2–6 record.

By the time the Steelers turned the season around, winning six of their last eight games, it was too late to salvage the season. They ended up with an 8–8 record, finishing third in the AFC North, and failed to reach the playoffs.

Five days after the season ended, Cowher announced his retirement. Spending his entire fifteen-year head coaching career with the Steelers, Cowher retired with a record of 149–90–1, with one Super Bowl championship, two total Super Bowl appearances, and six AFC Championship Game appearances.

Chapter 28

A NEW ECONOMY CITY & ANOTHER SUPER BOWL CHAMPIONSHIP

The G20, also known as the Group of Twenty, is an intergovernmental forum comprising nineteen countries and the European Union, or the EU, which itself is an economic and political union of twenty-seven separate countries. But, hey, G20 has a better ring to it than G46.

Formed in 1999 as the direct result of several global economic crises, the G20 meets annually. In 2009, Pittsburgh hosted the annual summit, and it was quite the coup—and honor—for the city.

US President Barack Obama volunteered to host the 2009 summit, with initial plans calling for it to be held in New York. After coordination issues emerged with the Big Apple, the Obama administration moved the summit site to Pittsburgh, in great part to highlight the city's transformation and economic recovery.

The 2009 G20 Summit was centered at the David L. Lawrence Convention Center, the first Leadership in Energy and Environmental Design (LEED) certified convention center in North America—and for many years the world's largest LEED-certified building. And, of course, the G20 Pittsburgh Summit drew its usual gaggle of protestors.

But let's not allow that to overshadow why the summit was there in the first place. It was in Pittsburgh because world leaders wanted to show the art of the possible for cities around the world. Pittsburgh, born of an industrialized past, was now a beacon of the New Economy.

In 1970, about one in three jobs in the Pittsburgh region were in manufacturing. Today, about one in five jobs lie in health care. In addition to health care, Pittsburgh also boasts a strong foundation in business and financial services. Then, there's the tremendous foundation Pittsburgh has built in the technology world.

The Pittsburgh Supercomputing Center (PSC) was founded in 1986 as a joint effort between the University of Pittsburgh and Carnegie Mellon University, and it was one of the original five National Science Foundation Supercomputing Centers.

Its mission has always been to facilitate and harness the full range of information technologies to enable discovery in US science and engineering, and it placed Pittsburgh as one of the leaders and influencers of the Information Age.

Like its healthcare and medical research professions, Pittsburgh's technology presence can trace its origins to the city's academic pedigree. Carnegie Mellon created one of the first computer science programs in the world, and the institution continues to rank among the top schools in the discipline. As such, CMU enjoys collaborative tie-ins with leading technology companies like Apple and Intel, further expanding the high-tech base in Pittsburgh.

Related to technology entrepreneurism and early-stage tech startups, in 2013, the University of Pittsburgh launched its Innovation Institute as a hub for innovation and entrepreneurship. The Institute provides services, such as protecting intellectual property, commercializing new discoveries, mentoring, and more.

Built on academia and entrepreneurship, the high-tech sector in Pittsburgh continues to blossom and bear fruit. In June 2022, *Startup Genome* ranked Pittsburgh thirteenth among the world's emerging startup ecosystems.[12] At this rate, the next Silicon Valley just might be in the Steel City.

In April 2022, data from the Computing Technology Industry Association (CompTIA) pegged Pittsburgh's regional high-tech employment at over 60,000, making it the twenty-ninth largest metropolitan area in the United States for technology. It's estimated the regional technology industry delivers upwards of $12.2 billion in economic impact, reflective of national trends accounting for approximately 8.5 percent of the total local economy.[13]

In 2021, the Pittsburgh Technology Council released its State of the Industry Report, where it reported the technology establishments in the thirteen counties across southwestern Pennsylvania employed over 305,000 people, comprising over 25 percent of the total regional workforce.[14]

Tech jobs tend to be good jobs too. According to that CompTIA report, tech workers in Pittsburgh earn a median of $82,820 annually, or 92 percent more than the median wage for the region.

Pittsburgh's technology prowess doesn't come without its challenges, however. The local industry continues to struggle with representation in its workforce. Racial and ethnic minorities are moderately underrepresented in the regional technology workforce, and women are drastically underrepresented. That underrepresentation threatens the sector's ability to maintain its growth rate regionally.

A turning point in Pittsburgh tech happened in 2006 when Google made its presence known beyond that of its almost ubiquitous web browser. That year,

Google hired Andrew W. Moore, a Carnegie Mellon University professor of computer science and robotics, to head up its new engineering office built within CMU. It wasn't long before that office outgrew its confines and moved into a new facility in Bakery Square.

Facebook, Uber, Microsoft, Amazon, Apple, and Zoom—all have a presence in the yinzer technology community. In the fields of artificial intelligence and robotics, among others, groundbreaking work takes place daily where steel mills once ruled the roost.

The tech web in Pittsburgh connects so many of the region's New Economy sectors, bridging industries like software and hardware technology, medical and scientific research, health care, and other verticals. In addition, it connects Pittsburgh tech to other tech concerns around the globe.

One of many examples is a collaboration that is near and dear to the heart of one of the authors of this book. Two Carnegie Mellon alumni have a company, Emerald Cloud Lab (ECL), headquartered in the San Francisco Bay area, and their concepts are helping CMU build the world's first Academic Cloud Lab. Researchers who use the Cloud Lab order experiments over the internet, and a combination of robotic instrumentation and trained technicians in the Cloud Lab perform the experiments exactly as specified. Data is then returned to the researchers, typically within a day.

Why Carnegie Mellon and not some other institution? Well, CMU is perfect for the application, with world-leading expertise in artificial intelligence, machine learning, robotics, biologics, genomics, proteomics, materials science, and computational biology.

You can't get that just anywhere. You have to go to . . . Pittsburgh.

On January 21, 2007, the day of the AFC and NFC Championship Games, the Steelers chose Mike Tomlin to become their next head coach. His selection ended a two-and-a-half-week search in which Tomlin was considered a longshot for the position, behind more notable and experienced coaches like Steelers' offensive coordinator Ken Whisenhunt and assistant coach Russ Grimm.

In fact, that Sunday's *Pittsburgh Tribune-Review* sported a headline that stated Grimm would be announced the following day as the Steelers' head coach.

Tomlin may have been a beneficiary of the NFL's so-called "Rooney Rule," a policy that Dan Rooney lobbied in support of that requires teams to interview ethnic-minority candidates for head coaching and senior football operation jobs.

The rule, still controversial in its impact on minority hiring in the NFL, was adopted in 2003.

Tomlin had begun his coaching career in 1995 in the college ranks, where his assistant coaching duties covered offense, defense, and special teams. In 1999, he moved to professional football, first with the Bengals for two years, and then on to Tampa, where he joined the staff of former Steelers player Tony Dungy to coach defensive backs. Tomlin stayed in Tampa after Jon Gruden took over as head coach, and the defense proved instrumental in the Buccaneers' march to victory in Super Bowl XXXVII in January 2003.

Tomlin then moved on to Minnesota, where he served as the Vikings' defensive coordinator for the 2006 season. Immediately following, Tomlin interviewed for the head coaching positions at both Miami and Pittsburgh. Pittsburgh won out on his services.

Like Cowher before him, Tomlin was just thirty-four years old when he was hired, and continued Pittsburgh's trend of hiring relatively young coaches—Noll had been thirty-eight years old when he was hired in 1969.

The 2007 season was the Steelers' seventy-fifth anniversary season, and the season started on the road, with the club visiting its long-time divisional rival, the Browns. The Steelers dominated the game, jumping to a seventeen-point lead in the first quarter on the way to a 34–7 victory.

The victory was not only a win in Tomlin's head coaching debut, but, for the first time, it moved the Steelers ahead in the all-time series against the Browns, fifty-six victories to the Browns' fifty-five.

Two more victories followed in succession before the Steelers tumbled in Week Four. After a Week Five 21–0 shutout victory over the Seahawks, the Steelers moved into their bye week with a 4–1 record.

The Steelers came out of their bye week with a 31–28 loss at Denver but then ran off wins in five of their next six games, the only blemish being a 19–16 overtime loss to the Jets in New York. The Week Eleven game against the Dolphins, coming on the heels of the disappointing loss in New York, remains one of the Steelers' more memorable games in recent history.

In front of a nationwide *Monday Night Football* audience, a torrential thunderstorm blanketed Pittsburgh, and the start of the game was delayed nearly a half hour due to lightning strikes. When play got underway, the rain continued to fall in buckets.

We're talking cats and dogs.

On the sodden turf of Heinz Field, players could barely move, and the impact was most evident on the two offenses. Both teams slogged around, struggling mightily to move the football, and for the game, the two teams combined for just twenty-two first downs, 375 total yards of offense and eleven punts.

The game remained scoreless until the Steelers' Reed converted a twenty-four-yard field goal attempt with only seventeen seconds remaining in the ballgame. The fact that the game had remained scoreless for fifty-nine minutes and forty-three seconds made it the NFL's longest scoreless tie in sixty-four years.

A week later, the Steelers defeated the Bengals, and with their record at 9–3, they enjoyed a comfortable position atop the division, holding a two-game lead over the Browns.

Down the stretch, though, the Steelers stumbled a bit. They lost two consecutive games, first on the road at New England, then at home against Jacksonville, spoiling their unbeaten record on the season at Heinz Field.

In a Thursday night game in St. Louis against the Rams, the Steelers ended their skid with a 41–24 victory. When the Browns lost three days later, the Steelers were handed their first divisional title in three years.

With a playoff berth clinched, Tomlin and his staff rested a good number of players for the season finale against Baltimore. After the Ravens jumped to a 17–0 first-half lead, a Steelers' rally fell short, and they closed the regular season with a 27–21 defeat.

Still, the Steelers had finished Tomlin's first season with a 10–6 record and the AFC North crown. For their reward, they would host a first-round playoff game against the wildcard Jacksonville Jaguars.

The Steelers looked to gain a measure of revenge for their loss to the Jaguars three weeks earlier, and they delivered the first blow in the contest when Najeh Davenport scored on a one-yard touchdown run early in the first quarter.

It took almost no time for the Jaguars to respond, however. Maurice Jones-Drew returned the ensuing kickoff ninety-six yards, setting up Fred Taylor's one-yard run to tie the score.

The big plays kept coming for the visiting Jaguars. In the second quarter, cornerback Rashean Mathis intercepted a Roethlisberger pass and returned it sixty-three yards for a touchdown. Before the first half ended, Jones-Drew scored on a forty-three-yard touchdown completion from quarterback David Gerrard. With the three unanswered scores, the Jaguars entered halftime holding a 21–7 lead.

After Jacksonville held strong deep in their own end of the field, the Steelers settled on a short twenty-eight-yard field goal by Reed to open the second-half scoring. However, the Jaguars pulled ahead even more when Jones-Drew scored from ten yards out to give the visitors an eighteen-point cushion heading into the fourth quarter.

Roethlisberger then led a furious comeback, connecting first with Santonio Holmes, and then with Miller on touchdown passes. After the Miller touchdown, however, a two-point conversion failed, leaving the Steelers trailing by five, 28–23, but with over ten minutes remaining.

With 6:21 remaining, Davenport scored on another one-yard touchdown run to give the Steelers their first lead since early in the contest, 29–28. But another failure on a two-point conversion left them with a precarious single-point advantage.

That was all the opening the Jaguars needed. At the end of what proved to be a game-winning drive, Jaguars kicker Josh Scobee booted a twenty-five-yard field goal with only thirty-seven seconds remaining.

The big plays of the first half and the missed two-point conversions had come back to haunt the Steelers. Their 31–29 defeat ended their season somewhat prematurely.

The playoff game marked the last game in a Steelers uniform for left guard Alan Faneca, a fixture on Pittsburgh's offensive line for ten seasons, the last seven of which he earned Pro Bowl honors. He would finish his career with two more Pro Bowl seasons with the Jets before a final campaign with the Cardinals in 2010.

The lead-in to the 2008 season included several tragedies. In January, Ernie Holmes was killed in an auto accident in Texas. In February, Myron Cope, the renowned, award-winning journalist and Steelers' team announcer for thirty-five years—not to mention the creator of The Terrible Towel—died of respiratory failure at the age of seventy-nine. Then, in June, Dwight White died of a suspected blood clot in one of his lungs after surgery.

All three passed members of the Steelers family were honored before the seasoning-opening game, a 38–17 romp over the Houston Texans in Pittsburgh. It was a great start to the season in which the Steelers were scheduled to play ten games with teams who finished the previous season with winning records.

The Steelers finished the first half of the season with a 6–2 record, the only losses coming to the Eagles in Week Three in Philadelphia and the Giants in Week Eight at home. Importantly, though, the Steelers had pinned a loss on the Ravens in the fourth game of the season, winning 23–20 in an overtime Monday night thriller. The Steelers/Ravens rivalry was taking shape to become one of the league's fiercest.

The first half of the season also saw the Steelers establish a firm team identity. Yes, they had a capable offense. But this team was similar to its Steelers predecessors in that it featured a tremendous defense, led by linebackers James Harrison, LaMarr

Woodley, and James Farrior, as well as safeties Troy Polamalu and Ryan Clark. In the first eight games, the most yardage the defense had given up was 282 yards to the Giants, who had also scored the most points, but only twenty-one at that.

Opening the second half of the season, the Steelers squandered a fourth-quarter lead to lose to Manning and the Colts, 24–20. They then reeled off five consecutive victories to push their record to 11–3. In those five victories, the Steelers allowed ten points or less in four of the games. In the other game, they surrendered just thirteen points.

The last of those five wins came the second Sunday in December, against the Ravens in Baltimore. The game featured the Steelers' number-one-ranked defense against the Ravens' number-two-ranked defense.

Trailing by three points in the fourth quarter, Roethlisberger led the Steelers on their best drive of the game when it mattered most. They drove ninety-two yards in less than three minutes and took the lead with a four-yard touchdown reception by Holmes with fifty seconds remaining. The defense then sealed the victory when William Gay intercepted Raven's quarterback Joe Flacco deep in Steelers territory.

The victory over the Ravens clinched both the AFC North title and a first-round bye in the playoffs. It also allowed the franchise to boast about being the first in the AFC to win 550 games.

In Week Fifteen, the Steelers visited the Tennessee Titans to determine which team would top the AFC regular season standings. The Steelers took a 14–10 lead deep into the third quarter, but in the end, they could not overcome two interceptions and two lost fumbles by Roethlisberger. The Titans pulled away late to win 31–14.

The next week, the Browns put up little resistance, and the Steelers rolled to a shutout victory, winning 31–0 to cap the regular season with a 12–4 record. However, the game wasn't without concern, as late in the second quarter, Roethlisberger went down with a head injury. He had to be immobilized on the field and carried off, later diagnosed with a concussion.

Linebacker James Harrison was a beast throughout the 2008 season. He had 101 tackles on the year, including sixteen tackles for a loss behind the line of scrimmage. In addition, he set a new team record for sacks, recording sixteen. His seven forced fumbles led the league, and he also intercepted a pass. For good measure, he also recorded a safety.

For his season, Harrison finished fourth in the vote for the Most Valuable Player in the entire league. He easily won the Defensive Player of the Year Award, though, and in doing so, he became the first undrafted player so honored.

Harrison joined the Steelers out of Kent State University, Jack Lambert's alma mater, where he was a walk-on, non-scholarship player on the football team. Signed to the Steelers in 2002, he spent most of the season on the practice squad, suiting up for only one game when he played on special teams.

He was released by the Steelers three times and was signed by the Ravens, who shipped him off to Europe to play with the Rhein Fire of the NFL Europe League. Eventually, the Ravens released him too.

When Steelers linebacker Clark Haggans suffered an offseason injury while training ahead of the 2004 season, the club signed Harrison for a fourth time. It turned out the fourth time was a charm.

Ahead of the 2007 season, linebacker Joey Porter was released for salary cap reasons, and Tomlin appointed Harrison the replacement as starter. It was a surprising and controversial decision, and it turned out to pay off in spades as Harrison broke out to become a star, earning his first Pro Bowl honors.

Over his sixteen-year career, fourteen of which were spent with the Steelers, Harrison was named to the Pro Bowl five straight times, from 2007 through 2011, when he was one of the most feared, most dominant players in the game.

Harrison had a knack for making memorable plays in the biggest of games, as he had throughout both the 2007 and 2008 seasons. But his biggest moment in the spotlight was yet to come.

With their 12–4 record deserving of the second seed in the AFC playoffs, the Steelers enjoyed a bye the week after the regular season ended, and the extra time off ensured Roethlisberger was healthy enough to play in their first postseason game.

On Saturday, January 11, the Ravens traveled to Tennessee and upset the number one-seeded Titans 13–10. Thus, the Steelers took to the field the next day, January 12, knowing that the AFC playoffs would have to go through Pittsburgh and the Steeler Nation faithful at Heinz Field.

Their opponent, the Chargers, started the game looking to end any thought of a Steelers homestand all the way to the Super Bowl. On the game's opening drive, they struck first on a forty-one-yard touchdown pass from Phillip Rivers to Vincent Jackson.

The Steelers squared things after Holmes returned a punt for a score midway through the first quarter. They then scored again just before the half to take a 14–10 lead into the intermission.

The Steelers never looked back from there. Roethlisberger connected with tight end Heath Miller for a third-quarter touchdown that gave the Steelers some breathing room, and the defense took care of the rest. For the game, the defense held the Chargers to just fifteen yards rushing, a new Steelers record for postseason play. The Steelers ended up winning convincingly, 35–24, to advance to the AFC Championship Game.

A berth in Super Bowl XLIII was the prize awaiting the victor of the third Steelers-Ravens matchup of the year. The setting was a cold January evening in Heinz Field, with light snow falling.

The Steelers put together a nice opening drive and took a 3–0 lead on a twenty-four-yard field goal by Reed. They then let their league-leading defense go to work.

The Ravens' four first-quarter possessions ended with a punt, an interception, another punt, and a turnover on downs. In total, the Steelers allowed just seventeen yards. In the meantime, Reed hit another first-quarter field goal to extend the lead to 6–0.

On the second play of the second quarter, Roethlisberger, under heavy pressure, scrambled and found Holmes on the right side, just past midfield. Holmes cut back against the grain to the left side of the field, diving into the end zone to complete a sixty-five-yard catch-and-run for a touchdown. After Reed's extra point, the Steelers held a 13–0 lead.

With less than four minutes to go in the first half, Ravens safety Jim Leonhard returned a punt forty-five yards to the Steelers' seventeen-yard line. After a pass interference penalty moved the ball to the three-yard line, Willis McGahee scored on a run off left guard. The extra point narrowed the Steelers' lead to four, 13–7, going into the halftime intermission.

The only points of the third quarter came at the end of the Steelers' second possession, when Reed converted on his third field goal of the game, this time from forty-six yards away. Heading into the final quarter, the Steelers held a 16–7 advantage.

After a modest Steelers drive to open the fourth quarter, a short Mitch Berger punt set up the Ravens in good field position at their forty-two-yard line. From there, Flacco and the Ravens sought to close the gap.

Several short passes moved the ball into Pittsburgh's side of the field. Then, the Ravens benefited again from another pass interference call, this one in the end zone. By rule, the ball was placed on the one-yard line, and McGahee scored on the next play. With the extra point, the Ravens crept to within two points, positioning themselves to win the game with just a field goal.

The Ravens then forced the Steelers to punt, taking over possession at their own fourteen-yard line with 6:50 remaining in the game. With the margin at just two points, tension swelled across the Heinz Field crowd.

Fittingly, the defense put that anxiety to rest. On the fifth play of the Ravens' drive, Polamalu intercepted Flacco and returned it forty yards for a touchdown, delivering a death blow to the Ravens' chances.

Two more Ravens turnovers ensued, and when Roethlisberger took a knee to let time expire, the Steelers had earned their seventh Super Bowl appearance with a 23–14 win.

Super Bowl XLIII was played in Tampa and pitted the Steelers against the NFC Champion Arizona Cardinals. The Cardinals were coached by Whisenhunt, who had lost out to Tomlin for the Steelers' head coaching position a couple of years before and had finished atop the NFC West with a 9–7 regular-season record.

Interestingly, Super Bowl XLIII featured the oldest franchise in the AFC, the Steelers, playing against the oldest franchise in the NFC, the Cardinals. Also, as you might recall, both of the franchises had played one year, the 1944 season, together as a merged team, Card-Pitt, due to depleted rosters during World War II.

The Cardinals were led offensively by thirty-seven-year-old quarterback Kurt Warner, a former league Most Valuable Player and the winning quarterback in Super Bowl XXXIV, and receivers Larry Fitzgerald, Anquan Boldin, and Steve Breaston, all three of whom recorded over 1,000 yards receiving on the season.

Defensively, the Cardinals had displayed a lot of inconsistency and ranked just twenty-eighth out of thirty-two teams in points allowed. They featured, however, great players like lineman Darnell Dockett, linebacker Karlos Dansby, cornerback Dominique Rodgers-Cromartie, and Pro Bowl safety Adrian Wilson.

Pittsburgh opened the game with possession and immediately set off on a nine-play, seventy-one-yard drive that took up 5:15 of game clock. Roethlisberger appeared to score on a run from the one-yard line, but after the Cardinals appealed the on-field ruling by game officials, the call was overturned. Wanting to get points on the board, Tomlin and the Steelers elected to kick a field goal on fourth down. Reed's eighteen-yard field goal was good, and the Steelers went out to a 3–0 lead.

The Steelers' defense forced a punt after five Cardinals plays, and Roethlisberger and crew took over on their own thirty-one-yard line. From there, they took off on another methodical drive.

Short passes and runs moved the ball deep into Cardinals' territory and kept the clock moving. Two plays into the second quarter, on the eleventh play of the drive, Steelers running back Gary Russell scored from one yard out. With Reed's extra point, the Steelers led 10–0.

After the Steelers' impressive display of playing keep away with the football, the Cardinals finally got moving on their second possession. Warner completed six of seven passes, the last of which was a forty-five-yard completion to Boldin that moved the ball to the Steelers' one-yard line. On the next play, after nearly falling after taking the snap, Warner connected with tight end Ben Patrick for a touchdown to get the Cardinals on the scoreboard.

The two teams then exchanged punts, allowing the Steelers to take over for their fourth possession at their own sixteen-yard line, with 2:46 remaining in the half to try to extend their lead. However, on second down, Roethlisberger was intercepted by Dansby, setting up Warner and the Cardinals at the Steelers' thirty-four-yard line with a golden opportunity to either tie the game or take the lead going into halftime.

Warner completed four passes to move the ball to the five-yard line, where the Cardinals called their final timeout of the half with eighteen seconds remaining. They were knocking on the door for a go-ahead touchdown, and momentum seemed to be building behind them. Then, everything changed in one of the most famous plays in Steelers history.

Warner took the snap out of the shotgun formation and tried to hit Boldin on a quick slant at the goal line. Harrison jumped the play, intercepting the ball and taking off down the right sideline.

At his own forty-yard line, Harrison was almost forced out of bounds by Warner, but he shrugged the quarterback off and kept running behind the protection of a couple of teammates. At the Cardinals' thirty-yard line, Harrison cut back to his left briefly to avoid Cardinals running back Tim Hightower. However, in doing so, it allowed offensive tackle Mike Gandy to close the distance to Harrison.

Gandy dove at Harrison's heels at the five-yard line, but Harrison high-stepped his way out of the tackle. Fitzgerald then draped himself on Harrison at the two-yard line as Breston came in from the left and collided with Harrison. Fighting through the tackles, Harrison tumbled into the end zone helmet-first to score the most improbable touchdown on a one-hundred-yard interception return—the longest play in Super Bowl history—as time in the first half expired.

It was the Immaculate *Inter*ception. What looked to be a 14–10 deficit going into the intermission was now, in fact, a 17–7 Steeler lead.

The third quarter began with the Steelers forcing another Cardinals punt, and they took over at their own eighteen-yard line. There, Roethlisberger took to repeating what the Steelers' offense did in the first quarter.

Sixteen plays and seventy-nine yards later, Reed's field goal from twenty-one yards out extended the Steelers' lead to 20–7. The drive ate up over eight and a half minutes on the clock, leaving the Cardinals just 2:11 in the third and the entire fourth quarter to mount a comeback.

Warner's next drive finished the third quarter, but the Cardinals were forced to punt just four plays into the final quarter. However, the Cardinals' defense rose up to force the Steelers' second punt of the game. Warner and the offense took possession at their own thirteen-yard line.

It took Warner just six plays, all completed passes, to move the ball to the Steelers' ten-yard line, forcing Tomlin to call a timeout to regroup his troops. The break in play didn't faze Warner, though, and two completions later, the Cardinals were in the end zone on a one-yard Fitzgerald touchdown catch. Neil Rackers' extra point closed the gap to six at 20–14.

The two teams then exchanged punts, first the Steelers, then the Cardinals. The Cardinals' punt, however, left the Steelers buried back at their own one-yard line. When Steelers center Justin Hartwig was called for holding in the end zone on a third-down play, the Cardinals were awarded a safety and two points, narrowing the score to 20–16. Moreover, they also received possession after the Steelers' free kick.

The Cardinals needed just two plays to strike again. On second down, Warner's exceptional second half continued as he hit Fitzgerald on a crossing pattern in the middle of the field. Fitzgerald cradled the ball in at his forty-three-yard line, planted his left foot, and immediately streaked down the middle of the field, splitting both Clark and Polamalu to complete the sixty-four-yard touchdown play.

Remarkably, the Cardinals took a 23–20 lead with just 2:47 remaining in the game.

The clock was down to 2:30 when Roethlisberger and the offense took the field at their own twenty-two-yard line looking to make some Super Bowl history of their own. Three short completions and a short Roethlisberger scramble pushed the ball to just past midfield, where the Steelers called their second timeout of the half with 1:02 remaining.

On a second-down play, Roethlisberger completed a pass to Holmes, who hauled it in at the thirty-five-yard line, his back to the defense and the goal line. When

Holmes spun to his left, toward the sideline, Cardinals defender Aaron Francisco slipped and fell trying to change direction. Freed, Holmes sprinted down the sideline, then cut back to his left. Francisco caught up to him and tackled him at the six-yard line, where the Steelers called their final timeout with forty-nine seconds left.

When play resumed, Roethlisberger tried Holmes again on the left side of the field, but the pass fell incomplete. On second down, Roethlisberger looked toward the middle of the field but found his receivers covered. Blessed with time from great pass protection, he spotted Holmes on the right side, deep in the end zone, and lofted a high pass just over the outstretched reach of defensive back Ralph Brown. Holmes, fully extended with his toes on the ground, reached up and snagged the reception, falling out of bounds after gaining possession. The touchdown gave the Steelers the lead with just thirty-five ticks left on the clock.

But the game wasn't over, certainly not for a future Hall of Fame quarterback like Warner. Two passes and two timeouts later, the Cardinals had the ball at the forty-three-yard line, looking for one long pass to steal a victory. Woodley, though, ended the threat by stripping the ball from Warner, and defensive end Brett Keisel recovered the fumble to end the threat.

The Steelers had won a thrilling Super Bowl XLIII with a come-from-behind 27–23 victory, giving Tomlin a championship in just his second season as head coach and making him the youngest to ever coach a Super Bowl winner. It was the Steelers' sixth Super Bowl championship, surpassing both the Cowboys and the 49ers for most Super Bowl triumphs. Holmes was named the Most Valuable Player after catching nine passes for 131 yards and a touchdown, including four receptions for seventy-three yards on the game-winning drive.

Super Bowl XLIII was also noteworthy for being the final game of John Madden's broadcasting career.

Before the AFC Championship Game against the Ravens, Pittsburgh Mayor Luke Ravenstahl had unofficially changed his name to "Steelerstahl." After the Super Bowl XLIII victory, the Pittsburgh City Council followed suit by ceremonially changing the name of the city to "Sixburgh" to commemorate the Steelers' sixth Super Bowl title.

Just as Noll had left a solid foundation for Cowher to enjoy immediate success, so too had Cowher helped Tomlin. Tomlin had been named the Coach of the Year and won the Super Bowl in just his second season as a head coach. And success kept coming—although not always at the level of expectations by Tomlin, the organization, and fans alike.

Befitting their role as Super Bowl champions, the 2009 Steelers team kickstarted the NFL season with a Thursday night game ahead of the league's opening weekend. At Heinz Field, they squeezed past the Titans 13–10 in overtime when Reed connected with a game-winning thirty-three-yard field goal.

After losing their next two on the road, the Steelers reeled off five straight victories to complete the first half of the season with a 6–2 record, level with the Bengals atop the North Division. However, in a case of easy come, easy go, they lost five consecutive games, a streak that included not only back-to-back overtime losses, but also losses to all three divisional opponents.

It was too much to overcome. Despite winning their final three games to finish with a 9–7 record, the Steelers finished third in the division and were on the outside looking in as the playoffs took shape.

The 2010 season started under a cloud of uncertainty. First, Holmes, the Super Bowl hero from two years before, was traded to the New York Jets. Then, Roethlisberger drew a six-game suspension—later reduced to four games—for violating the NFL's personal conduct policy.

With an unknown entity in the offense, the Steelers responded in a manner true to their history by fielding a staunch defensive led by safety Polamalu. Without their starting quarterback, the Steelers started the 2010 campaign with three victories, holding their opponents to scores of nine, eleven, and thirteen points. Even in Week Four, they surrendered only seventeen points to the Ravens in their first loss.

After Roethlisberger returned for the fifth game, the Steelers finished with a 9–3 run, completing a 12–4 regular season. Once again, they won the North Division title, this time in a tiebreaker with the 12–4 Ravens. When the Ravens romped over the Chiefs in the Wild Card Playoff game on January 9, it set up the third Steelers-Ravens matchup of the season the next week in an AFC Divisional Playoff game.

Troy Polamalu was named the NFL's Defensive Player of the Year after the 2010 season, an award he narrowly missed out on in 2005 and 2008, the latter of which he finished behind teammate Harrison. It was a deserving honor for one of the Steelers' most iconic players.

Troy Benjamin Aumua was born on April 19, 1981, in Garden Grove, California, the youngest of five children from his mother, Suila Polamalu. While he took on the name Troy Polamalu as a child, he didn't legally change his name until February 2007, when he became Troy Aumua Polamalu.

At age nine, Polamalu went to live with his aunt, uncle, and cousins in Oregon, and he later starred in football at Douglas High School in Winston. After graduating, he attended the University of Southern California, where he played for four years with the Trojans.

After a standout career at USC, including All-America honors his last two seasons, the Steelers selected Polamalu in the first round of the 2003 NFL Draft with the sixteenth overall pick. The Steelers wanted Polamalu so badly, they packaged two later draft picks and their twenty-seventh overall pick to move up to the sixteenth position in the first round.

Polamalu ended up playing his entire twelve-year career with Pittsburgh, where he ascended into the starting lineup his second season and never left. Instantly identifiable with his mane of long, dark, curly hair flowing out the back of his helmet, Polamalu played a hustling style of defense, in perpetual motion until the referees' whistles signaled play was dead.

Polamalu never once took a play off or loafed on an assignment, just going through the motions. And Steelers fans loved him for it.

An eight-time Pro Bowler, Polamalu retired after the 2014 season. In 158 career games, he was credited with 783 tackles, twelve sacks, fourteen forced fumbles, and thirty-two interceptions. Over his career, he scored five defensive touchdowns, three on interceptions and two on fumble recoveries and returns.

Troy Polamalu was inducted into the Pro Football Hall of Fame in 2020.

On January 15, 2011, Pittsburgh played host to the archrival Ravens in the divisional round of the playoffs. If the Raiders marked the Steelers' biggest rivalry in the 1970s, the turn of the century paved the way for the Ravens to take the mantle as their most heated rival. It stands true still to this writing.

In this late afternoon game, the Steelers opened the scoring on running back Rashard Mendenhall's one-yard touchdown run midway through the first quarter. From that point on, though, it was all Ravens in the first half, as they scored three touchdowns, including a defensive score on a fumble return.

The Steelers fought back methodically, though, scoring twice in the third quarter on two short Roethlisberger touchdown passes, first to tight end Miller from nine yards, the second to receiver Ward from eight yards. When Steelers kicker Shaun

Suisham hit a thirty-five-yard field goal early in the fourth quarter, Pittsburgh once again assumed the lead.

Benefitting from a long punt return, the Ravens' offense inherited the ball in great field position with six minutes remaining. However, the Steelers' defense held strong against three plays inside their ten-yard line to force a field goal. With 3:58 remaining, it was a tie game, 24–24.

Roethlisberger then led one final drive, converting two third-down plays, the last a completion to receiver Antonio Brown that went for fifty-eight yards and moved the ball to the Ravens' four-yard line. Mendenhall scored from two yards out, and the Steelers won 31–24 to advance to the AFC Championship Game.

Against the Jets the next week, the Steelers' defense stymied their opponents early, allowing the offense to jump out to a twenty-four-point second-quarter lead. From there, the Steelers held on to win, despite giving up a forty-five-yard touchdown reception to their former teammate, Holmes. With their 24–19 victory, the Steelers earned a berth in Super Bowl XLV against the Green Bay Packers.

Super Bowl XLV, played in Dallas, was the Steelers' league-tying eighth Super Bowl appearance. Unfortunately, the game didn't go the Steelers' way.

The Steelers fell behind early, 7–0. Then, a Roethlisberger interception was returned for a touchdown by Packers' safety Nick Collins to press the Green Bay advantage to 14–0. After a thirty-three-yard Suisham field goal got the Steelers on the board, the Packers responded with yet another touchdown to take a 21–3 lead. Fortunately, just before the half, Roethlisberger connected on an eight-yard touchdown pass to Ward to make the game more interesting at the half, but with the Steelers still down 21–10.

A Steelers' touchdown in the third quarter was matched by a Packers' touchdown in the fourth. But when Roethlisberger threw a twenty-five-yard touchdown pass to receiver Mike Wallace and the team then made good on a two-point conversion, the Steelers narrowed their deficit to just a single field goal, trailing 28–25 halfway through the fourth quarter.

The Packers, however, were the team to get a field goal when kicker Mason Crosby converted a twenty-three-yard attempt just in front of the two-minute warning. Roethlisberger wasn't able to muster up a game-winning drive, and three straight incompletions ended the Steelers' hope and turned the ball over on downs. The Packers won 31–25, denying the Steelers their seventh Super Bowl title.

In the eleven years from the 2011 season through the 2021 season, Tomlin and the Steelers have advanced to the playoffs seven times. They haven't advanced to the Super Bowl since that fateful last appearance in February 2011, but they have played in another AFC Championship Game, a loss to the New England Patriots after the 2016 season.

Since Tomlin took over the head coaching position in 2007, the Steelers have never had a losing record, a span of fifteen consecutive seasons of records .500 or above. Incredibly, since Noll took the reins in 1969, the Steelers have had just three head coaches.

To put three head coaches in over fifty years in perspective, consider the Jacksonville Jaguars had three head coaches in thirteen months between January 2021 and February 2022.

Chapter 29

THE LITTLE CITY
THAT DOES BIG THINGS

n 2010, *Forbes* magazine named Pittsburgh "America's Most Livable City." In its study, *Forbes* mentioned the city's strong university presence—a dozen colleges and campuses—and Pittsburgh's cultural arts scene, jobs, income growth, safety, and affordability.

For those who lived outside of the area, the ranking came as a shock, particularly those who had not visited since the 1970s and 1980s. Those who lived in the area, though, were already in the know.

Over time, Pittsburgh's lofty ranking proved to be no fluke. The city has been recognized by *National Geographic Traveler* as one of the "best places in the world to visit," by Jetsetter.com as one of the "best world-wide destinations," and by *The Huffington Post* as one of the "40 prettiest cities in the world." And, of course, Pittsburgh remains a steady presence on those livable city lists.

The *Forbes* mention wasn't the first, actually. *The Economist*, the international journal of global economies, first designated Pittsburgh as the most livable city in America in 2005. But you have to go back twenty years to get to the very first "livable" mention.

In 1985, Rand McNally listed Pittsburgh as its most livable city, despite an unemployment rate at the time hovering a little over nine percent.

It's often easy to make light of clickbait headlines and listicles. Some would argue that Pittsburgh is not so much a livable city, but a *listable* city.

But the fact of the matter is that Pittsburgh, more often than not, shows up in those lists of most livable cities, not only in the United States, but often in the top fifty cities *in the world*. It's a testament to the resilience of the city and its citizens, and each mention should be received with a sense of civic pride.

This book has been decades in the making. Not writing—that was more like two years. Rather, it was the thought of Pittsburgh, its plight, then its upward flight, that rattled around the head of one of this book's authors for over twenty-five years.

Simply, what separated Pittsburgh from its Rust Belt cousins and empowered it to transform and succeed? How has Pittsburgh prospered, in general, while other Rust Belt cities, like Detroit, for example, have continued to struggle?

Are yinzers smarter, tougher, grittier, harder working, and more resilient than others? Probably not. And it's important to note there are a lot of factors that worked in Pittsburgh's favor as it transformed itself, just as there were a lot of factors that worked in the settlement's favor when it was just beginning.

This book argues that the Steelers saved Pittsburgh. There's no question that Pittsburgh was built from steel. The steel industry allowed the city to grow and prosper for generations. Up until, of course, it didn't.

It was that pivot point, in the 1970s and 1980s, that proved critical in Pittsburgh's ongoing development. The Steelers and their sustained success proved to be much of the fuel driving transformation.

The Steelers teams of the early 1970s were built very much in the image of Pittsburghers—hard-working, gritty, resilient, with maybe a bit too much never quit and never back down for their own good. The Steelers were Pittsburgh's team.

When the steel industry began its decline, the identity of Pittsburgh didn't go with it. Rather, the identity of Pittsburgh became its football team. The Steelers won four Super Bowls in six seasons, and they sustained a level of success during and after that stretch that hasn't been paralleled in NFL history.

The Steelers were—and still are—more than a source of civic pride. They were heroes, they were role models, and they were Pittsburghers, yinzers to the core. Pittsburgh's relationship with its football team is unlike any other in professional sports. It's similar to a big-time college football or college basketball program in a small town.

When times got tough for Pittsburgh, the city's identity remained strong because of the Steelers. When times got tough for Detroit, the city's identity wasn't tied to the Detroit Lions football team—one of only four NFL franchises to never have appeared in the Super Bowl. Therein lies the difference.

Of course, the subject is open to debate. We'd be happy to sit down over a cold one or two and discuss.

On the forty-ninth anniversary of the Immaculate Reception, December 23, 2021, Pittsburgh Mayor Bill Peduto awarded Franco Harris an honorary key to the city. During the ceremony, Peduto noted Harris was a hero not only on the field, but off the field, too, "for how he exemplifies everything that's good about Pittsburgh."

"He's a hero to everyone in the city of Pittsburgh that needs a little bit of help," Peduto remarked. "He is someone who will always give his time, whether he has it or not."

Upon receiving the key, Harris said, "How fortunate was I to come to Pittsburgh in the '70s and to find out that this is a little city that does big things."

Harris continued and remarked, "We have to believe that each of us can make a difference. We also have to realize that not everything can be an Immaculate Reception. There are many more four-yard runs when it takes more time and effort to cross that goal line, and I knew I couldn't do that by myself. I needed my teammates, and together we accomplished some amazing things."

Amen, Franco. Together, Pittsburgh has accomplished some amazing things.

ACKNOWLEDGMENTS

From Tom O'Lenic

I would like to thank Ray Hartjen for making my passion project possible. What a blast it has been! His literary talent is off the charts, and his ability to overcome my many weaknesses is nothing less than amazing. He has also been an inspiration for me and so many others as he battles cancer with courage and positivity.

To my wife, Chris Anne, my children, Lindsay and Danny, and my neph-son Bryan Wilson for their support and encouragement.

To my childhood friends Tom Carroll, Joe Sikora, and Andrew Berman, as well as Joe's dad, Mr. Joe Sikora, whose feedback and enthusiasm for the book inspired me. And to my college bud, Tony Frezza, for his all-important advice.

To Morgan James Publishing for expediting this book to market with the same passion we have for the content inside of it.

Lastly, Jim Baker, whose generosity and dedication to family is something I will emulate.

From Ray Hartjen

I would like to thank Tom O'Lenic for entrusting to me the story he had juggled around in his head for some twenty-five years. After speaking about his idea for a book for several years, one day we decided to write it. After all, if not now, when? And when proved to be an important consideration when we looked at the calendar and realized that December 23, 2022, would be the fiftieth anniversary of the NFL's most memorable play. Thank you, Tom, for letting me partner with you on this book, your passion project. I greatly appreciate it.

I would also like to thank my wife, Lori, for her unwavering support, as well as that of my children, Olivia and Raymond. Additionally, with the time taken to develop the *Immaculate* manuscript, it took me away from my guitar-playing duties with my band, the Chronic Padres—thank you, Scott Sorochak, for your patience while I juggled activities.

I also want to express my gratitude to both Donna and Paul Truex for all their support and encouragement. When I was diagnosed with multiple myeloma in March 2019, they took the proverbial bull by the horns and . . . got . . . stuff . . . done. Thank you, too, to the entire cancer patient, cancer care provider, and cancer patient caregiver communities for providing the daily inspiration to #punchtodayintheface.

Additionally, thank you to Fran Carpentier for all her publishing industry know-how, as well as editorial input on the draft manuscript. Furthermore, a big thank you to Cortney Donelson for editing the manuscript and getting it ready for publication.

Lastly, thank you to David Hancock, Naomi Chellis, Chris Howard, Shannon Peters, Jim Howard, and the entire team at Morgan James Publishing for helping Tom and me share *Immaculate's* wonderful collection of stories with Steeler Nation and beyond.

ABOUT THE AUTHORS

Tom O'Lenic is an accomplished biotechnology executive, sports enthusiast, and boutique winemaker, born in Donora, Pennsylvania, and raised in Pittsburgh. His passion for competitive athletics was seeded in his youth in the Iron City and fueled by his family; Tom's father played minor league baseball, and his uncle was Baseball Hall of Famer "Stan the Man" Musial. Tom is fascinated with history and how the past influences the future, or, in some cases, doesn't. His experience with the steel industry collapse of the mid-1970s was deeply personal, as his father, an engineer at U.S. Steel, was one of the many thousands of employees who were adversely impacted by the declining business. *Immaculate: How the Steelers Saved Pittsburgh* is a passion project for Tom, who has long held the opinion the community of Pittsburgh steeled itself through its deindustrialization transformation with the galvanizing presence of the Pittsburgh Steelers. Tom currently resides in Pleasanton, California.

Ray Hartjen is a content marketer, writer, musician, and songwriter living in Northern California. In a professional career that has spanned parts of five decades, Ray has pivoted on many occasions, from investment banking to pharmaceuticals and from consumer electronics to SaaS software. One constant throughout his career path, however, has been storytelling. Ray has been a frequent source for quotes from the national media on both the consumer electronics and retail industries, and he has spun his fair share of yarn as a contributor to a number of online outlets, including pieces for Yahoo, where he published articles about the San Jose Sharks hockey team, and Salesforce AppExchange, where he writes about sales and marketing. A cancer fighter every day of the week that ends in a *y,* Ray periodically chronicles his experience as a multiple myeloma patient on his blog at memyselfandmymultiple-myeloma.com. And, with life's soundtrack constantly playing in his head, Ray also tours and records with his two-piece acoustic band, the Chronic Padres.

ENDNOTES

1   Fantel Hans, William Penn: Apostle of Dissent, (New York: William Morrow & Co. 1974) p. 23.

2   Dobrée Bonamy, William Penn: Quaker and Pioneer, Houghton Mifflin Co., 1932, New York, p. 128.

3   Anne T. Wilbur, Ralph Try Ballou, M. Maturin, and Durivage, Ballou's Pictorial Drawing-Room Companion. Boston: M.M. Ballou, 1857. First Edition, June 20, 1857 issue, Volume XII, No.25, Whole No. 313.

4   "'Whizzer' White to Play Football with Pittsburgh," The Gettysburg Times. August 1, 1938. p. 3.

5   Kim Gamble, "The Immaculate Interception," October 19, 2012, accessed September 6, 2022, https://grantland.com/features/the-immaculate-reception-franco-harris-pittsburgh-steelers-owners-ball-play/.

6   Ibid.

7   John Singer, "The Strongest Brand in Sports," IP Spotlight blog, November 9, 2007, accessed September 7, 2022,
https://ipspotlight.com/2007/11/08/the-strongest-brand-in-sports/.

8   Christina Gough, "Facebook Fans of National Football League Teams as of September 2022," Statista, accessed September 7, 2022, https://www.statista.com/statistics/240028/facebook-fans-of-national-football-league-teams/

9   Al Cataline, "Ranking the NFL Teams by Fanbase Size," Major League Sports-cations, April 25, 2022, accessed September 7, 2022, https://www.mlv.com/blog/ranking-the-nfl-teams-by-fanbase-size-these-are-the-10-biggest-fandoms-by-the-numbers/.

10 Arpan Thapa, "Top 10 Teams with Most NFL Fans," Players Bio, July 29, 2022, accessed September 7, 2002, https://playersbio.com/most-nfl-fans/.

11   Adam McCann, "Best and Worst Metro Areas for STEM Professionals," Wal-
     letHub, January 12, 2022, accessed September 7, 2022, https://wallethub.com/
     edu/best-worst-metro-areas-for-stem-professionals/9200.

12   Nate Doughty, "Report: Pittsburgh's overall ranking among global emerging
     startup ecosystems improves despite funding gap," PITTSBURGHINNO, June
     14, 2022, accessed September 6, 2022, https://www.bizjournals.com/pittsburgh/
     inno/stories/Inno-insights/2022/06/14/pittsburgh-emerging-startup-ecosystem-
     rank-2022.html.

13   Sophie Burkholder, "Pittsburgh tech is seeing the most tech job growth in
     software and cybersecurity," Technicality, April 5, 2022, accessed September
     6, 2022, https://technical.ly/software-development/pittsburgh-comptia-report-
     tech-jobs/.

14   2021 Pittsburgh State of the Industry Report, Pittsburgh Technology Council,
     September 20, 2021, accessed September 6, 2022, https://www.pghtech.org/
     news-and-publications/SOI_2021.

A free ebook edition is available with the purchase of this book.

To claim your free ebook edition:

1. Visit MorganJamesBOGO.com
2. Sign your name CLEARLY in the space
3. Complete the form and submit a photo of the entire copyright page
4. You or your friend can download the ebook to your preferred device

Morgan James BOGO™

A **FREE** ebook edition is available for you or a friend with the purchase of this print book.

_____

CLEARLY SIGN YOUR NAME ABOVE

Instructions to claim your free ebook edition:
1. Visit MorganJamesBOGO.com
2. Sign your name CLEARLY in the space above
3. Complete the form and submit a photo of this entire page
4. You or your friend can download the ebook to your preferred device

Print & Digital Together Forever.

Snap a photo

Free ebook

Read anywhere

CPSIA information can be obtained
at www.ICGtesting.com
Printed in the USA
JSHW031120101222
34657JS00004B/227

9 781636 980546